Back Bearings

Dedication

To Joan
– for seventy years

Back Bearings

A Navigator's Tale
1942–1974

Group Captain Eric Cropper

Pen & Sword
AVIATION

First published in
Great Britain in 2010
By Pen and Sword Aviation
An imprint of
Pen and Sword Books Ltd
47 Church Street
Barnsley
South Yorkshire
S70 2AS

ISBN 978-1-84884-151-2

A CIP record for this book is available from the British Library

Typeset in 11/13pt Palatino
by Mac Style, Beverley, E. Yorkshire

Printed and bound in Great Britain
by CPI UK

Pen and Sword Books Ltd incorporates the imprints of Pen and Sword
Aviation, Pen and Sword Maritime, Pen and Sword Military,
Wharncliffe Local History, Pen and Sword Select, Pen and Sword
Military Classics and Leo Cooper.

For a complete list of Pen & Sword titles please contact
PEN & SWORD BOOKS LIMITED
47 Church Street, Barnsley, South Yorkshire, S70 2AS, England
E-mail: enquiries@pen-and-sword.co.uk
Website: www.pen-and-sword.co.uk

CONTENTS

Introduction

When we are travelling – through life or across the earth – we want to know where we are and how to get to where we want to be. This is the purpose of navigation, which is both a science and an art: very often science alone or art alone will not help us, especially when chance plays its part. This book is the story of one navigator in the days when air navigation was still rudimentary and open to error.

On the cover of the Air Almanac – the bible for those who sought to find their position by observing heavenly bodies – there used to be a vignette of a doleful medieval individual using a backstaff, a primitive sextant, below which was a scroll bearing the legend 'Man Is Not Lost'. This phrase was adopted as a motto by the air navigation fraternity, usually used ironically. I originally chose it as the title for this book, and wrote six chapters before Group Captain Dickie Richardson (of a slightly earlier era) used it for his memoirs: I suppose I should have expected it. My present title refers to the way in which a navigator can get some idea of his present position by looking backwards, an occupation most of us tend to indulge in as we get older.

My career as a practising navigator covered some twenty-five years, from 1943 to to 1968, when enormous advances were being made in aviation in general and navigation systems in particular. This book lies somewhere between an autobiographical memoir and a not too technical review for the general reader of the development of air navigation as I knew it. I kept no journals, only engagement diaries in some years, and so I have had to rely largely on fickle memory, aided by my flying logbooks and those of my navigation logs and charts which still survive. Any errors of fact are therefore almost sure to be my own, although I have referred to supposedly authoritative sources from time to time.

Inevitably the story includes the strands of family and domestic life inextricably interwoven with the demands of the job in the Royal Air Force, and indeed I have probably not placed sufficient emphasis on the part played by my loyal, long-suffering and enterprising wife in a variety of circumstances and climates. This book is a tribute to her and our marriage of nearly sixty-five years.

The trade of air navigator is a dying one, and in civil aviation it has been dead for some years. Satellite navigation systems can position an aircraft, a ship, a vehicle and even a humble walker anywhere on the earth's surface with an accuracy and a reliability undreamed of sixty years ago. Perhaps this book will give some flavour of more primitive days when man in the air was very frequently lost and navigation was often 'by guess and by God'.

CHAPTER ONE

Starting

A file of khaki-clad figures, each man clutching the bayonet scabbard of the man in front, stumbled and cursed their way across rough farmland in pitch darkness. This was a night marching exercise, and as far as I was concerned, my introduction to the practice of navigation. I joined the Home Guard, aged 17, at the end of 1940 when it was still known as the Local Defence Volunteers (or, more colloquially, 'Look, Duck and Vanish'). The members of our section were mostly boys about my age, having left school but not being old enough to join or be conscripted into the Armed Forces. Our NCOs were aged Great War veterans (probably between 40 and 50 years old), and we all took ourselves very seriously. The immediate threat of a German invasion had receded somewhat by this time, and we were adequately uniformed and equipped, armed with Canadian 0.30 rifles (later Sten guns), and well drilled in infantry tactics.

We had had training in map reading, using the incomparable one-inch Ordnance Survey maps, and in using a hand-held marching compass. We were taught to measure on the map the true bearing of the required line of march (that is, its angular relationship with True North) and to follow this line using the same reading on the marching compass. As I was to discover later, navigation is never so simple: no magnetic compass ever points to True North, which is the direction of the Geographic North Pole – the one at the top of the terrestrial globe. The earth's magnetic field is not only asymmetrical but varies slightly year by year. At that time the magnetic pole was somewhere in Northern Canada, and compasses pointing to it read about 12° west of True North, known as the magnetic variation and shown on maps. We had therefore to make a correction to the true bearing before marching off into the night.

Off we went, in the time-honoured formation probably used before Waterloo, falling into hollows, tripping over bushes, and swearing bitterly. After three-quarters of an hour or so our objective was nowhere in sight; we should have reached it after fifteen minutes. A halt was called and a torchlit conference ensued. Navigation error was to blame: we had applied magnetic variation the wrong way, east instead of west, and were consequently marching 24° (nearly an hour on the clock face) out of the required direction. We then evolved the magic formula 'Map to compass – add'. Like most simple solutions, this of course only applied in certain circumstances – in that particular place and date in the northern hemisphere – but this did not affect the gallant Home Guard.

At the beginning of 1942, when I had just reached the age of 18, I decided to join the Royal Air Force and, naturally, to be a fighter pilot. I had thoroughly enjoyed the Home Guard but I felt that if I was going to fight, I would rather do it sitting down and with some substantial firepower under my control. I reported to the RAF Recruiting Office in the city of Leeds, and was interviewed by an elderly flight lieutenant wearing a pilot's wings and Great War medals. He did not seem to be very impressed with my ambition to be a fighter pilot, and after looking at my educational qualifications and giving me some mental arithmetic problems, announced that I was more suited to be an observer. However, he would send all my details to the Aircrew Selection Centre at Cardington and I would be called for more rigorous selection tests 'in due course'. With that I had to be satisfied, though the thought of sitting in the back of an aircraft shuffling maps and making calculations did not seem very attractive.

The call came in April, and I took the train down to Cardington, near Bedford, wearing my only decent suit and feeling apprehensive. This was the first RAF station I had seen: it was dominated by the huge airship hangars built in the twenties, and was largely hutted, though tidily laid out and fearsomely clean, painted and polished. In a couple of days we were given thorough medical examinations, a variety of written tests, and some aptitude assessments. I had no difficulty with the written tests but did not perform well on the pilot aptitude assessor, a machine consisting of a dummy cockpit and controls, where a spot of light had to be kept centred in a ring on the instrument panel by use of the controls. Various other lights flashed on at random and had to be switched off immediately.

When it was all over we were called for interview, and I was told that I had been selected for training as an observer. The recruiting officer had been right. I swallowed my disappointment and was attested (sworn in) as 1625303 Aircraftman 2nd Class, u/t (under training) observer. However, there were hold-ups in the RAF flying training system at that time, and I was placed on deferred service and would not be required for some months. Meanwhile I should join the local Air Training Corps and learn something about the RAF.

Back home again, I felt very unsettled. In one mood I was anxious to get into uniform and start my flying training; in another, I knew that this was the end of a phase in my life and I wanted to cling on to the familiar things and people. I was an introspective youth with little in the way of social knowhow, but I had a wide circle of friends, and a girl I loved (she has been my wife for nearly sixty-five years). This was all going to change and I wasn't sure that I liked the idea. But there was a war on, in the current phrase, and I was one of thousands in the same situation.

I sadly resigned from the Home Guard, turning in my rifle and bayonet, uniform, boots, steel helmet and respirator. My last few months in Dad's Army had been enjoyable and interesting, as I had been seconded to the Northern Command Home Guard Infantry School as a member of the infantry demonstration squad, showing other part-time soldiers how a section should be deployed and controlled, and the various fighting tactics. I had also done a short stint as a drill instructor for new recruits. All in all, the Home Guard had taught me a great deal; among other things, I fired a greater variety of personal weapons in eighteen months than I ever did in thirty-odd years in the RAF. I gained a new self-confidence through the ability to perform drill and handle other physical skills, and from comradeship with men from a variety of backgrounds and age groups – a broadening experience.

The Air Training Corps in Leeds had a special Deferred Service Squadron, No. 2031, with headquarters over a shop in the insalubrious district of Sheepscar. It wasn't worthwhile to give us uniforms, but we attended evening classes conscientiously once or twice a week and were given instruction – and very competent instruction – in air navigation, signals, maps and charts, and various other aviation-related subjects. Later we moved up to Leeds University and took over some surplus premises from the University Air Squadron. In recognition of my Home Guard experience, I was given the temporary rank of cadet sergeant, and had the pleasure and embarrassment of drilling the other members of the squadron in public on nearby Woodhouse Moor. Since we were all in not particularly smart civilian clothes, we must have looked a motley crew, and inevitably attracted onlookers and ribald comments.

I found that, contrary to expectations, I enjoyed the lectures and exercises in very elementary navigation. I still have my rough notebook and a small textbook entitled *Examples and Exercises in Elementary Air Navigation for use of the aircrews of the RAF, Army Co-operation, Fleet Air Arm, and Cadets of the ATC*, by M.J. Hearley BSc, published by Longman at one shilling. I found this subject fascinating: I had never liked mathematics at school, with the sole exception of trigonometry. Measuring triangles was a practical business and I could see the application of it in all sorts of ways. We were taught geometry and algebra by well-qualified and experienced masters at school, but no one ever related these subjects to adult life, professions and trades – the way in which they are used as scientific tools to unlock problems ultimately of interest to everyone. Air navigation in its most basic form is the business of measuring triangles, and I found no difficulty in understanding the very simple theory and doing the exercises. (Readers who have got this far and are uninterested – or knowledgeable

– in the theory of air navigation may like to skip the following few paragraphs.)

Ships at sea use their compasses to steer in a particular direction and can log their speed through the water. Winds, tides and currents affect the ship's course and speed and have to be allowed for in calculating the path and speed actually achieved over the sea. In the air, an aircraft is similarly affected by wind, so that if your engines were producing a speed in the air against a headwind of 50 mph, your speed over the ground would only be 150 mph. This is the most simple example and there are infinite variations.

The basic problem is solved by the use of what is known as the Triangle of Velocities. Each side of this triangle is a vector – a line drawn in a certain direction relative to north, and of a length proportional to the speed of movement. The three vectors in the triangle are the aircraft's course and airspeed (determined by a compass and airspeed indicator); its actual path and speed over the ground, known as track and groundspeed; and finally the prevailing wind, called wind velocity, and made up of the direction from which the wind is blowing and its speed.

With any four of these factors known the other two can be found, so that if you fly directly between two points identified on the ground, you can measure your track and groundspeed and compare them with your course and airspeed to find the direction and strength of the wind.

In practice things are not quite so simple: your compass must be corrected for magnetic variation (as we found out in the Home Guard) and other errors; your airspeed indicator reading must be corrected for altitude and other errors; you cannot always see the ground; and winds change with the aircraft's altitude, the progress of the flight, and the whims of the gods of the weather.

In our ATC classes we did these calculations by drawing out the triangle to scale on paper, using dividers, rulers and protractors – a primitive but effective method. We also learned the Morse code, much about map projections, a smattering of meteorology, and a little about the workings of aircraft instruments, plus some star recognition. When I came to study these subjects during initial training in the RAF, I realized how lucky I had been to get this early grounding.

This period in limbo came to an end all too soon, and I was ordered to report to the Aircrew Reception Centre at Lord's Cricket Ground on 9 November 1942. Since my life was about to change irrevocably, for better or worse, perhaps this is the place to say something about my origins and background.

* * *

I was born in Leeds five years after the end of the First World War (echoes from which permeated my childhood). My mother, one of the daughters of William Moxon, the Headingley blacksmith, died when I was a few months old and I was brought up by a much-loved aunt until the age of four. My father, born in North Wales to a working-class family, had come to a military hospital in Leeds at the end of the war when he was still an acting lance-corporal in the Royal Army Medical Corps. He stayed on in the same hospital as a civilian clerk, and then became an insurance agent, that familiar figure in poorer areas between the wars who called weekly to collect a few coppers towards a decent funeral. He was a self-educated man, a strong Labour supporter in the Fabian mode, and very bookish; he had been a Nonconformist lay preacher in his youth but was reluctant to admit to any specific doctrine, although he acknowledged Christian principles and loved to hear a good preacher.

He married again in 1927. Lilian Kay was the daughter of a Bradford wool merchant, who claimed to be descended from John Kay of the 'Flying Shuttle' and Richard Arkwright, who invented other innovations in the cotton-spinning industry. Lilian's father was not very successful, apparently, and died early, leaving a large family in not very wealthy circumstances. Exactly how she and my father met I was never told, and find it hard to imagine. She was a Catholic and had had a convent education, at St Monica's in Skipton, and also in Belgium. Her family lived in Melbourne Terrace, then a 'good' area of Bradford, but she had earned her own living (from necessity or choice) since the war. She had trained as a pharmaceutical assistant and worked in a chemist's shop in Bradford before she married. A difficult, prejudiced, prickly person, she was a good stepmother to me in many ways; she had ideas about diet well ahead of her time and was always keen to see that mine included the proper nutritional values.

We lived in a poor part of Leeds – Woodhouse – in a small back-to-back house, one of thousands like it, and I suppose we belonged to what the writer Julian Critchley has called 'the thin line that divides the lower-middle from the respectable working class.' When I was about seven, we moved to a new council house in the northern suburbs, and eventually achieved the goal of a mortgage on a small semi-detached house in Far Headingley, where my father lived until he died.

My father passed on to me his love of books, nature and music. My stepmother passed on to me her idea of good manners, acceptable speech, and respectability, and was determined to see that I got a good education. I accordingly won a scholarship to Leeds Modern School, a boys' secondary or grammar school of good reputation on the northern outskirts of the city. There I travelled daily by tram, even coming home for the midday meal when we had moved to Headingley. I realize now that the Modern School gave me an excellent education; to my mind, the standards achieved there in the sixth form were the equivalent of (if not an improvement on) the degree courses in many universities today. As I have said, I think the teaching of maths and physics could perhaps have been more imaginative, but my indifferent performance in those subjects was no doubt mainly because of my own inclinations; many boys went on to get BScs and MAs in science subjects.

I passed School Certificate in 1938, and ended my first year in the sixth form in the summer of 1939, passing the subsidiary level of the Higher Certificate. By this time I had abandoned science and was taking French, German, English Language and Literature, and so-called History-with-Geography.

On 1 September 1939 (two days before the declaration of war) the school was evacuated to Ilkley, only a few miles away in Wharfedale. I spent two or three not unpleasant months there, but as we were sharing Ilkley Grammar School, with lessons for half-days only, and as I was a prefect with some responsibilities for the younger boys, we did not get much work done. Much against the wishes of our revered headmaster, Dr 'Geoff' Morton, my parents and I agreed that I should go home and look for a job. If I had stayed on at school for the full Higher Certificate and been lucky enough to get a university place, my degree course would in any event have been interrupted by call-up for the Forces, since arts students were not exempt.

Back in Leeds, I found a junior clerk's job in the headquarters of the Leeds Permanent Building Society in modern offices in the city. Building societies then pursued their traditional roles of helping people to buy houses and save money, and had not yet started aping the banks and the insurance companies. Management was strict but paternal, and I progressed from post-desk boy at 17/6d. (about 87p) a week to the War Damage Department (an education in itself) at £2.

This was where I met my future wife, Joan. We were both sixteen and fell in love almost immediately and certainly irreversibly. We both had romantic ideas and ideals suitable to our age (and some of them persist nearly seventy years later). Joan came from a family background not dissimilar from mine, although her family was in more prosperous circumstances – they had a car and lived in a larger semi-detached. We had some shared interests in books, music and nature, although I must often have bored her by my diatribes and the assumption of knowledge in these and other subjects which I did not possess.

Leeds had a rich cultural life at this time, partly stimulated by the war, and we took advantage of it: chamber music concerts at lunchtime in the City Museum (before a bomb fell on it); symphony concerts (of varying quality) in the Town Hall on Saturdays; touring London orchestras, and ballet and opera companies; and choral music at Leeds Parish Church (often conducted by Herbert Bardgett from the Huddersfield Choral Society). Looking back at that time, I find it hard to believe that I crammed so many activities into it: I was doing Home Guard duty every fifth night, manning the guard post at a local viaduct; going out with Joan one or two nights a week and at weekends; concert going; and for a time I was the acting secretary of the Parish Church Oratorio Choir. I read voraciously and wrote a great deal of poetry, mostly derivative free verse, and though a lot of it was waffle, some of it still moves me. We would also get out into the Dales whenever we could, although in those days there was pleasant country within walking distance of our homes.

I must subconsciously have been attempting to live life to the full with the shadow of the war constantly darkening the horizon. We were lucky in Leeds to have few bombing raids, little damage and few casualties, but one could never forget what was going on in the theatres of war elsewhere. I knew that my time was running out.

*   *   *

The new entry assembled on the empty terraces of Lord's Cricket Ground on a dull and cold November morning. There were several hundred of us, mostly of my age but with a leavening of older young men such as ex-policemen, who were just being allowed to volunteer for aircrew. It took some time to sort us out into flights and squadrons, and our flight was then marched off by a dapper corporal to the block of luxury flats in St John's Wood taken over by the Air Ministry for our accommodation. Needless to say, the luxury had departed, but our rooms were perfectly adequate and reasonably comfortable, with the standard iron-framed beds and three 'biscuit' mattresses, rough blankets and white sheets.

In the course of the next few days, we were kitted out with uniform and boots, medically inspected ('Cough!') and told to get haircuts; I had had one before coming down to London, but had another two in the first week. A lot of time was taken up by marching to and from the dining-hall (in the basement of another block), where hundreds queued sometimes as long as half an hour for a meal. But there was not much grumbling – the food was indifferent but edible, and at our age we were hungry enough to eat anything.

In the succeeding weeks we were given lectures on health and hygiene (surprising revelations to the innocents among us, including me), Air Force law, administration and history, and other suitable subjects. We were drilled, taught unarmed combat in the park, and given plenty of time for cleaning our kit and buttons and learning how to lay out our beds and equipment in the prescribed style. We were nannied and bullied alternately by the little corporal, who was exclusively ours, and saw little or nothing of the Flight Commander.

Such time off as we had was spent in the local NAAFI and occasionally at the cinema. I remember seeing the film *Coastal Command* and being fired by the ambition to fly in a Sunderland flying boat (I never did). Some of us went up to the West End occasionally, but on our pay of three shillings a day (15p) we could hardly paint the town red. One other memory of that time is of walking back to the 'billet' from the NAAFI along Avenue Road in a traditional pea-souper, and having to walk with one foot in the gutter and the other on the pavement for guidance. Fogs were fogs then.

At last we received the expected posting to Initial Training Wing: we travelled by rail to Devonshire to become 'A' Flight, No. 1 Squadron, No. 1 ITW, billeted at the Oswalds Hotel, Babbacombe. Many seaside resorts (Scarborough, Blackpool and Torquay among others) were homes to aircrew ITWs, and flights of cadets wearing white flashes in their caps could be seen marching smartly up and down the promenades and doubling in PT kit on the beaches.

Discipline was strict at Babbacombe, but we were all volunteers and most of us were keen to learn as much as we could. There was foot drill or arms drill (or both) every day; we aspired to Guards drill, with foot stamping and marching at 120 paces to the minute. I have always enjoyed military drill when it is done properly, and there was real pride when a flight performed some intricate manoeuvre perfectly. As we became more proficient we learned continuity drill, where a flight of fifty men would go through a sequence of different drill movements for ten or fifteen minutes without a word of command. We all knew that on the face of it this had no direct bearing on becoming a proficient aircrew member, but I think we all realized that the ability to act with mind and body together, with others, in an ordered sequence had a value beyond the immediate one.

Flight Lieutenant Addinell, an Education Branch officer who was a fluent, sympathetic and persuasive teacher, took us for lectures in navigation, meteorology, instruments, engines, the theory of flight and some other subjects. I have a clear memory of standing outside the lecture room with him on a cold, fine winter's night, learning to recognize the principal stars used in astro-navigation.

We learned to read Morse to a speed of twelve words per minute, and to use an Aldis lamp. We would stand in groups in the park trying to keep warm, watching a lamp blinking from a distant window, and taking down the Morse code groups with numbed fingers. Now and again we had a route march around the deep Devon lanes, stopping to eat haversack rations on a windswept beach with splendid views of the hills and coast.

In our off-duty time we would get the bus down to Torquay, go to the cinema, walk on the sea front, or have a cheap meal at a Forces canteen run by volunteers; here there were regular record concerts of classical music, always well attended and much appreciated.

To say that we were a mixed bunch in 'A' Flight would perhaps give a wrong impression. We were mostly the same age, 18+, with a few slightly older men who had already served in the RAF and had managed to transfer to aircrew. The majority were grammar-school boys with respectable family backgrounds and mostly acceptable standards of behaviour. I don't remember any from the larger public schools or university, but most of us were well able to cope with the academic side of the course. I shared a room with three others, two of whom were Jewish; one of these, Basil Felt, came from my home town of Leeds, and I still remember him with affection. I last saw him in 1944 on Leeds station wearing a pilot's wings, but I don't know if he survived.

Those two of my room-mates and I were able to miss Sunday morning church parades, since I had formally been enlisted as an agnostic, and shown as such on my identity discs. As an idealistic 18-year-old I had found that despite earlier convictions I was unable to declare myself as a member of any Church; agnostic (that is, ignorant) seemed to describe my state of mind most accurately, although I think one or two of the senior NCOs were under the impression that I was a member of some esoteric sect. However, this did enable Basil Felt and Harris and me to stay in bed late on Sunday mornings and have a leisurely breakfast at a café down the street in Babbacombe – bliss.

After twelve weeks or so we had our examinations, and having passed, we became leading aircraftmen on the enormous sum of 7/3d. a day (36p). We had a week's leave and then returned to learn that the next step was postponed because of further hold-ups in the training system. Our routine became easier, with no regular lectures or examinations, and we were able to enjoy South Devon in the spring. During this time we were called together to be briefed about a new aircrew training system, the so-called PNB scheme (pilot, navigator, bomb aimer). We had originally been selected either as pilots or observers, but now we were told that we would all get the chance to be pilots at a grading course of twelve hours' flying on Tiger Moths. The RAF was looking for natural pilots, and they would be identified on this course, those who were not naturals becoming navigators or bomb aimers. We all knew that Bomber Command was still expanding rapidly at this time and that this was where most of us would be posted at the end of our training. Aspiring fighter pilots most of us still were, but at least we were grateful for a second chance to sit in any pilot's seat.

This came in May, when some of us were posted to No. 3 Elementary Flying Training School at Shellingford in Berkshire: this was an old-fashioned grass aerodrome with hutted accommodation, in pleasant countryside near Faringdon. There was an immediate change in atmosphere from ITW; discipline was more easygoing, drill was non-existent, and we were left more to our own devices when we were not required for flying, although there were occasional ground lectures.

We were kitted out with flying clothing, including rather antiquated Sidcot flying-suits, helmets and goggles. The de Havilland DH82a Tiger Moth was a biplane with two open cockpits, and looked very much like a First World War aeroplane, although it was not introduced into the RAF until 1932. It was an improved version of the DH Moth light aircraft so popular in inter-war flying clubs, and became the standard initial trainer for the RAF. With its reliable Gypsy Major engine, dual controls, and its low stalling speed of 43 mph, it was an ideal aircraft for its purpose at the time.

I made my first flight on 17 May 1943 in DH82a T6565, with Sergeant Dyer as instructor. 'Air familiarization and effect of controls' is recorded in my log. Seated in the rear cockpit with goggles down, the engine roaring, and the horizon tilting and turning, I felt like one of the intrepid aviators in the 'Biggles' stories or the film *Dawn Patrol*. But it was soon borne in on me that this flying business was hard work. Precise heights, airspeeds, and engine revolutions had to be remembered and adhered to for every manoeuvre, and good airmanship required a constant look-out in our immediate airspace.

We progressed to take-off, climbing, descending, right-hand and left-hand turns and eventually stalling and spinning. I enjoyed spinning and did not find the recovery process too difficult – full opposite rudder, stick forward when the rotation stopped, and away again. Circuits and landings followed, and although I could usually make a reasonable landing, my circuits were too ragged for the taste of my instructor, and I never really improved them.

When we had had about seven hours of instruction, taking about a week, the Flight Commander's check measured our progress, and some fortunate (or more competent) cadets were allowed to go solo. I was not among them, and I think that by then I had realized that I was not the sought-after 'natural' pilot. It was no surprise when, after a total of twelve hours' flying, I had not gone solo and did not shine in the final Chief Flying Instructor's test. In mitigation, I should say that I caught little of what Flight Lieutenant Imeretinsky, the CFI, was saying to me through the Gosport tubes – the archaic intercomm system with which the Tiger was fitted. He was rumoured to be a White Russian, and certainly I found his accent impenetrable.

Well, I had had my chance to become a pilot, and it was evidently not on the cards. We were next sent to the enormous aircrew holding unit at Heaton Park, Manchester, there to pass several weeks while the cogs and wheels of the training system slowly turned. There was a short period under canvas at what was called an Elementary Training Wing at Ludlow, and then back to Heaton Park, where we were paraded on a rainy August morning to hear our final aircrew categories and destinations. '303 Cropper – Navigator', read the Flight Commander from his long list. The majority of cadets were destined for units of the Empire Training Scheme in Canada, South Africa, or USA, but I was posted to No. 1 Elementary Air Navigation School, Bridgnorth, Shropshire, for yet another ground course preparatory to flying training.

For the second time I resigned myself to becoming a navigator, but this time knowing a little more about it, and not now entirely disliking the prospect.

Chapter Two

Learning

In a curious way, we RAF trainees were insulated from 'the War', as many servicemen in the United Kingdom must have been. We were mostly stationed at a distance from any bombed areas, and in any event the worst of the blitz was over for the moment. We had no worries about clothes and food, and no need to stand in queues or (except in transit from one unit to another) travel in cold, crowded trains and buses to our daily work. In general, the war news mostly passed over our heads; there were of course no personal radios in those days, and the most we heard was the occasional BBC news bulletin on the NAAFI wireless or a newsreel at the cinema. We rarely had the time or inclination to read newspapers, and certainly not the serious press.

We knew that the war would in due course impinge on us more directly, but we did not let this worry us: we were young and had a strong belief in our own invulnerability. The only glimpse of the unpleasant face of war was one day at Babbacombe, when four Focke-Wulf 190 fighter-bombers roared in from the sea (Harvards, said our aircraft recognition expert), shot off a few bursts of cannon fire and dropped a bomb behind the church at St Marychurch, doing little damage.

Meanwhile, during that summer of 1943, the tide was turning in the Allies' favour in the Battle of the Atlantic; Sicily was invaded; and an ever-expanding Bomber Command continued increasingly heavy attacks on the German heartland. Most of this did not register with us, although we did hear, in the NAAFI at Bridgnorth one day, that the Allies had landed in Italy. There was some subdued cheering and a shared feeling that perhaps the war was now going our way.

Bridgnorth was a well-established hutted camp, rather like Cardington in its paint and polish and tidiness. We slept in long barrack huts where the floor was gleaming linoleum (polished by us) and the corporal in charge had his own tiny room near the door. Again the change from the relaxed atmosphere of a flying station was marked: we marched everywhere, had frequent kit inspections, and paraded regularly.

The aim was to teach us all that could be taught about air navigation short of practising it in the air. When, in the 1950s, I was involved at the Air Ministry in planning navigation training, I often marvelled that, at our particular phase of the war, such training could be (or appeared to be) well organized in a cohesive pattern. With the pace of change in the conduct of the air war, the constant re-equipping of front-line squadrons with new types of aircraft, and the rapid scientific progress in navigation systems, it must have been a planner's nightmare.

What we were being taught at Bridgnorth was the basic methods of navigation, some of which were no doubt regarded as obsolescent even at that time, but providing a very sound framework on which we could progress later – much later – to more modern systems. If there was an emphasis it was on DR navigation – Dead Reckoning or Deduced Reckoning navigation – which is in essence the estimation of position by the use of the known compass course and airspeed adjusted to allow for the best-known wind velocity. We had already done this in a primitive way in initial training, but it now assumed added importance and complexity. Instead of drawing our triangles of velocity out with rule, protractor and dividers, we now used the Dalton computer – not a bit of electronic wizardry, but an instrument like a small box, about five inches by four by one; on one side was an Appleyard scale, a circular slide-rule used to work out speeds and times and other calculations; and on the other, an analogue computer which reproduced the triangle of velocities in a semi-mechanical way so that varying vectors could be manually set on it. This took a lot of drudgery out of plotting, once we learned to use it.

We were at the same time introduced to RAF Form 441 (all forms had and no doubt still have serial numbers in the RAF), the Navigation Log, on which all flight calculations and events were recorded by the navigator. It was impressed on us from the beginning that the log was of the greatest importance on operations: if the navigator was put out of action, another member of the crew would have a chance of carrying on if the log had been properly kept. It was also needed for post-flight interrogation and for analysis of the navigator's competence (a use which did not commend itself to the average navigator). There was a laid-down method of log keeping, with standard abbreviations and codewords, so that everyone was working to the same rules. Log keeping was something of an art in itself, and many old and wily navigators were able to produce logs which enhanced their reputations while not requiring too much activity: this worked well providing that the actual navigation was sound.

We progressed from DR plots in the classroom to working in the DR Trainer, a hut equipped with several mock-up navigation tables and their basic instruments, in which we received instructions through headphones and worked against the clock (sometimes set to run faster than real time). Aircraft noise from a loudspeaker was supposed to add to the realism, but did not greatly help our muddled brains to assimilate and process the many sources of information. In fact, it was a useful exercise, and most of us felt some satisfaction when we had completed a synthetic flight successfully.

The other familiar subjects – maps and charts, instruments and compasses – were taught at a rather deeper level than before, and we were introduced to astronomical navigation to the extent of taking sights of heavenly bodies with a bubble sextant and working out the resulting position lines using the Air Almanac and Air Navigation Tables. We were not to know it, but the use of astro-navigation in Bomber Command at this time was mainly restricted to emergencies when other aids were not available, but it was still important in Coastal Command where long sorties over the sea were flown, and in places like the Middle and Far East where navigation aids were few. At least the sun, moon and stars could not be jammed through enemy action.

We learned about wireless direction finding and the theory of taking bearings of ground stations with the loop aerial fitted to almost all aircraft which carried a wireless operator. This worked on a principle something like that of modern television aerials, which can be turned on an axis to point in the direction of the strongest signal and thus get the best picture. Aircraft loop aerials would usually be used by the wireless operator, who would tune in to a ground beacon or transmitter (the more powerful the better) and then rotate the loop aerial by hand until the minimum signal – giving a more accurate reading – was received and its bearing relative to the aircraft's nose could be read off on the aerial scale; this would then be plotted by the navigator to give a position line, and with two or more bearings he could construct a ground position or fix on his chart. This system, too, was being superseded by other radio aids, but of these, as of so much else, we were blissfully ignorant.

For the first time, some of our instructors were pilots or observers with operational experience. We listened carefully to the pearls they occasionally dropped before the swine, and picked their brains when they would let us. Our civilian meteorology instructor, Harry Maggs, was not only academically well qualified but was an experienced forecaster and was able to put across this not always easy subject in a comprehensible way. He was a pleasant, approachable man, and I was to meet him again in later years. (I have a memory of him trying to lecture with a great deal of noise going on from a workman just outside the classroom window, and of our mirth and surprise when Harry, a most quietly spoken and mild-mannered man, flung open the window and shouted, 'Bugger off!')

We worked hard, but had the occasional Sunday or evening off. The Black Lion in Bridgnorth was a favourite haunt, and we enjoyed wandering around the town with its ancient buildings on its unusual split-level site, Upper and Lower Town, with the Severn running by. I was also fortunate enough to be taken home by two fellow cadets and friends: with David Duignan to Kidderminster and 'Les' Henson in Birmingham. I have lost sight of David but exchanged Christmas cards every year with Mary and Les Henson until his recent demise.

At last we came to our final navigation plot and the written examinations. My results were good and I realized that I had been enjoying the course, and particularly the practical navigation exercises. Then we were on our travels again, the course being split up as usual, and my posting was to No. 5 Air Observers' School at Jurby on the Isle of Man. We took train to Fleetwood and sailed on one of the regular ferries to Douglas, on a dull day in October. At least if we could not go overseas in the usual sense of the word, we were crossing the sea to our next destination. The island loomed up ahead, with Snaefell at 2,036 feet seeming like a real mountain. Douglas was an archetypal British holiday resort out of season, but we spent little time there, and caught the toy train north through Laxey and Ramsey to Sulby Glen, whence we were transported across to Jurby on the west coast.

Jurby was another hutted camp, but not quite as spit-and-polish as Bridgnorth. It was close to the sea, and in my memory it was constantly windswept with wet westerlies. We were allocated Nissen huts holding eight men, and another thing I remember about Jurby is the chance happy comradeship of those of us in Hut 27: Nigel Hawkins, Ken Purdy, Johnnie King, George Smith, the inseparable Pybus and Simcox, and Derek Hughes. Most of us survived the war (George Smith did not), and some I met again in later years.

The small airfield had three concrete runways, from which the Avro Anson was flown. This was a legendary aircraft, one of the RAF's workhorses, introduced into service before the war as a light bomber and (among other things) used for coastal patrols very early in the war. Its two Armstrong-Siddeley Cheetah engines produced a rattling note which was instantly recognizable; the cabin had two front seats for pilot and second navigator, a navigation table, and a wireless operator's position. The Anson was noisy, smelly and not particularly comfortable, but it was reliable and often regarded with affection by those who flew it. We trainee navigators were due for about a hundred Anson hours before we qualified (if we did qualify) for our flying badges.

So here we were at the point for which eleven months' training had prepared us. Our course of about fifty cadets was divided into two sets for classroom work, and we flew in pairs, acting as first and second navigator alternately. The first navigator was the responsible one, keeping the log and chart going at the navigation table, plotting the position and giving the pilot directions. The second navigator sat in the right-hand front seat and gave what assistance he could by passing visual positions and any other useful information, such as coast crossings. Another and more onerous task of his was to wind up the undercarriage manually just after take-off – over a hundred turns of the handle. These Jurby aircraft were mostly Anson Mark 1s with few modern refinements, and on some you could see, on top of the fuselage aft of the cabin, the fairing over the former position of the old hand-operated gun turret of the operational version. I spotted just such a fairing on an Anson flying freight and passengers between the DEW Line and Yellowknife in Northern Canada in the late 1950s – a robust aircraft indeed.

For reasons which I will mention in a later chapter, my flying logbook does not include details of each individual flight I made at Jurby, but I do know that I flew a total of about sixty hours by day and forty-four by night, for fifty-one of which I was first navigator. My flying partner was Ken Bender, a tall, lanky Guianan with a strong sense of humour but a tendency to fly off the handle if things went wrong.

I remember my first flight well. We set course over Maughold Head on the north-east coast of the Isle of Man and then flew south-east to cross the Welsh coast at Point of Air just north of Prestatyn. I was sitting up front with the staff pilot while Ken slaved away at the navigation desk. I now had leisure to observe the ever-changing pattern of land, sea and sky, and I found it fascinating. On this first easy daylight exercise I found no problems with map reading, using the splendid RAF 1:500,000-scale topographical maps which showed every ground feature you needed.

This was a lucky start. I found that, whatever the turbulence, I never felt airsick sitting 'up front', whereas on bad weather days I sometimes felt very sick when crouched over the navigation table, breathing glycol and heating fumes and trying to get my brain to function in order to make the next calculation.

There were detailed briefings for each flight, when the first navigator would complete his flight plan using the forecast wind velocities, and draw out the given route on his 1:1,000,000-scale Mercator chart, the standard RAF plotting chart with red outlines on a white background. We would be briefed on the route, on the expected weather, on which navigation aids were to be used, and on any flight hazards such as high ground or barrage balloons. We were issued with one sheet of edible rice-paper, in a Perspex envelope, which contained the 'colours of the day' denoting the appropriate Very cartridges to fire if challenged, to show that we were not the enemy: this was sometimes necessary, as we discovered in broad daylight over the Irish Sea when we were fired on by a naval vessel (fortunately not very accurately).

This briefing sheet also contained details of airfield beacons (the 'pundits', or red lights, flashing two Morse characters, changed every day) and landmark beacons ('occults', or white flashing lights, also coded). Our flights were mostly over the Irish Sea and the Western Isles, and coastal lighthouses were invaluable aids at the heights we flew, usually around 2,000 feet; their characteristics were shown on RAF maps and charts, and I still remember that Chicken Rock light, on the very southern tip of the Isle of Man, flashed once every thirty seconds. I also remember that on some night flights in dirty weather, all that could be seen was Chicken Rock light on the way out and the same on the way back.

The staff pilots and wireless operators were a varied lot. Some were helpful and informative, some talkative, and some rarely said a word throughout the flight. I recall one Canadian sergeant-pilot who was particularly monosyllabic. We were night-flying west over the sea from Rathlin Island off the north-east corner of Northern Ireland; our next planned leg was south-east towards Belfast. Ken was first navigator and gave the next course to the pilot, who set his compass without comment and began a slow turn. I was busy checking my map for the next leg, and when I looked up we were steady on course again. The coast should have been coming up to starboard (right), but I could see nothing; it was a dark night with no stars, and I looked round for anything visible. Over on the port side I could see marine lights winking – the wrong side for the coast if we were going in the right direction. I checked the pilot's compass: he had set 'red on blue' and was flying the reciprocal course, so that instead of flying south-east we were steaming north-west into the Atlantic. I nudged the pilot and gestured at the compass; he looked at it, reset it and without a word turned on to the correct heading. We never knew whether this was a deliberate error to check on our alertness or if he just made a mistake; I fancy the latter.

On another night flight over Northern Ireland, I was first navigator and we were flying south, with Dundalk as our next turning point. At my estimated time of arrival (ETA), nothing could be seen of the bay on which it stands. We pressed on for a minute or so and then became aware of a lighted area ahead. I had never seen a town from the air without a blackout, and realized that we had crossed the Eire border and were approaching Dublin. I gave the pilot a hasty course correction, and he grunted 'About time, too' as he turned. As far as I know he did not report this breach of international flight rules, and I suspect that this sort of thing was not infrequent and that the Irish were more or less tolerant.

We made many flights over the Inner and Outer Hebrides, and to me it was endlessly absorbing to see the remote crofts and the tiny communities and fishing villages. It seemed incredible that people could work and make a living on some of the smaller islands, especially in the sort of weather we experienced that winter.

Our navigation aids were very basic. Besides the standard air speed indicator, altimeter and magnetic compasses, we had a drift recorder, an astro-compass and a hand-held observer's compass for taking bearings. Looking down through the drift recorder's eyepiece, we could line up the movement of objects on the ground (or the sea surface) and read off their direction on a bearing plate to give the difference between the direction in which the nose of the aircraft was pointing and the direction of the movement over the ground or sea – the drift. By doing this when flying successively in three directions sixty degrees apart, we could plot on our trusty Dalton computers a wind velocity obtained from the three drift readings. This was usually very accurate.

The astro-compass was a mechanical device which could be mounted in the astrodome (a perspex bubble in the cabin roof). It had a bearing plate with sights on it which could be levelled and used to take bearings of objects on the ground; from one object at a known position (such as a headland or a lighthouse) several bearings could be taken as the aircraft tracked past and changed its angle. Three of these bearings would give a very satisfactory position fix when run up to the time of the last one. Similar fixes could be obtained using the hand-held observer's magnetic compass, which was not so accurate, but the main advantage of the astro-compass was that the direction and altitude of a heavenly body could be set on it, the body sighted, and a check on the aircraft's true course obtained. Magnetic compasses were subject to all sorts of errors, and the accurate check provided by the astro-compass was particularly useful on long oversea flights. It did, however, require careful use of the Air Almanac and the Air Navigation Tables to find the correct settings, and in the weather we often flew in, sight of the sun, moon or stars could not always be relied on.

All these aids depended on sight of the ground, sea or sky. If none was visible, we could fall back on bearings obtained by the wireless operator, either by use of the direction-finding loop aerial or through contact with base or another DF station which would transmit a QDM message – 'The magnetic course to reach me is xyz degrees.' The accuracy of these bearings varied with the atmospheric conditions and the skill of the operator, and was not particularly good. The saving grace of QDMs was that if you steered the course given by your own base you were almost bound to get there in the end. .

Nevertheless, in poor weather the Anson navigator was working 'by guess and by God', as the saying went, and aircraft did get lost. One Anson from Jurby came to a grinding halt on the summit of Snowdon in thick cloud; the crew got away with injuries, but a few feet lower and the aircraft would have been totally destroyed. This accident certainly sharpened us up somewhat, especially where safety heights were concerned.

There were occasional and pleasurable flights when the navigation worked out exactly right. One of these for me was a curious exercise known as 'Radius of Action to a Second or Moving Base'. In flying terms, the Radius of Action is the greatest ground distance an aircraft can fly from a base or a known point before returning to the same point (or somewhere else) in a limited time, allowing a reasonable fuel safety margin. It depends on the amount of fuel the aircraft can carry, the rate of fuel consumption, and the winds encountered out and back. A typical use for this sort of calculation was in Coastal Command, where reconnaissance or anti-submarine aircraft flew long patrols over the sea and had to be sure of getting back to base with some fuel in hand. In some cases, one would have to return to another airfield or, as in the Fleet Air Arm, to your aircraft carrier, which by the end of the patrol would be in an entirely different position.

On this occasion I was first navigator, and we set off through the North Channel between the Mull of Kintyre and Rathlin Island into the grey Atlantic. It was a fine day for a change, and I was able to get a good departure fix as we left the land, flying north-west. From then on we were entirely over the sea, but I was able to establish our track by measuring the drift, and found a good wind by the three-drift method. Our second base in this case was the south-west corner of Islay, and after an hour or so over the sea I did my calculations with a certain amount of scepticism, and gave the pilot a course for Islay. On that day we had a Czech pilot, and although he was pleasant and cheerful enough, he was a man of few words, and those not very comprehensible.

However, as we got closer to our ETA for Islay, the pilot waved me up to the front with thumbs up and a beaming smile. There was Islay dead ahead, our target headland right on the nose, if a minute or two out in ETA. When I later read C.S. Forester's *The Happy Return*, in which his naval hero, Hornblower, makes a perfect landfall in South America after eight weeks out of sight of land, I knew exactly how he felt.

Unlike the marine sextants Hornblower used, which measured the altitude of the sun, moon or stars against the sea horizon, we used a bubble sextant where the instrument was kept level by a captive bubble as in a spirit level, and the altitude measured from that datum. In the small Anson at comparatively low level, it was difficult to keep the bubble steady for the required two-minute shot, no matter how carefully the pilot flew. (The Mark IXA sextant had a clockwork device which averaged all the shots taken over those two minutes.) Rather worse was the scramble beforehand necessary to extract the required astronomical data from the Air Almanac and the Air Navigation Tables, often under a poor cabin light fitted with a red filter. Three star sights had to be taken to obtain a fix at the crossing-point of three position lines, and very often the triangle thus drawn on the chart was so large as to be useless. A great deal of practice was required to reach an accurate result in astro-navigation, and this we did not get at Jurby. It was many years before I achieved satisfactory astro results, and this was with better sextants, better and steadier aircraft, simpler astronomical tables and improved plotting techniques.

Much more fun was reconnaissance photography, when we were required to identify some small ground feature and photograph it from low level. This was done with a huge and heavy hand-held camera, and I remember flying round Anglesey in atrocious weather trying to get a picture of the railway station at Llanerchymedd. We were successful, but I doubt if the resulting print would have been of much use to a photo-interpreter.

The course was not all work. We would get most Saturdays free, unless the flying programme was badly in arrears, and our little coterie from Hut 27 would take the bus down to Ramsey on Friday night. We would stay at the Queen's Hotel, run by two sisters who treated us as family, feeding us mightily and seeing that we did not drink too many half-pints of beer. We would play darts in the bar and talk the hind legs off several donkeys until a late hour, but the highlight was breakfast on Saturday morning with lashings of bacon and eggs, and ever more buttered toast. In that largely rural Manx community, food rationing did not seem to be as oppressive as on the mainland, and a good meal could usually be had.

Christmas Day 1943 fell on a Saturday, and for most of us it was our first taste (in every sense) of Christmas dinner at a proper RAF station: we cadets assembled in the Airmen's Mess, suitably decorated, and turkey and all the trimmings were served up to us by the officers and NCOs. On New Year's Day there was further entertainment on the parade ground, where some of the staff pilots, evidently Scots, since they were wearing the kilt below their uniform tunics, demonstrated sword and other Scottish dances, accompanied by a piper in full Highland dress. It was difficult to say who enjoyed it most, the dancers or the spectators, none of whom could have been described as stone cold sober on this Hogmanay.

The end of the course approached rapidly. I and several others had had a commissioning board, and our commissions as pilot officers were announced a couple of weeks before we were due to pass out, to take effect then. I was able to go down to Douglas and be measured for uniform at Simpson's the military tailor, but it would not be ready before we left Jurby and would have to be sent on to my leave address. But I bought a service dress cap, a raincoat and the necessary rank ribbon to sew on to my battledress, and had to be satisfied with that.

Our passing-out was something of an anti-climax. There was normally due ceremonial and presentation of flying badges at a passing-out parade, but on the appointed day heavy Manx rain came down without ceasing and the parade was cancelled. We sat in the classroom while Sergeant Bill Batt, our course NCO, handed out our flying-badges direct from a stores box – no pomp, no ceremony. The historic flying 'O', the badge awarded to observers since the First World War, had just been superseded by the 'N' badge, and we were not too pleased about that either. But we had made it, and that was all that mattered.

At that stage our postings were unknown. Most of us expected to go to Bomber Command and to join an Operational Training Unit (OTU), where we would be crewed up to fly twin-engined Wellington bombers and learn the appropriate procedures before converting to the heavies. We were to go home on leave and await our instructions.

Travelling back to Fleetwood by bus, train and boat, those of us in officers' uniforms had to stand some good-natured ribbing from our fellow navigators wearing three stripes on their sleeves. Some would be disappointed and others would feel that they had had a lucky escape. I was proud to hold the King's Commission (although it never entered my head that I would still be doing so in thirty years' time), but more pleased to have won my flying-badge with a good result on what had seemed to me a tough course. The stalwarts of Hut 27 broke up with regret and hoped to meet again – as some of us did.

There had not been much leave since I had joined, and the week or so at home in Leeds went like a flash. My service dress uniform arrived and I was duly admired and the ritual studio photograph was taken. Looking back now, I can see that the pleasure expressed by my parents at my progress must have been tempered by the knowledge that my future was somewhat uncertain; they had gone through the first war with its enormous casualty lists when few families remained unaffected. But for the moment I was safe, healthy and in good spirits, and I was selfishly content to be so. Joan and I made the most of our time together and were not too dismayed when the expected orders arrived.

*   *   *

I was required to report to RAF Station Wratting Common in Cambridgeshire, a place I had never heard of and could not find on the map. The nearest railway station went by the pleasing name of Six-Mile-Bottom, and I arrived there on a cold February afternoon, humping my large new suitcase and two kitbags of flying-clothing. I telephoned the MT Section at Wratting Common, and the voice on the other end, with conspicuous lack of enthusiasm, said that they would try and send something out for me. In due course a truck arrived and took me the few miles to the aerodrome.

With some surprise I saw that several Stirling aircraft were lined up by the perimeter track, looming out of the twilight like prehistoric monsters. The Stirling was the first of the four-engined heavy bombers to be produced for the RAF, and was still in operational service, although now outperformed in height and bomb-load by the Lancaster and Halifax. I could not imagine what these aircraft were doing at an airfield I assumed to be a Wellington OTU.

Wratting Common was a dispersed Nissen-hutted camp built in wartime amid a sea of East Anglian mud. Flat farmlands stretched for miles around the airfield; the messes were a mile from the living-quarters and another mile from the flight offices and aircraft – bicycles were the order of the day. The Officers' Mess, a none-too-spick-and-span Nissen complex, was full to overflowing with aircrew from all over what was still called the Empire, and from the USA, Poland, Czechoslovakia and elsewhere. I discovered that this was No. 1651 Heavy Conversion Unit, but was still baffled as to why I had been posted there and not to an OTU.

I shared a Nissen hut with two others, and there were certain comforts which I had not had as a cadet – a small wardrobe, a wash-stand, and a WAAF batwoman; but the hut itself was just as cold and draughty as any other I had lived in. Ruby, our batwoman, was cheerful but inexperienced: she brought hot water for us in the morning, made our beds, and cleaned the hut (to some extent). She also cleaned our shoes, no easy task since the local mud was ubiquitous and clinging. Her method was simple – knock the worst of the mud off and then put blacking over the rest. We protested in vain.

On the morning after arrival I reported to the Chief Ground Instructor. He told me that as there was a temporary shortage of navigators at the heavy conversion stage, it had been decided to try the experiment of posting in some trainees direct from Air Obervers' School, missing out the OTU stage and putting them into crews already formed but lacking a navigator for a variety of reasons. I was somewhat taken aback by this news, and not at all sure that I liked it. We had always been assured that the OTU was a vital part of the training process, where crews learned to work together and were given a chance to practise new procedures in a course of some months and sixty to seventy flying-hours. Now I would have to pick up new knowledge quickly, and would, in terms of flying-hours, be much less experienced when I reached an operational squadron. The CGI said that I would not be crewed up immediately and he would see how I got on – not very encouraging words.

There were one or two others in the same situation, and we commiserated with each other in the Mess. But within a few days of starting the ground school lectures our spirits rose as we encountered new navigation aids which, to us, were a tremendous advance on anything we had used hitherto.

One such was the distant-reading gyro-magnetic compass, usually referred to as the DRC. The magnetic compasses we had used in the Anson suffered from instability (they wavered) during turns and other manoeuvres, and were also affected by the metal in the aircraft structure. For this reason the pilot had a directional gyro on his instrument panel which he would use for a steady reading, but this had to be reset frequently to agree with the magnetic compass (when spinning, a gyroscope's axis remains steady, a useful property known as rigidity in space).

The DRC combined the north-seeking properties of the magnetic compass with the stability of a gyroscope, housing both these elements in a master unit mounted in the rear of the aircraft, well away from the main sources of magnetic disturbance. It was electrically driven and could power up to six repeaters which provided a compass reading anywhere in the aircraft, normally in the pilot's and navigator's positions. The magnetic element and the gyro monitored each other and gave accurate course readings, remaining stable during manoeuvres. An additional and most useful facility was a variation-setting control which allowed the magnetic variation (the source of our night-marching troubles in the Home Guard) to be catered for so that the repeaters showed courses in relation to True North. It was the navigator's job to to adjust this control, as the variation changed from place to place. The DRC was to be used for many years in the RAF, and gave good accuracy and reliability.

The second new device we met at Wratting Common was called Gee, and as far as I was concerned this transformed the whole problem of position finding. In the early days of the war, the aircraft of Bomber Command were little better equipped navigationally than our old Ansons at Jurby. Finding the target at night and in poor weather was usually difficult and sometimes impossible. Not until a majority of bombers was fitted with night cameras, automatically photographing the ground in the light of a photo-flash at bomb release, did it become obvious that few aircraft were reaching the target. An analysis of target photographs for June and July 1941 (those where the crews claimed to have bombed the target) revealed that only one in three had come within five miles of the aiming point.

This stimulated the development of a radar fixing system already known in theory. A master and a slave station simultaneously transmit a radar pulse, and a special receiver in the aircraft measures the time difference in the receipt of the two signals, showing the difference in the aircraft's distance from each station. This can be plotted as a line on a specially prepared Gee lattice chart. Signals from the master station and a second slave can be received at the same time and in the same way, giving another position line and thus the aircraft's position at the crossing of the two lines.

The Gee system was first used to any extent in 1942, by which time there were several Gee chains operating in the United Kingdom, giving a range of about 350–400 miles, sufficient to reach targets in the Ruhr. The Germans soon developed janmming transmitters which considerably cut down the operating range and made Gee unsuitable for accurate target finding, but the system was invaluable for navigation around the UK and for keeping the bomber force together and therefore less vulnerable on the outward and return routes. Equally important, the numbers of aircraft unable to find their bases on return in poor weather declined sharply.

We navigators were taught to operate a Gee receiver set on which a cathode ray tube showed sets of pulses received from the ground stations.

The time differences were measured on an electronically generated scale on the CRT, and the result plotted on the red, green and purple lattice lines on the Gee chart. We soon became proficient on the ground trainers and looked forward eagerly to using the system in the air.

At the same time we were being trained in the use of another new radar aid, H2S, sometimes called by the single code letter Y. A rotating scanner fitted beneath the aircraft transmitted a beam of radar energy at centimetric wavelengths (very short waves); this energy, meeting the land or sea surface below, was reflected back to a receiver in the aircraft and the results were shown on a circular CRT known as a plan position indicator. There would be few reflections from a smooth surface (the sea), varying reflections from a rough surface (the land), and intense reflections from a large collection of buildings (towns and cities). Thus a shadowy map of the terrain below, showing coastlines and towns, was built up on the screen; this was independent of the weather or any ground stations. Interpreting the PPI picture needed training and experience, but a good operator could take accurate fixes and also undertake blind bombing runs.

H2S was first used in Bomber Command in January 1943, mainly in Pathfinder target-marking aircraft. As, unlike Gee, its range was unlimited and there were no ground stations to jam, it proved to be a valuable aid, and the whole of the Command was slowly being equipped with it. The system was naturally treated with great secrecy, and there was an armed guard on the door of the H2S training section at Wratting. I find it remarkable that no inkling of this system – or Gee – had leaked down the chain to flying training units; its impact was all the greater, and we felt that we were taking part in a technical revolution in air navigation, as indeed we were.

My first two flights in a Stirling were with a crew flying night circuits and landings. This gave me an opportunity to operate the Gee set and familiarize myself with the DR compass without being preoccupied with route navigation. My logbook records that on the second of these flights we witnessed part of a Luftwaffe bombing raid on London, and saw one aircraft shot down. I retain no recollection of this, no doubt concentrating hard on all the features of the new aircraft.

I found the Stirling spacious: the navigator's position was generously proportioned and I could stand upright between the two pilots' seats, with a good view forward. As the Gee receiver was positioned above the centre of the navigation table, I tended to crash my head on it from time to time until I learned to avoid it. Serviceability was not very good on these Stirlings, as most of them were ex-operational with a good few hours' flying time. In addition, controls and other systems were operated electrically rather than hydraulically and seemed to develop faults rather more frequently; the flight engineers spent much of their time in the bowels of the aircraft rectifying minor failures.

On two day cross-country flights I flew as second navigator and was able to get a little more experience with Gee and the DR compass, and also do some map reading. At about this time I was finally slotted into a crew. The time-honoured method of forming new crews at the time was for newly graduated aircrew to meet at OTU and to sort themselves out into crews to suit their own inclinations. This was important, since crews who could not get on with each other were unlikely to perform efficiently, and more than likely to come to grief.

In my case there was no such choice, but my luck held and I found myself as the only officer in a crew of NCOs captained by Flight Sergeant Alan Moore of the Royal Canadian Air Force; he had lost his navigator through illness. Al was about a year older than I and came from the Toronto area, where his father ran a coal business; he was shortish and stocky, dour at times, but with an impish sense of humour. He was a strict disciplinarian in the air, and I found that the rest of the crew rated his flying ability very highly. They were not mistaken.

Our bomb aimer was Sergeant Michael Bartlett, from the Channel Islands, always called Mickey, chunky in build and full of irrepressible energy. Sergeant Ken Grosse, flight engineer, had joined the crew at Wratting Common, since his job had not been required on the OTU Wellingtons; he was tall and good-looking, with something of an eye for the opposite sex. The wireless operator, Sergeant Willy Williams, was a Londoner, thin, dark, and always cracking jokes. Another Canadian was the mid-upper gunner, Sergeant Tex Savard, who claimed to have Irish, French and Red Indian blood; he came from Alberta and showed something of his Indian ancestry in his features, usually smiling. Finally our rear-gunner, Warrant Officer Pat Wade, was two or three years older than the rest of us and had already done one tour of operations on a Bomber Command Wellington squadron. With his greater experience, he naturally felt some responsibility for the rest of the crew, and we tended to look on him, with affection, as something of a father figure.

I can pinpoint the date on which I joined the crew as 24 February 1944, as this was Mickey's 21st birthday. We all went out for the evening to a local pub and downed many pints of rather watery beer. I finished up in a spare bed in the crew's Nissen hut, and luckily we did not have to fly the following day.

Our first flight together was on 29 February – an auspicious date, we thought. It was a day cross-country in which the navigator did not shine but scrambled through without too much loss of dignity. The following flight was our introduction to H2S, when Mickey and I worked closely together and found the new system rewarding. These flights and one more were captained by a staff pilot, but for our final cross-country, at night, the crew was at last allowed out on its own, with some success. It was early days yet, but we seemed to have the makings of a capable team.

So after some thirty hours on Stirlings, we were posted to Hemswell in Lincolnshire (via a dreary transit camp at Lindholme, near Doncaster) for conversion to the Lancaster. This was now the mainstay of Bomber Command, together with the Halifax, and we were not sorry to exchange the ponderous, lumbering Stirling for it. The Lanc was leaner, trimmer, and looked like a thoroughbred after a carthorse. Although smaller than the Stirling, it carried a greater bomb-load and flew faster and higher. Al was delighted with its handling qualities and was soon sent off solo.

Hemswell was an interesting station for me because it was my first permanent pre-war RAF station. Instead of temporary wooden buildings and Nissen huts there were solid brick-built structures laid out to a pattern, with messes and married quarters (not occupied as such in wartime) separate from the technical site, with its four large hangars at the edge of the airfield; the taxiways, perimeter track, dispersals and three concrete runways were designed to cope with heavy bombers. To my eyes the Officers' Mess was luxurious, a handsome building with a hint of Lutyens, though sadly overcrowded as usual in wartime.

Our flying in the Lancaster Mark 3 at Hemswell was confined to circuits and landings, day and night ('circuits and bumps', as they were universally and pessimistically called). I was able to get in more Gee practice, and flew several flights in the rear turret, from which the view was breathtaking and absorbing. For the first time I was able to study the Lincolnshire countryside which I was to come to know so well.

Early in April, Al was satisfactorily checked out by the Flight Commander, and our long-awaited posting to an operational squadron arrived. This was No. 103, part of No. 1 Bomber Group, and was located at RAF Elsham Wolds, near Scunthorpe in north Lincolnshire. Pat was particularly pleased since his first tour had been with 103 when it flew Wellingtons from Bourne, and he insisted that it was a first-class squadron.

By this time we had got to know each other well and were working together enthusiastically. I suppose we must have been apprehensive to some extent, but we were all confident of the excellence of our training and felt that this was the culmination of many months' preparation and hard work. We were under no illusions about the casualty rates in bomber squadrons, but we were young enough and perhaps arrogant enough to feel that we would come through.

CHAPTER THREE

Learning Again – the Hard Way

A rattling crew bus took us from Hemswell to Elsham Wolds on a fine spring day in early April. The driver, a somewhat cynical WAAF, told us that Elsham had suffered a Ju 88 intruder attack on the previous night. We eyed each other silently; this particular hazard was not one we had hitherto considered.

But our spirits rose in the sunshine and we arrived at our new station laughing and joking. It was indeed on the wolds, the highest part of that otherwise flat Lincolnshire country. We reached it through Brigg (which meant Delius to me) and Barnetby-le-Wold, from which it was a mile or so uphill. Grimsby was some twelve miles or so to the east, with the Humber to the north. Elsham was another wartime hutted camp, but rather less dispersed than Wratting Common. No. 103 Squadron, then flying Wellingtons, had arrived there in July 1941 when the station had been newly constructed, and had converted to Halifaxes in the summer of the following year. By November 1942 it had been re-equipped with the Lancaster, much to the delight of the crews, who had found the early version of the Halifax less than satisfactory.

The squadron was formed in 1917, and operated over France in the First World War, flying DH 9s. The squadron badge is a black swan, with the motto 'Noli Me Tangere' (Touch Me Not), and many Australians flew with 103 in both wars. Disbanding in 1919, the squadron re-formed in 1936 at Andover with Hawker Hind day-bombers, re-equipping with Fairey Battles and joining the Advanced Air Striking Force in France in September 1939. After Dunkirk, and having suffered heavy casualties, 103 returned to the UK at RAF Newton in Nottinghamshire and converted thankfully to the Wellington late in 1940, later moving to Elsham.

Despite only three years of existence, Elsham had an oddly settled feel about it. In retrospect, this was perhaps because our crew was now part of a proper operational unit and would not be continually moving on for further training. I was given a bed in a hut near the Officers' Mess, and then walked over to the sergeants' quarters to see how the crew had fared. They had been allocated the usual Nissen hut ('A Nissen hut is a Nissen hut', Al said philosophically) and were making themselves at home. It was time for tea in the Sergeants' Mess, and they persuaded me to go with them, wearing a spare tunic of Pat Wade's. I felt self-conscious, not so much at acting contrary to service regulations and custom, but at being under false colours – wearing campaign ribbons to which I was not entitled. However, if anyone thought I looked a little young to be a warrant officer they didn't say so, and we had a pleasant meal, sitting outside and drinking tea in the spring sunshine.

Later I went across to the Officers' Mess: entering the ante-room I felt like a new boy at school, but a tall, dark wing commander looked up and came across to me, introducing himself as Eric Nelson, my new Squadron Commander. For half an hour or so he chatted to me, bought me half a bitter, and generally made me feel welcome. This was something new to me, after the indifference shown at training units, where we rarely spoke to senior officers. Wing Commander Nelson was a pre-war officer who believed in the old-fashioned virtues of courtesy and positive leadership, and he was justly a well-liked CO. Arriving in the Mess as I did, with no other crew member for support, his welcome did wonders for my morale.

My solitary state did not last long, since Al had received his commission a week or so previously and now found time to be properly kitted out with his pilot officer's uniform. Almost at once he moved into my room, and we began an even closer relationship, which helped us both in the coming months. The third bed in our small room was occupied by Flight Lieutenant Stan Slater, who was a pilot from No. 576 Squadron, with whom 103 shared the airfield. To us he was a figure to respect – he wore the DFC and had flown many operations; in any event, those were the days when pilot officers still called flight lieutenants 'Sir'. But he was a friendly character, who shortly moved elsewhere.

We duly reported to the Squadron Headquarters and were allocated lockers in the crew room and shown around the station by members of another crew. I went along to see the Squadron Navigation Leader, Flight Lieutenant Farquharson, and was given a kindly reception. He was another figure to treat with respect, since he had survived one tour of operations on Hampdens and another on Bothas (a terrifying product of Blackburn Aircraft which had been withdrawn from service after some disastrous operations). He told me that we would fly one or two training cross-countries before we were allowed to go on 'ops'.

The first of these took place in daylight on 10 April, and as far as I was concerned was a disaster. I felt unwell, was thoroughly airsick, and spent most of the flight staring hopelessly at the chart and trying to summon up enough energy to take a Gee fix. Somehow we got round the route, over north-east England, and Al and the rest of the crew forbore to make the obvious comments. The worst moment came when I took my log and chart to the Navigation Leader. He looked at my face and said: 'How was it?' 'Terrible,' I said, 'I don't know when I've done a worse trip.' He took the log and chart from me and, without looking at them, threw them into the waste-paper basket. 'Right,' he said, 'try again to-morrow.'

We did try again the next day and this time there was no difficulty. A night cross-country followed and again I coped successfully, as did the other members of the crew. By 23 April we had flown a further day and a night cross-country using H2S as the primary navigation aid and also for bombing. We were now considered ready for operations, and in fact Al had already done the standard 'second dickey' trip, on which he had flown as an extra pilot with an experienced crew to Cologne in the Ruhr. He was very quiet when he came back, and would only say that the flak had been terrific – in the true sense of the word.

*   *   *

We had joined the squadron at a transitional stage in Bomber Command's war (although it had been continuously changing and developing since 1939). For the previous year the Command had concentrated mainly on attacking the major industrial centres of Germany, inevitably located in or near cities. The inaccurately styled 'Battle of the Ruhr' and 'Battle of Berlin' were now about to give way to the softening-up of rail communications and other targets in France in anticipation of the coming invasion by the Allies.

The aircrews were of course unaware of this, and it was clear from those on 103 Squadron who were coming to the end of their tours (thirty operational flights) that it had been a long, hard winter. Trips to Hamburg and Berlin were uncommonly long and hard grinds, facing bad weather and icing, heavy flak concentrations, night-fighters, and then the problems of landing at base in fog or low cloud. Losses had been heavy, and the squadron became inured to seeing empty places in the messes and the crew room.

Only a couple of weeks before we arrived, ninety-six aircraft failed to return from a total of 795 dispatched to bomb Nuremberg. The weather played a great part in this disaster, although there were other factors, and Elsham was lucky to lose only two Lancasters, one from each squadron. I sensed, in the more experienced crews, not so much a lowering of morale as a dogged resignation and a longing to have done with the weary battle against the enemy and the elements. There was plenty of humour and banter, but the sense of strain was palpable, and we in our crew could only be thankful that we were starting our tour at the beginning of the summer, when at least one of the factors would be more favourable.

Our first operational flight was to Karlsruhe in southern Germany. Old Bomber Command hands say, 'You never forget your first op', but in truth I have no clear recollections of it, although I have my log and chart in front of me. I see that we were routed close to Dieppe, Reims and Saarbrucken at 21,000 feet. We were one of 637 aircraft taking part in this attack, but we saw little sign of the others; occasionally we would bump across the slipstream of another aircraft – a comforting feeling, since it indicated that we were within the 'bomber stream' and thus less likely to be picked off by a night-fighter. The weather over the target was poor and we bombed a few minutes early, not a critical error since we were well down the bombing order, as befitted a new crew. Eleven minutes after 'Bombs gone' my log records 'Fighter on tail – corkscrewing – shaken off'. We landed safely back at Elsham after six and a half hours' flying, the longest flight to date for any of us. Twenty aircraft were missing that night: of the eleven detailed from Elsham, none was missing, but one landed at base severely damaged and another ditched in Sandwich Bay (all the crew survived but were missing on a later operation).

Squadron life now fell into a sort of pattern, albeit an irregular and sometimes unpredictable one. Depending upon how late we had been flying the previous night, we would get up perhaps mid-morning and go down to the flight offices to see what was happening. If there was a likelihood of flying that night, Al and Ken would probably go to the aircraft dispersal and carry out a run-up, a thorough engine and control check; Mickey might check his bombsight and Tex and Pat their guns and turrets, and Willy and I would see that our navigation and radio equiment was serviceable. Fairly early on we were allocated our own aircraft, G-George, and would normally fly it exclusively. We got to know our ground crew and came to respect and trust their work, out on the dispersal in all weathers and at all times of the day and night.

Some time during the afternoon we would hear that 'Ops are on'; the station gates would be closed and the GPO telephone box secured so that no one could make private calls. Details of the bomb-load and fuel load would be learned from the ground crew, and there would be much speculation as to the target; 2,154 gallons was a full load and meant a long trip, probably deep into Germany.

Navigators and bomb aimers would report to their own briefing a little earlier than main briefing, so that they had time to prepare charts and calculate the flight plan from the route and forecast winds. The rest of the crew would join us, and the briefing room would be full of conversation and cigarette smoke, cross-crew banter, and groans if the target was an especially difficult one. Cigarettes would be put out and we would get to our feet as the Station Commander came in; he would say a few encouraging words and the specialist briefing officers would then get on with their jobs. The Met man was heard with particular concentration – weather at the target and for the return home was everybody's concern.

These were the days when a Bomber Command operation was planned down to the last detail; no longer did captains make decisions about the form of attack. Every aircraft had a laid-down route, height, take-off time and time on target, and deviation from these called for explanation on return. Targets were marked by Pathfinders of No. 8 Group, using various methods, depending on weather and other conditions, and we would be fully briefed on these for each operation.

At the end of the briefing we would empty our pockets of all personal items and receive a small escape pack in exchange. All aircrews were given ground training in parachuting, in crash-landing on land and water, on sea survival ('dinghy drills') and on escape and evasion, as well as our conduct if captured (name, rank and number only to be divulged to the enemy).

If we had some time before take-off, we navigators would put the finishing touches to our charts and flight plans, and check our topographical maps. One unpopular chore was the delineation on our plotting charts of the searchlight zones and heavily defended areas, which we coloured in green and red respectively. In Germany and Holland these changed little and we were able to put them in quickly, but when targets in France became more frequent these zones were liable to change, especially after D-Day.

Finally, we would foregather in the locker rooms and pick up our flying-clothing, parachutes and harnesses, and those inflatable waistcoats known only as Mae Wests. The gunners would wear flying-suits to beat the cold in the partly open turrets, and Pat in the rear turret also wore a bulky flotation suit at times. The crew in the Lancaster cabin – pilot, engineer, bomb aimer, navigator and wireless operator – would usually be warm enough to dispense with extra flying-clothes, although Al and Ken up front might wear an aircrew sweater under their battledress blouses. At the navigator's table Mickey and I sat on a backless bench elbow to elbow, with dark curtains drawn either side so that light did not get out nor daylight in. Unfortunately the cabin heating vents were positioned between these curtains, and at times the heat was unbearable. While Mickey and I were sweating, Al and Ken would be turning the heat up if they were cold at 20,000 feet.

In the locker rooms, last cigarettes would be smoked and there would be laughter and joking, with crews leg-pulling and exchanging insults. I suppose this was partly a nervous reaction, a way of ignoring the ever-present shadow of death and destruction, but I cannot remember our dwelling too much on this: we were only too well aware of the high loss rates in the Command, but my recollection is that we were more afraid of letting the crew down by not doing our particular jobs properly and efficiently. I well remember having vivid dreams, almost nightmares, not of flak and fighters, but of air plots which would not come right and symbols on my chart which I could not interpret.

We would ride the crew bus to our dispersal and arrive there in good time to do our checks, talk to the ground crew, and get ourselves aboard without haste. Agricultural land lay all around, and occasionally one of the family from the nearby farm would come down to the fence with glasses of milk for us, a way of showing their appreciation, although they cannot much have appreciated the almost nightly roar of our Merlins in their back yard. On summer evenings we would stand around G-George savouring the sun, if any, and the fresh air. Then we would hear the stutter of engines starting from across the airfield and we would climb aboard, up a short ladder and into the rear of the aircraft. Wearing parachute harness and Mae West and carrying navigation bag, parachute and flying helmet, I found the journey up the fuselage rather hazardous, and often suffered grazes or bruises. As we became more experienced we evolved a sort of controlled rush which carried us over the rear and main spars – formidable obstacles – with only minor collisions. Crew comfort was certainly not one of the major considerations in the Lancaster design.

Arrived at my seat, I would clip my parachute into the holder, plug in my intercom, and set out my chart, log and navigation tools – pencils, Douglas protractor, computer, dividers, straightedge and so on. Mickey sitting next to me would be doing the same with his H2S log and chart, and Al and Ken would be going through the ritual of start-up. The familiar smell of oil, fuel, glycol, paint and dope would be all-pervasive as the Merlins would come to life one by one, and we would all go through the checks peculiar to our crew position. Al would check us all on intercom and at the due time wave away the chocks and the ground crew, and we would taxi out of dispersal on to the perimeter track. Ahead of us and behind us, twenty or more Lancasters would be doing the same.

At take-off, as the power came on and the brakes off, the crowd of watchers by the Flying Control Tower would wave – WAAFs, HQ staff, Met men and usually the Station Commander. Al would tell Ken to stop looking at the girls and keep his mind on the engines.

Getting airborne was always a relief after the long preparation. We were on our own and knew what was to be done. As the airfield fell away below us there would be many aircraft visible in the air above and around us. Using the Gee lattice we would navigate around a small triangular pattern close to Elsham until the precisely prescribed time came to set course. Climbing steadily as the light failed, we would cross the coast near Cromer or Orfordness if we were bound for Germany, and soon everybody would be on oxygen, with the masks clamped tight to our faces. There would be little conversation on the intercom – alterations of course or height, perhaps a short warning from a gunner if another aircraft came close, and the occasional check from Al to see that everybody was functioning and alert.

Soon we would run out of the navigational cover of Gee as the enemy jamming took effect, reducing the ratio of signal to noise until the transmitter pulses on the cathode-ray tube gradually became lost in the 'grass'. Mickey would be taking H2S fixes, and we usually got an accurate one as we crossed the Dutch or French coast. The navigation compartment was a little world on its own, with my attention wholly concentrated on plotting position symbols on the chart, logging the multiplicity of readings, and working out wind velocities for the next course, while constantly checking our progress against the briefed time.

As we crossed the enemy coast, those who could see out increased their alertness, and the gunners would keep their turrets slowly moving to cover their full range of vision. As we came closer to the target, Mickey would relinquish the H2S to me and struggle down under Ken's legs to the bomb aimer's position in the nose, setting up the Mark XIV bombsight and checking on his bombing controls.

Occasionally Willy would pass me a list of wind velocities he had received in a Group broadcast. More experienced members of the bomber force, flying at the head of the main stream, would send their found winds by W/T back to Group, who would retransmit them, adjusted by the Met officer if necessary, for the benefit of the force as a whole. If my navigation was going well I would tend to ignore them, but sometimes – if we had had no fix for some time – they would come in useful.

Al, Ken and Mickey up front would now be looking out for target markers, and if I had done my job properly they would be dead ahead at the appointed time (not invariably the case). Mickey would then start the bombing run, directing Al to fly 'left left' or 'right' or 'steady' until the time came for 'bomb doors open'. We would hear and feel the rumble as the doors moved beneath us, and a draught of cool air would play around our feet. This was a reminder that we were sitting on top of several tons of high explosive and incendiaries, and somehow it made us feel much more vulnerable during the bombing run.

I had time now to move the blackout curtain aside, first carefully turning my desk light down. There was suddenly a real and unfriendly world outside; all sounds were masked by the roar of the engines, but fires, explosions and bursts of flak were only too visible. Occasionally the silhouette of a Lancaster or Halifax could be seen below. Looking out over the target was a pleasure I could easily forgo and did not often indulge in. In any event I had to record airspeed, course, height and precise time at 'bombs gone', to take a fix if possible, and be ready to give Al the new course out of the target area, much to everyone's relief.

On our second trip the target was Essen in the Ruhr, where the defences were heavy, and as we ran up on the markers Mickey's directions came to a halt. We ploughed on, bomb doors open, for a few long seconds, and then Al sent Ken down the nose to see what was going on. Mickey was lying on his oxygen tube, stopping the flow, and had passed out. Ken reconnected him, and when he was fully conscious Al decided that we should 'go round again' to drop our bombs on the target now behind us, a hazardous procedure against the bomber stream. Somehow we got back on the right course and dropped our bombs on the markers, Mickey now functioning satisfactorily. The relief from the rest of the crew as the bomb doors were closed and we left the target area was almost palpable. It took Mickey some time to live this down, especially as some wag chalked 'Oxygen Bartlett' on his locker door.

The long run home would be lightened by the knowledge that we had done the job. But we all knew that the bomber stream was at its most vulnerable to night-fighters as we left the target, and the tension would remain high until we crossed the enemy coast going homeward.

Our third operation was to Friedrichshaven, a very long haul on which we logged nine and a half hours in the air. For the return we were routed south of Paris, but with no Gee reception and poor H2S fixing we strayed north of the briefed track, and later Gee fixes showed that we must have flown over or close to the city. We were accurately targeted by predicted flak, bursting very close to us, and during the slow turn which was the prescribed escape manoeuvre the flak bursts maddeningly followed us round. After we had landed, the ground crew dug out several pieces of shrapnel from the fuselage near the mid-upper turret. Tex kept one as a souvenir of Paris.

There was inevitably some relaxation among the crew once the English coast was in sight, although the gunners and Al remained alert for intruders. As we lost height, Mickey and I would take off our oxygen masks, slump against the fuselage behind our backless bench, and perhaps pop a piece of chewing gum or barley sugar into our mouths. I would line up the Gee set for a homing down the lattice line leading to Elsham, and as we approached Al would call base for landing instructions. With up to twenty Elsham aircraft detailed for one operation, and similar numbers at the two airfields whose circuits overlapped ours – Killingholme and Kirmington – we could sometimes circle in the stack for twenty minutes or so, a tricky business if we were in cloud or poor visibility. 'G-George, pancake' were the words we were waiting for, and the squeal of the tyres as we touched down on the runway was a heartening sound.

Back at dispersal the ground crew would be waiting for us, and when the engines were stopped we would clamber out stiffly and savour the fresh air and the silence. Richard Morris, in his biography of Guy Gibson, catches this moment exactly: 'One by one the engines fell silent. In the sudden quiet the faint metallic tinkling noises of the cooling Merlins mingled with the sound of skylarks …'. I recall clear mornings when we landed around dawn and stars were still glittering in the sky; our ears would still be singing from the long pounding of the engines, but we could hear birdsong and the occasional farm noises, and aircraft still in the air overhead. We were grateful for these signs of normality and for the fact that we had returned to enjoy them.

The crew bus would take us to interrogation and we would be given a mug of tea with a generous lacing of rum. We would sit round the intelligence officer's table while he picked our brains – how and when we bombed, what the target looked like, the performance of the markers, aircraft shot down, and any grains of information which might add to the general picture of the operation. Hundreds of these reports would have to be sifted and collated at Group and Command HQ so that an accurate and comprehensive raid report could be made. In my mind's eye I can see us now, our scruffy aircrew battledress contrasting with the intelligence officer's No. 1 uniform, sipping our tea and smoking, with the deep grooves from the oxygen masks still showing on our grey faces. Then we would be off to bed, sometimes after a bacon-and-egg breakfast, and to long-awaited sleep, in my case often with troubled dreams.

Squadron life was not all grim and earnest, stress and strain. Unlike the early days of Bomber Command, when the full moon helped the crews to find the target, the moon period was now usually avoided as making the night-fighters' task easier. So at these times we had squadron parties or trips to the theatre in Scunthorpe, our local 'big city', or just pub crawls in the friendly town of Brigg, where the Dying Gladiator or Lord Nelson would be full of bomber crews celebrating the temporary stand-down.

One of these moon periods was particularly memorable for me since Joan was able to come to a dance in the Mess. I found a place for her to stay in Barnetby-le-Wold, our nearest village, and she came down from Leeds on the train – every place of any size (and some very small places) had their own railway stations in those days. It was a strange experience, seeing her for the first time in the setting of an RAF station; it was a mingling of two worlds, and I don't know what Joan made of the Mess at Elsham and its inhabitants. However, she looked enchanting in a red dress, and there were many envious glances.

On other off-duty occasions, the crew would sometimes cycle around the Lincolnshire lanes and find a place to have a meal. We had one expedition round the far side of the airfield, and down a long, bumpy, unmade road through green fields and hedges to a farmhouse kitchen, where we had ham and eggs and home-baked bread and cakes.

There was a good station library at Elsham and, as always, I managed to read a good deal. One day I found a book of mine on a library shelf; I had lent it to somebody on another crew who had gone missing, and the Committee of Adjustment (charged with the disposal of effects) had passed it on to the library. Luckily my signature was on the flyleaf and I had no trouble in claiming it. I still have it: *The Fire Was Bright*, by Leslie Kark, a journalistic account of earlier bomber operations (hardly escapist literature).

We were usually able to have a few days' leave every month. On the morning after an operational trip we would check the leave roster on the flight office noticeboard, and often our names would have moved up the list because there were crews missing. We would make black jokes about this – callous in retrospect perhaps, but part of the way in which we coped with the slow drip of losses, the non-appearance of friends and acquaintances. We were in fact grateful if leave did come round more frequently and we could have a few days away. Al and Tex usually went to London, a magnet for 'colonials', but the rest of us would go home. I would hitch-hike to Leeds, normally with little difficulty, and drop back for a while into what I thought of as another life. There was one summer evening when again our two worlds intermingled: Joan and I were walking near her home when a distant hum grew into a steady roar, and the evening sky was filled with Lancasters and Halifaxes, aircraft from the many Yorkshire airfields of 4 and 6 Groups preparing to fly east. I hardly knew whether to wish I was among them or to be thankful that I wasn't.

*   *   *

I had not been long on the squadron – it was 29 April – when we received an informal visit from Marshal of the RAF Lord Trenchard, the 'father' of the RAF and a legendary figure. I was lucky enough to be in the Mess when he arrived and to be introduced to him with other young officers. At this time he was not directly concerned with the conduct of the war, but a Marshal of the RAF never retires, and he was spending some time talking to operational aircrews of all commands. I cannot remember the details of the brief conversation but I clearly recall the great impression he made – tall, erect, grey and slightly shabby in his ancient uniform, but an undoubted personage. This was my first contact with a really senior officer – not just that but a historical figure – and I and the other green and would-be cynical young men felt a real pride in what he represented.

Shortly after this, Wing Commander Nelson, our Squadron Commander, was posted away amid general regret. He was replaced by Wing Commander Goodman, who had come from the South African aircrew training scheme and had little experience on Lancasters. He made an unpopular start by announcing that in future all 103 aircrew would be reporting for physical training sessions when they were not required for flying. Putting myself in his place with hindsight, I can see how shocked he must have been at the sloppy, unfit and generally scruffy appearance of both officers and NCOs, and the reluctance to do any duty not concerned with operational flying. His views were not well received, and there were mixed feelings when he was shot down over Hasselt in Belgium only a few days after his arrival.

This tragedy was heightened by the fact that Wing Commander Goodman had taken with him the crew of the senior Flight Commander, Squadron Leader van Rolleghem ('Van'), who had completed one tour with 103 Squadron in 1943, and had managed to get himself back on ops with most of his old crew. He was ill in hospital at the time of the Hasselt raid and was greatly upset when he learned that all his crew had been killed. Van was a Belgian of tremendous character and with much experience of civil flying before the war. After the war he returned to the Belgian Air Force and reached high rank.

Another Elsham character was 'Doc' Henderson, the Station Medical Officer, who was reputed to have flown more ops than anyone on the station, and was deservedly popular. One of the sights of the Mess on a non-flying evening was Doc and his fellow MO playing table tennis with great spirit but steadily declining co-ordination as the alcoholic evening wore on.

Our crew's tour of operations was grinding steadily on, at a much quicker pace than for those unfortunates who had battled over Berlin and the Ruhr through the long winter. After three trips to targets in Germany we were switched to France and Belgium for a varied list of objectives – ammunition and transport depots, an airfield, coastal gun batteries – in preparation for the Allied landings, though for us at the time this was purely surmise.

It was during this period that Headquarters Bomber Command dropped another sort of bombshell. It was announced to the incredulous crews that all targets in France would henceforth count as one-third of an operation towards the required total of thirty. I can recall the slightly sick feeling with which this was received: since most targets were likely to be in France for the next few months, we could see ourselves flying something like fifty or sixty trips to complete our tour. While there was agreement that trips to French targets would be shorter and against lighter defences, we felt that this was an unreasonable shortening of the odds against survival. Crews who had already lived through twenty-five or more operations, mostly against hazardous German targets, were particularly bitter about this new ruling.

There was certainly serious discontent among bomber crews generally, but the situation was not long in resolving itself. On 3 May, 362 aircraft (including ours) attacked a large German military depot and tank park at Mailly-le-Camp, thought to be housing the 21st Panzer Division. The attack was a success, but problems with the voice communications in the target area meant that many aircraft were 'going round again' while awaiting instructions to bomb; we did so for nine minutes, a long and anxious time in the circumstances. The night-fighters got to work, and forty-two aircraft were lost, mostly to them. A week later, twelve out of eighty-nine aircraft were lost in an attack on marshalling yards at Lille. After these disasters, nothing more was heard of the 'one-third of an op' rule.

After a few more French targets, we were dispatched on a mining sortie in Kiel Bay on the night of 15 May. Bomber Command had been laying mines off the Kiel Canal since the beginning of the war in a campaign mainly directed against U-boat traffic, and this was being stepped up preparatory to the invasion of Europe. We were to use H2S to indicate our dropping-point, using a bearing and distance from a small, easily-identified island. Both Mickey and I had by now become more proficient in the use of H2S, and we had no difficulty in getting to the right place and laying the mines. Although we were the only aircraft operating in that particular area, we met no opposition and returned to base congratulating ourselves on a quiet trip.

Before the end of May we flew on sorties to Duisburg and Dortmund in the Ruhr, and at the beginning of June we were allocated a new G-George with 'paddle-blade' propellers, which greatly improved performance. As a bonus the aircraft was fitted with an air position indicator, an analogue computer receiving inputs from the DR compass of the course we were flying, and from air pressure sensors giving our true airspeed (as opposed to the information from the existing air speed indicators to which corrections for height and temperature had to be made). The marvel of the API was that instead of laboriously (and mostly inaccurately) constructing a manual air plot on the chart, the navigator could now read off the air position at any time in latitude and longitude from the veeder counters on the face of the instrument, positioned at the back of the navigation table. Providing the magnetic variation was reset as necessary on the variation setting control of the DR compass, the API's accuracy was within 2%, and its reliability was equally high. The API was still in use in the RAF twenty years later, and represented a great advance in a less spectacular aspect of air navigation.

By this time we were beginning to gain more confidence in our individual jobs and also to work together as a crew with growing efficiency. Al's obvious competence as pilot and captain inspired us all to give of our best, and there was the added spur of knowing that our better performance would increase our chances of survival – enlightened self-interest, indeed.

CHAPTER FOUR

D-Day and After

At the beginning of June our crew took part in raids on coastal batteries at Calais and Wimereux, and on the evening of 5 June we were briefed to attack another at St Martin de Varreville on the Cherbourg peninsula. There was nothing unusual about the briefing and no untoward incident during the flight. We bombed just before midnight (Double British Summer Time, which was in force then) and as we came back across the Channel I noted in my log: 'Convoy below, approx 50 vessels.' We were one of 1,136 heavy bombers which attacked ten coastal batteries in the D-day assault area, and 'with a single exception the batteries offered no serious resistance to the ships of war approaching the coast of France, or to the invading forces' (Bomber Command Quarterly Review No. 9).

We were operating again the following evening, 6 June, and by this time we knew that the long-awaited invasion had started. We bombed a road and rail junction at Vire, in the south of the Cherbourg peninsula, one of over a hundred aircraft on this target, from which three were missing. As far as we were concerned, the five-hour trip was uneventful.

D-day was a great boost to morale, and the atmosphere was now infinitely more cheerful. After an attack on a landing ground at Flers in Normandy and a trip to Gelsenkirchen in the 'Happy Valley' (the Ruhr), we flew our first daylight operation on 14 June, the target being submarine pens and E-boat concentrations at Le Havre. This was Bomber Command's first daylight operation for many months, and although we had the inestimable benefit of fighter cover from Spitfires of No. 11 Group, we did not really feel at home away from the cloak of darkness. There was what the official Command report called 'a formidable curtain of light flak', and since the smoke puffs from the flak bursts lingered for several minutes and were visible in the daylight, it indeed seemed impenetrable. In fact, no aircraft was missing from this raid, although five were damaged by flak.

After two more night ops – one to the Ruhr and one in France – we flew a further daylight trip, with the target a flying-bomb installation at a place called Mimoyecques in the Pas de Calais. Although the first flying-bomb, or V1, did not fall in south-east England until 13 June, Bomber Command and the US Eighth Air Force had been attacking known launch sites (nicknamed 'ski-sites' from their long double ramps) for some months, with a great deal of success. The original German plan was for 6,000 weapons a day to be launched, but up to the last V1 at the beginning of September (when most of the sites were overrun by the Allied armies) this was reduced to an average of ninety-five a day. This at least was one campaign in which Bomber Command prevented more devastation than it caused.

Again we had fighter cover on the Mimoyecques raid, and there were no missing aircraft, although fourteen suffered minor flak damage. This was our first trip for which Pat was not in the rear turret. He had completed the twenty operations needed for his second tour; this was the rule at the time, and a very sensible one: a total of fifty ops must have reduced the possibility of survival very considerably. Pat was posted away as an instructor, and we were very sorry to see him go, missing his skill, his experience and above all his wise advice. He was replaced by Flight Sergeant 'Robbie' Roberts, another experienced gunner who got on well with the crew, but it wasn't quite the same.

Our crew flew three more night ops to French targets, and then on 7 July we were briefed for a daylight trip attacking German tank and troop concentrations at Caen, preparatory to a ground assault by Allied forces to capture the town and break the stalemate in the Allied advance.

We took off from Elsham shortly after eight o'clock on this fine Friday evening, flying our usual triangular pattern around the base area to gain height, and were grateful for the daylight and the good visibility since scores of aircraft were doing the same thing. We set course nearly an hour later at eight thousand feet, just a minute late on our briefed time.

As we flew south, descending to six thousand feet to avoid heavy cumulo-nimbus cloud, Al and Ken were discussing a problem with the starboard outer engine, which had started losing power. They decided not to shut it down, as it was not greatly overheating, but to watch it very carefully. There was no thought of turning back, but it did mean that if we lost any further time it would be difficult to increase speed.

We crossed the English coast just west of Worthing, and soon were able to see the extraordinary sight of Mulberry Harbour just off the French shore. There were heavy bombers everywhere, with the occasional friendly fighter over the top, which the gunners kept a close eye on. Our target, Caen, was just ten miles inland, and we were also able to see the tremendous flak barrage being put up around it. This was alarming, as it looked almost solid, much as at Le Havre; we knew that most of what we were seeing was smoke, but we also knew that the flak would be much more accurate at less than half our usual height. However, we all had a job to do and I ducked back into the navigation compartment and carried on with my calculations.

We had a five-minute spread for our time on target, 2150 to 2155, and my estimated time on target was now 2155. At 2151 we started our bombing run; Mickey at last said 'Bombs gone' at half a minute before 2154, which I pencilled into my log. Almost immediately there was a shuddering crash somewhere aft and we were thrown into a steep banking dive. There was little time to experience fear or to understand what had happened, and I hung on to the navigation table, unable to make much movement because of the 'G' forces, and feeling fresh air from the rear of the aircraft.

Al was battling with the controls, and we lost nearly three thousand feet before he was able to level out and assess the situation. He checked each crew member on the intercom and got responses from all except Robbie the rear gunner. The aircraft was hard to steer, and Tex from the mid-upper turret told us that the starboard fin and rudder and part of the tailplane were missing. What he could see of the rear turret appeared to be damaged.

G-George was now on an even keel, although Al was having to exert great force on the rudder bar to keep the aircraft straight, with only one rudder taking effect. (It occurred to me afterwards that the loss of power on the starboard outer engine might have worked slightly in our favour here.)

Al called Willy and asked him to go down from the wireless operator's position to the rear of the aircraft and report. After a minute or two he came back and plugged in his intercom again; I can hear him now saying, 'You've had your rear gunner, Skipper, and a lot of the turret as well.' We realized then that another aircraft must have collided with us from behind and presumably from above.

Why had Robbie not alerted us? He too may have been checking on fighters overhead, but we shall never know.

There are at least two reports of what happened to our aircraft over the target, one official and one personal. The formal Bomber Command report says:

Of the two Lancasters that crashed near the beachhead one was hit by flak and crash-landed; the other was involved in a remarkable incident. Lancaster G had just bombed when A, above it, released its bombs, some of which removed G's tailplane. A's port outer engine then struck G's rear turret. A turned away to port with one engine on fire and was engaged by flak which put out of action two more engines. Three of the crew baled out. The pilot made for a landing ground on one engine and crash-landed near it, saving the four men still aboard, who were back in this country soon after … The incident was accurately reported by a third crew.

I wonder if this third crew was the one in which Eric Simms, the ornithologist, was flying. He says in his autobiography (*Birds of the Air*, Hutchinson, 1976):

> We ran in over the Normandy beachhead. It was a clear summer evening and the air was full of Lancasters and hundreds of bursting flak shells, each leaving a round black cloud. Two Lancs in front of us flew steadily on, committed to their bombing runs and timed flights, converging slowly and with dreadful inevitability until they collided. Pieces of engine cowling flew past us and bits of wreckage struck the leading edges of our wings. One aircraft lost height and disappeared below us; the other flew on.

Some four minutes after the collision we turned north-west close to our briefed track, but at only three thousand feet. Al managed to gain a little height, but the rudder became increasingly heavy and he judged that he would be unable to fly the aircraft back to base. We knew that Tangmere, on the south coast near Chichester, was an active fighter airfield often used for emergency landings, and I gave Al a rough course to steer and worked out an estimated time of arrival. We called them on the emergency frequency, gave a short explanation of our problem, and were told to stand by as there were other damaged aircraft in the circuit.

Al gave us the option of baling out, but we all had complete faith in him, and took up our crash positions in the body of the aircraft aft of the main spar. I suppose that we must have felt fear and apprehension, but I have no recollection of that. As far as I was concerned this was less frightening than the sight of the flak barrage when we had run into the target.

Al put G-George down on the grass with the undercarriage up, and we ground and screeched to a halt in a cloud of dust. We scrambled out as quickly as possible after collecting aircraft papers and my navigation bag. The crash waggon and ambulance were waiting for us and we were whisked off to the Station Sick Quarters for a check-up, despite our protests that we were fit and well. The MO looked us over and prescribed medicine which he gave us on the spot: I can't now remember whether it was Scotch or Bourbon.

We were found beds and had a meal. Al spoke to Elsham on the telephone and I rang Joan in Leeds to make sure she would disregard any message that we were missing – our conscientious Adjutant had been known to send out 'Missing' telegrams before a crew turned up next day.

I find it hard to put myself in the place of that 20-year-old and say what my feelings were. There was certainly some exhilaration at having survived a closer acquaintance than usual with the 'Grim Reaper'. At the same time we were shocked and saddened to lose Robbie; however little we knew of him, he had been a member of our crew for a short space of time and therefore one of us. We were young enough and resilient enough to recover quickly from what is now called 'trauma', and we all felt the irony of being almost destroyed by someone on our own side on a short daylight operation, when we had come safely through trips at night over the Ruhr and deep into Germany.

We went down to the airfield and had a look at G-George. There had been no fire, and she lay forlornly on her belly with a single black fin standing upright. She was a write-off, and before they dragged her away I unscrewed the navigator's clock from my desk as a small memento.

A final irony in the Caen episode came to light in the post-war histories of the Normandy campaign. The attack on Caen was at the request of General Montgomery's 21st Army Group, and was intended to facilitate a breakthrough on the ground. Over 450 heavy bombers dropped their bombs where they had been briefed to drop them, against intense heavy and light flak. But according to John Terraine's monumental book on the RAF in the European war, *The Right of the Line* (Hodder and Stoughton, 1985): 'So great was the fear of bombing short and causing British casualties that the bombline was fixed 6,000 yards ahead of the nearest troops. This meant that the bombs would fall ... some three miles behind the strongly defended forward area which the infantry and tanks would have to capture.' On top of that, the ground attack was not mounted until over six hours after the bombing had finished. The enquiry afterwards (*vide* Terraine again) commented: 'Apart from the enormous lift to morale which the appearance of the heavy bombers had given, their view was that the bombing had made no difference to the whole operation.' It was just as well that the crews did not know this at the time.

Nevertheless, Montgomery sent Bomber Command's Commander-in-Chief a congratulatory message after the Caen raid. Our Station Commander read it out in the briefing room, and when he came to the final passage referring to 'your brave and gallant pilots' there was some good-humoured derision from the assembled aircrews, of whom, of course, only one in seven were pilots.

On 12 July we were one of more than a hundred Lancasters bombing an important railway junction at Revigny, just over a hundred miles east of Paris. We were given an alternative target at Culmont Chalindrey nearby, and flew a long diversionary route west of the Channel Islands and between Le Mans and Tours. There was low cloud over the target, and although we came down to 5,000 feet we could see no target indicators. Mickey in the nose reported flares, and as we turned to come in on them the gunners reported a combat ahead. Finally, after some minutes in the target area we received the codeword meaning no bombing on the Revigny target. Al decided to have a crack at the alternative target of Chalindrey, where in about thirteen minutes we bombed on red and green TIs and thankfully turned for home. There was low cloud over Elsham, too, and we were diverted to Lindholme near Doncaster, landing after nine hours and ten minutes in the air, our second-longest trip after Friedrichshaven. From these two targets twelve aircraft were missing (including one from 103 Squadron) – a high proportion out of 210 attacking, partly due to night-fighters from the nearby St Dizier airfield, but also to light flak and a collision over Revigny between two Lancasters. Again luck had been with us, and we were not detailed for a second strike at Revigny a few nights later, when twenty-four aircraft were missing.

On 18 July we took part in a massive dawn raid on targets in the Caen area in support of the Allied ground forces; more than 1,000 heavy bombers were used. Our crew had no problems and losses were light, but again it appears from subsequent accounts that this enormous effort was not followed up on the ground and achieved very little.

Somewhat ominously, we thought, for our last trip we were switched to a synthetic oil target (Scholven) in the Ruhr, with its well-organized flak and night-fighter defences. My log notes two combats reported (one before and one after bombing), many searchlights, and heavy flak on the bombing run. We left the target area with Al weaving to avoid any lurking night-fighters, and I logged light flak and searchlights before we left the Ruhr. We landed back at Elsham with thankful hearts after a four-and-a-quarter-hour flight. No Elsham aircraft was lost on that night.

The remaining six of our original crew were all deeply relieved that we had come through safely, but there was a genuine regret that we now had to dissolve the unique partnership that we had built up, with its strong and satisfying interdependence. In particular, Al and I had developed a close relationship, and we agreed that after a few months we would try to get ourselves posted to a Mosquito squadron, where we could once again fly together, but in a superbly fast aircraft with a greater chance of survival.

We felt that we had been an efficient crew for most of our tour and that this had been in our favour, but we knew that luck had also been on our side – not only in the Caen incident but in the timing of our posting to Elsham. In just over three months we had completed a full tour of operations, flying in summer weather, when many of our fellow aircrew who had been on the squadron when we arrived had had a long haul through the previous winter, flying mostly to German targets – the Ruhr and Berlin – and suffering severe losses. We recalled how, on at least one occasion, new crews had arrived, had been told to leave their luggage in the Mess, and had reported to briefing for operations that night; in the morning the bags were still lying in the Mess, ownerless. Yes, we had been lucky.

Both Al and Pat were in due course awarded the Distinguished Flying Cross, richly earned – Pat with fifty operations under his belt and Al as a competent and successful captain; the crew had felt that he should have received an immediate DFC after the Caen flight, where he had undoubtedly saved our lives, but we were happy and proud that he had his award at the end of the tour.

We left Elsham on leave to await our postings; I was certainly at home by 21 July, since this was the date on which Joan and I got engaged before going to Scarborough for a short holiday.

The crew was now dispersed, mostly as instructors at training units within Bomber Command. The plans Al and I had to convert to Mosquitoes never came to fruition since he was soon posted back to Canada, as was Tex, who spent some time in hospital with lung trouble. I lost sight of Ken Grosse and Willy Wiliams, but was still in touch with Michael Bartlett and Pat Wade until they died recently. Tex Savard in Alberta sent Christmas cards every year until a couple of years ago, when they ceased; he too must have gone. Al and I never met after 1944, although we exchanged letters, and he died some years ago in Ontario.

* * *

A significant phase in my life had ended, and I feel that I should be able to write something significant about it. All I can say is that, after more than half a century, what stays with me is the sense of pride and achievement in taking part in that terrible war, and a feeling of deep gratitude that I am still alive to write about it. Bomber Command lost over 55,000 aircrew, many more than the total of British officers lost in the Great War. Was this a total waste? There have always been critics of what we did in the bombing offensive, mostly using that distorted glass, hindsight. At the time we had no doubt, rightly or wrongly, that what we were doing was helping to win a just war and possibly shortening it; I still think that this was the case. Bomber Harris has been reviled for his part in laying waste German cities: but whatever he did was in line with directives from above, and though one must bitterly regret the death and destruction that was caused, we should never forget that our nation was fighting for its life, its existence, its identity – something that in the twenty-first century we are again in danger of losing by more insidious means.

Enough of generalities and controversies. I left Elsham with the knowledge that I had been able to hold my own in a testing job. Coming from a background in which youth, in general, was not encouraged to think well of itself and was kept in its place, this was a satisfaction to me: I was actually beginning to think of myself as a competent professional. In truth, I still had a great deal to learn. At the end of our operational tour my total flying hours were 330, a pitiful figure when I think of the thousands of hours built up by professional aircrew in the later RAF. Being able to use some of the latest navigational aids had made it possible to meet the requirements of the job at the time; what I did not realize for several years was that the constant availability of an accurate fixing system like Gee, while good for efficiency and safety, tended to work against acquiring some of the qualities of a first-rate navigator – a sixth sense, if you like, in dealing with sparse and inaccurate information and using it intelligently, the practice of an art as much as a science.

Our time at Elsham certainly changed me in several respects. There are two old photographs, one taken just before we started operational flying and another six months later. In the earlier photograph there is a boyish, almost innocent, look; in the later one my aspect is much older and a little dour, almost grim. This might be a trick of the camera, but I think not. I was beginning to grow up.

CHAPTER FIVE

Staff Navigator

No. 1662 Heavy Conversion Unit, RAF Station Blyton, lay just north of Gainsborough and in the flat and featureless part of Lincolnshire amid heavily agricultural land. Its job, like that of Wratting Common, was to convert potential bomber crews to four-engined aircraft, in this case the Handley-Page Halifax Marks 2 and 5. These two types, though fitted with Merlin engines, never equalled the efficiency and reliability of the Halifax Mark 3 with Hercules engines, and their operational ceiling and performance were generally inferior to those of the Lancaster. Blyton's Halifaxes, too, were mostly ex-operational aircraft and not in the best of condition.

All this I was to discover later as I organized a bed, checked in at the Mess, and reported to the Navigation Section. The station was hutted and dispersed, like most of its wartime vintage, but to my eyes it did not appear as spruce and cared for as Elsham. The Navigation Section was a long hut with offices at one end, a lecture room at the other, and a crew room between. The Navigation Leader was Flight Lieutenant Bill Bentley, an avuncular man who seemed middle-aged to me but was probably no more than thirty. The navigation staff were a varied selection – an Australian, a Canadian, a New Zealander and several RAF navigators – but they had all done at least one tour of bomber operations and several wore the purple and white ribbon of the DFC.

The atmosphere was friendly and leisurely, and I was not given a specific task straightaway. Familiarization with the Halifax was my first aim, and I was taken over an aircraft and shown the navigator's position and instruments, the emergency equipment and exits, and the general layout. Provision for the crew was more generous than in the Lancaster, and to my surprise both navigator and bomb aimer were accommodated in the nose compartment beneath the feet of the pilot and flight engineer, as was the wireless operator. What I particularly liked was that the front escape-hatch was also in the nose and easily accessible from the navigator's position.

After a couple of not very active days I asked if I could have a flight. An aircraft was about to take off on a Gee cross-country, and Flying

Control asked the captain if he would stop in front of the tower and pick up a new member of the staff for an experience flight. I went out with my parachute and helmet and climbed aboard, shutting the hatch and then plugging in my intercomm to ask the captain where he wanted me. 'How about the rear turret?' he said, 'we only have a mid-upper today.' So as the aircraft taxied on I inserted myself into the rear turret, stowing my parachute, and waited for take-off, closing the turret doors behind me.

I had flown several times in a Lancaster rear turret, but I found that the Halifax Boulton-Paul turret was of a different design, with a single joystick control instead of the double-handled Frazer-Nash system in the Lanc. The control system was also much more sensitive, as I discovered just after we were airborne, when I grasped the joystick to rotate the turret to one side. In a flash, or so it seemed, the turret had swung to the beam position, and its doors, which I had not locked properly, flew open behind me in the slipstream. The ground at the edge of the airfield looked uncomfortably close as it streamed past, and I moved the turret, more carefully this time, back to its fore-and-aft position, and closed and locked the doors: so much for familiarization with the Halifax. However, later in the four-hour flight I moved around the aircraft and began to feel more at home.

I had hardly been at Blyton more than a week when Bill Bentley buttonholed me in the Mess one day after lunch. 'Better get your bags packed,' he said, 'you're off to Shawbury on a Staff Nav Course.' I had never heard of Shawbury or the Staff Navigator Course, but I was told that this was a prerequisite to becoming a competent instructor. I have little doubt now that Group Headquarters had told Blyton to nominate someone, and that as the latest arrival and most underemployed dogsbody, I had drawn the short straw. But however it happened, this was a significant step in my career, though I had no idea of it at the time, and indeed no concept of a 'career' as such. My chief aim was still to survive the war.

Shawbury, a few miles north of Shrewsbury, was the RAF's Central Navigation School, at which all post-graduate navigation training was based. Starting in 1918 with the 'School of Naval Co-operation and Aerial Navigation' at Calshot on the south coast, the RAF had a long and varied history of specialized navigation training at several locations. Trenchard, as well as setting up the RAF College at Cranwell for officer training, introduced several specializations for officers of the General Duties (GD) Branch, who were then all pilots: Armament, Photography, Engineering, Signals and Navigation. The so-called Long Navigation Course, of one year's duration, started in 1920 and in 1929 became the Specialist Navigation Course, qualifying its graduates for the symbol 'N' in the Air Force List and for a number of staff, instructional and research and development posts. The Spec N Course, as it was universally known in the RAF, continued through various changes and vicissitudes until 1966, when

I was intimately involved in its evolution into the present Aerosystems Course, still active and still one year long in 2006.

Although there were officer observers in the First World War, their main task was reconnaissance and artillery spotting rather than navigation, and it was not until 1940 that the requirements of the Second World War caused aircrew other than pilots to be trained as navigators. They were still called observers, however, and continued to be so until late in 1943, when the 'O' flying badge was replaced by the 'N' badge, much to my chagrin and that of my fellow students at Jurby (still called No. 5 Air Observers' School) in January 1944; the flying 'O' was much prized, and those who had qualified for it continued to wear it for many years, sometimes in defiance of regulations.

With the rapid expansion of Bomber and Coastal Commands, the need for navigators led to the creation of several air observers' schools in the United Kingdom and in Commonwealth countries. This in turn led to a need for navigation instructors, for whom the long and relatively expensive Spec N Course was not justified. In 1942 the Staff Navigator Course was introduced at Cranage, which became known as the Central Navigation School (CNS); the course was of three or four months' duration, and used Ansons for flying exercises.

In March 1944 CNS moved to Shawbury, and by this time was operating forty-two Wellingtons Mark XIII and four Stirlings Mark III. All unknowing, I arrived there in August at a time when great things were happening in the RAF navigation world. On 1 September Air Commodore Philip Mackworth was posted in as Commandant, with Group Captain F.C. ('Dickie') Richardson as his deputy and Director of Studies; both were pre-war Spec Ns. In his book *Man Is Not Lost* (Airlife, 1997), Dickie Richardson describes how he and others had pressed for 'what amounted to a service university of air navigation ... a central repository of navigation knowledge covering every aspect of military aviation ... a common forum where the air forces of the Dominions and ourselves could study and research side by side,' co-ordinating the development of navigation from the user's point of view and maintaining 'continuous liaison with the Dominions and Allies by frequent flying visits and by drawing out staff and students from the RAF, the Dominion and Allied air forces.' All this came to pass: Shawbury's title, changed to the Empire Central Navigation School just after I arrived, became the Empire Air Navigation School before I left (presumably in recognition of the fact that the Royal Navy and the Army also were also involved with navigation). The Empire Air Armament School and the Empire Flying School were set up round about the same time – all this under a Socialist government! I have to admit that most of these significant changes went on over the heads of the humble Staff Navigator students.

I had already had a taste of the Welsh border country at Ludlow and Bridgnorth, and the rolling Shropshire hills were a pleasant change after

Lincolnshire. Shawbury had been built just before the war as a training station, and its permanent buildings were well laid out and reassuringly solid. The Officers' Mess was a large and splendid one (with a minstrels' gallery over the dining room), but uncomfortably overcrowded as usual in wartime, and some of us were given rooms in one of the pre-war married quarters now used to house the overflow from the Mess. My room-mates, Jimmy Treen and Ward Thomas, were about the same age as myself, and at around 20 we were probably the youngest (and the most junior) on the course. No. 95 Staff Navigator Course had about forty students, all with a bomber background, but including several from overseas commands and all with operational experience.

I still have a copy of the course syllabus, with the 'Man Is Not Lost' motif on the front cover. The foreword explains that the aim of the course is to equip graduates to fill staff and instructional navigation posts throughout the RAF. Since it was primarily designed to meet the needs of the service as a whole and not those of any particular command, it would be mainly concerned with 'those permanent and fundamental principles on which the practice of navigation depends' (a suitably resounding if rather pompous phrase). The foreword continues:

The graduate will have a sound basis on which he can continue to build his technical knowledge and he will know where to find information which he may require in the course of his duties. He receives training in the art of instruction … he must combine the ability to state a sound case with some knowledge of administration and organization in the Royal Air Force …

And an ominous conclusion:

Written examinations are set in all subjects, except in lecture technique, administration and organization; for these latter, marks are awarded on lectures given by students.

We could see that this was going to be no picnic. Many of my fellow-students had, like me, recently finished a tour of operations and were not particularly enamoured at the prospect of hard and unremitting work for thirteen weeks; the easy-going atmosphere of a bomber squadron seemed a distant dream. Still, to most navigators the subject of navigation cannot fail to be absorbing, and we had nearly forty hours of flying to look forward to – in my case in a new type of aircraft, the Wellington. There was talk, too, of an overseas flight (and not in an easterly or southerly direction).

Our classroom was the regulation wooden hut, heated by coke stoves but well maintained and highly polished; permanent buildings were reserved for the upper classes, the Spec N students, who were treated with respect on the few occasions on which we came into contact with them.

As I recall, the course administration was excellent and the instructors experienced and competent. I began to realize how little I knew about navigation; in particular (and in common with most of my fellow students) I was apprehensive about the maths examination which took place early in the course and which we had to pass if we were to continue. Looking at the maths syllabus – starting gently with logarithms and plane trigonometry, but culminating in a detailed study of spherical trigonometry – we could see that this was a substantial hurdle to be surmounted.

We need not have worried. Our mathematics instructor, Flight Lieutenant Pratt, was an Education Branch officer of unprepossessing appearance but outstanding teaching ability. He led us lucidly through the maths syllabus, resuscitating what most of us already knew about logs and plane trigonometry, and bringing us confidently into the mysteries of spherical trig. As a bonus, we discovered that he played jazz skilfully and with fervour on the Mess piano. He also taught us lecture technique, something he was well qualified to do.

Why did we need to study spherical trigonometry? This was a question most of us asked on the course, and the answers were not entirely satisfactory. The earth is a sphere (or to be pedantic, an oblate spheroid – a bit squashed at the poles), and position on it is identified by latitude (angular distance above or below the equator) and longitude (angular distance east or west of the Greenwich meridian). Given the positions of two different places, the distance between them and the bearing of one from the other can be calculated by solving the spherical triangle formed by the two positions and the nearer pole. There are several other calculations on the earth's surface which can be made by solving spherical triangles, but for the navigator – at that time – the more important use of the technique was concerned with the so-called celestial sphere.

This is a convenient fiction used by astronomers and astro-navigators, and is a supposed projection of the earth's sphere into infinity; on this celestial sphere, heavenly bodies can be located by using a celestial latitude (declination) and longitude (hour angle). For all practical purposes the stars occupy fixed and recorded positions on the celestial sphere, but the sun, moon and planets are peripatetic bodies whose wanderings are accurately predicted by astronomers in almanacs. In theory, if a navigator can measure the altitude of a heavenly body (its angular distance above the horizon – obtained by using a sextant), he can look up its position at that time in the star tables or almanac, relate this to his estimated position on the chart, and finally draw a position line – or more correctly, an arc of an enormous position circle – on which he must be positioned.

I have so over-simplified this process that it is hardly recognizable, and I have omitted mention of all the various corrections for sextant and other errors which are usually needed. Observations of two different bodies at a respectable angle to each other produce two position lines whose intersection gives the position of the observer; better still, three observations provide what the navigator hopes will be a small triangle (a 'cocked hat') on the chart within which is his position. But on dark and dirty nights with poor cockpit lighting the three-star fix often turned out to be labour in vain.

In the great days of the Royal Navy under sail (once accurate chronometers were available after Cook's day), sights were worked out using only the almanac(k) and spherical trigonometry, a process no doubt dreaded by young midshipmen, who would gather on deck and nervously compare their results. 'Hats off, gentlemen!' said a ship's captain after one of these sessions. 'The ship appears to be within the precincts of Westminster Abbey.' At sea, of course, at a speed of a few knots, there was plenty of time to take and calculate sights; in an aircraft flying at 200 mph, time was of the essence.

After this short lecture, the question remains: why did Staff Navigators need to study spherical trigonometry? I suppose it was analogous to the need for primary school children to learn simple arithmetic including multiplication tables; nowadays they can find the answers to their sums using electronic calculators, but unless they know how such answers can be derived by basic means they are liable to come up with gross errors or, if no calculator is available, with no answers at all. In astro-navigation, spherical triangles were solved in practice by the use of almanacs and tables, but the received wisdom was that occasions might arise when the basic calculation was called for; most of us could not conceive of such an occasion, and probably most of us never met it, but oddly enough I was one of the few who in later years did need to use basic spherical trig to solve problems in my daily work.

Jimmy and Ward and I plodded on with our noses very close to the grindstone, and I don't remember much in the way of relief until the maths examination was safely behind us. I see from the syllabus that we worked a 42-hour week, with a lot of private study on top of that. Did we have Saturdays or Sundays off? I don't remember which, but I do remember rattling down to Shrewsbury in Ward's little open-topped Austin from time to time and visiting the local pubs. Petrol wasn't always obtainable, and on at least one occasion we missed the last bus to Shawbury and had to walk the six miles back.

Towards the end of August we started our flights in the Wellington, flying in pairs; Jim Treen and I flew together. The Wimpey was a reassuring aircraft, with its deserved reputation for surviving a great deal of punishment, and there was much more workspace for the navigator than in the Lancaster.

There was a DR compass, an API, Gee, and an aid new to us, ASV (air-to-surface vessel) – a radar set to detect and home in to ships or submarines on the surface. Our first flight was an astro and dead-reckoning exercise up to St Kilda, and the second practised Coastal Command drill using astro, ASV, and good old-fashioned pin-points and drift readings around the Scillies.

We pampered bomber navigators had tremendous admiration for those in Coastal Command, who would fly long oversea patrols with perhaps one sight of land on departure and another on return. By this stage of the war the Battle of the Atlantic had been won, and coastal navigators had Gee and improved ASV, but earlier in the war the Catalinas and Sunderlands would fly for ten hours over the sea with no navigation aids but the sextant and the drift recorder, apart from an occasional wireless bearing. The drill was to keep a careful manual air plot, find an accurate track made good from the drift recorder, and take a three-drift wind velocity every half-hour, giving a dead-reckoning position in which one could have some confidence, especially if it could be checked by a sun sight. Flying usually around 1,500 feet, an experienced pilot or navigator could judge the wind direction from the wind lanes on the sea surface and the wind speed from the sea state. Some miracles of navigation were performed by the unsung Coastal navigators, but not until such aids as ASV, Consol and Loran came into use did their task become easier.

ASV, like H2S, transmitted radar pulses downwards from the aircraft which could be reflected from objects on the sea surface. On a single vertical baseline display the echo would be shown as a blip on either side of the baseline, the size and shape of the blip giving a measure of the size and direction of the object, and the distance up the baseline indicating range. So a ship or a submarine on the surface could be detected and a homing carried out from above or within cloud, whatever the visibility. This was ASV 2, later replaced by ASV3 with a rotating baseline building up a picture as in H2S, and it immeasurably increased Coastal Command's ability to find and attack enemy U-boats and shipping. The use of ASV and other tactics, such as the Leigh Light, helped in the dramatic reduction in Allied shipping losses from their peak at around 600,000 tons in May 1942 to well under 100,000 tons in July 1943, although we now know that perhaps a principal factor was the reading of German signals traffic by the Ultra operation at Bletchley Park.

The development and use of Consol makes a fascinating story. Consol stations had three medium-frequency radio transmitters sited close together and radiating a directional pattern of dots and dashes which could be picked up by any standard aircraft radio receiver. By counting the number of dots and dashes before an equisignal, the operator could plot a position line on a special Consol chart, and readings from two stations would give a fix. In poor reception conditions or at long range it was sometimes difficult (and tedious) to count accurately, but no special equipment was needed other than a radio receiver and a Consol chart. Accuracy was not high, but if you had no other aid Consol was of great assistance; over the sea it could be received at up to 1,000 miles from the transmitters by day and 1,500 by night, though at these ranges accuracy would indeed be poor. But the special joy of using Consol in the Battle of the Atlantic was that it was a system developed by the enemy and called by them 'Sonne', with two stations in Spain erected and operated by the Germans, mainly for the use of their long-range maritime aircraft and U-boats. Through diplomatic contacts with Spain, a neutral power, British scientists were able to visit both stations (at Lugo in northern Spain and Seville in the south) and glean enough information to produce Consol charts for our use. The German High Command must surely have known of this, but evidently the stations were so valuable to them that they did not stop transmissions and were apparently unable to code them satisfactorily. After the war, stations were built in the UK, and were still in use more than twenty years later.

Loran (LOng RAnge Navigation – an early acronym, like SPiced hAM) was a system devised and manufactured in the USA. It worked on radar frequencies and on a principle very similar to that of Gee, with master and slave stations transmitting pulses received in the aircraft by a specially designed CRT receiver. As in the Gee system, time differences in pulse reception would be measured and could be plotted on a hyperbolic lattice chart. Again, two readings were needed for a fix. The main difference from Gee was the much longer range available from more widely spaced masters and slaves, and the greater distances between transmitters. However, at that time there were stations only on the US eastern seaboard and Greenland, and the use of Loran on the European side of the Atlantic was therefore limited. Nevertheless it was a great boon to long-range Coastal Command aircraft at the western end of their patrols, and was also used by ships.

We had only a cursory look at Loran in the classroom, and were not able to use it in the air; we did operate ASV in the Wellingtons and found it helpful for locating islands like the Scillies and making landfalls; we did not have the opportunity to use it with surface vessels.

Towards the end of September our promised overseas flight took place, to Reykjavik in Iceland. At this stage of the war there was little enemy air activity in the area north of the British Isles, and we flew via Stornoway in the Hebrides, again using Coastal Command navigation techniques. Some of us, including myself, had never been abroad before (except for our flights over Europe). After we had checked into the RAF Mess at the airfield (with Beaufighters and Hudsons at the dispersals), we went into town and were enchanted by the coloured wooden houses, the brightly lit streets and shops, and the good-looking Nordic blonde girls – I think some of us had had a vague mental image of Eskimos in our youthful ignorance. Also memorable were the cakes in the cafés after Britain's wartime austerity, with coffee in glass cups, and a wonderful meal at the Missions to Seamen down on the docks: succulent fresh cod as I had never tasted it.

After the luxury of a free day in Reykjavik, we flew back to Shawbury by a similar route, a seven-hour flight. By this time, with the dreaded maths exam behind us, we were deep into the mysteries of advanced astro-navigation; radar theory; meteorology (including weather chart plotting and analysis and forecasting); compasses and magnetism; maps and charts; tides; and dead-reckoning theory and plotting. The last-named subject also included a look at techniques and drills in use in other commands, and some practice in analysing and assessing other navigators' efforts.

There was some light relief in the lessons in lecture technique presided over by Flight Lieutenant Pratt, although we had to prepare and deliver six short lectures using the ever-present chalk and blackboard – there were few sophisticated lecture aids in those days. Criticism was forthcoming not only from the staff but from one's fellow students, the latter usually more severe and less polite. I found this subject, with complementary sessions on administration, of great interest, covering syllabus planning, examination setting and marking, and the way in which navigation was organized and administered in the RAF. Most wartime aircrew types professed to have no interest in 'admin and org', but it was well taught and we were immeasurably better informed than we had been at the start of the course.

Two more Wellington flights concluded the flying programme – the final flight a low-level exercise to Tintagel, the interception of an aircraft in the Irish Sea, and low level back to Shawbury. The little low flying I had done had been illicit (Al buzzing the beach at Mablethorpe, for instance), and it was exhilarating to fly a properly planned and authorized exercise at nought feet or thereabouts. About halfway through the course there was a short weekend break, and rather than my using most of it travelling to Leeds and back, Joan came down to Shrewsbury and we stayed at a bed-and-breakfast place in the town which someone had recommended (separate rooms, of course, in those conventional days). We had a happy weekend, dinner at the Lion, walks by the river and in the town with its curious street names (Dogpole, Butcher Row, Wyle Cop), and a cheerful goodbye at the railway station, Joan wearing her engagement ring and I thinking how fortunate I was. Back to work, with the examinations looming up. In the lectures on radar we were given a brief acquaintance with airborne interception radar (AI) used by our nightfighters; with Rebecca/Eureka, in which an airborne transmitter triggered pulses from a ground beacon to give range and homing information; and with the radio altimeter, which measured the return time of radio transmissions bounced off the ground immediately below the aircraft, thus giving an absolute and accurate height above the ground. Two other systems were included which were of particular interest to Bomber Command navigators. One had been developed from the experience gained during the blitz in 1940 and 1941, when the radio beams used by the Luftwaffe as navigational aids were bent by interfering transmissions from our special ground stations. This was Oboe, in which two ground stations were used, one to keep the aircraft on a given track and the other to measure how far it was along that track. It was accurate enough to be used for blind bombing, when the signal for bomb release was given by the ground station, but since only one aircraft could be controlled at a time Oboe could not be used for large-scale bombing, and was mainly used by Mosquito aircraft to mark the target for the main force; in this role it was a success. Gee-H (or GH) worked in a similar way to Oboe and was of similar accuracy, but the aircraft transmitted pulses first to the ground stations and was able to determine its position using its own receiver. Up to a hundred aircraft could use GH at the same time, and the system was used successfully in blind bombing, mainly by Lancasters. Sir Arthur Harris, in his book *Bomber Offensive*, says that the use of GH 'made all the difference between the success and failure of the offensive against oil.' However, it was not until we were learning about the system at Shawbury in October 1944 that large numbers of aircraft were being equipped with it.

Looking back from sixty-odd years on, it is a cause for wonder that the necessary scientific and engineering effort and expertise could be harnessed to develop these systems in response to operational requirements, and to manufacture and install them and train the operators in incredibly short periods of time. As the air battle over Europe continually altered its patterns, so each side strove to meet new technical and tactical problems and keep a step ahead of the enemy: on our side there were certainly muddles and mistakes, but the advances in navigation aids alone in five and a half years of war would probably have taken a quarter of a century in time of peace (if indeed they had emerged at all). A modern analogy might be that of the digital computer, except that perhaps profit rather than national security has been the principal spur: as soon as a computer system is on the market it is obsolescent, since work is in continual progress to reduce, size, cost and user complexity, and to increase capability, capacity and speed of operation. The PC and the laptop were a long way in the future as No. 95 Course contemplated the analogue computers then in use. The API I had already met, and now there was a development called the GPI – the ground position indicator; this used the same sources as the API to evolve an air position from true airspeed and compass course, but a wind velocity could be manually set to produce what was virtually a dead-reckoning position, and this was projected on to a chart on the navigation table as a cross of light. Providing the chart or map was properly adjusted, that the system was started at the right position, and that an accurate wind was fed in, the GPI gave acceptable accuracy over short times and distances. This was about the first attempt to display the aircraft's position automatically, and it had its limitations.

In our daily absorption with the work under our noses, we had hardly taken in what was going on in the rest of the world. A few days after we arrived at Shawbury the Allies had entered Paris. By the time we left in November, the Germans had been driven out of France and Belgium. Allied troops were fighting in Germany, and the Japanese navy had suffered a great defeat at the hands of the US fleet in the Pacific. What we did notice, as we walked past the hangars, were preparations at Shawbury for an epic flight by the EANS Lancaster PD328, given the name of Aries. Captained by Wing Commander D.C. McKinley, this aircraft left Shawbury on 20 October 1944 and flew via Canada and the USA across the Pacific to Auckland, where the crew – all EANS instructors – undertook a lecture tour of Royal New Zealand Air Force training and operational units. They then went on and did the same in Australia for the RAAF, altogether giving some 400 lectures and showing more than 4,000 service personnel over the aircraft. They returned via Ceylon and Malta and landed at Shawbury on 14 December, having logged 202 hours in fifty-three days and a total of 36,000 nautical miles, the longest flight having taken 15 hrs 8 min. Throughout the tour, new navigation systems and techniques were studied. The Aries flight drew headlines in the press of many countries, perhaps providing a welcome relief from the unrelenting war news. Flying through every type of climatic condition (temperatures varied from below zero to more than 125°F), the Lancaster was only delayed once by unserviceability – a convincing demonstration of the type's versatility. The official Australia–UK record was broken by more than fifty hours, and other records were set. Aries made further record-breaking flights in later years, and was the first of a series of pioneering RAF aircraft with the same name.

The last few weeks of the course were taken up by examinations and were marred by a minor catastrophe. We turned up one morning to find our classroom a smoking ruin; the cause was thought to be a careless use of an open stove at night by an airman and a WAAF engaged in amorous dalliance (snogging, in the contemporary vernacular). Most of us lost our course notes and textbooks: in my case it was my flying logbook and all the notes I had ever taken in the RAF. To add insult to injury, we had just finished a three-hour examination in dead-reckoning navigation theory, and all the answer papers had gone up in flames. A re-sit was inevitable, with much lowered morale. We heard nothing of the fate of the airman concerned, but we would all have gladly acted as prosecutor at his court martial. The end of the course came at last; we could call ourselves Staff Navigators and have the symbol 'Sn' after our names in the Air Force List.

I was not too pleased with my end-of-course report: 'A student of average ability who reached a fairly good standard. A good average instructor but somewhat lacking in drive.' Fair enough, I can say with hindsight, but what annoyed me was that I missed the coveted Distinguished Pass – 85% of the total marks – by 1.7%. However, those of us who reached a certain standard in the Meteorology examination were allowed to apply for Fellowship of the Royal Meteorological Society; this I did, and was a Fellow for many years, although I have a strong suspicion that the only real qualification was an ability to pay the annual subscription. We had made many valuable friendships and contacts, and I was to meet several fellow-students again later in my service life: one at least became a lifelong friend, although I lost touch with Jimmy and Ward; the latter made a name for himself in the commercial television world as G.E. Ward Thomas. It had been a hard three months, but most of us felt that it had been worthwhile. If some time had been spent on what we saw as barely relevant, this had been largely balanced by work on current techniques and new systems. We now felt able to teach other aspiring navigators, and I am sure that at the back of our minds was still the thought that better knowledge of our trade might help survival in the future. As far as I was concerned, greater self-confidence had been engendered (tempered by the not exactly glowing final report). This was not the last I was to see of Shawbury and the Empire Air Navigation School.

*   *   *

After the hilly Shropshire countryside, Lincolnshire in November was not inspiring, but I was given plenty of work to do, both on the ground and in the air. Blyton was in the process of converting from the Halifax to the Lancaster – a popular move – and I made my second and last Halifax flight as an H2S instructor early in December. Not long before Christmas I was sent on two short detachments as a follow-up to the Shawbury course: one to No. 75 (New Zealand) Squadron at Mepal near Ely, and the other to the Pathfinder Force Navigation Training Unit at Worboys near Huntingdon. At Mepal I was given practice in GH, with which 75 Squadron (part of No. 8 PFF Group) was equipped; I hoped to fly an operational sortie, but in the few days I was there I was only able to use the GH trainer and get some tuition from an experienced operator. At the PFFNTU I was again unable to fly in one of their Mosquitoes, but was given a short course in PFF navigation methods and target-marking techniques. At this stage of the bomber offensive, No. 8 (Pathfinder) Group was well into its stride. Formed in August 1942, its job was to mark the target precisely so that the main force of bombers could make a more concentrated and accurate attack. It was something of an élite force, commanded by Air Vice-Marshal Donald Bennett, probably the youngest

Group Commander in the RAF at that time. He had held a Short Service Commission in the 1930s and then gone on to civil flying, becoming a specialist in navigation and publishing a book called *The Complete Air Navigator* in 1936; its intention was to prepare civil pilots or navigators for the First Class Navigation Licence, and its title was not an exaggeration – it went into four editions and I still have my copy. He rejoined the RAF and was shot down in a Halifax while attacking the *Tirpitz* in 1941; he was then a Squadron Commander. He escaped and returned to England, and in due course was given the job of running PFF. Under his command the group went from strength to strength, using almost exclusively second-tour aircrew, who wore distinguishing badges and in some cases got accelerated promotion. They used Lancasters and later Oboe-equipped Mosquitoes, and developed a range of target-marking techniques which I learned about at Worboys. Starting with flares or incendiaries in the early days, PFF later used coloured ground and sky markers, sometimes as a guide for a flare-dropping force which lit the target area for a longer period, and sometimes directly for the main force. All their various techniques had codenames, often derived from Antipodean locations such as Wanganui and Parramatta, calculated to baffle the enemy when he monitored the passing of instructions on the R/T. By 1944 a master bomber was used, usually in a Mosquito and with a deputy in another aircraft in case he got shot down; he would control the raid as it took place, checking the accuracy of the marking and directing the main force to bomb on the most accurate markers. PFF was thus a formidable weapon of war.

Back at Blyton again, my time was divided between marking students' logs and charts, lecturing, briefing for navigation exercises, and flying as an instructor (or 'screen', as the contemporary jargon had it). Many Polish crews came through the Conversion Unit, and although they were all supposed to speak adequate English, I had the feeling that most of my lectures went over their heads, however simplified I tried to make them. Polish crews seemed to be either very good or very bad, and I had a sobering experience with one of them. I stood in for their navigator, who was unwell, on a bombing exercise, but left the aircraft when they landed back at Blyton, since they were going on to fly 'circuits and bumps' for an hour or so. That aircraft crashed and all were killed.

It was a long hard winter in 1944, and I recall starting for a few days' leave with a colleague who was taking me the five or six miles to Gainsborough station in an open car. It took us an hour or so to get there and we had to get out and push several times, both of us looking like snowmen when we arrived at the station. But as the weather improved after the turn of the year we would cycle to Gainsborough to the cinema and the pubs, and once or twice I borrowed binoculars from Flying Control and went bird-watching at a nearby marshy lake; sitting there among the new spring green and the silence was like being in another world. At the beginning of March I was one of a staff crew which flew on a six-hour diversionary operation over the North Sea near the Friesian Islands, intended to distract enemy attention from a large bomber raid aimed elsewhere. This was uneventful, and turned out to be the last flight I was to make over enemy territory, although I naturally didn't know this at the time.

I find that I have a lapse of memory about my last few weeks at Blyton. My flying logbook records that for almost all of April 1945 I was engaged in 'transport' or 'ferry' flying, not on instructional duties. This suggests that the station was about to change its role and that the Conversion Unit was closing down or moving elsewhere, with aircraft, equipment and people being moved to other stations. The Allies had crossed the Rhine on 23 March, and there was little doubt that the end was in sight in Europe. Several of the instructional staff, myself included, had made up crews earlier in the year and applied to be posted back to operations. Our wishes were in part granted at the end of April, but the crews we had formed were disregarded and we were posted to many different units. Notwithstanding our operational experience and our tours as instructors, we all had to go back through the training machine, and I found myself posted to No. 1656 Heavy Conversion Unit at Lindholme, near Doncaster, to be crewed up again.

CHAPTER SIX

An End and a Beginning

I arrived at Lindholme on 3 May, just five days before VE-Day, the formal end of the war in Europe. Celebrations went on in every city, town and village. I don't remember a great deal about my own celebrations: Doc Henderson turned up from somewhere and took a few ex-Blyton and Elsham people back to Blyton for a tremendous party. He drove us back to Lindholme next morning in his ambulance (in which we lay sleeping soundly), and since the station seemed to have stood down by general consent, we had the rest of the day to recuperate. With many others in my position, I did not know whether to be glad or sorry. Of course it was an unqualified relief to see the end of a war so costly in lives and misery. And yet I had, against all common sense, been strongly drawn towards flying again on operations, and there was a feeling of disappointment that this was not to be. This was not unaffected by the knowledge that the war in the Far East was still going on fiercely and showed no signs of coming to an end; there was little doubt in the minds of bomber crews that Japan would provide our next targets, and there were few who were overjoyed at the prospect. Flying over jungle and ocean did not appeal to us, especially as we knew of the treatment handed out to prisoners of war by the Japanese. When I went home to Leeds on a few days' leave shortly after VE-Day, Joan and I decided it was time for us to get married. We had been 'going steady' for five years but had waited to get engaged until I had finished my tour of operations; I had been lucky once, but with the threat of the Far East war over our heads we knew our luck might not last. 'Wait', said Joan's parents, but we did not want to wait, and with their eventual consent we fixed the wedding date for 21 July, exactly a year after our engagement. We would get married at St Matthew's Church, Chapel Allerton, where Joan had been a regular attender and where I had gone to church as a child. We went to see the vicar, the Reverend Mr Sampson, who knew Joan well, and we were able to allay his fears that this was a quick wartime affair where the couple hardly knew each other.

Back at Lindholme, I was crewed with Hugh (Tommy) Thomas, a lean, laconic Londoner, 'laid back' as we say today; he had a DFC from his

Lancaster tour, was an excellent pilot, and didn't take life too seriously. Flight Lieutenant Neale was the bomb aimer, a larger-than-life character from Birmingham; Flying Officer Bert Muge was the wireless operator, both second-tour aircrew. About the flight engineer I have a memory lapse, but the gunners I remember well – both sergeants in their first crew, one a Scot and the other from Stepney. We settled down well together, and after some eighteen hours' flying were posted to No. 7 (PFF) Squadron at Oakington, a pre-war station near Cambridge. So at last we were part of the élite Pathfinder Force, but a force that was now out of a job. Nobody was sure to what extent PFF's expertise, developed at such cost, would be of any use in the Far East war. It was thought that operations would most likely be in daylight, and the squadron was practising formation flying, as in the USAAF. Although Bomber Command had flown in daylight formations in the early days of the war in aircraft like the Blenheim, this had proved to be expensive in losses, and soon ceased. However, our first flight with 7 Squadron was a formation bombing exercise, in which we were lead aircraft, and for us it was a novel and exhilarating experience. On later flights we found that flying a Lancaster in close formation was no picnic for the pilots, who were constantly juggling throttles and controls and would finish the flight in a muck-sweat and physically fatigued.

By the end of June the preparations for the General Election were in full swing. Our Group Commander, Donald Bennett, had obtained permission to stand as a candidate in Middlesbrough, and our Squadron Commander, Wing Commander 'Bobbie' Burns, who knew him well, was asked to give him some assistance. On 29 June I found myself navigating the Station Oxford to Topcliffe in Yorkshire, with Wing Commander Burns as pilot; he had miraculously survived a fall from a burning Lancaster without a parachute, losing an arm in the process, had been a prisoner of war, and had later been awarded the DSO. When I knew him better, he struck me as a man (not surprisingly) under considerable stress, and one who perhaps should not have been given command of a flying squadron at that particular time. However, he was reputed to be a good pilot, and I watched with interest as he detached his artificial arm and screwed in a metal gadget with which he could operate the throttles and perform other tasks. He was indeed a good pilot, but what I remember most about that flight was the look on the face of the young airman at Topcliffe who held the aircraft door open as Bobbie Burns emerged, screwing one gloved hand round and round with the other.

In the first half of July we made two flights codenamed 'Cook's Tour', whose object was to give ground crews some idea of what their bomber aircraft had achieved. Flying in daylight and at comparatively low level over the Ruhr area, we viewed with some disquiet the desolation caused by the Allied armies, Bomber Command, and the USAAF. Duisburg, Dortmund, Cologne, Aachen – all were in ruins. I think the worst sight was the small town of Wesel, just north-west of the Ruhr: hardly a building seemed to be standing. It was a grim experience and one which we did not discuss in any detail among ourselves. What our groundcrew thought I cannot imagine.

The day came for our wedding. I had ordered a new No. 1 uniform, but it had not materialized; my only No. 1 was hurriedly cleaned and pressed, but still looked shabby. Joan had made her own light blue wedding dress and looked radiant with pink roses. Tommy was my best man (Al Moore was now back in Canada), and brought his new wife, also Joan; I had been at their wedding only a few weeks before. My Joan and I were married at 10 a.m. by Mr Sampson at St Matthew's, and went back to her parents' house for a wedding lunch. There were twenty-one guests and the meal exceeded expectations in all departments – there was even a two-tiered wedding-cake, a triumph of organization in that immediate post-war period when rationing was at its most severe. Joan and I had no doubts or reservations; we both knew that this was for life, as it has proved to be (at any rate, so far – after sixty-five years). We had our short honeymoon at Grassington in Upper Wharfedale, and walked in the fields and woods and by the Wharfe in the summer weather. The result of the General Election announced on 26 July largely passed us by, though I remember being surprised (and not displeased, as the son of a committed Socialist father). But we had other preoccupations. At the moment there was little chance of Joan joining me; there were already rumours that 7 Squadron was to move from Oakington, and we should have to wait and see what happened before making any decisions.

In the event, the squadron moved to Mepal, near Ely (where I had had my short detachment with 75 Squadron the previous December) at the beginning of August. From a navigator's point of view, Mepal was uniquely placed for recognition from the air: the Old and New Bedford Rivers ran in two ruler-straight parallel lines north-east from Earith for about twenty miles to Downham Market south of the Wash. In the three-quarters of a mile between them lay the Hundred Foot Washes, in these days partly maintained as a bird reserve and famous for winter wildfowl. The airfield lay in a small triangle made by the Bedford Rivers, the Chatteris–Ely road, and the minor road from the village of Sutton-in-the-Isle to Earith. All one had to do was to locate the Bedford Rivers and fly up or down them until the airfield came into view.

It was a typical wartime bomber airfield, with dispersed Nissen-hut sites, the standard three runways and black hangars, and the inevitable bicycles for transport. We settled into the Mess and waited uneasily to hear what the future held for us. We were to be part of the somewhat melodramatically named 'Tiger Force', given the task of finishing off Japan – not a campaign we were looking forward to with any pleasure. It was thought that a most likely role for the bomber force would be massive support for ground armies, as in the Normandy campaign after D-Day. Since such support would probably be needed at short notice for tactical rather than strategic targets, we were to practise holding ourselves available for such operations, rather in the manner of Fighter Command in the Battle of Britain. We worked a three-shift system – stand down, stand by, and stand to – for twenty-four hours each. Standing down meant, naturally enough, time off when we could go off camp and explore the pleasures of Ely and Cambridge; the stand-by shift had to be spent on the station, ready to prepare for flying at little notice; and standing to was done in the crew room, using makeshift beds when necessary, but ready to get into the air within minutes. The theory was that we would be quickly briefed on the general area and requirement for the operation, and would then receive a target briefing by radio when airborne. Whether this system was universal throughout 8 Group at this time or a brainchild of our very keen Squadron Commander, Bobbie Burns, I never discovered. Nor do I remember how the problems of bombing up and bomb-load changes at short notice were solved, if in fact they were.

Although most of the 7 Squadron crews were experienced operators, they were not really at home with this changed method of working. With the war in Europe over and the war in the Far East still an unknown quantity, it was difficult for us to take things seriously, and there was an undercurrent of dissatisfaction. But in mid-August the picture changed dramatically: we read in the papers, with some incredulity, the story of the two atomic bombs dropped on Hiroshima on 6 August and on Nagasaki three days later, with the end of the war coming on 14 August, now known as VJ-Day. We were astounded and impressed by the power and effects of these A-bombs as reported in the press, and most of us felt that they marked a significant change in the waging of modern warfare. The historians now say that neither the atomic bomb attacks nor the coincident Soviet declaration of war on Japan was the decisive factor in the Japanese surrender, although they probably caused it to be made earlier. It is thought that the submarine blockade of the Japanese islands had brought economic defeat, and that this, coupled with the virtual destruction of Japan's navy and air force, had precipitated the final surrender. At Mepal we were not vitally concerned with the causes of the end of the Second World War; we were thankful that the black cloud had been lifted from our future, and enthusiastic about the prospects of a world without war after nearly six years of slaughter and sacrifice. On VJ-Day, it so happened that our crew was on a 'stand-to' shift and unable to leave the crew-room area. That night the rest of the camp was in chaos, with ground staff and aircrews drinking the messes and local pubs dry, WAAFs reportedly running about the WAAF site in various stages of undress, and the stand-by crews departing by any available means for Cambridge, or even London. Bobbie Burns gathered the remnants of the squadron together the following morning and tore us off a gigantic strip – lack of discipline, dereliction of duty, etc., etc. Since those to whom he was speaking had mostly not left the station (and indeed the 'stand-to' crews had remained standing to) we felt that his strictures were unjust, but on the whole we were too elated to care, and in the event most of us were able to take a few days' leave before the end of August. We knew that the business of demobilization would take some time, and had no idea what use would be made of the bomber force during this period. I think most of us hoped that we would be able to continue flying for the remainder of our time in the service, and that crews would be able to stay together and increase their experience. Many pilots and navigators who had enjoyed their flying felt that they would like to continue in civil aviation, and I remember several who started studying for their civil licences. I was in a good position here, since my Staff Navigator qualification entitled me to the RAF Second Class Navigation Warrant, which in turn would exempt me from some of the civil examination requirements. Now that I had a wife to think about, it was time to consider the future – something I had avoided doing during the previous couple of years, since the probability of any future at all had at times seemed fairly small.

The immediate requirement was to find somewhere for Joan to live near the station and to get permission to 'live out'. There was no suggestion that 7 Squadron would move again in the near future, and no bar now to married men living off camp with their wives (some, of course, had managed to do this unofficially while on flying operations). Finding somewhere was another problem. Somebody told me about the possibility of lodgings in a house in the nearest village, Sutton-in-the-Isle. A long, straggling fen village, Sutton was only a few minutes' cycle ride from RAF Station Mepal, and one could take a short cut across the corner of the aerodrome. Miss Read lived at a small house in The Row, a back lane which ran parallel to the main street but a hundred or so feet lower. It was a mid-Victorian cottage, brick-built like most of the local houses, with a privy round the back and a longish garden and orchard stretching up to the main street. I could see an antique pump outside the kitchen door, but I was assured that water was laid on – and so it was, to a tap in the front garden. Miss Read seemed a pleasant, friendly sort of woman of about 50, and her charges for board and lodging for the two of us would be three pounds ten shillings a week. This I thought we could manage on my flying officer's pay of a pound a day plus an allowance – not strictly a marriage allowance, as I was not entitled – of 3s. 10d. a day. We would have a double bedroom, of course, and 'use of the sitting room', but we would eat with Miss Read and her elderly mother. I clinched the deal, not without misgivings, and some time in mid-September went up to Leeds and brought Joan and her modest effects back to Sutton. I didn't fully realize at the time what a culture shock this must have been for her; not only was she leaving home and parents for the first time, but she was exchanging suburban life in a big city for a rural existence in a village deep in the fen country, six miles from the nearest town of any size (Ely) and with few modern conveniences. May Read kindly brought us up soft water for washing, as the tap water was hard, but Joan's face was a picture when she saw wriggling larvae in the wash-hand basin and realized that this was straight from the water-butts. The trip to the privy (a one-and-a-half holer) was something to be avoided in the rain and dark, and chamber pots were in use in the bedrooms, which were of course unheated. Our bed was an enormous one, with a feather mattress and lace curtains round the head; it was mysteriously reputed to have belonged to the Churchill family, but we took that with a pinch of salt. May Read was a spinster who, like many another of her age, had lost her fiancé in the Great War and had never married. She considered herself slightly above the village women, but was under the thumb of her mother: old Mrs Read was well into her 80s, small in stature, and ruled May with a rod of iron. She tolerated us, no doubt because the small income we provided made life easier, but made few concessions; she considered that her great age brought privileges, and tended to lock herself in the pantry with the new bread and our cheese ration. But we rubbed along reasonably well and made friends with several village people through May's good offices. As far as I remember we never used the sitting-room (usually referred to as the parlour), nor did anyone else.

We now settled into a sort of routine: I recall that time as a kind of limbo in which we continued our squadron flying exercises desultorily and without a great deal of enthusiasm, not knowing what their aim was nor how long we would be required to continue them. The three-shift system of working was quietly dropped, and I would cycle up to the airfield (usually referred to as the 'drome) after breakfast to see what the day held and who was on the flying programme. We went on with the formation flying we had started before VJ-Day, and we also flew exercises designed to train us for closer co-operation with ground forces.

These exercises were mainly of two types – working with a mobile radar control post (MRCP) or with a visual control post (VCP). In the MRCP exercises a single aircraft or a small formation would be guided to a target by VHF voice radio from a mobile ground station which was a radar-equipped Army vehicle, manned by soldiers but with an RAF liaison officer. This could be done at night or above cloud, but the resulting bombing was not so accurate as with VCP, when the ground control vehicle gave the precise location of the target for us to find visually. This was done in daylight at low level, often over an area of the Sussex Downs near Pulborough; we would fly a prescribed pattern (a 'cab rank') between two known points, establish contact with the control vehicle (callsign 'Rover Joe'), and wait for a target location to be passed to us by six-figure grid reference on the Ordnance Survey one inch to one mile map; here my Home Guard training came in useful. Using the map and the Mark I eyeball, we would then find and bomb the target, usually representing a troop or vehicle concentration. Nothing could have been more different from the standard Bomber Command night operations, and I thoroughly enjoyed the detailed map reading required. Being Pathfinder aircraft, our Mark III Lancasters were fitted with the ground position indicator (GPI) which I had encountered at Shawbury but never used in the air. The GPI would show reasonably acceptable ground positions over a fairly short period of time, provided that the information derived from the API was accurate, that the manually set wind velocity was also accurate and that the indicator graticule (an arrow of light projected on to the map) was started at the right place on the one-inch map pinned to the chart table. But I don't remember ever relying on it completely, and indeed we flew all the VCP exercises in adequate visibility when we could find the target visually.

One of these exercises involved a demonstration for some senior Army officers (probably the Staff College Course) at Old Sarum on Salisbury Plain. We were briefed to bomb a simulated target in front of spectator stands at precisely 11.30 hours: this we did to within a couple of seconds, satisfactorily demolishing the wood and canvas target with our stick of small practice bombs. At once a plaintive voice came from our control vehicle: 'Could you please do that again? The spectators are only just assembling.' We told them smugly that we had used all our practice bombs and were now going home.

On many days, if our crew was not required on the flying programme or if the weather had caused cancellations, I would cycle home for lunch and probably not return in the afternoon. Discipline, while not exactly lax, was certainly relaxed, and those aircrew who had no specific job other than flying took the view that if their crew was not required they need not hang around the squadron.

On these occasions, Joan and I would go for walks on the fen droves, or take a bus into Ely for shopping. Excursions as far afield as Cambridge, also by bus, were reserved for legitimate days off, when we would find somewhere to have lunch and perhaps go to the cinema. To me this change of life-style, going back daily to a reasonably comfortable home, eating home-cooked meals, and above all being with a loving wife, transformed my life unimaginably for the better. Looking back, it cannot have been so enjoyable for Joan, spending much time with May and her tyrannical mother, helping with household chores as she felt bound to do, and having to cope with the somewhat primitive living conditions.

The winter of 1945/6 was a particularly hard one in the fens. There was skating down on the lower land below the village, known as the Gault, and we visited the Gay family (descendants of the poet John Gay) who lived in a sizeable house down there and told us of winters when they would open the French windows in the drawing-room and skate straight out into the garden. Going to bed was a cold business, and our fox terrier, who had joined us by this time, would scramble up on to our bed when the nights were cold and work her way down inside until she was below our feet. Getting up, washing and shaving were done as quickly as possible; but cold bedrooms were the rule in those days, and we did not think it unusual.

A task given to Bomber Command at that time was the return of service personnel from Germany and Italy who were due for release or leave. Our crew made one flight to Gatow, the Berlin military airfield, and one to Bari, in southern Italy, for this purpose. Many thousands of men and women who would otherwise have had to wait their turn for overloaded land and sea travel were brought back in this way (nearly 60,000 from Italy alone between August and December 1945). They were packed into the rear fuselage of the Lancaster with blankets and a snack, and must have been cold and uncomfortable for the six-hour flight from Italy. But for them it was a quick way home, and for us a valuable training experience.

At the end of January 1946 I had been commissioned for two years and qualified for time promotion to the War Substantive rank of flight lieutenant, a step up much appreciated, not just for the few extra shillings a day but for the enhanced status (not yet accompanied by any increase in responsibility).

I had by this time decided, with Joan's support, to stay on in the RAF for the time being. I had no professional qualifications for a civilian job except as an air navigator, and it was realized even then that, although many civil pilots would be needed, navigators would not be in great demand. I enjoyed flying and the comradeship and ethos of the service, and the thought of going back to office work in a city was not enticing. I applied for a four-year Extended Service Commission, had an interview with the Station Commander, Group Captain Rankin, and some time later was granted an ESC; our livelihood was now secure for at least four years, and there was always a chance, if I still wanted it, that I could in time get a permanent commission. I note from my logbook (and the diary I kept for a few months around that time) that my interview with the Station Commander was only a few days after I had flown with him in the station Oxford on a night cross-country, no doubt laid on to see what I was like as a navigator. I remember that flight well: it was a clear night and we saw the Aurora Borealis in all its glory. Navigation was easy with all the post-war town and city lighting blazing away, and I must have made a good impression.

We went back home to Leeds for a week's leave at the end of March, and from my diary I note that Joan saw her doctor on 1 April (an auspicious date) and then broke the news that a baby was due in September. I think we would have preferred to start a family a little later, but nature had taken its course and we were happy with the idea of becoming parents.

Later in April, our Squadron Navigation Leader, Frank Bond, was demobilized, and I was given the job, taking over his tiny office in the Navigation Section. This meant that I could no longer fly as a member of a regular crew, and in fact my logbook records that I didn't fly again with Tommy, who left the service shortly afterwards. The navigation leader was responsible for the training of the squadron navigators, planning and briefing flying exercises, issuing of maps, checking navigators' logs and charts, and giving the occasional lecture to the other aircrew on navigation subjects (duties also included sweeping out the Navigation Section from time to time). I was pleased to have the additional responsibility and to be able to use my Staff Navigator qualification and instructor experience. It did mean that I spent more time on the station and less at home, but both Joan and I had realized that this was inevitable.

Morale at RAF Station Mepal at this time was, not unnaturally, at a low ebb. Older airmen who had served throughout the war were now anxious to get home, and unhappy about what seemed to be a slow and unwieldy release procedure. Since many of them were senior NCOs in positions of authority, this unease had its effect throughout the station, and discipline and efficiency suffered. This was particularly so among the ground crews who serviced the aircraft and who, during the war, had performed miracles to keep the squadrons operational, working mostly in the open and in all weathers, day and night. They could hardly be blamed for not putting in the same scale of effort after the war was over. Aircraft serviceability accordingly suffered, and my diary records many flights being 'scrubbed': on one particular day, we were due to jettison unwanted bombs (inert, of course) at sea, with a morning take-off. First the flight was put back to the afternoon because of an engine fault. When that was cleared and we arrived back at the aircraft after lunch, we found that it was not bombed up. When this was done our flight engineer was missing, and when he turned up the groundcrew were not there for start-up and had to be called over the station Tannoy (loudspeaker) system. After finally starting up we found that one throttle lever would not function. At this stage we gave up, although I see from my logbook that we achieved an hour's circuits and landings the same evening.

One bright spot in the general gloom was the acquisition of new aircraft. The Lancaster Mark VII(FE) had originally been modified and equipped for Far East operations and was becoming available to replace our mostly war-worn Mark IIIs. I flew on several ferry flights taking our old aircraft to join the serried ranks of other Lancasters, Halifaxes and Stirlings awaiting break-up at the Maintenance Units – a dispiriting sight, especially when in the twenty-first century the surviving Lancasters and Halifaxes can be counted on the fingers of one hand and as far as I know there are no surviving Stirlings.

Our new aircraft were painted white and made the dispersals look more cheerful. Their navigation equipment was similar to that of the Mark IIIs, with the addition of Rebecca, a radar homing device triggering signals from a ground beacon designed to be mobile for use in air drops of troops or equipment. A vertical timebase ran up the centre of the cathode ray tube in the aircraft receiver, and the distance from the ground beacon could be read off from the bottom of the tube to the received signal or blip over a range of thirty to forty miles and more. When the amplitude of the blip was the same on either side of the baseline, the beacon was dead ahead and a homing could be carried out. It was a very successful system, simple to use, accurate and reliable, and it became a standard fitment to most multi-engined RAF aircraft, just as the ground beacon (appropriately named Eureka) was eventually installed at nearly all RAF airfields at home and overseas, and was still operational many years later.

Rebecca/Eureka also incorporated an aid known as BABS (Blind Approach Beam System) which allowed a landing approach in poor visibility using a BABS beacon sited at the end of the runway. As far as I recall, we had neither a BABS nor a Eureka beacon at Mepal, but we were able to use the equipment for trials elsewhere. I was to have a much closer acquaintance with these systems later.

Bomber Command was in a state, if not of chaos, of turmoil and change at this time. Groups and squadrons were being disbanded and stations closed, and there could be little clear direction on the purpose and tasks of the bomber force. Someone in the Command navigation staff must have been concerned about standards, since we received several directives on navigation procedures, logkeeping and so on. We also saw the beginning of an aircrew categorization scheme which aimed to improve standards by regular ground and flying tests. This had been adapted from Transport Command, where there was an obvious need to determine if a crew was properly competent to carry freight, passengers or VIPs, and to ensure that they did not do so unless they held the appropriate category. Although crews in Bomber Command could be (and were) assessed by their Flight Commanders and Leaders, there was no formal or universal basis for this; the proposed categorization schemes were not well received by the crews, of whom a large proportion were impatiently awaiting demobilization.

News came in the summer that Mepal was to close and that 7 Squadron was to move to Upwood, an airfield some ten miles to the west in Huntingdonshire. Since my own future was in some doubt – there was talk of a navigation leader's job elsewhere – we reluctantly decided that Joan should return home in preparation for the happy event in September.

We said a fond farewell to May Read (and her mother), and Joan left for Leeds as I returned to live for a few weeks in the discomfort of the Nissen-hut quarters on the aerodrome.

At the end of July, 7 Squadron, now fully equipped with Mark VII(FE) Lancasters, took off for the fifteen-minute flight to Upwood, carrying our personal belongings (in most cases, surprisingly few) with us in the aircraft. Upwood was a pre-war station built about the same time and on the same pattern as Oakington; it boasted permanent married quarters in which the more senior married officers and airmen were accommodated, and now, nearly twelve months after the end of the war, had a more settled and civilized feel about it than Mepal, where there were few creature comforts. There were the rudiments of a social life, and on my first stint as Station Duty Officer I was duly invited to the Station Commander's house for Sunday lunchtime drinks – civilization indeed.

The squadron settled down into its new accommodation in a permanent hangar, and I established some sort of order in the Navigation Section. Squadron Leader Johnnie Barrass, the friendly and helpful Station Navigation Officer, asked me to give him a hand from time to time, and listened to what I had to say about my job and its problems (not of a very high order). I had said that it was time for me to move on to some other job, perhaps more demanding than on a squadron which, although I still enjoyed the flying, was like other bomber squadrons in the doldrums. He asked me if I would be interested in a staff job, and I said that I wouldn't mind as long as it was concerned with flying operations and gave me a chance to fly now and again. He promised to think about it, but I was not very optimistic, and was accordingly surprised when, late in August 1946, I was posted to Headquarters Bomber Command.

CHAPTER SEVEN

Mahogany Bomber

In a phrase that was old-fashioned even in 1946, an aircrew officer posted to a staff job was said to be 'flying a mahogany bomber'. I had mixed feelings about this, but as I took the train south I reflected that at least the job I was going to was on the navigation staff of the Headquarters and would be using my specific skills and experience, such as they were; I could so easily have been sent to a personnel or admin job. Not only that, but I was going to what was reputedly a pleasant part of the country with which I was unfamiliar.

Headquarters Bomber Command was about five miles west of High Wycombe in Buckinghamshire, and was the only purpose-built Command Headquarters in the Royal Air Force, most of the others being in large country houses. It was completed in 1940, and was sited in heavily wooded countryside next to the village of Naphill. The headquarters was – and still is – among mature beech woods, and was presumably sited so as not to be easily identifiable from the air. Sir Arthur Harris says, in his book *Bomber Offensive*, that although the Germans were well aware of the location, the site was never bombed – surely a curious omission. However, the Operations complex, the heart of the headquarters, was deep underground and virtually bombproof. The Luftwaffe probably knew that, too.

I was given a share of a room in the Mess, with a pleasant woodland outlook, and in the morning walked up the path through the beech trees to the Air Staff block. The group of headquarters buildings included a Unit Headquarters where the Unit Commander, a squadron leader, had the unenviable task of providing the usual range of station facilities, but to a very senior clientele, from Air Chief Marshal downwards. There was also an administrative staff block for the personnel, equipment, legal, and other admin staffs; and a technical staff block where the engineering, signals, armament and other specialists did their very necessary work.

The navigation staff offices were on the ground floor of the Air Staff block and at the other end of the corridor from the Commander-in-Chief's office and that of the Senior Air Staff Officer. The former was then Air

Chief Marshal Sir Norman Bottomley, who ironically enough had been Deputy Chief of the Air Staff during Harris's reign at High Wycombe, and the recipient of much criticism and frequent disagreement by Harris. The SASO was Air Vice-Marshal Langford-Sainsbury, an officer of whom I had never heard, but was to come to know well, or as well as a junior flight lieutenant could know an AVM.

The Command Navigation Officer was Group Captain Hobbs, a pilot with a Specialist Navigation qualification. At this time there were not many navigators above the rank of squadron leader, since few had been commissioned before 1940, and pilots naturally predominated in command and staff appointments. During the war there had been a Deputy C Nav O at Bomber Command, but this post had now been dropped. My immediate seniors were Squadron Leader 'Johnnie' Johnstone, Nav 1, and Squadron Leader Dean (inevitably 'Dixie'), who was known as Nav 1R for Radar, showing the importance now given to electronic navigation aids. These two shared an office next to mine, which I was pleased to see was all my own – or would be after my handover week with Flight Lieutenant Curtis, my predecessor.

The job was known as Nav 2, and was largely to act as general dogsbody for the navigation staff, making routine returns, keeping records of navigation officers at groups, stations, and squadrons, looking after the navigation reference library (just up my street), and any other odd jobs going. But I had another hat to wear, as Command Map Officer, responsible for the supply of maps and charts to all stations in the command and to the headquarters. There were three map clerks and a large map store under my command, and I also had a map room on the top floor of the Air Staff block which carried small reference stocks of all available maps and charts, to which I could retreat when I wanted a tranquil half-hour. This part of the job gave me some quiet satisfaction.

At first I was a little apprehensive about working and living with so many senior officers; not only were flight lieutenants rare in the Air Staff, but at 22 I was the youngest officer there by quite a margin. Coming from a squadron manned mostly by wartime aircrew, I had become a little slack in dress, wearing a battered service dress cap and a coloured scarf when it was cold. I was told in no uncertain terms by an elderly group captain that I was improperly dressed, and I prudently adopted a tidier and more orthodox appearance. However, many people still wore slightly shabby uniforms, as new ones were expensive, cloth was still rationed, and few RAF officers had private incomes.

I had only been at High Wycombe for a few days when I was told that SASO wanted a navigator for a flight to Finningley. The Bomber Command Communications Flight was based at Booker on the other side of High Wycombe town; a small grass field, it catered for the Ansons Mark XIX and the Proctors of the Comm Flight, and also housed an Elementary

Flying Training School with Tiger Moths. Command staff officers could thus fly to stations on one-day staff visits and keep their hands in in the air at the same time.

AVM Langford-Sainsbury turned out to be an amiable man and an excellent pilot. However, he was very much overweight, so much so that he found it difficult to operate the undercarriage lever on his right, but as I was sitting in the right-hand seat I was able to do this for him. This was no problem as, unlike our old Mark I Ansons at Jurby, the Mark XIX had a one-movement lever rather than a handle to be turned more than a hundred times. I map-read to Finningley (near Doncaster) as it was a fine day, and paid a formal call on the Senior Navigation Officer, who, if he was surprised to receive a fresh-faced youth in the guise of a Command staff officer, didn't show it.

Headquarters officers, however junior, were encouraged to make staff visits to the stations throughout the Command, so that when they were presented with problems at any particular station they would have some idea of the circumstances and know with whom they were dealing. In my case I was also able to make fairly frequent visits to the Army Directorate of Military Survey at Bushey Park, who supplied our maps and charts and consulted us on mapping policy.

During my handover week I was taken down to the main operations room, always known as 'The Hole', two storeys below ground down dank, draughty and echoing passages. The great room was preserved more or less as it had been just before the end of the war, with its map boards showing planned raids and the enormous state board showing the aircraft available in all of the seven operational groups and four training groups. Eighth Air Force USAAF was also shown, and the total number of aircraft was in the region of 3,000. This was in remarkable contrast to the current Bomber Command operations room, much smaller and located on a higher subterranean level: its state board showed just two bomber groups, No. 1 Group with headquarters at Bawtry near Doncaster, and stations in Lincolnshire and Yorkshire; and No. 3 Group at Exning in Suffolk, with its stations mostly in East Anglia. The number of serviceable aircraft – all Lancasters and Mosquitoes at this time, if I remember correctly – was usually under 200, so rapid had been the post-war rundown. The ops room was manned on a 24-hour basis by elderly aircrew flight lieutenants who always seemed to be drinking tea and eating Marmite sandwiches. Later in my time at High Wycombe we used the main operations room for command exercises, when it regained a little of its old atmosphere, and I became quite familiar with it, conscious always of its historical significance. This was where, night after night for more than three years of war, Harris heard his staff's briefings and then made his decisions on the targets for the night. As he pointed out, unlike Army commanders he was committing the major part of his forces to battle every night, year after year – a terrible responsibility.

* * *

After the first few weeks in my new job, our daughter Susan made her appearance. In those days it was quite usual for births to take place at home if there were no complications, and it so happened (or was arranged) that I was spending the weekend with Joan and her parents when the happy event took place; the midwife was something of a character, a red-haired Russian Jewess whose air of authority and matter-of-fact approach gave Joan confidence. I kept in the background as much as possible (also the custom in those days). Joan's maternal grandmother was living with her parents at that time, and we have a treasured photograph of the four generations.

I now had an added incentive to find somewhere for us to live, and after some weeks of searching I found Loosley House Cottage, a lodge or gardener's cottage in the grounds of Loosley House at Loosley Row, a hamlet about three miles from the headquarters and a couple of miles from the small town of Princes Risborough. It was an unremarkable Victorian cottage of brick and flint with red-tiled floors; the front door opened straight into the living-room, and there was a small dining-room, a kitchen down two steps, and three bedrooms and a bathroom upstairs. It had the great advantage of central heating run from a large solid-fuel stove in the kitchen; there was no garden, but there was a magnificent view over the valley to Bledlow Ridge and the Chilterns. The house was adequately furnished, and though the rent at four-and-a-half guineas was a little more than we could really afford, I thought it worthwhile.

We moved down from Leeds by train in November, somehow coping with baby, dog, large pram and luggage – was there a bicycle as well? The Waites, our landlords from Loosley House, had lit a fire for us, and the house felt welcoming in the winter weather. We were to spend another two years there, and always remember it with affection as our first true home.

Looking at my flying logbook for the period, I was at first puzzled to see that I did no flying between the end of October and mid-April 1947. Then I remembered that this winter was one of the worst in living memory: from January to the end of March there was continuous snow and frost. Power supplies were cut for longish periods, and for some time householders were asked not to use electricity during certain hours of the day. Luckily Loosley House had a fair stock of coke left over from its wartime days as an evacuee nursery, and we were able to use it sparingly to keep our kitchen stove going. I remember cycling the three miles to the headquarters with a narrow and slippery channel cleared in the road and banks of snow higher than my head on either side. Flying throughout the Command was affected, and in the spring floods following the months of heavy snow, the Lancasters dropped food and other supplies to the stricken east coast areas.

Life in the headquarters was, on the whole, quiet and unexciting in this period of post-war doldrums. As I have said, my job was a fairly routine one and I was not privy to the policy-making discussions which were going on in the Air Staff on the future shape of the Command. At that time, although the Iron Curtain had already come down in Europe, there seemed to be very little guidance from government as to what the task of a national bomber force might be, and we were some way from being able to deliver nuclear weapons or to formulate a deterrent defence strategy. We were certainly already looking towards Russia for possible targets, but with little conviction of being able to operate effectively with our current types and numbers of aircraft. New aircraft specifications were being drawn up, and I recall seeing the Air Staff Target for the B3/45, eventually to become the Canberra, and being amazed at the rate of climb and operating heights and speeds required. The B14/46, the first of the V-bombers, was also being studied, but only the Command Navigation Officer and Dixie Dean were involved in planning the navigation equipment. Meanwhile the bomber squadrons were being re-equipped with the Avro Lincoln, an up-market version of the Lancaster designed with the Japanese war in mind and offering modest improvements in height, speed, range, and armament, but little change in the navigation systems. Its crew accommodation still left a great deal to be desired, although the bomb aimer's compartment in the nose was much improved.

I see from my appointments diary that I was taking driving lessons and reported for the driving test in Aylesbury on Friday 13 June, market day in this bustling county town. Much to my chagrin, I did not pass and had to make a second – successful – attempt a few weeks later. I recall with some shame and horror that on staff visits by road I cajoled the WAAF driver into letting me drive while I was still officially a learner; an accident would have had severe disciplinary repercussions, but my luck was evidently in.

By this time, as one of the few junior officers at the headquarters, I had been given the job of Unit Fire Officer, in charge of the small RAF Fire Section headed by a corporal and possessing one fire engine (or appliance, as I learned to call it); this vehicle I did drive legally when I had passed my test. The job was not very onerous, and we fortunately never had a fire while I held it. However, there was one embarrassing fire practice when the section was called to a fire obligingly lit in the woods between the Mess and the headquarters site. The fire vehicle arrived very promptly, unrolled hoses quickly and efficiently, and attached them to two nearby fire hydrants. When the hydrants were turned on, a few tired drops of water trickled out of the hose nozzles and dripped on to the ground. The C-in-C was watching and did not appear to be amused, and the fire went out of its own accord before the hydrants were cleared. I had an uncomfortable interview with the Unit Commander, and passed on the displeasure to my corporal immediately afterwards. The Fire Section smartened up somewhat – at least temporarily.

As the Command Map Officer, I became involved in the development of flight information documents, mostly airfield diagrams showing the flying facilities and approaches. Transport Command, flying as it constantly did to strange airfields, found this type of information essential, and had produced coverage of all its regular routes. Bomber Command too was now starting to make overseas flights both for training and for 'showing the flag', and we had had to obtain what flight information there was from the transporters. This was before the days of airways systems in the UK and Europe, although they had been in existence in the USA for some years. We were still often drawing straight lines on the chart from one airfield to another, but overflying foreign countries needed special routes and clearances, and crews needed accurate and up-to-date information that was easy to assimilate quickly. This was the beginning of a whole new flight information industry, which involved the production of airfield charts and route books with world-wide coverage, showing all *en route* and terminal navigation and landing aids, and kept current daily on the RAF teleprinter network – something of an advance on the wartime information sheet with a few codes printed on rice paper, to be eaten if shot down.

One other idea we adapted from Transport Command was the aircrew categorization scheme. Transport aircraft carried passengers or freight and sometimes both; for obvious reasons, the standard of crews required for passenger carrying was higher than that for freight, and the best crews were allocated to carrying VIPs. So transport crews were regularly examined, both in the air and on the ground, by a special categorization unit awarding categories ranging from A for VIP crews to E for crews unfit for transport flying. The system was a practical one which grew out of the role of Transport Command, and the crews knew that they had to perform adequately if they were to continue doing their job.

In theory there were advantages in applying such a scheme to Bomber Command, where to some extent standards had lapsed without the spur of operations over enemy territory; if you knew that your own life and the lives of your crew depended on your doing your job efficiently, then you would do it to the best of your ability, but on routine training exercises the incentive was not the same. One of our Station Navigation Officers (Flight Lieutenant Rex Sanders) had developed a scheme for assessing the competence of bomber navigators, and I got the job of producing a system for the Command based on his work. The tests involved a fairly basic ground examination and the detailed marking of navigators' logs and charts for three cross-country exercises, and were to be administered by Station Navigation Officers. One drawback was that Bomber Command had no equivalent to the Transport Command situation, where the crew category determined the type of work to be done: unless the categorization assessments were irredeemably low the bomber crew would continue doing what it had been doing. Nevertheless the scheme did help to pinpoint training problems and to ginger up idle or incompetent crew members, and (as I discovered later when I became more closely concerned at the working level) it did achieve the aim of improving standards.

My own practical navigation standards were certainly not improving, but I managed to keep my hand in on the odd Anson flight from Booker. I was also able to fulfil an old ambition and fly in a Mosquito. The Telecommunications Flying Unit (TFU) at Defford in Worcestershire provided test flying facilities for the Telecomunications Research Establishment (TRE), whose scientists had developed many of the new radio and radar aids which had helped to win the war. TRE had produced a miniaturized version of the Rebecca homing device, Rebecca Mark 4, which had been installed in a TFU Mosquito, and I was invited to go down and take a short trial flight to assess it from the operator's point of view. On a fine day in August I flew from Defford in a Mosquito B35, one of the latest bomber versions of the type piloted by a lieutenant-commander test pilot from the Naval Section at TFU. I had thought the Lancaster crew compartment not exactly spacious, but sitting in the navigator's position in the Mossie was like wearing an ill-fitting strait-jacket, and I was amazed at the amount of instrumentation that had been installed. The Gee set had to be operated over the left shoulder, and I could see serious muscular problems setting in after longish flights. The Rebecca 4 had a small hooded screen and presented no particular difficulties apart from the crouching position needed to read it; we did a homing on a local Eureka beacon, and then for a few minutes I was free to enjoy the speed and power of the Mosquito kindly demonstrated by Lieutenant-Commander Hudson.

On another occasion later that year, I flew to Upwood to act as navigator in a Lancaster from No. 214 Squadron taking part in a trial of minelaying methods off Weston-super-Mare. We used H2S Mark 3 for the dropping runs, and it was a pleasure to exercise my old skills and to be back in a Lanc again.

*   *   *

Although there were such visits away from time to time, on the whole I had regular working hours, and cycled home for lunch on most days.

Rationing was still strict but Joan worked miracles with what food she could get and with the none-too-generous housekeeping money we could afford; she was not a Yorkshire girl for nothing, and got on good terms with her butcher in Princes Risborough. She bought large bones for soup, extracted the marrow from them and used it in lieu of fat for cakes. The baker, Mr Janes from High Wycombe, called several times a week, and pulled up his horse and hooded cart outside the door. One of his local specialities was lardy cake, full of calories, very filling, but delicious. Our teatime favourite, especially at weekends if we had been for a bracing walk, was dripping toast eaten in front of a blazing fire.

Joan would push Susan in her large pram the two miles to Risborough on shopping days, and push it back again heavily laden up the steep hills. Often in the afternoons she would take Susan on wooding expeditions down a little unpaved lane to a place marked on the map as Wardrobes, picking up fallen branches and bringing them back on the pram.

Susan walked and talked early and proved to be a lively child with a mind of her own. Watching her grow up and develop was a delight, and we had the sense of being a cohesive family in a secure home, after all the vicissitudes of the last few years.

Joyce and Arthur Waite, our landlords at Loosley House, were very kind to us, no doubt looking on us as overgrown children. Their own daughter, Jan, was sixteen or so, and usually away at school, but often came down to talk to us in the cottage when she was at home. Her pony, Nest, was stabled in the adjoining building, and we would occasionally hear her moving and stamping in the evening quiet. The Waites had four dogs, a pair of Labradors, an elderly Airedale, and a nondescript hairy mongrel known as Puppy. Our own terrier, Sherry, had settled in well and enjoyed the country life with plenty of walks. The male black Labrador, Pan, was a good guard dog and usually loose in the grounds; the local people were wary of him, with his deep bark, but he would often sit drooling by Susan's pram outside our front windows and lick well-sucked rusks from her fingers. Eventually four Labrador pups arrived, and though Mrs Waite was strict with them, we were occasionally allowed to walk them down the long fields between the house and the Wycombe road, when they would gallop off into the distance and only come back when they were tired. Our own terrier was keen on rabbit holes, and once disappeared down a large one for some time, causing great alarm but finally coming out in her own time.

Although we were city bred, we had always looked towards the nearby countryside and the Dales for our pleasures, and took to the rural life like ducks to water. Loosley Row was truly rural, with no shop and no church, but with a small sub-post office and a pub called The Whip at the top of the hill, on which there stood the remains of a seventeenth-century smock mill named after Lacey Green, the next village towards High Wycombe.

Not far away was the Pink and Lily, where Rupert Brooke stayed and wrote poetry before the First World War.

The local small rattling bus, always known as 'Farmer's Bus', passed daily to go to Risborough or Wycombe and as far as Aylesbury, and we did not consider ourselves isolated through the lack of a car. The cottage was not on the telephone, but we had an extension from Loosley House which we were allowed to use for urgent incoming calls: the number was Princes Risborough 2.

The Waites introduced us to some of their friends, including John (J.H.B.) Peel, the writer, newly demobbed from the Navy and usually with a pretty girl in tow; we entertained them and friends from the headquarters to simple suppers or small parties when we could find something to drink and nibble. We were unsophisticated hosts, but people seemed to enjoy themselves. Occasionally we had friends to stay, and our parents came down once or twice for short holidays.

The WAAF map clerk in charge of the Command map store, Corporal Joan Lisle, was a charming girl and would come to baby-sit with Susan so that we could go out to dinner or to the annual ball at the headquarters Mess. These were grand affairs (or as grand as could reasonably be expected in this immediate post-war period). For the first one, Mrs Waite insisted on lending Joan a white ball-gown in the classic Grecian style, in which – with a few deft adjustments – she looked stunning and drew many admiring looks: a welcome change from being a busy mother and cottage-wife.

We found time to read and listen to music in the evenings; I had bought a second-hand pre-war radiogram and we played my own old 78 rpm records and the occasional new one. The BBC had some splendid evening concerts in those days, and one of my abiding memories of Loosley Row is always triggered when I hear the wistful third movement of Dvorak's Eighth Symphony: I am sitting quietly listening in the living-room of the cottage; Susan is asleep upstairs; Joan is ironing in the kitchen doorway, and we are communicating silently to each other our enjoyment of the music. It still brings tears to my eyes.

*   *   *

Nearly two years into my four-year Extended Service Commission, I had to start to think about the future. A career as a navigator in civil aviation was not a sound proposition; the chances of getting a permanent commission in the RAF were good and offered better prospects, especially with the experience I had gained at High Wycombe and my Staff Navigator qualification. Joan and I talked it over and we agreed that there would be advantages in staying in the service if this were possible. The problems of moving house every two years had to be balanced against a reasonable standard of living and the possibilities of promotion to higher rank. There would also be a small pension at the end of a service career, although at our age and stage I hardly think we considered that as a deciding factor. Certainly I would be lucky to find any comparable job in civvy street, with my lack of appropriate qualifications, and – probably in my case an overriding reason – I loved flying and many aspects of RAF life.

At about this time there was a shortage of officers in the middle ranks qualified on the Specialist Navigation Course. Pre-war Spec Ns were too senior, retiring or dead, and many of the wartime Spec Ns had not stayed in the service. They would be especially needed for research and development posts at flight lieutenant and squadron leader rank as the new generation of high-performance aircraft was brought into service. In Bomber Command it was also thought that by appointing Spec Ns as Station Navigation Officers (usually Staff Navigators hitherto) the overall standards of navigation might be enhanced: I did not take this view myself.

The Spec N Course then was of six months' duration, and including the flying required was consequently expensive at a time when service budgets were under scrutiny (when were they not?). Since the four-month Staff Navigator Course covered much of the basic studies which Spec N students needed, it seemed sensible to convert as many suitable Staff ns as possible via a specially designed shorter course, and this was introduced in mid-1947 at the Empire Air Navigation School (still at Shawbury) as the Specialist Navigation Conversion Course.

This seemed a natural progression for me to make, and after passing an entrance examination at Shawbury I was selected for No. 3 Spec N Con Course starting on 20 January 1948 for sixteen weeks. I was detached from HQ Bomber Command for the period, and my post on the navigation staff was filled by an officer posted in for the purpose. My boss said that I would probably come back to the headquarters after the course, but he pointed out that I would be well into my second year by then and would probably be posted elsewhere before long.

In the circumstances it seemed best for Joan to stay put at Loosley House Cottage while I was on the course. The Waites could keep a friendly eye on her and I would get home for weekends whenever I could. It was still a wrench for me to leave our first real home and embark on the long and weary journey across country to Shawbury – bus to West Wycombe, second bus to Oxford, train to Birmingham, second train to Shrewsbury, and whatever I could find to take me the last few miles to Shawbury; it was rarely less than a five-hour journey.

Nearly eighteen months in a staff job had taught me a great deal and had considerably broadened my horizons. Seven years later, when I had to produce a Staff College essay on what I had learned from my experience, I wrote:

... I began to comprehend dimly for the first time that an air force is not a machine rolling blindly along under its own impetus, but that its slightest motions are the result of the applications of intelligences at varying points in the line of control; and that the measure of control depends to a large extent on the transmission and interpretation of orders, instructions and information by staff officers. I also learned that, although a staff officer should possess a detailed knowledge of certain aspects of his work, the building-up of a knowledge of references, authorities, and contacts is of inestimable value – the ability, at a moment's notice, to put one's finger on the right paragraph of the right publication, or to be able to say 'I'm sorry, I don't know the answer myself, but X is the man you want, and you will find him at Y.'

This was all true, if expressed in rather a ponderous style, and I knew that I had been lucky to gain such experience so early in my service.

CHAPTER EIGHT

Specialist Navigator

After writing in the last chapter about the long and tedious journey to Shawbury, I find from my flying logbook that in fact I flew from Booker, in a Proctor of the Bomber Command Communications Flight, in exactly an hour, arriving the day before the start of the course. The wearisome train and bus journeys came later, when I went home to Buckinghamshire for weekend leaves. It was just over three years since I had left at the end of the Staff Navigator Course, at a time when significant changes in the RAF navigation world had got off to a flying start with the formation of the Empire Air Navigation School. In those three years Shawbury had become, as envisaged, a world centre for the study of air navigation, and the Lancastrian Aries had made several more record-breaking (and ground-breaking) flights. There was now an Aries II – a modified Lincoln aircraft which had arrived early in 1947 and had completed several long-range overseas flights. EANS had also established regular navigation liaison conferences at which the great and the good from industry, the scientific world, and the other services came together to discuss current problems and developments; people of the standing of Sir Robert Watson-Watt came to address these gatherings. A Test and Development Section had been set up at Shawbury to undertake 'projects relating to navigation techniques' and 'trials of equipment and ephemerides (astronomical tables) to determine their accuracy and suitability to service requirements'. So says the EANS Air Navigation Liaison Letter for the first quarter of 1948 – another innovation which had a wide distribution in the RAF and the Commonwealth air forces. The school was now equipped with Lancaster Mark VII aircraft. A new series of Specialist Navigation Courses lasting six months had started in 1946, and the Staff Navigator Course had been replaced for the time being with the so-called Advanced Navigation Course, slightly shorter and mainly concerned with producing navigation instructors rather than all-round Staff Navigators. No doubt some savings had had to be made; tinkering with the form and aims of the course continued for some years, but eventually it was re-established very much in its original form. The day I arrived at Shawbury also saw the appointment as Commandant of Air

Commodore L.K. (Kelly) Barnes, a well-known figure in RAF navigation circles who had played some part in establishing a vigorous navigation policy and was much respected. He was a pre-war Spec N, of course, and the only pilot in the RAF who had a special dispensation from the Air Ministry to wear the 'N' flying badge, which he did frequently, with a noticeable effect on navigators' morale.

As I walked in through the gates I saw that the physical aspects of the station had had something of a face-lift. Many of the wartime excrescences, such as hutted classrooms and Nissen huts, had disappeared; the married quarters were occupied by families; and the Officers' Mess, while still crowded, appeared to be comparatively comfortable and under sound management. I shared a room with Flight Lieutenant Johnny Whitlock, another bomber navigator on the conversion course, with a droll sense of humour and a cheerful temperament. Our classroom was in the main school building, alongside that of No. 5 Specialist Navigation Course, who were about halfway through their six months' stint and would graduate at about the same time as we did. Our Course Commander was Squadron Leader 'Pep' Pepperman, a pilot Spec N who was a short stocky character, down to earth but conscientious and always ready to help students with problems. Our senior student was Flight Lieutenant John Digman, who had just completed a tour of duty on the EANS staff; he became a life-long friend with whom I am still in touch. Sixteen of the twenty-strong course were navigators, with four pilots who, being outnumbered, were obliged to suffer a great deal of leg pulling ('Some of my best friends are pilots, but would you want your daughter to marry one?'). We had all experienced operational flying at some stage or other, and we all got on amazingly well, with a great deal of mutual support on the academic side of the course. My copy of the course syllabus has long gone the way of all flesh, but I have some of my own notes, and I see that the subjects studied were mostly those we had covered on the Staff n Course, but dealt with in greater depth, particularly in mathematics and physics. In the standard navigation subjects such as compasses, instruments, radio and radar, and maps and charts, there had been many advances in the past three years which had to be looked at. Meteorology and climatology were taught to a very high standard, and I was delighted to be again under the eye of Harry Maggs, who had been my Met instructor at Bridgnorth in 1943. Maths was, as ever, hard going, but now included a look at modern statistics, which had many practical applications, such as the theory of errors, and proved to be of great interest. Again we were lucky with our tutor, Flight Lieutenant 'Flash' Button, who I am sure earned his nickname by his lightning (and lucid) expositions of knotty mathematical problems. He was a true polymath with wide interests (including music), and went on to become head of the RAF Education Branch as an air vice-marshal.

* * *

EANS had been studying and developing several new techniques in the practice of air navigation, some of which had come about as a result of the Aries long-range flights. Grid navigation was a technique for use in high latitudes where the usual maps and charts in use had serious drawbacks because of the convergence of meridians at the geographic Poles; the standard RAF plotting chart, on the Mercator projection, could not be used beyond about 70 degrees north or south latitude because of the scale expansion (to infinity at the Poles). Constant-scale charts, such as those on the conical orthomorphic projection used in the RAF as radar plotting charts and in general use in the USAAF, could cover the polar regions, but there was still the problem of rapidly changing compass directions near the Pole. Superimposing a parallel grid on a constant-scale chart, with the grid lines parallel to a selected meridian of longitude (the 'standard meridian'), enabled a straight-line track to be flown across the converging meridians in polar areas. The grid variation ('grivation', or the angular difference between the grid meridian and the magnetic meridian at any one place) could be applied to the compass to obtain a course to fly which would take into account both the grid difference and the magnetic variation, both of which could be large and rapidly changing near the Pole. Charts could be overprinted with grivation curves which were used in exactly the same way as isogonals (lines of magnetic variation routinely printed on plotting charts). With the use of a variation setting control, such as on the DR compass, to offset gyro-magnetic compasses for grivation, the navigator's task was greatly simplified (though I can hardly say that about the foregoing explanation, drastically summarized for the purposes of this book). It is only fair to say that the principle of grid navigation was not entirely new: it had been originated by the Italian Navy in the 1920s when Italy was involved in airship flights over the North Pole. However, it seems that it was not until the 1945 Aries flights from Shawbury that there was any practical use of the technique.

'Pressure-pattern flying' was another new development under study at Shawbury. The wartime increase in long-distance overseas flights (especially those ferrying aircraft across the North Atlantic) and the introduction of the radar altimeter led to the use of atmospheric pressure patterns to aid navigation, and also improve fuel economy. The standard aircraft altimeter was basically an aneroid barometer measuring atmospheric pressure and showing it as height, whereas the radar altimeter gave the true height of the aircraft by bouncing radar echoes off the sea surface. By comparing the readings of these two instruments over a period at the same height, the navigator could measure the atmospheric pressure gradient along his track and calculate the wind component at right-angles to it, giving a position-line parallel to track. Since this method was only practicable over the sea, and since it took some twenty-five minutes to obtain the data, this was not a very widely applicable way of obtaining a single position-line. Single-heading flight was a technique using forecast pressure patterns to calculate one heading (or course) which would take an aircraft all the way to its destination. The theory was complex, and depended much on aircraft instrument errors, and on the validity of the assumptions in the calculation formulae, which were inaccurate at low altitudes. As far as military aircraft were concerned, there were obvious tactical drawbacks in keeping to one course and one pressure level for long periods. An allied method using pressure patterns was the optimum flight path, or 'least-time track' – finding the most economical flight path between departure and destination. This could be done by working out single headings for a number of altitudes until the best height to fly for minimum time *en route* was found. This method again relied on the accuracy of forecasting, and suffered from tactical disadvantages. EANS studies concluded that these pressure-pattern techniques were not likely to be of great use in the RAF, except for transoceanic flights in northern latitudes (and there were not many of these at the time). However, the fledgling post-war airlines were very interested in the possibilities of saving flight time and fuel by using pressure patterns. The Meteorological Office estimated in 1948 that an aircraft flying from London to New York at 18,000 feet and 200 knots could have saved 1.6 hours by using the optimum flight path technique compared with the great circle route. Such a saving was certainly worth considering, and there was confidence that upper air forecasting would improve substantially in the near future. Indeed, the optimum flight path technique combined with maximum range cruise-control was used by civil airlines in the 1950s with some success, as the operating speeds then had not reached those of later jet aircraft, and a worthwhile fuel and time saving could be made. The latest upper-air forecast charts were used by flight planning staffs to determine the flight profile, relieving the captain and the flight navigator of some of the tedious pre-flight work, and again saving precious time.

* * *

We were able to try these techniques ourselves in the EANS Lancasters, with several flights using grid navigation and one using the single-heading method from St Eval in Cornwall to Madeira, later landing at Gibraltar, where we spent a couple of days enjoying the unique atmosphere of the colony and visiting La Linea across the Spanish border. This was only my second time 'abroad', and I was particularly struck by the contrast between the Britishness of some aspects of life on the Rock (policemen, red pillar-boxes, egg and chips in the cafés) and the exotic Mediterranean backdrop and population. Most of us bought presents to take home, including quite a lot of tinned and other food which was unobtainable in the UK in 1948; I have a clear memory of going home to Loosley Row for the weekend, via the usual weary train journey, and walking the two miles from Princes Risborough station with a suitcase that nearly broke my back, filled as it was with Gibraltarian delights. Loosley House Cottage seemed like another world during these short weekends, mostly taken up by travelling. Joan was having something of a struggle to make ends meet, with the loss of my ration book and the extra expense of my living separately in the Mess while we still paid rent at home, and the cost of travel to and from Shawbury. With much embarrassment I asked Mrs Waite if she would consider reducing our rent a little in the circumstances, which she kindly did, easing the situation to some extent. At some time during the course there was a ball in the Shawbury Officers' Mess to which Joan was able to come, thanks to Pep Pepperman's kindness in offering beds to her and Susan. They arrived at Shrewsbury station and were met by Ron Davies, a fellow-student who owned a car and whose wife Rita was also there for the ball. It was a well-organized and enjoyable event, and it was a pleasure to see Joan forget her domestic cares for a while.

No. 3 Spec N Conversion Course came to an end on 10 May 1948 with much rejoicing among its weary students, who were now fully qualified Spec Ns, entitled to the symbol 'N' in the Air Force List. My own examination results were not as good numerically as for the Staff Navigator Course – 76.5% as against 83.3% – but constituted a so-called A2 Pass with Credit and a much more encouraging report: 'A hard working and conscientious student with above average technical knowledge. Justifiably confident of his own ability, he should prove a valuable asset in a staff appointment.' ('Justifiably confident' probably meant 'a little too big for his boots'.) But in the last few days of the course, when I was looking forward to getting back home, the picture changed. Kelly Barnes, our Commandant, with four months behind him in the job and ever an innovator, decided that there should be a moratorium on Spec N training and the other main activities of EANS to give a chance to stand back and look at the role and aims of the school in the light of rapidly changing RAF requirements. The Advanced Navigation Courses would continue, since the need for instructors was still pressing, but there would be a three-month study period during which members of the staff and some of the graduating Spec N students would take an all-round look at navigation in the RAF and come up with recommendations for future policy. This became known as the 'Interim Course', and to my surprise I was asked to join it. This was an offer I could hardly refuse, despite its meaning a further period away from home. Since those selected for this new venture were understandably to be people with some time to serve, I was urged to apply for a permanent commission. Joan and I had discussed this, and I had no hesitation in applying, although it was hard to tell her that I would be at Shawbury for another three months. I was interviewed by a local selection board at Shawbury, and in less time than I had thought possible my permanent commission was confirmed. Under the rules prevailing at the time I was now committed to the RAF to the age of 43 (or later, if promotion came my way), and I could forget about civil aviation or finding some boring job on the ground. There is almost nothing about the 'Interim Course' among my personal papers; most of the work done had a security classification, and I imagine that my notes and other documents were destroyed at some stage. A history of the Spec N Course compiled at the RAF College of Air Warfare in the 1960s refers to the 'rethink' at Shawbury, and says:

> In June, 1948, what would now be called a brain washing was held. Many changes in staff had been made earlier in the year and for a month all instruction was suspended. Instead, a conversion course for the staff was held rather on Staff College lines. Major lectures were given at SASO and Command Navigation Officer level, which were followed by major exercises in syndicates. The aim of the course was to develop forward thinking, and to write a new syllabus for the Specialist Navigation Course.

Though correct in essence, this account does not really square with my recollections: my flying logbook shows that I stayed on at Shawbury for the 'Interim Course' from May to the end of August, rather more than one month. While forward thinking was certainly part of the study, the aims were much wider than that, and I recall that the remit included recommendations on navigation and navigation training policy to higher authority. We had an array of speakers from industry, the Air Ministry and the Ministry of Supply (some of air rank) dealing with subjects as diverse as the Russian cartographic service, the results of the heavy bomber campaign in Europe, and the organization of navigation staffs in the RAF. I remember particularly the talk given by Air Vice-Marshal Pelly, who had been head of the British Bombing Survey Unit which had spent two years analysing the effects of the RAF and USAAF raids in France and Germany; this was the first really solid evidence most of us had had that, while devastating in its physical effect, strategic bombing had not had the decisive effect on the Third Reich's industry and on the morale of the German people which we had estimated at the time. Nevertheless, there was no doubt that Bomber Command had made a significant contribution to the final victory.

I never discovered what recommendations on future navigation policy were made by EANS, and I cannot recall seeing any reference to the 'Interim Course' in service literature in later years. Was it a waste of time? I know that Kelly Barnes fell ill and died not too long afterwards, and it may be that without his forceful and ebullient personality, such changes as he had recommended were not pursued. For me, at least, it gave a taste of wider and deeper considerations than those mainly hard facts we had had to acquire with much sweat on the Spec N Course, and also an insight into some of the issues facing policy makers in the ministries and scientists in the research establishments. If the 'Interim Course' did not have the far-reaching effects hoped for by its initiators, something else happened while I was at Shawbury which did have important consequences in the RAF navigation world: Air Ministry Order No. 410/1948 was published on 20 May, and offered equal careers to pilots and navigators in the Royal Air Force. As I have written elsewhere in this book, there were virtually no commissioned navigators before 1940, and the simple arithmetic of seniority meant that few would be available for consideration as Flight and Squadron Commanders; those who had achieved squadron leader and wing commander rank would be regarded as much more effective in navigation staff posts, where their expertise could be most valuable. When the AMO was published, Air Marshal Sir Ralph Cochrane, then the Commander-in-Chief of Flying Training Command, came down to EANS to talk to the assembled staff and students about it. While the move was generally welcomed among both pilots and navigators, it was realized that this was a long-term affair and would not mean immediate selection of many navigators for command posts; as I pointed out to Sir Ralph, as soon as a pilot goes solo he is an aircraft commander, whereas a navigator would normally be under command from the beginning. As I said, the only thing I had ever commanded was a WAAF map clerk; it would obviously take more time for the average navigator to gain the command experience equivalent to that of the average pilot. Nevertheless, this was a significant step in the right direction.

I must record another significant event during my time at Shawbury. At the end of a day's work I was walking across to the Mess and took a short cut through a back entrance. Someone had been disposing of a pile of papers in a dustbin, and one was lying on the ground. I caught sight of its title and picked it up: it was No. 1, Volume 1, of the *Journal of the Institute of Navigation*, published in January 1948 at six shillings. I had heard vaguely that such a body was being formed, but it had not been specifically brought to the attention of EANS students. I was impressed and intrigued by the excellent format and production and took it to my room to read further. An Institute of Navigation had been set up in the USA in 1945, and the UK followed suit in 1947 with an impressive array of founder members. Sir Harold Spencer-Jones, the Astronomer Royal, was the first President, with Air Chief Marshal Sir John Slessor (then Commandant of the Imperial Defence College) and Sir Robert Watson-Watt, the pioneer of radar, as Vice-Presidents. In his inaugural address, the Astronomer Royal said that the Institute had been formed 'to promote the interests of science and of practical navigation, by uniting together in a scientific body those who are concerned with or are interested in the science and art of navigation.' This first issue of the *Journal* included as contributors (as well as Sir Harold Spencer-Jones and Sir John Slessor) Sir Charles Darwin, the Director of the National Physical Laboratory; Sir Robert Watson-Watt; Donald Sadler, the Superintendent of the Nautical Almanac Office; Francis Chichester; and Air Vice-Marshal Donald Bennett. Dealing equally with the marine and the air aspects of navigation, the Institute went from strength to strength, later becoming the Royal Institute of Navigation, with Prince Philip as Patron, and it flourishes with much influence today. From the beginning much was due to the inspired day-to-day guidance of the Executive Secretary, Michael Richey, and the high standards he maintained as Editor of the *Journal*. I became a member while I was still at Shawbury, and remained a member for nearly forty years. I still have that first number of the *Journal*, and it is lying on my desk at this moment.

* * *

At the end of August 1948, I rejoined the navigation staff at Headquarters Bomber Command, where I was marking time until a posting elsewhere came up. There were a variety of odd jobs to do, including the final preparation of the Command's navigator categorization scheme for publication. Since I was most likely to get a job as a Station Navigation Officer, I thought it prudent to frame the details of the scheme in a way which would be workable and acceptable at station level. I was to find out in due course that this admirable aim was not so easily attainable. At home again in Loosley Row, I found that Susan at nearly two years old was out of the 'big pram' stage and trundling busily around with her small wooden wheelbarrow. We made the most of the Buckinghamshire autumn and walked around the lanes and fields, picking blackberries for jam, and for the first (and last) time picking quinces in a Princes Risborough orchard. Joan and I had been happy in what was our first real home together, despite the privations of the early 1947 winter and the separation for much of 1948. Now we knew we had to move, and were not looking forward to it with much pleasure. There were two SNO jobs coming up, at Lakenheath in Norfolk and at Waddington in Lincolnshire, and I took the opportunity, via the Communications Flight, to make a staff visit to each. Lakenheath, not far from Thetford and in the Breckland country, was not unattractive, but Waddington, close to Lincoln and a pre-war station, seemed to me to be the better bet. For the first and only time in my career I had a choice of specific postings, and I took it. We packed up our few belongings at Loosley House Cottage and said our goodbyes to Joyce and Arthur Waite (we were to meet Mrs Waite again in unusual circumstances). Some time in November Joan took Susan up to Leeds to stay with her parents, and I left High Wycombe for Lincolnshire.

CHAPTER NINE

Back to Lincolnshire

R AF Waddington stands on Ermine Street, some three miles south of Lincoln, on the long ridge that runs north and south through the west of the second-largest English county. There has been a military airfield here since the First World War; in the late 1930s a modern RAF station was built, with three concrete runways, hangars and the administrative and technical buildings on the east side of Ermine Street, and the messes and married quarters on the west. It is still an important operational station flying Tornadoes.

In 1948 the station was home to three Lincoln squadrons – 50, 57, and 61 – manned by a mixture of war-experienced and newly qualified aircrew, the former predominating. One major change since I had last been on a flying squadron was that a new system of non-commissioned aircrew ranks had been introduced: newly qualified aircrew were classed as Pilot IV or Navigator IV, moving up to III after a little experience, and then II as the equivalent to the former Sergeant; I for Flight Sergeant; and the Warrant Officer rank was replaced by a Master Aircrew designation. The bomb aimer (or air bomber) category was abolished, with all former bomb aimers who were staying in the service retrained as navigators; and wireless operators became air signallers. The new ranks were an attempt to differentiate aircrew from ground NCOs, giving them a separate mess and acknowledging that they had different responsibilities. In my view (and that of many others), this was a mistake, as it tended to divorce NCO aircrew from some of the realities of RAF life, the humdrum duties and disciplinary activities which help to make the service an integrated whole. The scheme lasted for some years and then reverted to the old NCO ranks, except that the Master Aircrew designation was (and is) retained. At about the same time, the non-commissioned ground technical ranks were changed, with Sergeants becoming Senior Technicians and Flight Sergeants Chief Technicians (at least the NCO i/c Servicing could still be called 'Chiefie', as always). In the airman ranks, Aircraftman 1st Class was abolished and a new rank of Senior Aircraftman introduced above Leading Aircraftman. All these changes were unsettling, but the times were unsettling in any event, with two-year conscripts forming a substantial proportion of the available manpower, and many officers and airmen still on short-term engagements. We had received one or two of the first post-war Cranwell products as co-pilots, and the squadrons on the whole were not impressed. With quite a number of the more senior officers being returned prisoners of war who had spent some years in prison camps, and whose flying experience (through no fault of their own) did not always match their seniority, morale generally was not high. I reported to Wing Commander Smith, the Wing Commander Flying, who seemed a pleasant chap, and then went across to the Flying Control Tower where my office was on the ground floor overlooking the airfield. My predecessor was anxious to depart, and did not spend much time with me. A WAAF clerk had been assigned to him but did not seem to be very interested in the job. I was somewhat shocked to find that the daily 'Notices to Airmen', received by signal from the RAF air traffic HQ at Uxbridge, were just filed away and forgotten. Since they included details of navigation hazards, flight restrictions and the activation of danger areas, they should have been sent to the squadrons and also made available for pre-flight reference to anyone who needed them. I could see that some changes were necessary. I was able to get rid of the lackadaisical WAAF almost immediately, and in her place got a young National Service clerk general duties, LAC Bell, a local boy from Barnetby near Elsham, who turned out to be a treasure. Willing, intelligent and capable, he made a big difference to my workload and the routine aspects of the job.

What was the job? I suppose the Station Navigation Officer acted as a focal point for all navigational matters: overseeing the Squadron Navigation Leaders, issuing maps, briefing crews on exercises, maintaining briefing material, arranging training sessions, and running the command navigator categorization scheme (with which I was already so familiar). Relationships with the squadrons could be tricky – the navigation leaders and some of the navigators were older, more senior, and more experienced than I, and they did not let me forget it. But on the whole it was recognized that I was there to provide a service to them and that I mostly put their requirements first. The fact that I was a Spec N didn't cut much ice, but at least the knowledge that I had done a tour of wartime bomber operations was in my favour. One early bonus was that Michael Bartlett, our old bomb aimer from Al Moore's crew, was on 61 Squadron, married and living on the station, and it was pleasant to see a familiar face. One of the first jobs I had to tackle was the reorganization of the station map store. Housed in a large room in the 61 Squadron hangar, the map stocks had evidently been left to look after themselves for some time. Maps and charts were stored in a random fashion, issues were not being recorded, and new map orders lay here and there unpacked; there seemed to be no inventory, and many out-of-date editions had not been replaced. Bell and I spent several evenings there after the day's work, and gradually we produced order from chaos, disposing of old and unwanted stocks, restocking where necessary, and setting up proper recording systems. This was work I enjoyed (and as a former Command Map Officer could hardly have neglected). Bell appeared to enjoy it, too, working late voluntarily and making a positive contribution. I began to get to know him well, and we worked together with mutual respect for the rest of my time at Waddington. Soon I was able to move out of the noisy and draughty office in the tower and into a building nearby which had been originally designed as a navigation section, with two small offices at either end (one with an astrodome in the roof) and an open lecture area in the centre. Bell and I each had a tiny office, and we were able to provide a secure store for navigation equipment – sextants, watches, and so on. By scrounging suitable furniture from other parts of the station, we were able to set up a respectable lecture room for training periods; life began to look a little rosier.

*   *   *

On the domestic front, permanent married quarters for the airmen were being built, and quite rightly had priority over those for officers. Some temporary prefabricated quarters were promised for junior officers, but they would not be ready for another six months or so. I scoured the local press and the countryside for a furnished house, but with the number of RAF aerodromes still active in the Lincoln area there were few to be had. At last I found a cottage in the village of Harmston, a couple of miles from the station, which was just about acceptable but rather primitive compared with Loosley House Cottage. There was electricity but no water laid on, the nearest supply being a Victorian public tap up the lane (with water gushing from a lion's mouth), and the convenience (or inconvenience) was an earth closet round the back – I was told that a local old man would empty it weekly for the price of a pint. The house was poorly furnished and had an antique range for cooking, but it would have to do for a few months, especially as the rent was only £2 a week.

I am sure that Joan's heart sank when she arrived with Susan and saw the cottage for the first time. Our few possessions – which had been standing forlornly in the Station Equipment Section – were delivered, we got a fire going in the grate, and (like the talented improviser she is) Joan made the place into a home in short order. 'Be it never so humble' took on a particular relevance. The old man who was reputed to empty the earth closet never materialized, promise of a pint notwithstanding, and I got the job, luckily with a large neglected garden in which to dispose of the evidence. We kept two water pails standing in the tiny scullery, one for drinking and one for washing, and I or Joan and Susan would go up the lane to refill them once or twice a day. One Monday morning Susan, dressed in clean clothes, had the misfortune to sit in one of these pails, and had to be comforted and changed from head to foot. The milk had to be fetched from a farm at the top of the lane; they had ferrets in cages in the yard, and Susan would look at these with mixed fascination and alarm. We had our own lidded milk can which Susan also used to fetch water in, proudly carrying it 'to help Mummy'. Our neighbours, Mr and Mrs Kirk, were a quiet elderly couple. She had been in service and he had been – and still was occasionally – a farm labourer, with all the skills and knowledge that that implied in those days. They mostly kept themselves to themselves, but were friendly and ready to give help if we needed it. They kept a pig in a sty at the bottom of the garden, and Susan would often go and throw scraps to him. There was also a pony in the field across the lane who could be given the occasional titbit. The Kirks had a fearsome wild and woolly dog kept chained to a kennel in the yard. His fierce bark could be heard whenever anyone passed by, and he was given a wide berth by the postman and others (and by our own fox terrier). Susan was missing one day, and after a frantic search in all possible places was found sitting with the Kirks' dog on the floor of the kennel in happy communion. I don't remember if she picked up any fleas. When the pig was killed, Mrs Kirk was busy for some days salting, curing, and making various appetizing dishes, some of which were very kindly passed to us. Joan said that if ever we were in the right sort of place she was determined to keep a pig.

* * *

During these first few months at Waddington I had been trying to familiarize myself with the Lincoln aircraft, but I see from my logbook that I had only one flight in December and another in January. The Lincoln Mark II, built up the road at Avro's Bracebridge Heath factory, was equipped with four Merlin 68 engines driving four-bladed propellers, giving more power and range than the Lancaster – 2,250 miles with a bomb load of 14,000 lb, with a maximum speed of 305 mph at 19,000 feet. On the other hand, the crew accommodation was not much of an improvement, although the bomb-aiming position in the nose was roomier and had a comfortable seat with an excellent all-round view. Navigation equipment was virtually the same as in the Lancaster – DR compass, API, Gee and H2S Mark III – so there was nothing new to me there. At that time, Bomber Command squadrons were regularly sent on overseas exercises to the Suez Canal Zone, where they would spend a month operating from RAF Station Shallufa, one of several RAF airfields in the Suez area. Especially in the winter months, this allowed intensive bombing and navigation training to be carried out in the usually better weather conditions. Both groundcrews and aircrews experienced the problems and difficulties of operating away from the home bases and in a totally different climatic environment.

So at the end of January I left our peasants' cottage at Harmston and was crewed with the Officer Commanding No. 50 Squadron, Squadron Leader R.A.G. Ellen, for the flight to Egypt, along with several other Lincoln aircraft from Waddington. We were routed via the south of France, with a night stop at Castel Benito, the RAF staging-post near Tripoli (named, of course, for Il Duce). We then flew across the Western Desert and down the Canal Zone to Shallufa. The British were still in control of Egypt, and the strip just west of the Suez Canal was virtually a fortified camp, with Army and RAF bases, maintenance units, and stores all within a wire-fenced and guarded area. Shallufa was a dreary place, with the constant smell of fuel oil, and for the first few days after our arrival, a westerly wind blowing sand from the desert so that everything was covered in a fine dust. The Station Navigation Officer, Freddie Brown, was just going off on leave, and kindly made me free of his office for the period of our detachment. I remember spending some time removing sand from maps, documents and furniture. My first task was to learn to be a bomb aimer; the specialized aircrew category had been abolished, and all navigators were now required to do this job as well, while former bomb aimers who had stayed in the service had been (or were still being) retrained as navigators. I had been fully briefed on the bombsight (still the trusty Mark XIV), the bombing computer, and the bomb-release equipment, and now went off to fly several bombing exercises with 12 lb practice bombs on the local range, risibly called El Shatt. After five of these flights, dropping eight bombs on each sortie, I was judged competent by our Bombing Leader, and was able to turn my attention to navigation again.

It was the custom to fly one night-navigation exercise from Shallufa to Khartoum in the Sudan, dropping bombs on the RAF range there. With few navigation aids available, I briefed the crews of the half-dozen aircraft to use astro-navigation and radio bearings; we were all relieved to note that there was a Eureka beacon at the Khartoum airfield. I flew as navigator with Squadron Leader Ellen, and we carried two newspaper reporters, one from *The Times*, who were accommodated in much discomfort on the metal step forward of the main spar and next to the signaller's position, just under the astrodome. So began a flight which I can never recall without a deep sense of embarrassment. For the first two hours or so we flew in daylight and were able to use ground features for navigation. Then the darkness dropped suddenly, as it does in Africa, and we were reduced to using radio bearings from Shallufa. One of the dead-reckoning navigation techniques in use at that time was that of calculating what was known as the most probable position (MPP). This was a statistical method developed at Shawbury for use when navigational information was scarce – in particular when only single position-lines were available, as was the case now. It involved drawing a circle of probability around the dead-reckoning position derived by applying the best-known wind velocity to the air position (from the API); this circle had a radius of eight nautical miles per hour flown since the air position (from the API); this circle had a radius of eight nautical miles per hour flown since the last positive fix, and purported to be an area of 50% probability. Zones of the same error probability were listed for various types of position lines, and the MPP would lie in the overlap of the two error areas; if they did not overlap, then the MPP would be halfway between the two error limits, although it was acknowledged that in this case the position obtained should be regarded with suspicion.

For a while this technique seemed to be working out fairly well, but as we flew further away from Shallufa, the error zone around the radio bearings became larger; there was nothing to be seen either on the ground or on the H2S, and I decided that the time had come to take an astro fix. I asked the second navigator, Nav 1 Paddy Sheppard, to come up and take some sights while I would do the calculations. His reply came up on the intercom from the nose position: 'Sorry, I haven't been checked out on the sextant yet.' He was a former bomb aimer whose conversion to navigator was evidently not yet complete. With a heavy sigh I reached for the sextant, simultaneously realizing that two large pressmen were squashed into the space below the astrodome. This gave me a good excuse to slump back into my seat again: in any event I had little faith in astro-navigation, and had not had to use it for some years. We Bomber Command navigators had become used to accurate fixing by Gee or H2S, and tended to neglect the older aids. It is perhaps appropriate here to quote from Air Publication 1234, Air Navigation, the edition of 1944 written by Group Captain Dickie Richardson, which was the RAF navigators' bible for many years. Under the heading 'Common causes of error in navigation' he says: 'Flying induces a form of inertia that strongly resembles laziness … there is a very strong inclination to be inactive during flight … errors in Navigation arise much more frequently from wrong assumptions being made on account of inactivity.'

Inertia was certainly what I was feeling as we roared on through the darkness, although I was fully aware that some 'wrong assumptions' were being made. We altered course ostensibly on to the last leg down to the bombing range at Khartoum. Nothing broke the blackness ahead, and I could neither pick up the Khartoum Eureka beacon nor get any sort of fix on the H2S. At last we heard on the R/T some of the other crews contacting the bombing range and preparing to bomb. The range control passed them the local winds, and I realized with a slightly sick feeling that they were very different in both direction and speed from those I had been using to construct my MPPs. I did some hasty replotting and decided that, wherever we were, our position was well west of the Nile and as much as forty or fifty miles from where we should have been. I asked Squadron Leader Ellen to fly due east, telling him that we were well off track, and carefully retuned the H2S to pick up the Nile. After some twenty minutes' flying, with the flight engineer checking the fuel state, the black streak of the river showed up on the H2S screen, and at almost the same time the blip of the Eureka beacon came faintly in on the Rebecca timebase. We had been flying against some unforecast headwinds, and by this time the bombing range had closed and we had to land at Khartoum with our practice bombs unused.

This was a severe lesson to me, and I took it to heart. Here I was, supposed to be setting an example to the squadron navigators with my specialist qualifications, and I had got myself well and truly lost. The captain and crew were very tactful and did not pull my leg too unmercifully, and at least one other navigator had made similar errors, but I felt humiliated – with good reason. I had failed to use all the navigation aids available, and in addition I had placed too much reliance on statistical methods ('lies, damn lies, and …'). But life had to go on, and we spent much of the following day sleeping after our eight-hour flight. We were destined to see rather more of Khartoum than originally planned, since on our take-off for Shallufa we had an engine failure, landed again, and found that an engine change was required. In the end we spent ten days in Khartoum, a fine city by African standards at that time, and the capital of what was still the Anglo-Egyptian Sudan. The country around was fertile, being near the junction of the Blue and White Niles, on which we saw ancient paddle-steamers and a variety of other craft. The streets were wide, with palm trees and flowering shrubs; in one of them there was an impressive statue of Kitchener mounted on a camel (removed, of course, since independence). Once the new engine arrived from the Canal Zone, our sweating groundcrew had the unenviable job of replacing it, which took several days with the minimal equipment available. Meanwhile we idle aircrew mostly rose late and went to swim in the Civil Service Club pool, a fairly basic facility with corrugated-iron fencing around it. My daily task was to barter with the elderly Senussi who sat outside the building where I was quartered and sold local products such as crocodile-skin handbags and snakeskin shoes. He was a tall dignified man who spoke good English and must have been comparatively wealthy – he told me that he had a son training to be a doctor in England. He dropped the price a little each day and I was more than satisfied with a bargain handbag when we left.

We were very happy when we had air tested the Lincoln and were able to leave for Shallufa. The flight was in daylight and we were able to see some of the wild and dramatic country over which we had flown in the dark. I silently gave thanks that my navigation errors had been no worse than they were; running out of fuel and force-landing in some of that terrain would have been a disaster. We had only a few days at Shallufa before leaving for the UK again via Castel Benito, flying over the Qattara Depression in the Western Desert over which there had been much fighting in the Second World War; the occasional tank and vehicle skeletons could still be seen lying in the sand. The onward flight to Waddington was remarkable only for its length – we had an eighty-knot headwind for much of the route and the flight took us ten hours and forty-five minutes, still my longest as navigator.

There is one final memory of our month in Egypt. The CO of 50 Squadron, Squadron Leader Rippingale, was as determined as I was to see Cairo before we left, and we travelled from Suez on an Arab bus across the desert to the capital, getting up very early in the morning to do so. We stayed in an inexpensive hotel in the middle of the city, and were appalled at the noise and the hazards of the traffic, which continued unabated throughout the night. We made the ritual visit to the pyramids and the Sphinx at Giza, and were duly impressed despite the wearisome attentions of dragomans, guides and beggars. The heat and the dust of the return bus journey were equally wearisome, but we were glad that we had made the effort. As it happens, I have never been back to Egypt.

Back in Lincolnshire, life continued much as before, except that a new home was on the stocks. Joan, Susan and I (and the dog) moved into No. 4 Officers' Temporary Married Quarters towards the end of April and said goodbye to our Harmston hovel without too much regret. No. 4 OTMQ was a semi-detached prefabricated bungalow constructed mainly from sections designed originally for radar huts on bomber stations. It was not luxury but it was a great improvement on our recent cottage, fully furnished to the proper scale for officers' married quarters; this in fact proved something of a problem, since there was no provision for any reduction in the scale to match the size of the quarter, and most equipment officers tended to be less than flexible. So we had a full-size dining-table, sideboard, and eight chairs in the tiny dining area, and kitchen equipment designed in the days of cooks and other household staff (Kettles, Fish, Officers', 1).

There was a rough patch of uncultivated ground behind the house, and our kind former neighbour, old Mr Kirk from Harmston, came up on his ancient cycle (mounted by a step on the rear wheel) and dug it over for us. It was an education to watch him turning over the plot with his old spade as sharp as a knife and his skilful economical movements; he did it in half the time and half the effort I would have used.

This was the first time we had lived on a station, and we had very mixed feelings about it. On the one hand, there was only a short distance for me to go to work, we lived among people doing similar jobs to ourselves, and we could take advantage of what little social life there was (bearing in mind that RAF pay was not generous at that time); on the other hand, we missed the variety of village life and the ability to 'keep ourselves to ourselves'. Group Captain Mackay, the Station Commander, and his wife were a pleasant couple, and Mrs Mackay conscientiously had wives to tea from time to time, but ladies were still only allowed in the Mess as guests and there was no Wives' Club or similar body. We made one or two friends in the nearby quarters, and visited Ronnie and Michael Bartlett – now living in the old farm on the Station – from time to time. Susan liked her new home and rode her small red tricycle round it and the garden paths with great skill.

Two important events occurred that summer: Joan became pregnant again, and we bought a car, the two things not being unconnected. We had thought it time that Susan should cease being an only child, and with two children to consider we needed to be more mobile. Our luck was in, since I was paid the enormous sum of £200 in post-war credits, and the Royal Observer Corps officer stationed at Waddington had a car to dispose of for just that figure. It was a 1935 Morris Ten, a square-bodied car built before streamlining came in, with a spare wheel and a folding luggage rack at the rear. For the first time we were free agents and didn't need to depend on buses and trains to get about; this made a real difference to our lives, despite the cost of petrol and maintenance.

About this time, disturbing rumours were going about that station navigation officer posts in Bomber Command were to be upgraded to the rank of squadron leader. With my small peace-time seniority I could see that I was unlikely to be given an acting rank to stay in my post, and when the rumours were confirmed we knew that we were likely to be on the move again. Our baby was due in December, and we hoped that at least we could stay where we were until then. In fact, Squadron Leader Frank Moss was posted in at the beginning of November, and we began an amicable, if protracted, handover. I don't recall what his previous job had been, but he was an experienced navigator, considerably older than me, and had been through Lincoln conversion. I took him to see the Wing Commander Flying, by now Wing Commander Paddy Menaul (a very sharp operator who was improving standards generally), and introduced him around the squadrons.

My main concern now was my own future. As with Susan, Joan had planned to have our second child at home; the doctor had no objections and the local midwife visited regularly to see that all was well. We had expected the baby in November, but the time ran on and it became obvious that there had been a slight miscalculation. On the evening of Friday 9 December, Joan thought that it was time to contact the midwife; as I walked to the telephone box, snow was falling and there was a light covering. The midwife duly arrived, as did Jennifer an hour or two later, a large and healthy baby, but something of a struggle for my poor wife.

Luckily Susan slept through most of it, while I walked up and down in the kitchen, biting my nails and making cups of tea.

Life was now changed again, but Joan took it in her stride; our chief worry was now for the immediate future. My posting came through later in the month – to the Bomber Command Instrument Rating and Examining Flight (colloquially known as 'X' Flight) at Scampton, just north of Lincoln and also on Ermine Street. This meant that we could stay in our present quarters for the time being and I could drive to work daily; at least we would not have to uproot ourselves and move to another part of the country. I left my job at Waddington with some regret, having made many friends, gained some valuable experience and learnt some salutary lessons.

I reported to Scampton on 16 January 1950. Another pre-war station, it housed the Lincoln Operational Conversion Unit, where new crews learnt to fly the Lincoln; 'X' Flight was a self-contained lodger unit, commanded by a squadron leader, and consisting of two bomber crews (all officers) and two Lincoln aircraft with their own groundcrew. Each of the aircrew was a qualified instructor in his own category: my fellow navigator, Don Richardson, was an old friend from my Staff Navigator Course, and had been on the staff at Shawbury in my time. All had wartime operational experience and had been (we liked to think) specially selected for the job, which required us to visit all Bomber Command flying stations and check on the application of the aircrew categorization schemes; this involved examining aircrew in their efficiency on the ground and in the air, and also required the pilots to undergo instrument rating tests. The word had gone round the Command that the C-in-C was alarmed at the standards of aircrew proficiency in these post-war doldrums. In particular, as I have touched on already, many Flight and Squadron Commanders did not have the flying experience to match their seniority; the perceived need for an all-weather force was not matched by the instrument flying capability, and a programme of instrument rating – now being adopted throughout the RAF – was being pursued. Pilots were to undergo tests, both in the air and on the ground, to determine their rating, and would be awarded a 'green card' for the highest proficiency, or a 'white card' for average proficiency; these ratings would determine the weather limits to which they were allowed to fly, and the C-in-C wanted all Wing Commanders Flying and all Flight and Squadron Commanders to have the higher rating.

So 'X' Flight was in the thick of a programme which entailed (as well as their categorization duties) flying with senior officer pilots for instrument rating purposes, which called not only for skill and experience but cunning and diplomacy. Frank Woolley was the CO of the flight; son of a serving air commodore, he was an experienced pilot and instructor, and although I found him somewhat self-centred and not entirely sympathetic, he was a competent and popular boss of this rather peculiar outfit. We were left to our own devices by the station, and did no station duties, except that we were expected to turn up to station parades now and again. Most of our time was spent away from Scampton at the other Bomber Command stations, at each of which we would spend a week, but usually flying back each evening and off again the following morning. I suppose we were regarded by the stations and their squadrons as a necessary evil, like HM Inspectors in the education world. Having helped to plan and launch the navigator categorization scheme at Command HQ, and then to make it work as a Station Navigation Officer, I was now seeing it from yet another perspective. Luckily, Don Richardson and I knew most of the Station and Squadron Navigation Officers, and some were old friends (like John Digman at Upwood and Ted Grant at Wyton), and we had full co-operation and understanding in most places.

BABS, the Blind Approach Beam System working in conjunction with Rebecca, was now in general use in Bomber Command, with BABS beacons aligned with the main runway at each airfield. It was our job to check out navigators on BABS approaches, preceded by Rebecca homings, in which they used a prescribed procedure to talk the pilot around the approach pattern and put the aircraft in a position to land. My logbook shows that I examined many navigators on this procedure, and I must have become quite adept myself. BABS was certainly a factor in improving the ability to make a landing in poor weather, and we could have done with it in wartime when so many bomber aircraft were lost returning to base. I also sat in as navigator on the categorization and instrument rating tests for pilots. Occasionally these were hazardous: the pilot being tested would sit in the left-hand seat, his normal position, with the examiner (Jim Sullings or Paddy Forsythe) as co-pilot. He would be wearing an IF hood, which was simply an aluminium visor which allowed him to see the instrument panel but nothing outside the aircraft. Lack of experience and skill (or both), added to examination nerves, made for some very ragged circuits. We began to appreciate the C-in-C's views after we had staggered drunkenly round the airfield time after time with an unhappy and not too proficient Squadron Commander at the controls.

We would of course take time out regularly to keep our own hands in, flying night cross-countries, taking part in Command exercises, and doing our own instrument flying. I was once allowed to fly a Lincoln on several circuits of a nearby disused airfield while Paddy Forsythe practised his instructor patter in preparation for his own tests by Central Flying School to update his Qualified Flying Instructor category. We were also asked to test and report on the new crossbar lighting approach system designed by E.S. Calvert at the Royal Aircraft Establishment, Farnborough, and installed for trials at Heathrow. We did these flights at night and had to wait for poor weather with a low cloudbase, a reversal of the usual order of things. Our pilots found the system a substantial improvement on the existing approach lighting, with the higher intensity making it possible to pick up the threshold much earlier, and the crossbars giving a very good indication of attitude and distance to touchdown.

Our daily flights to the other bomber stations were enlivened by a childish game. The era of strictly controlled airways had not arrived, and it was still possible to draw a line on the chart from one RAF station to another and use that as the flight track. In 'X' Flight it became the custom for the pilot to fly the first heading given to him by the navigator and not deviate from it until he was at or abeam of the destination, thus affecting to assess the accuracy of the navigation by how far he was adrift – really a pointless exercise, since all sorts of things outside the navigator's control could affect the issue. This was demonstrated on several occasions when the aircraft finished up a considerable distance from the intended airfield, to the delight of the pilots and the puzzlement of the navigators, until it was found that Sid Bristow, one of the flight engineers, was bringing his autocycle with him and stowing it under the master unit of the DR compass at the rear of the Lincoln, thus causing inaccurate compass readings. It was all harmless fun, never indulged in if the weather was marginal.

* * *

Before long the family moved from our little prefab at Waddington to one precisely similar at Scampton, although this one had already been lived in. One of our chief memories of the summer of 1950 is of the plague of earwigs which infested the married quarters for some weeks. All food had to be covered and we draped a lacy shawl over Jennifer's carrycot for protection. On most evenings we would co-opt Don Richardson to come down and help spray the insects until the infestation gradually petered out, a proceeding usually accompanied by much mirth and the odd glass of beer.

The other memories of that summer are of two holidays we had at Bridlington on the East Yorkshire coast, then an old-fashioned seaside resort with which we had both been familiar as children. We took a furnished house on each occasion, and invested in a small trailer to carry all the paraphernalia needed for a holiday with a young child and a baby. I think it had been home-made by a local pig farmer, and had no such refinements as brakes or springs, but it did serve us well for some years towed behind our pre-war Morris 10. We also acquired a cheap snapshot camera, so we have many photographs over which we can reminisce. Joan's parents joined us for a few days on one of the holidays, making a happy family party. We particularly enjoyed the splendid gardens and grounds of Sewerby Hall, and we have an abiding memory of the 3-year-old Susan dancing unselfconsciously in the aisle at a concert in the Bridlington Floral Hall.

We seemed settled for a while, although, as always, there were rumours of 'X' Flight changing its role in anticipation of the new jet aircraft intended for Bomber Command. But in October I suddenly received a posting notice from Command Headquarters; as far as I recall this was out of the blue, with no preliminary discussion or warning. However, this had been the pattern of most of my postings in the service, and I don't suppose I was unduly surprised. I was to report to RAE Farnborough on 1 November, to take up the post of Navigation Liaison Officer in the Radio Department. Despite the family upheaval this would entail, and without knowing too much about the details of the job, I was naturally pleased at being selected for this plum Spec N post at one of the world's foremost aeronautical research establishments. I was sorry to be leaving the close camaraderie of a special unit such as 'X' Flight, but I had had my fill of examining, and looked forward to something entirely different. Although I did not know it at the time, I was leaving Bomber Command for good after seven eventful years.

CHAPTER TEN

With the Boffins

'Boffin, n. esp. Brit. colloq. – a person engaged in scientific (esp. military) research [20th c.: orig. unkn.]' – Concise Oxford Dictionary.

In 1862, a Lieutenant G.E. Grover of the Royal Engineers reported on the results of his investigation and experiments in the uses of balloons in military operations. The War Office did not see fit to give Grover a grant for further work, but in 1878 allocated £150 to the Royal Engineers to build a balloon at Woolwich Arsenal (perhaps the first British Air Estimates). A balloon factory was established at Aldershot (where else?) in 1890, and moved up the road to South Farnborough in 1905. HM Balloon Factory became the Army Aircraft Factory in 1911, and the Royal Aircraft Factory the following year, as the increasing interest in heavier-than-air craft was given a fillip by Bleriot's 1909 Channel crossing in his monoplane. The name had to be changed yet again on 1 April 1918 to avoid confusion with the Royal Air Force, formed on that date, and Farnborough became the Royal Aircraft Establishment. In the early 1950s the local people still called it 'the Factory' (and no doubt some of the older generation still do).

In the early days the Royal Engineers ran a Balloon Section, parallel with the balloon factory element, which trained aviators and handlers. When aeroplanes became the priority and the factory switched to their production, the Balloon Section RE became an Air Battalion in 1911 and the Royal Flying Corps in 1912. So, as this brief early history shows, Farnborough saw the very beginning of aviation and its military use.

I was very conscious of the weight of this history when I booked into the RAF Officers' Mess at Farnborough, built during the First World War. As I walked across to RAE I passed Cody's Tree, mounted on a plinth and with its skeletal form reminiscent of some modern sculpture. 'Colonel' Samuel Cody, first and most colourful of the early test pilots (indeed every pilot was a test pilot then), made the first aeroplane flight in Britain on 16 October 1908 from Laffan's Plain, now part of RAE. He used the tree to tether his aeroplane during ground tests to measure the amount of propeller thrust. In the 'black sheds', the ancient hangars still in use, hung a tailless flying machine designed by J.W. Dunne in 1907.

As I became more familiar with RAE, I encountered many such reminders and mementoes of the early days of aviation; after all, these were less than fifty years before my arrival, which is in turn sixty years ago – one's perspective of time alters with age. I had visited Farnborough once before, at the end of 1945 when I was detached from 7 Squadron for a short accident-prevention course at the Air Ministry. We were taken to RAE to be shown some of the work of the Accident Investigation Branch, but the highlight of the visit was the exhibition of German aircraft which the RAE had collected and evaluated at various stages of the war and after, including the Me 262 jet fighter-bomber and the Me 163 rocket-powered Komet, apparently a test pilot's nightmare. It was amazing to see this collection of almost all the major types of German military aircraft, mostly in airworthy condition.

Now, five years later, I was struck by the apparently random assortment of architectural styles comprising the establishment, with modern buildings from the recent war and post-war periods cheek by jowl with pre-1918 hangars, workshops and offices (often of corrugated iron). All this was crammed into an area of some fifty to sixty acres between the modern airfield, with its 2,400 yd main runway and control tower, and the main road through Farnborough town, with the semi-urban area of Cove limiting any expansion to the north and west. As I remember it, the main administration building alone was of substantial size and moderately imposing appearance. No. 160 Building, in which I was to work, was one of the more modern brick and concrete structures, built in 1944. This, with its neighbour and contemporary 161 Building, housed both the Radio and Electrical Engineering Departments, and was close to the west gate.

Almost my first sight of the interior of 160 Building was of the large radio laboratory on the first floor, fitted with long benches on which was a bewildering array of radio equipment in various stages of assembly. A bespectacled man of about my own age was sitting gloomily in front of a cathode-ray oscilloscope, and I remember clearly feeling that I was going to be out of my technical depth. However, my spirits rose a little when I saw this my first boffin, muttering imprecations, strike his oscilloscope sharply with his fist, a remedial measure not unfamiliar to the average navigator.

At this point it might be useful to give some idea of how RAE was organized when I joined it at the end of 1950. What the accompanying table makes clear is that it was a very large organization employing thousands of people, including a fair proportion of the local population. In very simple terms, there were research and development departments on the one hand, and all the supporting technical and administrative departments on the other. In addition, there were several 'lodger units', notably the Empire Test Pilots' School and RAF Institute of Aviation Medicine. Then there was the RAE Technical College, in which young people served excellent technical apprenticeships to provide a continuous stream of skilled personnel for the establishment. Several outstations, such as the weapons ranges at Aberporth in Wales, were also run by RAE. The large bulk of RAE personnel was civilian; such service personnel as there were in the R & D departments were mostly technical officers, RAF or RN. I and one other Spec N in the Instrument and Photographic Department were the only General Duties (flying) officers, apart from the Experimental Flying Department, which was manned by RAF and RN pilots and aircrew with one or two civilian test pilots. EFD was organized in flights, each of which (normally commanded by a squadron leader) provided aircraft and flying facilities to the appropriate R & D department. Radio Flight (still occasionally referred to then as Wireless and Electrical Flight) worked with the Radio and Electrical Engineering Departments, and was the one with which I would be most concerned. My disciplinary boss was the Commanding Officer of EFD, an RAF group captain with whom I had only occasional contact, mostly social. My working boss was Caradoc Williams, a Principal Scientific Officer who headed the Radio Navigation Aids Group within the Radio Department.

In very general terms, my job was to provide the user's point of view in the development of radio aids to air navigation. More specifically, I was required to work closely with the scientists involved in development projects, to organize and usually take part in flying test programmes, and to assist in the assessment and interpretation of test results. It was the sort of job that the RAF Specialist Navigation Course had been designed for – to be able to speak the language both of the service pilot or navigator and of the research and develoment teams.

I replaced Flight Lieutenant Paddy Carson, an Ulsterman who had obviously enjoyed his time at RAE and whose work was much appreciated in the Radio Department. We had a short handover, and I seem to recall that much of it was devoted to teaching me how to use a mechanical calculator essential to the analysis of results from one of the current test programmes – a laborious business I shall return to later.

I was to share an office with Major Al Shiely of the US Air Force, a pilot who was also a radio specialist, but he was not involved in the projects on which I would be working, although we became good friends before he moved on after a few months. My chief working partner throughout my time at RAE was Fred Stringer, an Experimental Officer about my own age, with whom I struck up an immediate rapport. He was an Army brat and so knew something of service life, and we shared a similar sense of humour, useful in some of the more frustrating test programmes we were to work on. Freddy worked hard: he was studying for an external BSc at

Organization of the Royal Aircraft Establishment Farnborough 1950–51

Director
2 Deputy Directors   Secretary & Chief Accountant

R & D Departments: Support Departments:

Aerodynamics   Accounts
Armaments   Air Ministry Constabulary
Carrier Equipment   Air Ministry Works Department
Chemistry   Central Administration
Electrical Engineering   Central Planning & Progress
Experimental Flying (see below)   Designs Administration
Guided Weapons   Experimental Aircraft Services
Instrument & Photographic   Fire Brigade
Mechanical Engineering   Heat, Light & Power
Metallurgy   Inspection (aircraft & workshops)
Naval Aircraft   Library & Info Services
Radio   Joint Factory Committee
Structures   Maths Services
                                           Medical
Experimental Flying Dept: Meteorological Office
                                           Patents
CO (RAF Gp Capt)   Personnel
Adjutant   Printing
Chief Test Pilot   RAE News
Senior Air Traffic Control Officer   RAF Detachment
Aero Flight   Safety
Armament Flight   Stores
S & ME Flight   Technical Facilities
Instrument Flight   Transport
Radio Flight   Workshops Management
Transport Flight
Naval Acft Flight   'Lodger' Organizations:
Met Research Flight   Empire Test Pilots' School
                                           Clothing & Equipment Physiological
                                           Research Establishment
                                           RAF Institute of Aviation Medicine
                                           RAE Technical College

Main RAE Outstations:
Aircraft Torpedo Development Unit, Gosport
Armament & Instrument Experimental Unit, Martlesham Heath
Guided Weapons Trials Wing, Aberporth
National Aeronautical Establishment, Bedford
Orfordness Research Station
R & D Establishment, Cardington
Rocket Propulsion Department, Westcott

London University in his spare time, but was always enthusiastic about the job in hand. He was also particularly enthusiastic about flying, and I can remember many years later introducing him at an aero-systems seminar and saying that whatever the R & D programme Freddy was involved in, sooner or later there would be an aeroplane in it. He later qualified as a pilot, and has continued flying and instructing until an advanced age. The success of his notable career in the aviation world can be judged by the fact that he was Master of the Guild of Air Pilots and Air Navigators in 1989/90, and was later awarded the title Master Air Pilot.

The head of our group, Caradoc Williams, had long experience in the field of radio aids. He was one of the scientists who travelled to Spain during the war to inspect the German Sonne navigation beacon system; their work enabled British aircraft and ships to use this aid under the name Consol when navigating in the Atlantic (and also for some years after the war with beacons in the UK and elsewhere). His special field in the early 1950s was radio wave propagation and its application to navigation systems, in which he was a recognized authority. He was a quietly spoken, unfussy man who gave us adequate guidance and then let us get on with the job; however, he could deliver adverse criticism or a reproof when this was necessary, usually in a constructive spirit. In due course Joan and I exchanged visits with Caradoc, his wife Eileen and their young family, and found that we had much in common.

*   *   *

One of the first things I did when I arrived at Farnborough was to walk across the road from the RAE main gate and visit Johnson's, the estate agents, in search of somewhere to live. I hadn't long to wait: a ground-floor flat in a large house in Mytchett, a couple of miles across the Surrey border from Farnborough, was offered, and I went to have a look at it. It was – had been – an imposing late Victorian or Edwardian house in large grounds, now rather unkempt. The two upper floors were also flats, occupied by an Army and an RAF officer respectively, and with separate side entrances. The ground-floor flat was entered through the front door into a large tiled hall; there were two living-rooms (one obviously a former drawing-room of enormous proportions), and three bedrooms of varying sizes (but none small) which had been converted from other uses – one had evidently been a kitchen, and still had a row of bells for the staff to answer. There was an old-fashioned scullery kitchen, a small bathroom, and an impressive mahogany-throned lavatory. It was furnished with a not ungenerous selection of rather shabby pieces, some of which were of good quality: faded grandeur was the keynote. The rent was £5 a week, not including the charwoman whose services were available.

After some telephone consultation with Joan, I took the flat, both of us longing for the family to be together again, and feeling that if we were on the spot we should be able to find somewhere better. After a dreary 'marching out' of our Scampton married quarter on a wet wintry day, we drove down to Surrey (via a night stop in Aylesbury) in the faithful Morris 10 with pig-trailer, and moved into Mytchett Heath before Christmas.

As always, Joan made the best of things, and soon had the place feeling like a home, dispensing with the useless charwoman after a week or two and rearranging the mostly tatty furniture to better effect. The house belonged to the widow of a brigadier-general in the Royal Army Medical Corps who had bought it on his retirement in the 1930s. Before that, we heard from local gossip, it had belonged to an elderly maiden lady who had kept the garden and grounds immaculate – the donkey which pulled the lawn-mower wore slippers over its hooves to avoid damaging the lawns. There was certainly plenty of space in and around the house: a vegetable garden, an extensive overgrown shrubbery, even a pond, and the now untidy lawn. There was a garage round the back of the house, and also a chicken run and a duck run, which Joan noted with a gleam in her eye.

We stayed there just over a year, and found many things to enjoy, as well as the inevitable drawbacks and problems – the house was damp and expensive to heat, but at least we had plenty of space. Joan was now able to fulfil some long-held ambitions. First we bought three point-of-lay pullets (Light Sussex/Rhode Island Red cross, for the record); we called them Milly, Molly and Mandy from Susan's current reading, and they kept us generously in eggs, which were of course still rationed then. Next we acquired some Khaki Campbell ducks, and finally a three-month-old Middle White pig, inevitably named Percy by the children.

Percy lived in a concreted pen, already on the premises, with a sty that the occasional gardener and I built for him, and fed well on all the household scraps and on meal from the corn-chandler in Farnborough, obtained by giving up one year's bacon ration. Susan and Jennifer helped to feed this menagerie, and knew from the beginning what Percy's fate was to be. He grew rapidly and was a large pig by the time I took him down to the Farnborough abattoir (in our pig-trailer, of course). We had arranged for a local retired butcher to come and cut up the carcass and to salt down the hams and other joints, but he failed to appear as we waited with the carcass on scrubbed boards in the greenhouse. When we finally ran him to earth we found that he had poisoned hands and could not do the job. However, he loaned us his salting-trough, and we got the abattoir to cut the carcass into appropriate joints. Then Joan and I sorted out the mountain of pig-meat, and salted down the hams and other portions by carefully following the instructions in the Ministry of Food handbook (we still have it somewhere). We of course had pork for Christmas, and our friends and neighbours also benefited; we even sent parcels off through the post to our parents in Leeds, entirely practicable in those days. Our salting, too, was successful, and we ate the last ham nearly a year later. There are many other tales we could tell about our husbandry at Mytchett Heath, but this is probably not the place for them.

We found time for a short holiday in the Isle of Wight in the spring of 1951, taking the car and trailer (with child paraphernalia) across on the ferry. This holiday was almost disastrous, since the place we had booked had evidently forgotten about us and nothing was ready. But we moved on after the first night and found a pleasant hotel in Newport for the rest of the week, at greater expense but more comfort. This holiday was also memorable for the fact that Jennifer took her first unaided steps on the ferry pier at Yarmouth.

*   *   *

Meanwhile, I was driving daily the few miles to RAE and picking up the threads of my new job, unlike anything I had done before. There was one other RAF liaison officer in the Radio Department, Squadron Leader Tom Pratley: he was a member of the Technical (Signals) Branch and very much concerned with the engineering aspects of radio, so we did not see much of each other in the course of our normal work. But we built up a very good relationship with him and his family, who all became good friends; he had two small boys and we often went out for joint family picnics.

As soon as I could I made my number with Radio Flight, and I see from my logbook that I was flying with them a couple of weeks after I arrived. They had several aircraft, usually referred to as 'hacks', which were used to mount tests of various types of radio equipment: these were mainly a Vickers Viking, a twin-engined aircraft in use then by British European Airways; a Valetta, similar to the Viking but designed as a navigation classroom for the RAF; and an Avro York, produced at the end of the war for RAF Transport Command – a large four-engined aircraft with plenty of space inside. These were crewed by RAF pilots and navigators, and the odd flight engineer, all the pilots being qualified at the Empire Test Pilots' School; there was one civilian test pilot, Tich Tayler (later Chief Test Pilot for Shorts), with whom I flew frequently, and who was an outstanding pilot with a dry sense of humour. There were six or seven civilian test pilots in the Experimental Flying Department, and I remember their jubilation when they all received a substantial and justified rise in pay, plus a few months' backdate; Tich went out and bought a Jowett Javelin, a sporty car in those days.

Coming from the Bomber Command Examining Flight, where aircrew emergency procedures were given great importance, I was a little shocked by the casual attitude in EFD towards flight safety. On my first flight I asked as a matter of course where the emergency exits and equipment were, but got no satisfactory reply. I understood that with pilots and crews flying in half a dozen different aircraft in a week, it would not have been easy to be familiar with all the emergency drills, but there seemed to be no organized emergency training and no concern that this was the case. This situation changed for the better after a few months, when a new CO of Experimental Flying, Group Captain S.W.R. Hughes, was appointed. He told me, years later when he was Commander-in-Chief of Far East Air Force, that he too had been disconcerted by the lack of training and awareness in aircrew emergency procedures at RAE, and had made it one of his priorities.

One of my first tasks was to familiarize myself with the Decca Navigator system, which was installed in most of our 'hack' aircraft used for experimental work. The system had been used in ships on the D-Day landings in 1944, and there was now a well-developed ground network in Europe for both maritime and air use. As in the Gee system, a Decca chain consisted of a master station and three slaves, but transmitting continuous-wave signals at low frequencies. The slave stations were automatically phase-locked to the master signal, and the ship or aircraft receiver was designed to detect the phase difference between the master and slave signals and display it on an indicator called a Decometer. With three of these decometers (designated red, green and purple) each giving a reading, the position could be plotted on appropriately coloured lanes on a hyperbolic lattice chart similar to a Gee chart. By 1950/51 there were six chains covering the whole of the UK and a large part of western Europe, and the accuracy of fixes was very high – as it had to be for marine use. The Decca system was, however, susceptible to precipitation static and other kinds of static interference, as are all medium- and low-frequency receivers; this was one reason why the RAF was not generally equipped with it. But with newly designed receiving aerials and the use of wick dischargers on the aircraft, the effects of interference had been much reduced.

A recent development of the system was the flight log computer (analogue, of course), in which readings from two decometers were converted into geographical position on a moving chart display unit in the cockpit. Thus, providing he had set up the original position on the chart cursor, the pilot could see his current position at any time – a dream come true for most pilots. There were drawbacks and limitations to the flight log, but it was refined and improved, and used with success in civil aviation for several years. Radio Flight's chief use of the Decca Navigator was to provide an accurate position reference in the performance assessment of other navigation aids and in various flight studies of radio system performance. Freddy Stringer and I would set up a console somewhere in the aircraft with a camera recorder noting the decometer readings, time, and probably indications from the system under study. In later post-flight analysis, I would calculate the accurate position of the aircraft throughout the flight from the Decca Navigator, and compare this with readings from the system being assessed. This was a laborious business: first the readings had to be recorded for each photograph, usually taken at intervals of two or three minutes, so that for a four-hour flight there could be 80 or 120 readings for each system. The Decca positions would be plotted on a lattice chart and the latitude and longitude noted. In some trials we compared these datum positions with those obtained from other systems by solving the spherical triangles bounded by the North Geographical Pole and the two latitude and longitude readings (thus justifying the training in spherical trigonometry at Shawbury). This work was done on the mechanical calculator which my predecessor at RAE, Paddy Carson, had so painstakingly taught me to use, and the complete process usually took two or three times as long as the flight being analysed. I remembered ruefully this painfully slow process when, years later, I flew in a Comet IV of the Aeroplane and Armament Experimental Establishment at Boscombe Down on system evaluation trials. The airborne digital computer produced the answers as the flight progressed, and adjustments to the trial programme could be made if necessary while still in the air.

One of the first trials I was involved in was a research project for the Cavendish Laboratory at Cambridge, a study of the effects of ionospheric and other atmospheric conditions on the propagation of radio waves in the medium-frequency bands, a reminder that Farnborough (unlike, say, Boscombe Down) was involved in a great deal of basic research as distinct from work on system development. We were using Radio Flight's York aircraft for this task as there was some bulky recording equipment to be accommodated, and my job was to make arrangements for the flights with the Cavendish Laboratory and to take part in them as an observer, usually with Freddy, who had set up the position-recording consoles. I was told that the person in charge of the Cavendish Laboratory work was Sir Claud Alexander, with whom I should confirm arrangements. This sounds like an eminent scientist, an FRS at least, I thought, and accordingly spoke to him on the telephone with great respect, dropping the odd 'Sir' now and again. In fact he turned out to be a few years younger than I, a hereditary baronet doing post-graduate work at Cambridge. When he came down to fly with us, Claud became one of the team, and since he had a similar sense of fun, Freddy and I enjoyed the dozen or so flights for his project. Our task was to record the aircraft's position via the Decca Navigator, and the flight routes were arranged with this in mind. Several of the flights made use of the English and Danish Decca chains, whose coverage was excellent, and on one occasion we landed at Kastrup, Copenhagen's airport, to make a night flight from there, and were able to spend a couple of days in

Copenhagen. To us, coming from a country still recovering from the Second World War, and with food and many other things still rationed, Copenhagen was a revelation, with handsome shops full of luxury goods and fine clothing, and the hotels and restaurants serving delicious food. The Scandinavian sense of style – soon to be popular in the UK – was in direct contrast with the 'utility' look and the drabness and shabbiness we had got used to at home. My only regret was that Joan could not share this with me, but at least I brought presents back for her and the children. I was to make several visits to Copenhagen during my time at RAE, and each time I savoured the refreshing atmosphere in this sparkling capital city.

*   *   *

On the domestic front, we moved house at the end of 1951 to Cove, a village more or less swallowed up by North Farnborough and on the north-east edge of the RAE. Though we had in some ways enjoyed the 'big house' aspects of Mytchett Heath, it was damp, costly in fuel, and too large and shabby for us. We found a small modern house in Cove which had a garage and a garden to which we were able to move our three hens (the ducks and Percy the pig having gone the way of all flesh by this time). There was a small financial advantage to the move: the Air Ministry had recently introduced a so-called hirings scheme under which, if no married quarters were available, suitable houses to let could be leased to the service and then to the officer or airman concerned, who would pay the standard married-quarter rent rather than what the owner was asking. The house itself was an unremarkable one, built not long after the war and with corresponding utility features, but we were to stay there for over three years, and got used to the place. Cove still had some village features – a good butcher, handy post office, a corner shop and so on – and one great geographical advantage: the RAE west gate, next door to Radio Department, was a five-minute cycle ride away. Susan was five now, and having started at the Ash Vale village school, was able to go to the Cove primary school quite close by. Elmsleigh Road was typically suburban, with both old and newish houses. Our neighbours (some of whom also worked at 'the factory') were friendly, and we settled in quickly, having undertaken our own removal via the faithful pig trailer. There were some good if neglected rose bushes in the front garden (soon sorted out by Joan), a plum tree in the back garden, and a peach tree growing on the south wall; at the right time Joan skilfully fertilized it and it bore fruit for the first time, much to the disbelief of Susan's teacher, who had to be asked to tea for a private view. There was also a large garden shed which the children appropriated for wet-weather play, and we made them a sandpit and a swing in due course. As I usually worked in civilian clothes except when flying, we were very much like any other young couple in the neighbourhood, and did not feel out of place. We were certainly living a more suburban life than we had done since we were married: although the RAF station umbrella had been largely removed, we had access to good dental and medical facilities in Farnborough town, with a public library and varied shops. Pleasant countryside was not too far away, and we particularly enjoyed picnicking near rural Odiham in Hampshire and at The Moat at Elstead near Farnham, a large pond set in the Surrey heathland and offering the joys of paddling with newts. We were also able to use the Army NAAFI shop in Aldershot, some three miles away, for basic food shopping, another help financially.

*   *   *

One long-running test programme which occupied me for much of my time at RAE (and Freddy Stringer for longer than that – some four years in all) was a study of the performance of a British version of the radio compass. This was a development of the aircraft direction-finding loop aerial I had first encountered at Bridgnorth during ground training, and had first used at the Air Observers' School in the Isle of Man. At that time a loop aerial, in conjunction with a standard aircraft W/T receiver tuned to a ground transmitter, would be rotated by hand (usually by the wireless operator) until the minimum signal was received and a bearing could be read off on the aerial scale relative to the way the aircraft was heading. The radio compass used a similar type of loop aerial, but used the induced voltage of the received signal to drive a motor which turned the loop until minimum signal, when the bearing would be read off on a remote indicator visible to the pilot or navigator.

Radio compass systems, manufactured by Bendix and others, were well established in the USA even before the war, and there was an extensive system of airways making use of ground radio beacons. In wartime these could be jammed and had other operational drawbacks, but once the RAF started operating on regular overseas routes after the war, radio compasses were obviously going to be useful, if not essential, for larger aircraft. Marconi and the General Electric Company each developed a radio compass, and the RAF selected the GEC system for its use: the prototype was designated ARI (Airborne Radio Installation) X303 – the 'X' denoting 'experimental'. This was the model the RAE Radio Department was given for performance tests in 1949, but by the time the test programme was completed and the results published in 1953, the RAF (in particular Transport Command) was equipped with the production version, ARI 5428. It was not surprising that the programme was so long in completion: the only people working on it (and at no very high priority) were Freddy, my predecessor Paddy Carson, and I, with several other projects going on at the same time. As an aside, Freddy and I were smugly pleased when, shortly after the publication of the results in an RAE Technical Memorandum of about forty pages, an enormous inch-thick tome was received from the USA, bound in green leatherette with gold lettering, reporting on a parallel study; this work had also taken several years and had been done by a largish team from one of the American universities, possibly MIT. However, they had not produced anything more detailed or of better quality than our two-man job, and their conclusions were similar.

In fact our study was not just limited to the performance of this particular radio compass system, but looked at the effects of ionospheric reflections by day and night and at sunset (when errors were greatest); at reception quality at different frequencies and ranges within the 150–1,500 megacycle (megahertz) band; and at comparative performance when using conventional external and 'suppressed' loop aerials. This was a time when, with new types of jet aircraft constantly pushing up operating speeds, radio aerials of various types protruding into the slipstream were affecting aerodynamic efficiency, and flush-mounted aerials were being designed whose effect on system performance needed to be assessed.

One of my earliest jobs in the Radio Department was to produce a departmental memorandum summarizing the progress in this test programme and the plans for further trials. I am looking at a copy as I write and marvelling at the technical expertise apparently displayed – but in fact resulting mostly from picking other people's brains. I see that this memorandum is entitled 'Research on Homing and Direction Finding in Aircraft', which indicates that we had some wider aims than testing the performance of one system.

For the flight trials we used a Viking aircraft with a loop aerial mounted externally, and a Lincoln with the loop mounted in a 'dish' let in to the top of the fuselage and covered with a Perspex plate. In fact, most of the aerial comparison work was done on the ground using an old wooden aerial tower at Cove in which two complete radio compass systems were mounted, one with an external loop and one with a 'suppressed' version. Freddy and I did several night vigils in this curious building, with the sets tuned to various transmitters at different powers, ranges and frequencies. With the co-operation of the BBC we were able to use transmissions from Droitwich and Brookmans Park at times when these stations were not usually operating; we also used several Continental transmitters. Pen recorders followed the fluctuations of the radio compass bearing indicators throughout the night, and particularly through the sunset period. One of the first things that aircrew were taught about low- and medium-frequency reception was that it was particularly unreliable around sunset, and I was not surprised to see the bearing indicators oscillating wildly at this time; however, Freddy and I watched with some incredulity as, with the receivers tuned to Lille radio, both indicators rotated through the full 360 degrees, a convincing demonstration that the received wisdom was correct.

One of the flights in this trials programme sticks in my mind. With Spud Murphy flying the Viking, Freddy and I directed the aircraft along a so-called logarithmic spiral flight path which ended at RAF Wunstorf in Germany. This flight path, flown at night, was calculated (by Freddy) to simulate a velocity of 100 knots relative to the transmitter we were using, and the return flight, also at night, was on a circular flight path centred on the transmitter to simulate zero relative velocity, so that the errors in each case could be compared. Luxembourg was the station used, with a camera recording the radio compass bearings and the Decca Navigator indicators; I remember that the resulting analysis work was extremely laborious, but demonstrated that errors tended to reduce when the receiver was at a constant range from the transmitter. Why I particularly remember this flight is that, despite our landing at Wunstorf around midnight, the Station Commander had kept the bar open and was keen to pick our brains about the trials. Group Captain Stapleton was a pre-war Specialist Navigator, and I think he expected some high-powered RAE scientists, instead of two rather scruffy young men who needed a shave. All we really wanted to do was sleep, but he was kind and hospitable and we were well primed with suitable drinks. We had some difficulty in explaining the theory behind the logarithmic spiral flight path, but then I didn't fully understand the mathematics myself. Luckily Freddy did, having done all the calculations, but I think our audience was somewhat baffled, especially as the hour grew later. We eventually got away to bed, and as we were not taking off again till the evening, were able to have a long, refreshing sleep.

Since the comparison of the performance of the suppressed and external aerials was of particular interest, Freddy and I produced a separate report on this aspect. In very general terms, we found that the daylight bearing errors of the suppressed loop were very similar to those of the external loop, but that at night, with sky-wave operating, they were slightly greater. The suppressed ('dishpan') loop was more susceptible to quadrantal error – a well-known effect with loop aerials due to reflections of the incoming signal from the aircraft's metallic structure, greatest at the four quadrantal points. Loops or radio compasses would be routinely calibrated for this error – which could be substantial – and a correction card produced. With the ARI X303 model we were using, a metal correction strip was incorporated in the loop-drive mechanism, but we found that some additional correction would be necessary with the suppressed version; this was in due course provided in the production models.

We also found that there was a reduction in the maximum operating range by both day and night with the suppressed aerial, as might have been expected.

As a result of this work, we were asked by the Ministry of Civil Aviation to do a similar aerial comparison for the Decca Navigator system, with emphasis on the performance at night as affected by ionosphere reflections. We wanted to use a reasonably high-performance aircraft, but at that time there was no suitable RAE aircraft fitted with Decca and the requisite aerials. Our group leader, Caradoc Williams, was keen for us to do this work, as radio-wave propagation by the ionosphere was his special subject; he at first tried to borrow an Avro Ashton (a prototype pure-jet airliner doing trials at Boscombe Down), but this did not materialize. Eventually we were offered the use of the Vickers Viscount prototype, known as the 630: this was G-AHRF, the very first of a long and successful line of civil turbo-prop aircraft. G-AHRF was to be flown for our trials by the Civil Aircraft Testing Section (CATS) at Boscombe Down, but had previously been flying for some months on the London–Paris route, and was still in British European Airways livery. Luckily it had already been fitted with suppressed and mast aerials for the Decca Navigator system.

The aircraft was at Vickers-Armstrong's factory at Weybridge for servicing, and Freddy and I went down towards the end of July 1951 to see it and to work out what would be needed for the trials installation. Allen Greenwood (later chairman of British Aircraft Corporation) was our contact, and took us into the hangar. We were immediately impressed with the elegant lines of the 630 and by the comfortable interior; it was fitted with airline seats (some of which we would have to remove), and the usual military aircraft smell of glycol, fuel and so on was entirely absent, as one would expect in a civil airliner.

There were the usual delays in setting up the trials, especially as so many organizations were involved – Vickers, Boscombe Down, for some reason the Ministry of Supply, MCA, and the Decca Navigator Company to install and calibrate a Decca Navigator Mark 6 system. While this was going on Freddy and I were still working on the radio compass trials (our Wunstorf flight was made at about this time), as well as designing and setting up the recording system in the Viscount. Finally we made our first familiarization flight from Wisley airfield at Weybridge (next to the old Brooklands motor-racing circuit, and the scene of some of the earliest flights in British aviation). We had been told that flight in the Viscount was so quiet and smooth that a pencil could be balanced on end on the table; we tried it and found that it was perfectly true. Flying in that aircraft was a pleasure, a great contrast to the noise and vibration we usually suffered in the York or the Lincoln.

After a further short flight from Farnborough with Group Captain 'Bruin' Purvis of CATS at the controls, we were ready for the first of the two planned trial runs. With the comparatively short operating range of the Viscount 630 and the need to fly in an appropriate area of Decca chain coverage, we had selected Geneva and Copenhagen as the terminal airports, as we would not be able to return to the UK without landing. The first trial flight was made on the night of 11 October 1951, piloted by 'Nippy' Knight of CATS. All the equipment – the Decca Navigator, the recording console, and the Gee set we used for navigation – performed satisfactorily, and we landed at Cointrin airport, Geneva, feeling remarkably fresh and well satisfied with the way things had gone.

We were due to fly back the following day, but as this was the first appearance of the Viscount at Cointrin, and there was a great deal of interest in it, Nippy Knight agreed to take several airline and airport representatives for a short demonstration flight. It was a beautiful day as we flew over Mont Blanc and the Matterhorn, a memorable sight with the blue sky and sparkling sunlight, and I was able to take a few photographs. The aircraft was flown on three engines, then two, and finally one; as we were lightly loaded it was very manoeuvrable and the passengers were duly impressed.

When we landed and taxied in, I happened to be the first out of the front door and down the steps as the Rotol propellers were slowly winding down, and noticed that one blade of the No. 1 (port outer) prop had a nick in the tip. It transpired that as we had taxied out for take-off we had used a very narrow taxi track edged with small metal lighting pylons, just high enough to clip one of the propellers, which in the Viscount had a very low ground clearance. The pilot had noticed no vibration or other effect, and had not used that particular engine for the single-engine demonstration; nevertheless he thought it prudent to get a Rotol specialist to inspect the damage, and we had another enjoyable couple of days in Geneva waiting for the Rotol representative to fly out. When he came, he advised that a prop change was not necessary and that if the nick on the blade tip was carefully filed down there should be no trouble, as indeed was the case when we flew back.

We found Geneva a pleasant city, with its well-to-do air and expensive shops contrasting (as we had found on earlier trips to Copenhagen) with our austerity at home. We walked by the lake with its spectacular fountain, and were amused by the many patisseries full of well-built ladies enjoying coffee and cream cakes.

The second flight, to Copenhagen, was made a week later, and again all the test equipment functioned satisfactorily. But we seemed fated to suffer minor mishaps: after a long, low night approach to Kastrup airport, we were informed by air traffic control that we had touched a power cable a mile or so short of the runway and had put a village in darkness. Nippy Knight and his engineer made a thorough inspection of the underside of the fuselage, especially the landing-gear, but there was not the slightest sign of damage. If we had indeed touched a power line we were lucky to have got away with it, literally without a scratch.

Before our return flight we had a relaxing spare day in Copenhagen, with which Freddy and I were already familiar. Our only regret was that our families could not be with us, but before we took off from Kastrup I bought a box of smorgasbord from the airport restaurant so that Joan could have a taste of Denmark.

The return night flight, landing at Blackbushe near Farnborough to clear customs, was the end of the Viscount flying for us. Freddy and I went over to Boscombe Down the following day to collect the recording equipment, and then we had to get down to the usual painstaking (and sometimes unutterably boring) post-flight analysis. As I explained earlier in this chapter, the Decca Navigator system operated by phase comparison, and we found that phase error was the determining factor for maximum reliable coverage at night: for the mast aerial this was about 230 nautical miles from the centre of the ground system, reducing to about 170 nautical miles with the suppressed aerial. The comparatively low efficiency of the suppressed aerial (a small metal plate on the port side of the tailfin) meant that for its performance to equal that of the mast aerial, higher power from the ground transmitters would be needed. However, we recommended that the efficiency of the suppressed aerial should be improved by better design, and this was later done.

*   *   *

Looking at my flying logbook when I was writing this account of the Viscount 630 trials, I found that it was fifty years to the day since the flight to Copenhagen. So much has changed in the British aircraft industry in that half-century. There was so much happening during my time at Farnborough that it is hard to remember it all: the roll-call of active aircraft manufacturers seemed endless – Armstrong-Whitworth, Avro, Blackburn, Bristol, de Havilland, Fairey, Handley-Page, Hawker, Saunders-Roe, Short, Vickers …. All these firms were producing new and experimental types of aircraft which were breaking all sorts of records. The B3/45 Air Staff Target I had seen at HQ Bomber Command had turned into the English Electric Canberra, one of the most successful light bombers ever built (and as I write in 2001 a PR version of the Canberra is in action over Afghanistan). In my own field, new radio, radar and instrument systems were in production or under development. Aircraft were flying at over 50,000 feet and at supersonic and transonic speeds, and in many of these projects the UK was leading the world.

This feeling of progress and achievement, of optimism, was all about us at Farnborough then. Every day we saw a variety of prototype and experimental aircraft landing and taking off (and often heard the sometimes caustic post-flight comments by the test pilots). We got used to the regular explosions from the Naval Aircraft Department's steam catapult trials, and witnessed many rubber deck landings by the NA Flight Vampires. At the annual Farnborough Air Show sponsored by the Society of British Aircraft Constructors we were able to see the latest aircraft, both when they demonstrated their performance in the air and when we had a close look at them on the ground. I recall standing at the main gate one day as the giant Bristol Brabazon passed overhead on finals to the main runway – a magnificent sight and sound, with the deep musical hum from six turbo-prop engines. Alas, a splendid white elephant.

Pushing aeronautical science to the limits was sometimes a hazardous business. In September 1952 Joan and I and the children were on holiday at Minehead in Somerset when we heard the news of John Derry's death flying the DH 110 at the Farnborough Air Show; the aircraft disintegrated and fell partly among the watching crowd, killing twenty-seven and injuring many more. We were shaken and appalled, but selfishly thankful that we had not been on the spot.

Radio Flight had its tragedies too. I had a telephone call one morning from Dickie Bradwell, the OC, asking if I could navigate for him on a Canberra flight. I had a particular wish to fly in the Canberra, but had to attend a meeting that morning which I couldn't avoid. Dickie found a navigator elsewhere: both of them were killed when their aircraft crashed on approach to RAF Llandow in South Wales. Spud Murphy, the test pilot with whom I did most of my RAE flying on many types of aircraft, was also killed in a flying accident shortly after I left RAE. I don't recall – if I ever knew – the causes of these two particular accidents, but I still have an uneasy feeling about the casual approach to flight safety which was apparent when I arrived at Farnborough, although the situation had substantially improved before I left.

*   *   *

My desk diaries for 1951 and 1952 show that, in addition to the various trials programmes I was involved in, I seemed to be in constant communication with many people and organizations inside and outside RAE. As the RAF liaison officer in the navigation group, I was frequently visited or telephoned by people wanting information on the development and performance of radio navigation systems. I did a lot of work with the Navigation Division at Boscombe Down, which was responsible for system acceptance trials, both civil and military; among other things I produced for them a paper (grandly called RAE Technical Memorandum No. RAD 345) on the use of the Decca Navigator as an evaluation datum for other position-fixing systems they were working on. The Air Ministry Operational Requirements and Operations (Navigation) branches were also regular customers. Through Caradoc Williams we had contact with the Institution of Electrical Engineers on radio wave propagation, and also with the Department of Scientific and Industrial Research, for whom we did some low-level flight trials on a ground transmitter (I remember being very airsick on one of these flights until the MO produced some effective pills).

Within Farnborough I kept in close touch with my opposite number (Squadron Leader Tom Kitching, replaced by Mac Bunting) in the Instrument and Air Photographic (IAP) Department, which was working on a variety of new navigation systems, including inertial navigation, improved ground position indicators and compasses, automatic astro-navigation, and the navigation and bombing computer (NBC) for the latest version of ground-mapping radar (H2S 9) for the V-bomber force.

A regular task was arranging (and taking part in) visit programmes for a variety of service courses, especially the RAF and RCAF Specialist Navigation Courses. They would usually come for a day or a day and a half, and spend some time with Radio, IAP and probably Guided Weapons Departments. Other courses came from the RAF Staff Colleges and Flying College and from the Empire Test Pilots' School, and I would usually give them a short resumé of current Radio Department projects, as we were only one of several departments they visited.

Occasionally I found time to further my own career concerns. In my previous posting at Scampton I had sat and passed the RAF 'C' examination for promotion to squadron leader, and now I had to think about the RAF Staff College qualifying exam, another necessary step. Luckily I was able to take a one-week course in current affairs at Hertford College, Oxford, designed specifically for RAF officers taking the 'Q' exam. The work was intensive but it was a wholly absorbing experience and I felt a little envious of the academic life. Then there were evening lectures in the Prince Consort's Library at Aldershot, arranged by the Army and including such speakers as Arnold Toynbee, Arthur Bryant, and the then CIGS. RAE also had an occasional lecture programme, mostly on aeronautically related subjects, at which one of the speakers was the eminent atomic scientist Sir John Cockcroft.

With all this help I managed to pass the 'Q' exam in 1952 – another hurdle over.

* * *

In my second year at Farnborough, Freddy and I were involved – concurrently with other tasks – in a project centred on fighter aircraft. With the drastic improvements in performance of types like the Swift and the Hunter, Fighter Command was concerned that there was no really suitable navigation aid to give the single-seat fighter pilot the ability to fix his own position; changes were being planned in the system of fighter control by ground radar stations (GCI) – so effective in the Battle of Britain – so that larger numbers of aircraft could be handled by a method known as broadcast control. It would not always be possible to keep each individual aircraft under close GCI control, and pilots would need their own navigation systems. Equipment like the radio compass, the Decca Navigator and Rebecca/Eureka, though they could be miniaturized, were still too bulky and heavy for most fighters, and there was little room on the instrument panel for suitable indicators.

Interest centred on so-called R-Theta (distance and bearing) systems which could be used for homing as well as position fixing. New VHF ground beacons were being introduced for civil and military use, such as the VHF omnirange (VOR) and the Voice Rotating Beacon, which would give better performance than current radio compass systems using LF and MF bands which were susceptible to atmospheric conditions. If such beacons could be coupled with distance-measuring equipment (DME) now being developed (mostly using reflected pulse measurements, as in Rebecca/Eureka), range and bearing fixes could be obtained. In civil aviation, the discussion was still continuing on whether to use the Decca Navigator or a VOR/DME system as the standard.

As far as fighter navigation was concerned, none of these systems seemed to be particularly satisfactory, but towards the end of 1951 we heard about a development in the USA for military air defence aircraft which employed a ground beacon in the 1,000 megacycle band transmitting both range and bearing to an airborne receiver. In American nomenclature the transmitter was designated AN/URN3, and the receiver AN/ARN21; the project had a high security classification, but we were given all the necessary information. The display was a combined range and bearing indicator capable of installation in the instrument panel of a single-seat fighter, though possibly at the cost of some other function. The Federal Telecommunications Laboratory in Nutley, New Jersey, was the manufacturer.

Fighter Command was naturally very interested in URN3/ARN21, and we had several visits from its navigation staff and from the Central Fighter Establishment at West Raynham. One of their problems was that, even if an accurate range and bearing could be provided by one meter in the cockpit, a single-seat fighter pilot would find it difficult to plot his position with a pen or pencil on a normal map on his knee; his workload was already high, and he needed to keep his attention outside the cockpit for much of the time. We considered a series of cards, one for each beacon with range rings and bearing lines already printed, held in a kneepad like those used by test pilots to record flight test data. But CFE had seen the Decca flight log and was keen to have an automatic display.

Freddy and I were asked to look at the possibilities. Talking to our radio engineering specialists, we first of all established that it would be perfectly possible to use the received signal impulses for both range and bearing to produce a moving spot of light relative to the centre of a circular screen. But the minimum size for such a unit would be about 7 inches square by

1.5 or 2 inches deep, and this was not the sort of space which was available in current and pending single-seat fighter instrument panels. Thinking of the kneepads routinely strapped to the thigh by test pilots to note down in-flight performance data, we canvassed our test-pilot colleagues for opinions on such a unit for a map presentation. On the whole their comments were favourable, although they pointed out that some way would have to be found of quick disengagement if the unit was in use in an aircraft fitted with an ejector seat.

Having made suitable sketches, we went down to see Mr Cody in the model shop. (Was he a son or grandson of the great Colonel Cody? I shouldn't be surprised, as he had certainly been at 'the factory' for some years.) He made us some wooden space models approximating to the size of the unit we had in mind, with thigh-straps attached and a specimen map face for verisimilitude. My logbook shows that we took them up in a Radio Flight Anson – 'R-Theta space model trials' – but I don't remember what the results were. Presumably they were not unfavourable, since we then embarked on a round of the aircraft manufacturers to look at cockpits in various new aircraft types, including the Attacker and the Hunter. We also tried the space models in the Fairey Gannet, an anti-submarine aircraft being built for naval use, and as this had a large cockpit area it was the one type where we felt sanguine about the credibility of the map presentation unit.

But before we got much further with this project I was posted away from Farnborough and lost sight of it. As far as I know, no working model was ever produced, although the evaluation of the URN3/ARN21 navigation system showed that it was acceptable for British use. It later became well established in the USA and Europe under the designation TACAN (Tactical Air Navigation system), and I came across it again a few years later.

* * *

In January 1953 I was posted to the Air Ministry in Whitehall, to a job concerned mainly with RAF post-graduate navigation training policy (the Staff and Specialist Navigation Courses). This was something of a surprise, as I had hoped to carry on at Farnborough for another six months at least, and then to go to another research and development post. But the Whitehall job was for a squadron leader and I was naturally pleased to get promotion to the acting rank after having been a flight lieutenant for seven years. Another benefit was that we could continue to live at Cove; I would be joining the ranks of the daily commuters to Waterloo Station via British Rail from Farnborough.

I was sad to be leaving RAE and the variety of tasks I had been involved in. I would particularly miss working with Freddy Stringer on absorbing and challenging projects with which we were usually given a free hand. Another thirteen types of aircraft were now in my logbook, including two marks of Meteor, the Vickers Viscount, the Fairey Firefly, and even the Avro Shackleton Mark 1 in which I had done some Loran familiarization from RAF Kinloss. I had driven all sorts of vehicles, from 10 and 15 cwt vans and 30 cwt staff cars to 3-ton lorries. Flight trials had taken us to Denmark, Malta, Switzerland and Germany, and the subsequent analyses and reports had given me an insight into the production of technical papers, greatly assisted by the use of the RAE Library. Above all I had relished working in a scientific and experimental environment in which I was able to use some of the knowledge laboriously gained at Shawbury and elsewhere, and being in touch with the developments going on in a flourishing aviation world.

Looking back over this chapter, I see that it is much the longest so far in this book. And yet there are still areas of our work at RAE which I haven't touched on: for example, instrument landing systems (ILS), radio altimeters, and single-sideband radio, all being worked on in various forms; and I recall seeing, in one of the Radio Department labs, a cigar-box-sized receiver which I was told used transistors instead of valves – the commercial implications passed me by.

What stays with me after all these years is the sense that we were working in the very birthplace of British aviation, with its living history all around us, at a time when the UK aviation industry was breaking new ground and producing new and innovative aircraft and systems. It saddens me to think that, in the last few years, Farnborough seems to have become a shadow of its former pre-eminence.

Its title was changed in 1988 to 'The Royal Aerospace Establishment', not unreasonably in view of the wider scope of its work and the fact that the RAE initials could be retained. But in 1991, following the end of the Cold War, the government was pursuing a policy of rationalizing and reorganizing (dread words) some Civil Service departments into 'cost-effective business centres'; the Defence Research Agency was born and Farnborough became its Aerospace Division. By 1994 all research flying at Farnborough (and RAE Bedford) had been transferred to Boscombe Down (still the Aeroplane and Armament Experimental Establishment), and the remaining laboratories, workshops and staff became known in 1995 as the Defence Evaluation and Research Agency. The airfield at Farnborough is now used mainly by small civil airline operators, although the annual Air Show is still held.

From Cody to commerce: truly the end of an era.

CHAPTER ELEVEN

Whitehall Warrior

Having handed over at RAE to Ted Bullock, late of Shawbury, I reported to the Deputy Directorate of Flying Training (Navigation) – colloquially known as DDTNav – at the Air Ministry in Richmond Terrace, Whitehall, on 5 January 1953.

Now began a completely different lifestyle, one I had never contemplated or imagined. I became a commuter, one of thousands travelling up to London from outlying towns and districts. I wore civilian clothes (my only good suit) and carried an umbrella and a briefcase, though I drew the line at the bowler hat which many serving officers at the Ministry still wore. I would cycle up to the station in North Farnborough for the 8.31 train through Woking to Waterloo, using my season ticket. The journey would be spent reading the paper or looking at work I had brought home the night before (not too frequent an occurrence). Then a walk across Westminster Bridge, a right turn into Whitehall, and up to Richmond Terrace, almost opposite the Cenotaph; it was a former town house of one of the Dukes of Richmond, backing on to the Thames, and in its day had been a splendid residence. Its lofty rooms had been partitioned when it was taken over by the Air Ministry, and it was now a rabbit warren of undistinguished and somewhat dingy offices. From the first-floor room in which I was to work there was an uninterrupted and useful view of Big Ben – referred to as 'the office clock'. Although we were not required to be at our desks before 9.30 in the morning, work went on until six o'clock and I was usually home about seven-fifteen – a long day away from the family, when at Farnborough I had been a mere five minutes away from home.

Richmond Terrace housed the staff of the Assistant Chief of the Air Staff (Training), whose job was to oversee the policy for RAF flying training in all aircrew categories. When I arrived, ACAS(T) was Air Vice-Marshal The Earl of Bandon, a larger-than-life character known throughout the RAF as Paddy Bandon, or the Abandoned Earl. I shall have more to say about him later.

I shared the office with my immediate superior, Wing Commander Peter Meston, a pilot Spec N whom I remembered as the Chief Instructor at Shawbury in 1948; and Squadron Leader Vic Gotham, a navigator who was mainly concerned with basic navigation training. Our Deputy Director was Group Captain Charlie Bale, a colourful character who had spent much of the war flying in Coastal Command, and a genial and undemanding boss with whom we occasionally had boozy lunchtime sessions. His Personal Assistant, Mrs Joan Goldspink, was one of those civil servants who are invaluable in their own departments – she had been in the job for some years and knew most of what was going on and where to find the papers you particularly wanted; as a bonus, she was a pleasant and friendly personality.

My own job was to supervise navigation training at the Central Navigation and Control School at Shawbury, where the Staff Navigator Course still continued alongside the Staff Navigation Course (Pilots) training pilot navigation instructors, and where were also housed the Flying Training Command Navigation Instructors' Categorization Flight and the Navigation Investigation and Training Research Section. So Shawbury still retained some of its old functions from the heady days of the Empire Air Navigation School, but the Specialist Navigation Course (now nearly a year long) had removed to the RAF Flying College at Manby in Lincolnshire, where the Flying College Course trained more senior officers for air staff and flying command posts. The Spec N Course was also my concern, plus liaison on navigation training with the USA, Commonwealth and foreign air forces; the provision of radio aids in Flying Training Command; and supervision of overseas training flights from navigation schools.

Two ex-officio jobs were as Secretary to the RAF Synthetic Training Committee, chaired by the Deputy Director of Operational Training, and meeting regularly to consider the provision and use of synthetic trainers for all aircrew categories; and as a member of the Institute of Navigation's Technical Committee.

One other job which came my way, and which I particularly enjoyed, was the proofreading and general editing of the new series of RAF navigation manuals being produced at Shawbury in five parts (Air Publication AP 1234A to E). These replaced Dickie Richardson's splendid AP 1234 published in one volume in 1944 but still thought of as the RAF navigator's bible. The new publications covered techniques, instruments and radio aids developed during and after the war, and some were of necessity security classified.

So I had plenty of interesting work on my plate, and if I had wondered earlier what on earth the Whitehall warriors found to do other than shuffling paper, I now knew. Luckily this was still the era when aircrew staff officers were supposed to keep in flying practice, and a small fleet of Ansons and other light aircraft was maintained at RAF Hendon for this purpose. The pilots on ACAS(T)'s staff naturally took full advantage of this facility, and I was often asked to act as navigator; more often than not these trips could be combined with a necessary staff visit. I remember one flight from Hendon to Manby for which the two pilots were AVM Bandon and Air Commodore Mead (the Director of Flying Training); Paddy Bandon asked the Air Commodore to do the pre-flight ground checks and said to me confidentially, 'The last time I flew an Anson I took off with the tail-locks in.' That reminded me of the story that he had run out of runway when landing a Vampire at an airfield in Germany where he was a Group Commander after the war, and had later been presented with a model of the aircraft, engraved 'The first air marshal to break the barrier', that being the era in which supersonic flight was becoming more common. However, our flight proceeded uneventfully, although neither pilot was used to flying with a navigator and found it puzzling when I turned them off the direct approach to Manby to do a Gee homing in poor visibility.

Other stories of Paddy Bandon are legion, and mostly apocryphal (like the one in which he attended the 1937 Coronation in hired peer's robes, had to hitch a lift back to his RAF station, and was promptly booked by the Station Duty Officer for being improperly dressed). But I can vouch for one: at Richmond Terrace, entry security was provided by an elderly doorman who asked visitors to fill in a form stating their identity and business; they were then escorted to their destination and were required to hand in their copy of the form on leaving, signed by the person they were visiting. Paddy, wishing to test this system, wrote on the form of one of his visitors, 'This man is a dangerous Russian spy – arrest him immediately'. The hapless doorman merely spiked the form as usual without a glance at it, and the Earl came down soon afterwards and caused a minor explosion, after which security was considerably tightened up – as far as was possible in this ancient building.

* * *

Basic navigator training – with which, thankfully, I was not directly concerned – would undergo substantial changes by the end of 1953. With successive reductions in the RAF manning plan, fewer navigators would be needed in the operational commands (then still Bomber, Fighter, Coastal and Transport), and as the number of Air Navigation Schools was reduced there was a backlog of trained navigators who were having to wait some months to enter operational training and were employed in various dogsbody capacities until places became vacant in the Operational Conversion Units. The so-called 'all through' training, in which all students worked to the same syllabus at the Air Navigation Schools (still including some in Canada, whose graduates needed acclimatization courses when they returned to the UK) was to be superseded by a shorter basic ANS course followed by one of three 'functional' courses – Coastal/Transport, Bomber and Fighter – which would prepare them for a particular operational role.

I was grateful that this somewhat complex transitional period was not my problem. Post-graduate navigation training was still a firm requirement, and no great changes in policy or content were envisaged. The fifteen-week Staff Navigator Course and the twelve-week Staff Navigation Course (Pilots) still carried on at Shawbury, as I wrote at the beginning of this chapter, plus instructor categorization and the research section. There were some tentative plans to remove the navigation element from Shawbury to re-form a Central Navigation School at Thorney Island, possibly to include the Specialist Navigation Course, but this was not likely to happen in the near future (and in fact never did happen in that form).

The Spec N Course itself was still geared to training navigators and some pilots to fill senior navigation posts at the Air Ministry and Command Headquarters, and in research and development. Like many other Spec Ns, I had been surprised and not too pleased when the course was moved from Shawbury to Manby to join the RAF Flying College. The College had been set up to prepare senior officers (mostly wing commanders and squadron leaders) for flying commands and air staff jobs, covering technical subjects and flying experience in all roles which the broader Staff College courses, catering for all officer branches, could not provide. It had been established in the face of some opposition – no doubt cost was the main problem, as always – and I had the impression that the incorporation of the Spec N Course, which could share the flying facilities, was part of a hard-driven bargain.

Spec N flying was done mainly in the Lincoln, with some access to the other Flying College aircraft such as the Canberra; Lincolns were also used for the now retitled Staff Navigation Course. I was amused, but not surprised, to find that the old workhorse, the Anson, was still in use in basic navigator training along with the Vickers Varsity, a development of the Viking used for more advanced work and carrying two student navigators. The Valetta Flying Classroom, another Vickers development, could carry an instructor and about eight students, and was used to demonstrate various aids and techniques.

A new type, a version of the small Handley-Page Marathon four-engined passenger aircraft, was about to be brought into service for basic navigator training; as it happened I had already flown in a Marathon the previous year, when I went from RAE to London Airport for a demonstration of the latest Decca Navigator equipment, and not long after I arrived at the Air Ministry I went with Wing Commander Meston to

Handley-Page's at Woodley to view the navigation trainer version. It was not a great success when it came into service, with handling problems in icing conditions, and after a few years at No. 1 Air Navigation School it was withdrawn in favour of the Varsity.

There was also talk of using the Vampire NF10 – a two-seat jet fighter – for the planned fighter functional training, and this did eventually take place, with some success.

As one might expect, the Air Navigation Schools' aircraft were not equipped with any very advancd navigation aids, athough some did have Gee Mark 3 (the miniaturized version) and Rebecca 4. DR Trainers, somewhat improved on those in which we had sweated at Bridgnorth in 1943, were still in frequent use, and a new version, electronically operated and with some high-performance simulation, was under development. Synthetic trainers for H2S Mark 4a and Gee-H Mark 2 were planned for the proposed functional courses.

I lost little time in visiting Shawbury and bringing myself up to date with the current practices and people. It was pleasant to be back in the familiar srroundings, and it seemed at first as though little had changed, as indeed was the case with the syllabus and general aims of the Staff Navigation Course. The Staff Navigation Course (Pilots) was directed mostly towards Fighter Command, and was producing pilots well qualified to teach navigation, to be Station Navigation Officers, and to hold junior staff posts in that Command. But I sensed that the removal of the Spec N Course had somehow altered the ethos of the place, rather like a school without a sixth form; the lack of more advanced studies alongside what might be termed the 'bread and butter' work of CNCS had had its effect, although the presence of the Investigation and Research Section did provide some reference to a more scientific approach when required.

The Flying College at Manby was also early on my visit programme, and I was told on arrival that the Commandant wanted to see me. Air Commodore Walker (always known as 'Gus', and in due course Air Chief Marshal Sir Augustus Walker GCB, CBE, DSO, DFC, AFC, MA) had a pugnacious face but a pleasant and welcoming smile. He explained that he liked to see all visiting staff officers to make sure that he knew what was going on 'at a higher level' – a very wise move, in my view. I suppose Gus Walker was one of the most popular senior officers in the service; he lost an arm during the war when he was a Bomber Station Commander and was helping to rescue a crashed crew as the aircraft exploded. On my subsequent visits he always remembered my name and had a friendly word.

My main concern at Manby was of course the Specialist Navigation Course, and I was particularly interested to see how it had developed since (and partly because of) the reappraisal I had taken part in at Shawbury in 1948, and how it had fared since the move to the Flying College in May

1952. After 1948 the academic content of the syllabus had been substantially reduced in favour of the study of future navigational problems in each operational command. The Shawbury Investigation Wing had set up a special study group to assimilate and analyse all the available information on navigation techniques and equipment. This study group won a reputation for forward thinking outside the purely navigational field, and when the RAF Flying College was established in 1949 it was transferred to Manby and developed the Operational Studies Section, which became the backbone of all course studies at the College.

The Spec N Course was now the junior course at the Flying College, and had taken some time to settle down to its new status. The series of record-breaking Aries flights originally undertaken by the course was now done in the name of the Flying College, although Spec N staff and students were involved in many of them. The great benefit to the Spec N students was in the use of the Operational Studies Section, which could present the current and future operational picture against which to set the technical studies. I was pleased to see that maths and physics were still being taught as a sound basis for the other subjects. It was good, too, to note that the policy established at Shawbury of giving places on the course to students from the US and Commonwealth Air Forces was being continued. The USAF had no precisely similar course, but there were regular places for RAF officers on the Royal Canadian Air Force Spec N Course.

Neither the Spec N Course nor the Staff Navigation Course underwent any significant changes during my time at the Air Ministry, and although I visited both Shawbury and Manby regularly there were few policy decisions to be made. Selection for the Spec N Course, including the administration of the entrance examination, took up some time but was routine, if interesting, staff work.

* * *

Life at Cove continued much as usual, though I missed seeing as much of the family as I had done when I worked at Farnborough. Usually the children had gone or were going to bed when I arrived home from the station, but at least we had most Saturdays off, although the office was manned in the mornings and my turn came round about once a month. We had a day off for the Queen's Coronation on 2 June 1953, and bought a television set (9-inch screen, £30) for the occasion, when some of the neighbours came in and watched the proceedings. We did not go up to London as a family on many occasions, but I do remember that we took the children to see the *Nutcracker* ballet at the new Festival Hall: they were spellbound. Joan and I also attended a dress rehearsal for the Trooping the Colour on Horse Guards Parade, and on another occasion we went to tea at the House of Commons when the Old Modernians' Association was entertained by Wing Commander Eric Bullus MP, an old boy.

At the end of 1953 we sold our Morris 10 (now 18 years old) for the same price we had paid for it in 1949, and bought a Fordson 10 cwt utility vehicle from Peter Meston, my boss at the time. The conversion from a van to a passenger vehicle had been 'on a DIY basis', as we would say nowadays, and wasn't entirely successful, but when we visited Joan's parents in Leeds we invariably returned with a full load of odds and ends and household impedimenta which could never have been carried in a conventional saloon. But luxury travel it was not.

Susan left Cove Primary School for a small private school up the road towards Farnborough. It was run quite competently by two middle-aged to elderly ladies – Susan liked it, and Jennifer spent a few months there before we eventually left Cove.

Cove Green, a public open space (hardly a park), was quite close to our house, and we remember with affection the small occasional fairs held there, with old-fashioned roundabouts, swings and stalls. The children loved it, and Susan treasured for years the plaster 'lady's head' she won at one of the stalls.

Two holidays were spent at Minehead in Somerset, staying at the same hotel as Joan's parents. One memory is of bilberry picking on Porlock Hill; another, not so pleasant, of serious trouble with the old Morris on the way home – inconvenient and expensive, and probably why we decided to change cars.

* * *

As I wrote earlier, Air Ministry staff officers were able to fly regularly from Hendon, and my logbook shows that I made several flights as navigator to Eindhoven in Holland and Buckeburg in Germany, also to Guernsey, all in the now antique but reliable Anson. I note also that I had my first flight in a Canberra after a visit to Manby – the aircraft was returning to Farnborough and I was able to cadge a convenient lift.

Early in 1954 I got the job of organizing a flight on which the Astronomer Royal (then Sir Harold Spencer-Jones) could observe the total solar eclipse due on 30 June that year. I can't recall exactly how this task landed on my desk, but I was by then heavily involved with the Institute of Navigation, whose President at the time was Donald Sadler, the Director of HM Nautical Almanac Office: I think the first approach came from him.

This was the first total solar eclipse visible in the British Isles since 1927, and many scientific bodies worldwide would be making observations, many using aircraft. A total eclipse can provide information about the earth and the universe which can't be got in any other way: they are not frequent – counting the 1954 occurrence there had been only eight visible in the British Isles since 1400, and the next would take place in 1999. With the 1954 eclipse track spread over three continents, observers spaced out along it were able to get very accurate positions of the moon, which were then used as references to integrate geodetic data from each continent and so to provide more accurate mapping. Most of the other observers were concerned with fundamental physical research: one team was trying to check certain aspects of relativity theory, and another investigating solar radio emissions. Most were studying different aspects of the sun's atmosphere by looking at the inner and outer coronae, only properly visible during total eclipse.

The Astronomer Royal wanted to bring with him scientists from Cambridge and Edinburgh Universities and from the Greenwich Observatory, and as the plans developed the media became interested, and Ivor Jones from the BBC, a *Times* correspondent and a press photographer were added to the proposed passenger list. As luck would have it, the Flying College had recently acquired a Handley-Page Hastings four-engined transport aircraft which was used, among other things, for Spec N polar flights. The College needed no persuading to agree to do this particular task, and I acted as the link between it and the various bodies who were to take part in the flight.

When the moon passes between the earth and the sun to cause a solar eclipse, the tip of the shadow cone cast by the sun passes rapidly across the earth in a belt almost a hundred miles wide. In the 1954 eclipse, this belt started in Nebraska and moved eastwards at about 1,800 mph, passing south of Iceland at about midday, moving on through Scandinavia, Russia and Iran, and finally leaving the earth in India. The longest time for which the sun was totally obscured was about two and a half minutes. As it happened, the shadow path passed through the zone of maximum auroral frequency, and it was thought that there was a good chance of observing an auroral display (the Northern Lights) during the total eclipse in this area. By positioning the aircraft above cloud and in the middle of the eclipse track, flying with the shadow, the time of observed totality would be increased by about twenty-two seconds. So the scientists were hoping to get a good look at the aurora in daylight (or eclipse light, so to speak).

I naturally put myself down on the passenger list for this flight, and in the event I was roped in to help out with some of the auroral observations; Bennet McInnes, a young physicist from Edinburgh University, was to operate what he called an auroral colorimeter, and he needed someone to note down readings as he made them.

All went according to plan, and the Manby aircraft, captained by Wing Commander W.J. Burnett and with its proper complement of scientists and the media, took off from Leuchars in Scotland for the nine-hour flight over the Atlantic. Some of us were setting up equipment, some slept, and I noticed that the Astronomer Royal was deep in a book (for the record it was *Lady Chatterley's Lover*, well before the unexpurgated editions were available in this country). The eclipse duly took place and was a magnificent sight. I wrote afterwards:

> The light began to fade rapidly when the sun's face was about three-quarters obscured; the white clouds below us turned deep blue, and just before totality the horizon was a brilliant orange turning to pale green and, higher up, blue-black. The sun was a black disc with a silver circle round it – the inner corona – and outside this was a pearly-white glow with long equatorial streamers stretching out on either side to about three or four times the sun's diameter.

Unfortunately there were no aurorae to be seen; the scientists were disappointed but said that they had got some useful measurements. I was amused by Bennet McInnes' specially designed headgear for cutting out unnecessary light when he was operating his colorimeter: it was a tweed flat cap with part of the peak cut away, and made him look rather like a music-hall comedian.

When we landed at Leuchars, the BBC man was whipped off to Edinburgh in a Meteor jet, and later, when we were airborne in the Hastings on our way back to Manby, we had the unusual experience of hearing his recording of intercomm conversation during the eclipse flight broadcast on the Light Programme and coming through our headsets in the aircraft.

Donald Sadler and the Astronomer Royal were most impressed by the RAF's performance in this unique flight, and I had appreciative letters from them and from Bennet McInnes and his boss, Dr Paton, of the Department of Natural Philosophy at Edinburgh, plus a copy of the latter's paper on the observations for the *Journal of the British Astronomical Association*.

* * *

While I was completing the planning for the eclipse flight, an even more interesting flying opportunity presented itself. Shortly after I had joined DDT Nav, Paddy Bandon had been replaced as Assistant Chief of the Air Staff (Training) by Air Vice-Marshal McEvoy (later Air Chief Marshal Sir Theodore McEvoy KCB, CBE). After a comparatively short tour, he was due to take up the job of the senior RAF representative on the staff of the Imperial Defence College, whose alumni included high-ranking officers of all three services (and the Commonwealth) earmarked for higher appointments. Their one-year course included tours in various parts of the world, and one of West Africa was scheduled for the late summer of 1954; AVM McEvoy decided to accompany this tour but flying his own aircraft, crewed mostly by members of his former staff in the Air Ministry.

The two co-pilots were Wing Commander John Barraclough from IDC and Wing Commander Jackie Holmes from the Deputy Directorate of Training (Flying); I was to be the navigator, with Squadron Leader Taylor from Training (Air Sigs) as air signaller.

The aircraft chosen for the flight was the Vickers Varsity, now the standard trainer at the Air Navigation Schools, and in June I went up to the ANS at Swinderby near Lincoln to do some familiarization. The Varsity T1 was a development of the Viking, but with two much more powerful Hercules 264 engines, giving a very good single-engine performance – much more confidence-making for the crew. There were rear-facing navigation positions for two students sitting side-by-side, but although the navigation tables were reasonably spacious I found the seats uncomfortable, as they had been designed for back-pack parachutes, which we did not have. The navigation equipment was fairly basic, with a G4B gyro-compass plus the normal magnetic standby compass; the ARI 5428 radio compass, which was the production model of the GEC radio compass Freddy Stringer and I had tested at RAE; the standard Gee Mk 2; and Rebecca, I was pleased to note, plus the usual API, drift recorder, and astro-compass (of which I was to make a great deal of use in the days to come). I made two or three shortish flights as navigator and sat in as second navigator with a student on a five-hour cross-country (I noticed with some amusement that the young student never took his head out of the cockpit to map-read and position himself exactly, and did not seem to be interested in any pin-points I provided, but perhaps that was part of his briefing). By now I felt confident enough in the Varsity and was ready for some intensive flight planning.

The RAF had set up a central briefing unit at Ruislip to give advice and information on overseas flights, and they provided a detailed document with recommended routes for each leg; although the UK now had an airways system, this was not yet in existence for most of the countries we would be flying over. The brief showed danger and restricted areas, emergency airfields, high ground, and any peculiarities of the air traffic control systems into or over which we would be flying.

Our route would be via Luqa, Malta, to Idris (formerly Castel Benito, after Mussolini) near Tripoli, and then across the western continental bulge of Africa to Kano in northern Nigeria, continuing south to Lagos, the capital of Nigeria, which was of course still under British administration at that time. We would spend a day or so there and then go west to Accra in what was then the Gold Coast, also British-administered, where AVM McEvoy's main engagements were. Our return route would be via Bathurst in the Gambia, Gibraltar, and so home.

With the longish distances involved, I decided to use 1:2,000,000 plotting charts, half the scale of the standard RAF chart, starting with the Ordnance Survey chart as far as Malta and then using the USAF long-range navigation chart for the flight over Africa (all on the Mercator projection). This not only saved having to use several charts for each leg, but had the bonus of topographical and aeronautical information on the USAF charts; I found them very satisfactory.

We did all the usual performance sums for the Varsity, looking at various all-up weights, fuel loads, cruising speeds and altitudes, and the lengths of the runways we would be using. None of the legs seemed to present a particular problem in this respect, although the Bathurst–Gibraltar leg was nearly 1,600 nautical miles, and we should have to take on a full fuel load. Navigationally the leg from Idris to Kano was probably the most challenging, with few aids, few suitable diversion airfields, and some occasional high ground.

Having done one shakedown cross-country from Swinderby as a crew, with AVM McEvoy in the left-hand seat, we felt satisfied with the aircraft (Varsity WF416) and worked well together. The Air Vice-Marshal was a pleasure to fly with – calm, equable, apparently unflappable and a very competent pilot, as well as a friendly companion. All of us looked forward to the trip with keen anticipation.

We left the UK towards the end of August, clearing customs at Tangmere in Sussex and flying the well-used route across France and the Mediterranean to Malta in six and a half hours. After a pleasant dinner in Valetta we flew the short leg to Idris the following morning, and took it easy for the rest of the day before an early start for Kano. The weather was good and no headwinds were forecast, so we had no worries about endurance. Our track was virtually a straight line, with a slight diversion to overfly Ghat, a small airfield on the southern edge of the Sahara. Using mainly drifts and radio bearings across the featureless desert, as we approached Ghat there were mountains up to 6,500 feet which gave us good positions. South of Ghat was again featureless terrain, and mindful of my shame in getting lost on the way to Khartoum, I took a couple of sun shots, with a three-drift wind in between, and worked out a very satisfactory most probable position close to track. Further south there were more terrain features, and when we eventually picked up Kano Eureka beacon at seventy-eight miles we were close to the intended track and needed only a five-degree alteration in heading. We landed at Kano after a seven-and-a-quarter-hour flight, tired but pleased with the way this leg had gone. The town of Kano is in the province of the same name, the most northerly in Nigeria, and peopled mostly by Hausa Muslims, with their own emir. We had time to see the old walled city area with its unique houses of sun-dried bricks plastered over with mud and decorated with patterns of various colours.

Next day we flew on to Lagos, crossing the rivers Kaduna and Niger and flying over jungle and mangrove swamp. Shortly before reaching Lagos, we flew over Ibadan, now the second largest city in the Federation of Nigeria and the site of the University. In recent years Abuja, some 200 miles north-east of Lagos, has replaced it as the Federal capital. Lagos was then, and no doubt still is, a bustling city and a busy seaport, trading with all parts of the country and exporting palm oil, palm kernels, cocoa, and other products; oil was not yet a major industry. We had time to walk about the city, sight-see, and buy a few souvenirs, which in my case included a locally made picnic basket and two beautifully carved ebony heads, both of which I still have. We found the steamy heat trying, but there was something of a breeze off the Atlantic (the Bight of Benin, lapping the shores of what used to be called 'the White Man's Grave').

A short flight west along the coast took us to Accra, capital of what was called the Gold Coast and is now Ghana. Here we had several days as the guests of the Royal West African Frontier Force, the locally raised soldiery, which included a beach picnic with curry and local fruit, and surfing on the long rollers sweeping in from the Gulf of Guinea; I managed to crack a rib as I came off my board on one long fast glissade, but it was not a problem until I got back to the UK. We signed the book at the Governor's residence, a castle which was formerly a Portuguese fort, and we visited the mammy markets, still an important part of the Ghanaian economy, bustling places where almost anything could be bought or sold. One abiding memory of our stay was of walking back to our sleeping-quarters at night, and seeing clouds of assorted insects around the outside light, with enormous toads squatting beneath, ready to catch the casualties. We also managed to get seats on a short Hastings flight, laid on so that the Imperial Defence College students visiting the Gold Coast could see something of the local terrain; I remember little of this except the extensive areas of rain forest with the occasional plantation, which at that time would have usually been for cocoa production.

Then it was time to start the long journey back home up the west coast of Africa. Our first stop was at Bathurst in the Gambia, then a Crown colony and now a republic. It must be one of the smallest countries in Africa, occupying a 250-mile strip along the Gambia River and surrounded by Senegalese territory. It seemed to be mostly river, creeks and swamps, and it is a surprise to me that the country is now managing to attract some tourist activity, probably for the beaches in the coastal area and for the abundant wildlife, especially birds: this is one of the countries from which the ospreys migrate to spend the breeding season in Scotland.

The airfield then was primitive, with pierced steel planking runways probably laid down during the war, when it was on the route used by aircraft being ferried to Egypt. Our aircraft had to be refuelled from drums, a long and labour-intensive process during which I got out my performance graphs and tables and laboriously worked out how much runway we should need for take-off the following morning with a maximum fuel load for our longest leg to Gibraltar. Bearing in mind the high ambient temperatures, I could see that it was going to be a close thing, but AVM McEvoy was optimistic and felt that we should make it if we took off early in the morning.

Accommodation was difficult, and I was taken out to the RWAFF Officers' Mess a few miles outside Bathurst. Here I stepped back into the Africa of the turn of the century, the Africa I had read about so often in books of exploration, adventure and big-game hunting. The Mess was at the edge of the jungle; the ante-room looked as though it had remained unchanged since Edwardian times, with worn leather armchairs, a threadbare carpet, and a generally dark heavy appearance. The massive bookcases were full of old volumes of *Punch*, the *Army List*, and a remarkable collection of slightly moth-eaten books on the flora and fauna of Gambia, with some accounts of long-dead British administrators with titles such as *On Safari in the Gold Coast*, and *Native Customs Along the Gambia River*. Several even more moth-eaten game heads – mostly antelope, as I recall – were hung around the walls, and there was an all-pervasive atmosphere of rot and damp.

Dinner was served in the gloomy dining-room, with regimental silver on the table and the house servants dressed in white jackets and red cummerbunds. My dining companion was a young RWAFF subaltern who was apparently the only living-in officer. The main course was fish pie, with a crisp brown crust on the top and a pleasant anonymous sauce. I had missed lunch and tucked in hungrily: the pie was good, but, finishing the last mouthful, I found that I had swallowed a fishbone, which lodged somewhere deep in my gullet and was evidently sharp. Coughing, spluttering, and a finger down the throat did not help, and the RWAFF officer said that he would run me down to the hospital in Bathurst. We got into his jeep and started off down the red dusty road, the coughing and spluttering continuing. My young friend put his foot down and we bounced and bumped along the unmade surface. Troops of monkeys, the same colour as the road, ran across in front of us, and there was the occasional glimpse of exotic birds in the trees. After one particularly bumpy patch I felt the bone jump up in my throat, and I was thankfully able to pick it out with little damage. We turned around to drive back to the Mess, and this time I was in a state to appreciate such wildlife as showed itself.

Take-off in the cool of the morning was uneventful, although we used up nearly all of the old runway. The flight to Gibraltar was mostly along the west African coastline, and I again used the good old-fashioned methods of drifts, astro-compass position lines to make running fixes from ground features, sun shots and radio bearings as well as the Mark 1 eyeball for pin-points. Coming round the north-west corner of Africa, so to speak, and overflying Casablanca, we were glad to land at Gibraltar after over eight hours in the air. The next day we flew back to Swinderby, clearing customs at Tangmere as before, and thankfully having an early night before going our separate ways the following day – in my case a longish dreary train journey to Farnborough via London. The West African flight had been a rewarding experience, and among many other things we had had a last sight of part of the British Empire before it was handed back, we had experienced incredibly varied African terrain from the air, and in my case I had had an opportunity to practise some basic navigation techniques over strange (if, thankfully, not uncharted) territory.

* * *

I was pleased to be back home again and to have had the forethought to arrange a couple of weeks' leave. Two days in the office cleared up a few outstanding matters, and the family was then free to take a holiday. We decided to drive down to the west country and to take pot luck with hotels, which we felt would not be too busy in September (the bank holiday was then at the beginning of August). My cracked rib from inexpert surfing in Accra was now beginning to trouble me, and I had it strapped up with an enormous piece of sticking plaster around the chest. This did not stop me driving, and we set off in the Fordson for Dorset, finding a suitable family room at the King's Arms in Dorchester. Here the itching from my plastered torso grew intolerable, and on advice from the local pharmacist we took the plaster off – an excruciating business – and treated it with ointment, which did improve matters.

After a look around Dorset, inevitably visiting Lulworth Cove, we moved on to Devon, and found another family room at the Oswalds Hotel at Babbacombe, in which I had been billeted during my initial training in 1942/3, and which was now functioning as a hotel again. We found Babbacombe delightful, much as I remembered it; as it happened, Susan had her eighth birthday while we were there, and the cake shop which made her a birthday cake was the one we cadets had patronized for our morning breaks. Although it was nearly the end of the holiday season, a small orchestra played in an open-air bandstand overlooking the sea. One morning the orchestra was playing as usual, but without a single person in the audience, so the four of us sat down in the front row of deckchairs and enjoyed a concert of light classical music solely for us; our applause was warm at the end of each piece, and the young conductor bowed deeply and gravely, enjoying the joke.

* * *

After the longish break, it was back to the daily round of commuting and office work (although I notice from my logbook that I had a day's flying, for some reason photographing ships in the Thames Estuary, two days after I returned). By now my immediate boss, Peter Meston, had been replaced by Wing Commander Tom Whiting, who had early on in the war been Air Marshal Sir Basil Embry's navigator in Blenheims – a highly hazardous occupation. We got on well and I was left to get on with my job without too much interference. Charlie Bale had also moved on, and our Deputy Director was now Group Captain Hedley Boxer, a charming man who was a pre-war Spec N.

As I wrote earlier, I had two ex-officio jobs, one of which was as Secretary to the Synthetic Training Committee chaired by the Deputy Director of Operational Training, who was then Group Captain Gordon-Finlayson. He was something of a character, rather like a taller version of Winston Churchill, even to the cigar. Luckily the Committee did not meet very frequently and my duties were merely to write and circulate the minutes. I recall little detail of the subjects discussed: synthetic trainers for all aircrew roles were becoming more capable and sophisticated, but costs were escalating, as always, and it was not possible to match demand with the funds available. But the job was excellent training for me, and I certainly learnt something about the wheeling and dealing involved in policy making at Ministry level.

My other job, as a member of the Institute of Navigation Technical Committee, was much more interesting. The Institute had become a significant power in the navigation world (both marine and air) since its formation in 1948, as I wrote earlier in this book. In 1953 the President was Rear Admiral Day, the Hydrographer of the Navy, and the Vice-Presidents were Sir Robert Watson-Watt, the radar pioneer, and Donald Sadler, Director of the Nautical Almanac Office. Francis Chichester (not then knighted) was Honorary Treasurer, and Wing Commander E.W. (Andy) Anderson Chairman of the Technical Committee; he had been navigator on the historic Aries flights from Shawbury in 1944 when I was there on the Staff Navigator Course. Other members of the Institute's Council included the Astronomer Royal and the heads of navigation directorates at the Admiralty, the Air Ministry, and the Ministry of Supply (then concerned with research and development into navigation systems). The whole organization was held together by Michael Richey, the Executive Secretary, with a very small staff; he also edited the Institute's *Journal* to very high standards, so that it was influential in navigation circles around the world. The Institute's significance was heightened by the Duke of Edinburgh consenting to become Patron in 1954 (and it eventually became the Royal Institute of Navigation in the early 1970s).

Donald Sadler became President in 1954, and in his inaugural address he quoted the objects of the Institute as laid down in its constitution:

First, to unite in one scientific society those interested in the science of navigation; second, to advance the science and practice of navigation by means including the co-ordination of the knowledge and achievement of marine and air navigators, scientists and others, and the encouragement of research; and third, to encourage the formation of similar bodies in other countries.

From its inception in 1947, the Institute's membership had grown steadily, and now stood at 1,355 Fellows and Members and sixty-four Corporate Members. The new President paid particular tribute to Michael Richey, 'that co-ordinator *par excellence*', and also said, 'I have been amazed and gratified by the amount of effort and time given so freely by all who have taken a share in [the Institute's] working.'

To me it was a great (and largely fortuitous and undeserved) honour to be involved in the inner workings of the ION, and to rub shoulders with some of the great and good in the navigation world in the historic and impressive surroundings of the Royal Geographical Society in Kensington Gore. A further (and not particularly welcome) honour came my way when I was asked to chair a small working party of the Technical Committee to look into the accuracy of dead-reckoning navigation. The other members were C.S. Durst, a senior scientist at the Meteorological Office, and something of an authority on the accuracy of forecast winds, and J.B. Parker, a statistician and a former RAF navigator who had worked in the Investigation and Research Section at EANS Shawbury; in fact, he had written the original paper on the most probable position which had led to present standard practice in the RAF. Both had recently published relevant papers in the Institute's *Journal*: Parker on 'Determining the Most Probable Position', and Durst on 'The accuracy of route wind forecasts for aviation'.

Dead-reckoning (DR) – sometimes called deduced reckoning – is, as I have written earlier, a method of calculating a position without positive information such as a visual, astro or radio fix or a sight of the ground. In the air its viability depended on the accuracy of the pilot, the airspeed indicator and the compass in providing a still-air position and on the accuracy of the wind velocity applied to deduce a DR position. The advent of the air position indicator had improved air plot accuracy, and in general the accuracy of forecast wind velocities had also improved over the last few years. But there would always be an error in the DR position; some experimental work had been done in RAF Coastal Command during the war to calculate the likely DR error, and based on this the standard figure used in the RAF was at first ten per cent of distance flown since the last positive fix, giving a fifteen-nautical-mile error circle around the DR position for an hour flown at an average 150 knots without a fix. Later this was amended to eight nautical miles per hour since the last fix – a dubious figure statistically, and with ever higher airspeeds even more dubious. In the absence of positive fixes, this DR error circle had to be compared with information from astro, radio or visual position lines (each of which also had a fifty per cent error value assigned to it) to obtain a most probable position. Not unnaturally, most navigators had a healthy suspicion of statistics and little faith in the laid-down MPP procedure, which had certainly led me very much astray (helped, it must be said, by my own dilatoriness) on my flight to Khartoum in 1949 (Chapter 9).

The first thing our working party had to do was to state the problem, and after a couple of meetings with Durst and Parker I produced a so-called interim report to do just this, which appeared in the *Journal* in April 1954. This began by stating the obvious:

> At present, standard air navigation practice recommends the use of one D.R. error figure in all flight conditions; with the comparatively recent increase in operational limits in all fields of aviation, this figure is seriously in question, with regard to both size and form .... The present working party has, therefore, been set up to investigate the accuracy of D.R. in air navigation, and to attempt to produce error data covering a wide range of operational conditions.

The report went on to discuss methods of approach – analytical, using data and statistical evidence already available; and empirical, using data from experimental flights under controlled conditions. Since the empirical approach would 'require a flight programme of ambitious proportions, difficult to combine with military flights or civil flight schedules', it was inevitable that the only practicable method at that time would have to be analytical. A preliminary working plan was outlined, including definition of the terms in which DR error should be stated; specifying groups of operational conditions for each of which separate error values would be required; assessing, from published data, values of error in deriving still-air positions; resolving these data with that available on wind vector errors; and investigating methods of obtaining experimental figures to confirm (or otherwise) the theoretical analysis. The report continued by defining, as a working basis, criteria for error values as follows:

(a) To be stated in terms of a percentage of air distance flown since positive position data.
(b) To be quoted as standard deviations.
(c) To be considered under different operational conditions (three differing height bands, true airspeed below and over 250 knots, and with manual and automatic air plots).
(d) Calculations of wind vector errors to be confined to those due to inaccurate wind forecasts and the possible change of wind vector with time and distance.

It was further mentioned that the shape of the error zone – either circular or elliptical – would also have to be considered.

Having stated the problems, the working party realized that it had set itself an almost impossible task. We had one or two further meetings, and Durst and Parker went away to juggle with more statistics, but little of significance was produced before I had to step down from the Technical Committee after my next posting. Durst published a paper on the subject in the *Journal* of April 1955, with a critique by Parker in the same issue; unfortunately my copy of this is missing, but I can refer to a discussion on the subject (which I could not attend) noted in the October 1955 *Journal*, in which one W. Hudson (evidently a practising navigator) said, among other things and referring to Durst's paper:

> It is good to see his definition of dead reckoning: I have often wondered what it means in the subconscious minds of some navigators – perhaps a method of avoiding the necessity of acquiring more accurate information. To me it is a technique not without its uses and certainly not without its fun, but to be kept to the minimum by regular and definite findings.

He thought that MPPs were justifiable in certain conditions, but that

> The navigator will prefer to use his own figures based on his own opinions of the worth of position line or lines, and D.R. position. There is sometimes an indefinable something, a feeling, or almost a hunch, that helps.

I think he spoke for many navigators who still felt then that navigation was an art rather than a science.

Coincidentally, in the same issue of the ION *Journal* in which our interim working party report appeared, there were two short and general papers under the heading 'Methods of Air and Surface Navigation', the first by a mariner and the second by Wing Commander Andy Anderson. This included the comment:

> It is … easy to see why the air navigator is not greatly enamoured of dead reckoning. The classical concept of navigation as a picture painted by means of position lines on a tough canvas foundation of dead reckoning is the sort of concept that he tends to avoid. Instead, he uses dead reckoning partly as an invaluable independent check on the reliability, but not the accuracy, of his information and partly as a last resort if position finding systems fail and he can navigate in no other way.

None of these comments was particularly encouraging, and it seems that the working party never made a final report. Certainly in 1960 or so the

RAF Air Navigation Schools were still teaching the same DR navigation drills, and also in 1960 Andy Anderson again tackled the subject in the ION *Journal*, and concluded: 'Airborne dead reckoning is a dying art. The future business of air operations lies in data processing systems on the ground.' He was certainly right in the first statement, if a little astray in the second, but earth-orbiting navigation satellites were hardly more than a twinkle in some scientists' eyes in 1960.

* * *

Towards the end of 1954 I was told that I had been selected to attend the next course at the RAF Staff College Bracknell, starting in January 1955 and lasting for twelve months. This was good news in several ways: a Staff College qualification was an essential for further advancement; the posting would cut short the usual Air Ministry tour of three years to two; and we could continue to live at Cove, which was within easy driving distance of Bracknell. Since I had been promoted to substantive squadron leader in October, the future (though always problematical in the service) was looking rosier.

Yet I was sorry to leave many aspects of the job in Richmond Terrace – involvement in policy making, even though at a humble level, the unexpected opportunities for flying, and the work with ION, had made the two years pass quickly. I should also miss the long lunch hours we tried to have once a week when we would visit the National Gallery, the Tate, or the National Portrait Gallery or one of the museums, in search of culture (to quote Hermann Goering: 'Whenever I hear the word culture, I reach for my pistol'); and the walks in St James's Park or along the Embankment. What I would not miss was the daily commuting and the odd weekends in a deserted Ministry as Duty Air Staff Officer.

As I have already mentioned, prospective Staff College students were required to present an essay on arrival entitled 'An outline of my service experience and some lessons from it'. I quote from the paragraph dealing with my Air Ministry tour:

Experience here has underlined lessons learnt in previous staff work, and has demonstrated several new ones – the preponderance of non-operational considerations in the making of operational decisions in peace; the important part played by finance in the administration of a modern air force; and the extent to which co-operation between the R.A.F. and other air forces has developed since 1939. I have also discovered anew the value to a staff officer of personal contacts and of a wide knowledge of subjects entirely unconnected with the work in hand.

These conclusions were true enough as far as they went, though I circumspectly omitted the political influences (at least political correctness had not then been invented), the personal idiosyncracies of some of the policy makers, and what I perceived to be the inefficiency of middle-ranking civil servants, often resulting in ineffectual meetings and time-wasting conferences. But I had learnt a lot and mostly enjoyed myself; poor Joan had, as usual, to keep the family flag flying at home during my long working days and frequent absences.

I refer to politics, but with hindsight I realize that in the training world we were partly shielded from the harsh realities of the needs of the operational commands; the RAF was still involved in the Malayan emergency, the Korean war only ended in 1953, and the Cold War was getting into its stride with the coming development of Bomber Command's V-Force a major preoccupation against the backdrop of America's second H-bomb in 1954. My eyes were to be opened at Bracknell.

CHAPTER TWELVE

Learning Yet Again

In 1955 Bracknell was a small, pleasant market town, about ten miles from Farnborough and around twenty minutes' drive from Cove. It had a bustling high street with a complement of small shops, and there was a friendly feel about the place. But it had recently been designated as a 'New Town', and already work had begun on housing estates and light industry. From a population of around 11,000 in the late 1950s, the town grew to nearly 94,000 by 1991, and is no doubt still larger now. So we saw the last of the old Bracknell: we were lucky that the New Town work did not seriously impinge on the RAF Staff College (although in 1951 a bid by the Bracknell Development Corporation to take over the Ramslade estate in which the College was located had been defeated by the Air Ministry).

A staff college for the RAF was one of Trenchard's prescient and far-reaching plans for the service, made as early as 1919. Andover was its first location in 1922, using former wartime huts for accommodation, with twenty officers (including a Squadron Leader Portal) on a one-year course, with other students from the Navy, the Army, the Indian Army and the Dominions; the Commandant was Air Commodore Brooke-Popham. The College remained at Andover for the next twenty years, although limited to short 'War Courses' during the Second World War; in 1942 it moved to Bulstrode Park, Gerrards Cross, but in early 1945, with victory in sight, it was felt that a larger site with better facilities would be required for a longer, more comprehensive peacetime course. In 1939 the Air Ministry had requisitioned Ramslade House, a late Georgian country house and estate at Bracknell, and it was used for various purposes, including the HQ of Second Tactical Air Force and of Army Co-operation Command. It was now decided to move the Staff College to Ramslade, and in August 1945 the first post-war course started, with 122 officers.

At the same time the Air Ministry felt that there should also be a parallel course in the UK for Allied and friendly air forces, and the RAF Staff College, Bulstrode Wing, was formed with a syllabus close to that at Bracknell and with forty students, including ten RAF and Dominion officers. After some teething troubles this proved a success, and it was moved in 1948 to a more permanent location at Andover, where it remained, fulfilling the same function, until the amalgamation of both colleges at Bracknell in 1970.

(For this brief history I am indebted to a study by Wing Commander R.A. Mason MA, RAF, entitled 'The Royal Air Force Staff College 1922–1972', written at Bracknell in 1972, parts of which I have drastically summarized to include in the foregoing paragraphs.)

The post-war objects of the course were laid down in an Air Ministry Order in 1945:

> To assist officers to think clearly, to express themselves concisely and logically and to read wisely, … to provide a sound basic knowledge of the organization and operation of the Royal Air Force and a background to the work of the other Services which will enable officers to perform staff duties appropriate to their rank.

These aims were basically the same when No. 45 Staff Course assembled in January 1955. We were ninety-five strong, predominantly from the General Duties (flying) Branch of the RAF, with eighteen from the other branches, plus officers from the Navy, the Army, the RCAF, RAAF, RNZAF, and USAF, and four senior civil servants. I was delighted to find that my old friend from Shawbury and Bomber Command days, John Digman, was a fellow student, as was Paddy Forsythe, with whom I had flown in the Bomber Command Examining Flight, and Mike Vaux from the Spec N Course, plus the odd acquaintance from elsewhere. Our senior student was Wing Commander Andrew Humphrey, a well-liked officer who was to become Chief of the Air Staff and Chief of the Defence Staff (as was Wing Commander Neil Cameron, a member of the Directing Staff). The Commandant was Air Vice-Marshal Macfadyen, a figure of great authority, with Air Commodore Roy Faville as his Assistant Commandant. Among the several group captains on the DS was Eric Nelson, who had been my friendly CO on 103 Squadron in 1944, and among the many DS wing commanders was John Gilchrist, an instructor at No. 5 Air Observers' School in Jurby in 1943 and on the staff at Shawbury later. Many other fellow students I was to meet again later, and several reached very senior rank in due course.

I still have the copy of the 'Tutorial Information and Instructions' issued to each student on the first day, a comprehensive document covering the scope and general programme of the course, how to cope with exercises, publications to be issued (a lengthy list), daily routine, information on the College library, and a welter of administrative detail, complete with Appendices A to G (one of which includes a reading list of about a hundred books). I noted that twenty-one new married quarters were under construction to add to the fifty-one already occupied, and congratulated myself on not having that particular worry. The instructions began, of course, with a statement of the aim (the first principle of war, with which we were to become exceedingly familiar in the next few months – 'Selection and Maintenance of the Aim'). An Air Ministry Directive of 1949 was quoted: 'The Royal Air Force Staff College exists to afford an advanced service education to selected officers, thereby fitting them for command and staff appointments appropriate to their present ranks and preparing them to fit themselves for higher appointments' – a slightly broader aim than that of 1945 mentioned above.

The College Mess was in the original house of the Ramslade estate, which was extensive and included, as well as the married quarters, administrative buildings of a not very impressive type, a NAAFI shop, car parking and some pleasant gardens with trees. The Mess dining-room opened out on to a croquet lawn, which was usually in constant use in summer over lunchtime. The main lecture hall was something of a surprise, as it was a large Nissen-type building to the rear of the main house; however, it was well maintained and perfectly comfortable and adequate. It was not until 1969 that a new Tutorial Building was completed preparatory to the amalgamation with the Andover Staff College.

The daily routine normally started at 0930 (except on Mondays, when it began at 1000, a civilized concession much appreciated). The allotted programme time ended at 1900 on Mondays, Tuesdays, Thursdays and Fridays, with Wednesday afternoons usually set apart for games, a common proceeding in the RAF then. Saturday mornings were reserved for study, revision and flying (of which more later). The course was organized in three groups, each directed by a group captain, and each further divided into syndicates of six students directed by a DS wing commander; while remaining in the same group, the syndicates were changed twice during the year, ensuring a good mix of students.

In my first syndicate I was lucky enough to be with John Digman; yet another navigator was Eric Alcock, and John Mason and Bill Horsman were pilots, the latter from the RAAF who had flown on operations in Korea. The syndicate was completed by (John?) Brown of the RAF Regiment, so we had, appropriately enough, an Alcock and Brown (for those to whom this allusion is meaningless, Alcock and Brown were RAF officers who made the first transatlantic flight in 1919, and were both knighted). Our DS mentor was Norman Ryder, a Battle of Britain pilot, who treated us gently and kept us on the right lines. (Another, much decorated, Battle of Britain veteran on the DS was Denis Crowley-Milling, later an air marshal).

Our early lecture programmes concentrated on reasoning, writing and speaking, followed up by syndicate discussions and exercises, and practice in what was known as service writing – the form in which correspondence, orders and instructions, and papers were presented. I had a head start here, having just come from a desk job and having been a staff officer at an early age. For the non-RAF officers on the course this must have seemed an unnecessary evil, since most other services had a different way of doing things: for example, when framing an order the RAF convention was to say that 'X unit "is to" do so-and-so', whereas the Army would say '"will" do', a tiny but telling difference.

The principles of war were hammered into us, starting (as I wrote earlier) with the all-important 'Selection and maintenance of the aim', an essential in writing formal appreciations which discussed a particular military requirement and the possible ways of fulfilling it, ending with recommendations which then had to be translated into operation orders, saying with precision and clarity exactly what was to be done. These were sometimes in syndicate and sometimes individually, and the solutions would come back to us with DS comments in red ink, not only on the content but on the standard of presentation. There would also be a copy of what was always called 'the pink', a DS solution on pink paper which, our DS always said, was not the final answer and could be open to discussion.

We were also given opportunities to practise speaking, starting with the syndicate DS handing out topics at random and requiring us to speak in syndicate for five minutes at no notice. Later, students were required to give a short talk to the assembled course and DS on a subject of their choice. I chose to talk about the total solar eclipse of 1954, which was still fresh in my mind after the flight I had organized to observe it. Students giving these talks were able to use the full services of the College drawing office run by Ben Irish, a long-serving College character, to produce any charts or diagrams required – the College had not progressed as far as slide or overhead projectors in those days. Then there was the team lecture, in which half a dozen students would give talks on a connected subject: the team I was in was given 'The Colonial Empire', not one we would have chosen, but one we found full of interest – the British colonial territories were still very extensive and numerous then, and the job of governing them was complex, as most of them were being prepared for independence.

Life was not all drudgery, however. Apart from the social occasions (drinks with the DS on arrival, a cocktail party in February, and a summer dance), there was a constant stream of visiting lecturers and a running programme of visits to places of interest. I shall have more to say about speakers and visits later, but I have a particular memory of the first visiting lecturer for a special reason: he was a senior naval officer talking about the roles and equipment of the Royal Navy, and as the lecture progressed I became more and more annoyed, since he talked as though the heavy bomber had never been invented and the *Bismarck* and the *Tirpitz* never destroyed by air power. When the lecture ended, questions were invited (as was invariably the case): since this was the first such occasion, there was naturally some reluctance among the students to ask the first question, but I was so incensed by what I saw as the lack of recognition of the air role that I stood up and tackled the speaker on the point, feeling unduly self-conscious but encouraged by a murmur of approval from some of the RAF students. I received a fairly anodyne reply but was later pleased that I had broken the ice.

*   *   *

Meanwhile, family life at Cove continued much as usual. Although my working days were not always as long as at the Air Ministry, there was a lot of private study and homework to do, and I must have seemed very preoccupied. I was very grateful for the fact that, since Jenny was now of an age to leave her cot, she moved into Susan's double bedroom and I was able to turn her former tiny room into a study. I bought a second-hand table and an elderly Royal upright typewriter (£9, it cost, and I gave it away some twenty-five years later, still in working order), so was able to concentrate on the various individual tasks we were set.

We were well settled at Cove after more than three years – the longest we had lived anywhere since we were married. Our elderly fox terrier had been replaced by a boisterous Labrador/spaniel cross, and the children had pet rabbits in the garden which were becoming more prolific. Both girls were now at the same small private school nearby and seemed to like it. Then out of the blue we had a letter early in the year from the owner of the house, who was a widow: she was getting married again and gave us a month's notice to quit. This was a shock, and our first thought was to check the married quarter situation at Bracknell. With the progress of the building programme and our position on the waiting list (which was worked out on a points system, taking into account number of children, length of service and so on) it was unlikely that we would be able to move into quarters before June or July. Things looked black, but I checked the terms of the agreement drawn up by the RAF as standard when renting a hiring: this said quite plainly that the minimum notice to quit was three months. In the event this took us up to June, when we were able to move into a brand-new married quarter at Bracknell, a semi-detached four-bedroom house with John Digman and his family just across the road, and another student, Peter Mitchell, with his wife Anne and a new baby, next door.

Leaving Cove was something of a wrench (we gave the rabbit family to the milkman), but there were advantages in being back in the RAF atmosphere again after four years away; being a few minutes' walk from work was a bonus, though we had problems with the newly built house – the garden a wilderness, the smell of mortar and paint, and plaster falling off the walls, but there were compensations. Luckily a small private school had just been started within the College grounds which Susan and Jennifer were able to attend – not the best in the world, but adequate and thankfully close to home.

* * *

As we pursued our studies, the RAF was in a transitional period (when was it ever not?). Since 1952 Bomber Command had been building up the Canberra light bomber force while retaining the obsolescent Lincoln. By 1954 there were thirty-five Canberra squadrons in the UK, and RAF Germany was receving the first of them. The V-bombers were still undergoing development and production, with the first Valiants coming into service at the Gaydon Operational Conversion Unit early in 1955. The Vulcan and Victor followed, but not until 1957, and it was 1964 before the V-Force was at maximum strength and constituted the UK's strategic nuclear deterrent until this was taken over by the Navy in 1969, when the third Polaris submarine was declared operational.

We were in the Cold War period, and this dominated political and military thinking at the time and for many years afterwards. We students were given a copy of Field Marshal Montgomery's lecture at the Royal United Services Institution on 21 October 1954, entitled 'A Look through a Window at World War III'. Monty was Deputy Commander at NATO at the time, and his views carried some weight. It was a long lecture, but we picked out some plums from it which had a particular bearing on our studies. At the beginning of the lecture, he said:

> I consider that the present state of world affairs, and the present tension, will continue for a long period. Therefore the true objective of all military thinking today must be how to combine most economically the military measures needed for success in the cold war, with the development of the military strength needed to convince our enemies that a world hot war would result in their own destruction ....

After a detailed survey of possible scenarios for a hot war, looking at each of the air, sea and land forces (in that order), he concluded *inter alia* that:

> The air is coming to the front as the dominant factor in war, and the decisive arm. This is going to introduce difficult problems, and in solving them do not let us bother unduly about the colour of our uniform: khaki, dark blue, light blue.

And another conclusion:

I have forecast greatly increased responsibilities for air forces. Today, it is doubtful if the air forces could cope with those added responsibilities. If what I have said is true, then the air forces must be got ready over the years to handle the tasks that will fall to them.

Whatever our opinions of Montgomery, I think most of us agreed with what he said. We got on well with our Navy and Army colleagues at Bracknell, but there was still some deeply entrenched inter-service rivalry which worked against the best use of finance and resources; it probably still goes on to some extent despite all the recent integration in the three services.

So, among all these serious national and international problems, we were struggling with the detail of RAF Command organization, the principles of staff work, RAF manning, aircraft maintenance, the effects of nuclear explosions, the Navy, the Army, and even the use and misuse of graphs and charts (via a lecture by my old mentor from Shawbury days, 'Flash' Button). Many of the subjects we studied were illuminated by visiting lecturers of some standing – some of the RAF Commanders-in-Chief, for example; the Under-Secretary of State for Air; MRAF Sir John Slessor; Lord De L'Isle and Dudley VC; the Bishop of Croydon; Sir Vincent Tewson of the TUC; Brigadier Sir John Hunt (of Everest); and a long list of others (including Chuck Yeager, the US test pilot).

We had a USAF Week, when the Commandant of the USAF Air War College brought a team to expound current USAF air strategy and its problems; in July the Director, DS and students of the Royal Naval Staff College joined us for a week of combined study; and later in the year we had a joint study period with the Army Staff College, visiting Camberley for the purpose. I remember little of what was discussed at Camberley, but I have a very clear vision of sessions in the main lecture hall with the serried ranks of Army officers sitting opposite to the light-blue contingent, who made the (to us) surprising discovery that no two uniformed Army officers of the hundred or so present were dressed alike. Was there a moral here?

There was also, throughout the course, a comprehensive programme of visits, and I can perhaps do no better than to quote the article entitled 'Bracknell Caravan' in the RAF Staff College's Journal, *The Hawk*, for 1955:

The programme started in March with visits to Messrs Vickers-Armstrong at Weybridge and to RAF Halton. At Weybridge we were shown something of the Valiant production cycle; RAF Halton showed us how apprentices are trained. The end of April saw us cross the 'frontier' into South Wales ... to visit RAF St Athan and the Margam Abbey steel works. The latter visit was a revelation to most of us, the most impressive aspect being the degree of automaticity evolved by the industry for carrying out the weighty tasks involved in steel plate production .... We next paid a flying visit to the RAF College Cranwell, where we toured the College and learned about the training given to future permanent officers. At the same time, the other half of the course went to the RAF Flying College Manby, to learn about its mission in life. The following day, the two parties changed places, eventually returning direct to Blackbushe Airport ....

Visits to the Bristol Aeroplane Company, RAF Quedgeley, and the USAF Strategic Air Command base at Upper Heyford then followed in rapid succession. In the same period, we crossed from Portsmouth to the Isle of Wight in rather unfriendly weather to watch 'Operation Runaground', a stimulating spectacle in which the Royal Marine Commandos climbed cliffs with breath-taking abandon and generally ignored the dangerous combination of height and gravity ....

As a prelude to the naval phase of the course, we flew to the Joint Anti-Submarine School, Londonderry ... the school staff gave us a good insight into anti-submarine work and convoy escort; many of us also ventured forth in Shackletons from RAF Ballykelly, the captains of which sturdily defied low cloud and drizzle to give us a sono-buoy demonstration.

On the 20th June we again made our way to Portsmouth to go to sea in HMS 'Centaur' and watch 'Exercise Shopwindow'. A conducted tour around this modern aircraft carrier was followed by a series of demonstrations involving an anti-submarine frigate, motor torpedo boats and a submarine. ... The exercise finished with a demonstration of the capabilities of carrier-borne aircraft, and a polished display of aerobatics was given by Seahawk fighters as a grand finale.

For the week of the 4th July, the course divided into two parts to spend three days as guests of various naval establishments in Portsmouth. ... Submarine operation was discussed with the officers of HMS 'Dolphin' and we were able to scramble around inside a real live submarine. ... This very pleasant stay with the dark blue Service ended on a traditional note with a conducted tour of HMS 'Victory' and a visit to the Royal Navy Museum.

(Apropos of the submarine visit, I remember saying to one of the officers that I didn't think I could bear being shut up in a tin box deep under the ocean, to be told that it was better than a tin box up in the sky.)

We had a day at RAE Farnborough, and a visit to the London Fire Brigade to which families were invited: Jenny still remembers sitting next to the Chief Fire Officer as we watched a thrilling demonstration by rescue teams. There was a tour of the Port of London in a steam yacht and a look at Ford Motors at Dagenham.. In the autumn term, to complement the bomber and fighter phases of the course, we visited various Bomber and

Fighter Command units, and I was lucky enough to have a trip in a Canberra for a low-level cross-country and shallow dive-bombing. We also spent a week with Army units on Salisbury Plain, living in mess with the Army. I still shudder to recall some after-dinner games in one mess, when billiard balls were thrown about and one unfortunate subaltern was tossed out of a window; this was not in a cavalry or infantry mess, but with the Royal Army Service Corps – I think they were trying to impress us.

But one of the highlights of the course was the tour of Allied Air Forces in Central Europe (AAFCE), which lasted eight days over some 1,500 miles. We travelled in coaches supplied by a local firm, and they bore no resemblance to the luxury coaches even of the time – seats were hard and there were no 'facilities'; but this was all part of the experience. Crossing via the car ferry at Dover, we spent a night in Paris, and the following day at Fontainebleau at HQAAFCE, with a series of lectures on NATO organization and problems. After another evening in Paris ('sampling the entertainment offered by the gay city', says one report in the language of the time), we went on to Luxembourg, stopping for an hour on the way to see the cathedral in Rheims, and spent the night at the small spa at Mondorf. Here I recall choosing our dinner trout from those swimming in a tank outside, and sleeping under a duvet for the first time.

The next day we went to the USAF Tactical Air Force base at Bitburg nearby, where we were briefed on the base's role and shown some tactical weapons. In the afternoon we boarded the coaches again to drive to Cologne, through the Eiffel mountains and along the river Ahr until we finally joined the Rhine at Remagen. This was a splendidly scenic route, and we were able to make a stop in the Ahr valley among the vine-terraces, and sample the local wine. We reached Cologne via Bonn and found our hotels; unfortunately the one allocated to our group was not quite finished, and John Digman and I had to share a double bed in a room notably lacking in comfort.

The next two days were spent visiting RAF stations in No. 83 Group, RAF Germany – Wahn, Bruggen, and Wildenrath, mostly equipped with Canberras, where we were shown the function and organization of the group, and visited the mobile Joint Operation and Aircraft Control Centres, the Reconnaissance Wing and its associated Mobile Photographic Unit. A full Air Support demonstration was staged for us, showing how each individual unit functioned, and ending with a display of very accurate air-to-ground firing with guns and rockets. We also had a brief visit to the newly built Joint HQ at Mönchengladbach – HQ 2nd Tactical Air Force – which was like a well-laid-out modern town and most impressive.

This was the last visit of the tour, and we left Germany on the morning of 30 July, arriving in Brussels in the late afternoon with a chance to look around the city, have a meal, and do final shopping before boarding the coaches (of which we were heartily weary by this time) at ten o'clock in the evening for the drive across Belgium and France, reaching Boulogne just after daybreak. Following a night spent on hard seats, the Channel crossing and the final miles to Bracknell, we were all thankful to be home again, after a unique and memorable experience. To quote *The Hawk* yet again:

> There were many incidents and personal experiences which helped to cement friendships and which played no small part in our increased knowledge of each other. Some of these, no doubt, will become legends and will be retold to posterity in Officers' Mess bars and Service clubs.

As I mentioned when describing the course routine, Wednesday afternoons were devoted to sport when the programme made this possible. I have never been a devotee of team games, though of course I played cricket and football at school. Since there was a flourishing gliding club at White Waltham (a small grass airfield nearby), I and several other students opted to learn to glide, and very much enjoyed the experience. The gliders were winched off the ground, climbing at what seemed to be a phenomenally steep angle and then released at several hundred feet for a circuit of the aerodrome, or perbaps two circuits if the weather made any lift available (in hot weather lift could always be found off the hangar roof), followed by a landing. My instructor was an officer of the local Air Training Corps, and was very skilful and experienced; as I had discovered during my wartime training, I was not a natural pilot, but at least was now more confident and experienced, and managed to go solo and qualify for British Gliding Association 'A' and 'B' certificates. Interestingly enough, of the seven Staff College students who qualified, only one was already a pilot.

Intermittently throughout the Bracknell course we were able to fly from White Waltham, mostly in Ansons or Chipmunks (plus one flight in a Balliol trainer with Bill Horsman), with one short trip in a Westland-Sikorsky helicopter. With the odd flight in a Canberra and a Shackleton, I logged over twenty-eight flying hours at Bracknell – not bad for an academic course.

And much of the course was genuinely academic. Apart from the exercises in staff papers of various sorts, each student was required to write two essays on a subject of his choice. For the first I chose a theme I knew little about but found very interesting – 'The Problem of Germany'. This entailed a great deal of reading, and I spent quite a lot of time in the College library. The finished essay reviewed the progress of Germany (both Federal and 'Democratic') since 1945, and suggested a possible future scenario. John Gilchrist, who was now my syndicate DS, made

Members of the 9th (West Riding) Battalion Home Guard on guard duty at Seven Arches Viaduct in North Leeds in 1941. L to R: Pte Cropper, Pte Guest, Cpl Boyle and Sgt Sleightholme.

'Citizen's Army'. No 2031 Deferred Service Squadron Air Traing Corps on parade in Roundhay Park, Leeds, in1942. Author on left in front rank. (*Yorkshire Post*)

Under training at No 5 Air Observers School, RAF Jurby in January 1944. L to R: Ken Bender, Fisher, Joe, Higgins, Cropper, Reed and Nuttall.

Crewed up – No 1651 Heavy Conversion Unit, RAF Wratting Common in February 1944. Standing L to R: Tex Savard, mid upper gunner; Author, Navigator; Ken Grosse, Flight Engineer; Al Moore, Pilot and Captain. Sitting: Willy Williams, Wireless Op; Mickey Bartlett, Bomb Aimer and Pat Wade, Rear Gunner.

103 Squadron at RAF Elsham Wolds. L to R; Ken, Mick, Eric, Pat, Tex and ground crew of Lancaster G-George in May 1944.

Pat – Rear Gunner in a flotation suit in May 1944.

Bombing-up G-George.
Armourer with a 1,000 bomb,
May 1944.

Eric at Elsham Wolds in
May 1944.

Eric at RAF Blyton in February 1945.

Eric with his wife Joan on their wedding day on 21 July 1945.

Morning NAAFI break with 7 Squadron, Mepal on 17 June 1946. The tail of the new Mk VII (FE) Lancaster is just visible. *(Crown Copyright)*

No 3 Specialist Navigation Conversion Course, Empire Air Navigation School at RAF Shawbury in Spring 1948.The author is in the back row, 2nd from right. Centre front row Sqn Ldr Pepperman and 3rd from right Ron Davis.

Eric and his wife at HQ Bomber Command Annual Ball in September 1948.

A Lincoln Mk2 of 57 Squadron over Khartoum and the Nile, with port inner engine stopped, February 1949.

Grounded Lincoln at Khartoum, the problem under discussion. L to R: Eric, *Times* correspondent, Sqn Ldr Ellen, OC 57 Squadron in February 1949.

Lincoln engine being replaced at Khartoum in February 1949.

The faithful Morris 10 on a picnic in 1950.

Field work at Farnborough in 1952.

Vickers Viscount prototype G-AHRF. The mast aerials are visible behind the cockpit and the suppressed (plate) aerial high on the tail. July 1951. *(Crown Copyright)*

Freddy Stringer with Viscount G-AHRF at Geneva in October 1951.

Prop trouble on G-AHRF at Geneva in 1951.

The author in an Anson for continuation training at Hendon in 1954.

Wg Cdr Burnett and Flt Lt Pete Wells at the navigation table in Hastings 327 during the eclipse flight. *(Central Press Photos Ltd)*

The Crew of Hastings 327 of the RAF Flying College, Manby, before the flight to view the total solar eclipse in June 1954. Eric on left and captain Wg Cdr Burnett. *(Central Press Photos Ltd)*

The Astronomer-Royal, Sir Harold Spencer-Jones, viewing the eclipse from Hastings 327. *(Central Press Photos Ltd)*

The total solar eclipse
of 30 June 1954.
(Central Press Photos Ltd)

A visit by No 45 Staff College Course to the Bristol Aeroplane Co in 1955. Eric is 4th from right on the 2nd row. Centre of front row is Air Cdr Faville, the Assistant Commandant at the RAF Staff College.

The end of course pantomime at Bracknell in December 1955. AVM MacFadyen, the Commandant, front row centre.

The midnight sun over Port Clarence, Seward Peninsula, seen from a Civil Air Patrol Piper Pacer in June 1956.

Mount McKinley, seen from a T-33A jet trainer in May 1956.

A de Havilland Beaver (L-20) floatplane at Six Mile Lake near Elmendorf in 1956.

encouraging comments (apart from his view that I over-used the comma) as did the Group Director, Group Captain Prichard, who, however, felt that I could have been more adventurous and creative in looking at the future: I was in entire agreement. For the second and last essay I wrote about the problems of the Ministry of Supply and its responsibility for the production of military aircraft; at least this was a subject I knew something about after my years at Farnborough and the Air Ministry. This again was well received, but with some reservations about my over-use of 'long and impressive-sounding words in preference to the use of a more simple and direct style' and weak paragraph construction; I am still trying to deal with these weaknesses.

With the end of the course in sight, students were beginning to think about their next postings and to worry about what the Air Ministry 'P' staff might have in store for them. A list of provisional postings was circulated towards the end of November, and Joan and I were not particularly pleased to note that we were to go to Singapore so that I could take up a post on the Operations Staff of HQ Far East Air Force. Many people were keen to go overseas, but we were quite happy in the UK, where I had been lucky enough to be stationed for all my service, and we did not particularly like what we had heard about the climate in the Far East. One consolation was that John Digman was also posted to HQ FEAF, so that our families could plan and perhaps travel together with mutual support.

The last days of the course seemed to be upon us suddenly. There were no final examinations, but we had graduated and would qualify for the coveted symbol 'psa' after our names in the Air Force List – a significant help, we hoped, in our future careers. We had our end-of-course interviews with the Commandant, who, like all the DS, was encouraging; I cannot now remember what he said to me except for his final words, with a Biblical ring: 'Don't hide your light under a bushel.' I suppose this meant that I was seen as not sufficiently self-assertive, and I had no quarrel with that.

We had the final Guest Night followed by a hilarious pantomime put on by some of the students ('1955 and still Clueless'), with all the course's in-jokes and merciless leg-pulling of the DS. I sat just behind the Commandant in the audience and have a photograph of both of us roaring with laughter.

Then, suddenly, it was all over – the endless writing, exercises, discussion, lectures, the visits and tours, fascinating but exhausting; all behind us. It had been a truly valuable experience, an education in every sense of the word, and I shall always be grateful for that sabbatical year. An additional bonus was the formation of many friendships which would stand us in good stead throughout our service careers.

On the day after the formal end of the course, I had still had no confirmation of my provisional posting, although those of most students had now been confirmed. I walked up to the College Adjutant's office and was told that my final posting notice had just been received. To say that I was taken aback when I read it is a gross understatement: I was posted to Headquarters Alaskan Air Command, Elmendorf Air Force Base, Alaska, on the Operations Staff, to take effect at the end of March 1956. This was one of the exchange posts with the USAF which had been set up not long after the end of the war, when, following the Aries flights from Shawbury, the RAF had become leaders in polar navigation and the USAF felt that this expertise would be useful in Alaska; the post was established for a Specialist Navigator. The Americans soon overtook us in their polar experience, but apparently liked having an RAF navigator in Alaska, and retained the exchange. Before the posting took effect I was to undergo a short jet conversion course.

I walked home in something of a daze to break the news to Joan, and after fielding the usual boisterous welcome in the kitchen from our dog Bunty, said, 'You'll never guess where we're posted to.' I was even more shaken when Joan said, 'I suppose you'll tell me it's Alaska.' How she knew or guessed I still do not know to this day, but she swears that this was the most unlikely place she could think of. Since we had acclimatized our thinking to the Far East, we had to make a rapid readjustment. It was an honour to be accepted for a USAF exchange post, and it would be a new and exciting experience. But Alaska? We had visions of perpetual ice, snow and fog and perhaps primitive living conditions – igloos? We were of course well adrift in our initial reactions: we discovered that Elmendorf was a large well-established base close to Anchorage, the main city (though not the capital) of the Territory of Alaska. Married quarters would be provided and there would be a school for the children. We had three months' grace to get ourselves organized for a move to the other side of the world (I calculated that Elmendorf was around four-and-a-half thousand miles from Bracknell), and the College would allow us to occupy our house until then.

For the moment there was not a great deal we could do towards the move. We spent Christmas at Bracknell and then had a few days in Leeds over the New Year, where we told our respective parents what the future had in store for us. Back at home, the making of many lists and many arrangements began, but on 11 January I reported to No. 231 Operational Conversion Unit at Bassingbourn in Cambridgeshire for No. 37 Short Canberra Course.

*   *   *

Presumably the Air Ministry felt that officers going to USAF exchange posts should be jet-experienced; that seemed reasonable to me, and I was keen to get to grips with one of the most successful aircraft produced by the British aircraft industry. The Canberra continued in service for many years (and the Americans manufactured numbers of them under licence for the USAF). It was expected to be phased out in the early 1960s, but the cancellation of the TSR2 aircraft caused it to be retained as the main tactical strike aircraft until the early 1970s, and even as late as the 1990s it was still used in specialized roles – target towing, calibration of navigation aids and early warning. Since the first RAF Canberra flew in 1952, the type gave at least forty years' service, something almost unheard of in the twenty-first century, when a weapons system tends to be obsolescent as soon as it comes into service.

The four-and-a-half-week course at Bassingbourn started, as most flying courses do, with ground school, in which we were given a thorough grounding in the somewhat complex electrical systems of the aircraft, the aircraft performance data, the operating and emergency procedures, and the navigation equipment. All the students were experienced aviators and some already had jet experience (I could hardly count my few odd flights in Meteors at RAE and the Canberra at Staff College). I was crewed with a Wing Commander Marshall, of whom I remember little except that he was a pleasant personality and a competent pilot (most of the time). We had to accustom ourselves to an aircraft with a much higher performance than either of us had been used to, and to thinking of airspeed in relation to Mach number (the ratio of the actual speed to the speed of sound) as well as in knots, with operating heights of 40,000 or 45,000 feet at over 400 knots. At these altitudes the True Air Speed (TAS) could well be twice the figure being shown on the airspeed indicator, and we were taught several different ways of calculating the TAS, including the use of the (manual) Mark IV Height and TAS Computer. Luckily the aircraft were equipped with air position indicators so that an accurate air plot could be kept.

Navigation techniques were much as we had been used to in conventional bomber aircraft – a fix every six minutes, using Gee Mark II (or Mark III, the miniaturized version) with strict adherence to track and timing, and homings and let-downs using Rebecca Mark IV and the associated Blind Approach Beam System with which I had become so familiar in the Bomber Command Examining Flight. The speed of the aircraft meant that when plotting a turning point a turning-circle of about four nautical miles' radius had to be allowed for.

With a crew of one pilot and one or two navigators, the latter had to take a greater interest in the aircraft systems, and we carried a very comprehensive list of over a hundred different fuses, and had to become familiar with the electrical systems, controls and indicators, plus the oxygen and demisting systems. After a decompression chamber session to ensure that we had no medical problems at heights up to 50,000 feet, we had our written ground school examinations and emergency drills and were then ready to fly.

Our first few flights were in the dual-control Canberra T4 with a pilot instructor, during which I was able to familiarize myself with the navigation aids and practise let-downs and BABS approaches. We then progressed to the B2, and for the last two flights Wing Commander Marshall was solo. As I said, he was a competent pilot, but he made one error which I could only put down to absent-mindedness: as we were on finals for landing after local flying, the tower asked us if we were intending to land off this approach, and got the answer 'Affirmative'. Back they came with 'Your wheels are not down', and as we were almost on the runway at this stage Marshall had to put on full power and go round again. He apologized and we did not discuss it further, but I certainly was grateful for the alertness of the controller. Our final flight was a short cross-country which we managed without problems, and we were then Canberra qualified.

I enjoyed the challenge of a new type with greatly increased performance, but I cannot say that I enjoyed working in the confined conditions of the navigator's position in the rear of the aircraft, where there was little outside view. Not only that, but being attached to the ejector seat by a multiplicity of connections was not comfortable, though I suppose I would have got used to it in time. My idea of a suitable aircraft was still one in which I could stand up and walk about.

* * *

Back home at Bracknell in mid-February, all was action: getting removal and storage tenders, advertising the car for sale, organizing kit and other insurance, fitting in dental appointments, and a host of other things, including complicated financial arrangements.

We were due to 'march out' of our married quarter on 16 March and sail to New York on 17 March on the Cunard White Star ship RMS *Media*, and it was with great relief that we found ourselves on the train, with our hand-luggage, on the way to Liverpool with all the wearisome preparations behind us, and a new and very different two years ahead of us.

CHAPTER THIRTEEN

Northern Exchange

After a night in a Liverpool hotel and some last-minute shopping, we boarded the RMS *Media* on a cold, grey afternoon. Joan's parents and sister Enid had kindly driven over from Leeds to see us off, and we were able to entertain them in our family cabin before visitors had to go ashore. The ship left Prince's Landing Stage about half-past four in the afternoon, and we moved slowly down the Mersey with a final view of the Liver Birds as they disappeared into the gathering gloom; if I remember correctly a light drizzle was falling.

The *Media* was one of the smaller Cunarders, with a single funnel and first-class accommodation throughout. The standards of cabins, catering and stewarding were extremely high and we could not have been looked after more efficiently. Unfortunately the Atlantic weather was not co-operative, and the ship's log for the second day out read: 'Strong south-east breeze, rough sea, heavy north-west swell, overcast, showers'. Gales were experienced later, and the weather remained poor for most of the voyage, which instead of the scheduled seven days took nearly eight, with the ship sailing at reduced speed for almost two days. Susan, Jenny and I felt unwell for a day or so, but poor Joan was incapacitated for several days, spending most of the time in her bunk feeling ghastly ('Stop the ship!').

However, she recovered in due course and was able to spend time on the deck sitting in a comfortable steamer chair with rugs and waiting for the morning drink of beef tea.

Once the girls had found their sea legs they were able to explore the ship, and we have photographs of them skipping on deck in one of the few sunny spells, and playing with two other RAF children whose parents, Wing Commander and Mrs Iliffe, were on their way to Washington (I remember that the children were called Chaucer and Freya, sufficiently unusual in those days). We found in conversation that the Iliffes knew the Waite family, who had owned our cottage at Loosley Row in Buckinghamshire when I worked at HQ Bomber Command in the late forties. They told us that Jan Waite, their daughter, with whom we had been very friendly, now worked in Washington; they gave us her telephone number in the hope that we would be able to make contact in the few days we would have in the capital. That was the first coincidence.

We finally docked in New York early in the morning on Sunday 25 March, taking in that skyline which was so familiar but which we had never thought to see; dominated then by the Empire State Building, nowadays of comparatively modest dimensions. After clearing Customs we claimed the room already booked for us at the Governor Clinton Hotel opposite Pennsylvania Railroad Station – a rather old-fashioned establishment but our first taste of American living. After eight days at sea we were all a little disoriented, but found our way to Times Square and Broadway and to the top of the Empire State for the panoramic view of this tremendous city. One odd memory that stays with us is that of the smell of cigars in the street (was this purely a Sunday phenomenon?).

The following morning we crossed the street to Penn Station and caught the 1030 train to Washington, from which we were able to see something of everyday America as it appeared and disappeared alongside the railroad. We were met in Washington by someone from the British Joint Services Mission, which was responsible, among other things, for administering the hundred or so RAF exchange officers throughout the USA. I was due to spend the next three days being briefed and coping with various arcane administrative processes, and we were relieved to be taken to a self-contained apartment in a block known as the Gralyn and kept especially for British military transients – a large family room with bathroom and kitchen facilities where we could make ourselves at home for the short time involved. It was in a quiet part of the city but close to shops, and we made our first acquaintance with a supermarket – Magruder's, a small one by modern standards, but to us a novel and exciting experience, walking round the laden shelves with a trolley to buy a few basics such as tea and something for breakfast; the children were enchanted.

We telephoned Jan Waite's number and she was delighted to hear from us, arranging to pick us up from the apartment and take us all for a drive-in lunch. We hadn't seen her for some seven years (and of course Jenny had never seen her), but picked up where we had left off; she hadn't changed, but was understandably more sophisticated and slightly Americanized. Now came the second coincidence. We were driving down Pennsylvania Avenue, past imposing government buildings, and telling Jan about our job in Alaska. When we mentioned that we were to go to Elmendorf Air Force Base, she exclaimed and almost stopped the car, in the middle of the heavy lunch-hour traffic. Recovering, she told us that she was now married to an officer in the USAF, that he was being posted to Elmendorf, and that she would be joining him later. This was indeed an unlooked-for, not to say incredible, bonus – that we would have a friend in what we still tended to think of as the wilderness. This rather overshadowed the novelty of the drive-in restaurant, but the children enjoyed it. We arranged to keep in touch until we met again in Alaska.

Reporting next day to BJSM's Air Force Staff at 1800 West K Street, I found that most of my time was taken up with form filling, financial arrangements for pay and allowances, and reading endless instructions and regulations. There was little in the way of briefing for my particular job, and I got the impression that the administrative staff there knew little about it and cared less; I suppose this was to be expected in the circumstances. I did have an interview with the Head of the Air Force Staff, an air vice-marshal, but the only thing I recall is his concern that as I was shown in my personal documents as an agnostic I might offend the largely church-going Americans in some way. I thought this was somewhat small minded, but managed to reassure him that I should be keeping a low profile in religious matters. One thing I managed to achieve was to initiate arrangements for Susan to take what were known as Moray House tests – an overseas equivalent of the Eleven-Plus examination for progress to secondary education in the UK – since she would reach the qualifying age while we were in Alaska.

No doubt we spent any remaining time in looking around Washington, but I have no special memory of that. On our final day we rose early and caught the plane to Seattle – the first time Joan and the girls had flown since a short flight in a light aircraft at Waddington in 1949. Staging at Chicago, we arrived at Seattle in the evening after a very long day (I recorded that we had risen at 3 a.m. Pacific Standard Time and finally gone to bed at 10.30 p.m. PST). We saw nothing of Seattle except the hotel and the airport, but were glad to be on the final leg at last. Most of the flight was over cloud, but as we descended on the run in to Anchorage, we could see a mass of craggy mountains amid an inhospitable-looking landscape.

*   *   *

'Alaska' – 'the big land' or 'mainland' in one of the native languages. It certainly is big: as large as Texas, California and Montana put together, nearly 600,000 square miles. In 1956 it still had Territorial status, but there was a strong movement towards statehood, which finally came in 1959. The capital was and is Juneau in the southern 'panhandle' which runs alongside British Columbia in Canada, but about half of Alaska's population (mostly white but with some Indian and Inuit) lives in or near the city of Anchorage, in the Pacific Coast area facing the Gulf of Alaska; the total Alaskan population is now around half a million. This area is backed by the Alaska Range of mountains, which keep off some of the Arctic winds, so that the climate is comparatively mild in winter; the region was wryly called the 'Banana Belt'. Most of the farming land is in this area, but since the 1960s the oil industry has increased the population in the Kenai Peninsula just south of Anchorage.

Mount McKinley, in the Alaska Range, is the highest mountain in North America at 20,300 feet, and the Mount McKinley National Park has been set aside as a game reserve and is a major tourist attraction. On a clear day the mountain could be seen from the Anchorage area over a hundred miles away.

In the interior, between the Alaska and Brooks Ranges, Fairbanks is another centre of population and the terminus of the Alaska Railroad and Alaska Highway from the south. Much of the land in the interior is tundra, flat, treeless and wet in summer, when temperatures can be as high as 90° F in the shade, but really cold in winter – sometimes more than 60° below zero, or 90° F of frost. Also at Fairbanks is the University of Alaska, and there are gold-mining plants nearby, although large modern dredges have replaced the whiskered prospector with his mule and his hand-panning. Several thousand Athabascan Indians live in this area.

Western Alaska extends to the Bering Sea, with Russian Siberia only a few miles across the Bering Straits. Two tiny dots either side of the international boundary are the Diomede Islands – Big Diomede on the Russian side, Little Diomede in Alaska. There are many Eskimos – nowadays termed Inuit – in this region, and Nome is the largest town, still something like a Wild West frontier town with its wooden saloons and sidewalks. The climate is not good: strong winds and high humidity in winter, cool, rainy and foggy in summer.

South-western Alaska includes the Alaskan Peninsula, the curving Aleutian Islands chain and the Kodiak group. The Aleutians stretch another 1,500 miles out into the Pacific and form one of the world's most inhospitable regions – cold, wet, cloudy and foggy for most of the year. The entire region is mountainous from one end to the other and almost entirely treeless. This is a land of active volcanoes, and it is one of the world's most active earthquake belts; Mount Katmai erupted in 1912 and Mount Spurr in 1964 (causing a lot of damage in the city of Anchorage). About 5,000 Aleuts live in south-western Alaska, a people related to the Inuit but with their own customs and language.

The area north of the Brooks Range and bordering the Arctic Ocean (usually called the Arctic Slope nowadays) has average temperatures about 17° below zero F in winter and about 40° above in the summer, although there can be freezing temperatures at any time of year. There are more than two months of perpetual darkness in winter and about the same period of continual summer daylight. Until the early 1950s, when the Distant Early Warning (DEW) line of defence radars was built along the north coast, there were very few whites in the area, and the population was largely Inuit, mostly living in villages, with trading-posts and native schools. Things have again changed, more dramatically, in recent years with the setting up of the oil fields in the Prudhoe Bay area, from which the Trans-Alaska Pipeline runs all the way down to Valdez in the south; Alaska is now second only to Texas in oil production in the United States.

There is a long prehistory: it is thought that the earliest immigrants came across from Asia as much as 15,000 years ago and that these were the Indian groups which eventually spread to the rest of the Americas. Inuit and Aleuts seem to be much later arrivals, perhaps 8,000 to 3,000 years ago. Conversely the modern history of the country is short, and could be said to start in 1724, when Peter the Great of Russia sent Captain Vitus Bering, a Danish mariner, to explore the land areas of Siberia. In 1728 he sailed into the sea now named after him, and sighted some of the islands between the two land masses. In another expedition in 1740 Bering landed on the mainland near Mount St Elias, and another ship landed near Sitka. Gradually Russian fur traders and trappers began to enter the area, and by 1800 there were a few settlements at Kodiak and on the Pribilov Islands, mainly to exploit the fur seals. Other settlements were formed along the mainland coasts, with Sitka as the Russian capital, but Russia felt that the country was something of a liability and tried to sell it to the USA as early as 1855. Alaska was finally sold to the Americans in 1867 for just over seven million dollars, the Secretary of State of the day, Seward, coming under much criticism for this transaction – 'Seward's Folly' and 'Seward's Icebox', as it was called. Congress paid little attention to this new acquisition for nearly twenty years, during which time there was no civil government and the country was run at various times by the Army, the Navy and the Treasury Department. Little exploration was done and there was little use of the natural resources.

Then came the Gold Rush, first in the Klondyke in Canada, to which the most accessible route was via the Alaskan panhandle, and then in Nome and Fairbanks. This awakened interest in the country and helped to open up the interior. Later, from 1940 for about twenty years, the US government invested nearly two billion dollars in the development of military bases in Alaska: this brought thousands of residents into the country, created jobs, and improved transportation and communications.

The population increased from about 70,000 to nearly a quarter of a million, and half of this was in the Anchorage area, where Elmendorf Air Force Base had a population of about 25,000.

* * *

Some of this background I had read up before we travelled to Alaska, but when we arrived at Anchorage International Airport our first preoccupation was getting ourselves sorted out domestically. We were met by the two RAF exchange officers already at Elmendorf, Gerry Daly and

Flight Lieutenant Hugh ('Jimmy') James, a characterful fighter pilot flying F-89D (Scorpion) jets with the 10th Air Division; they were accompanied by their families and gave us a friendly and helpful welcome. The first stop was the 'Chateau' at Elmendorf, a sort of transit hotel (normally for VIPs) where we had kindly been booked in until we could move into the Dalys' married quarter. We were thankful to go to bed that night after another long day of travel; our rooms were comfortable but the building was stiflingly overheated although the outside temperatures were not particularly low. The Alaskan 'break-up' had started – that period between winter and spring when the snows start to melt and everything looks slushy and dirty, sometimes with rain and low cloud or fog.

We had corresponded with the Dalys and had some idea of what to expect, but were impressed at the sheer size of the base. Construction had started back in 1940, and the base had been named after Captain Hugh M Elmendorf, an Air Corps officer killed in an aircraft accident at Wright Field, Ohio, in 1933. Always strategically important for the USA's defence, Alaska had taken on added significance with the start of the Cold War, and Elmendorf had gradually increased in size and capability. It housed both the joint Alaskan Command headquarters and that of the Alaskan Air Command, the 10th Air Division providing fighter defence, and many other flying and support units. With plenty of real estate available, the base sprawled over a wide area; the Château stood on the wide main boulevard, on the other side of which and not far away were the blocks of married quarters where we would live, built round a rectangular 'quad'. Mount Spurr School, which Sue and Jenny would be attending, was just across the boulevard. Looking south and west the impressive Chugach Mountains could be seen, with the highest point around 13,000 feet, forming a backdrop which always lifted our hearts. Besides the necessary military buildings – accommodation blocks, offices, messes, stores, etc. – there were many clubs, three cinemas, two chapels catering for various denominations, a library, a post office, a bank, and many base exchange facilities: these included shops of various sorts, cafeterias, coffee bars, a service station, dry cleaning, barber shops, bowling alleys and so on and so on – the American way of life with which we were to become so familiar. It was said that many people never went off base, and we could understand why.

The first few days were taken up with a multiplicity of administrative processes – security clearance, getting a driving licence, registering at the bank and the mail office, passes for the commissary (meat and other foodstuffs for families), the base exchange, the officers' club and so on. I took over Gerry's middle-aged Dodge, which had been his predecessor's (and was handed on to my successor and then the exchange officer after him), and was indoctrinated into driving a left-hand drive car while driving on the right. We had arrived on Good Friday and the children were able to start school on the day after Easter Monday, while we moved into our quarters on the following Thursday, Gerry and his family having transferred to the Chateau. It was a relief to be in our own space again (and to control our own room temperature) despite our heavy baggage not having arrived. The house was one of a block fronting on to the main boulevard, with kitchen, combined dining- and sitting-room, three bedrooms and a bathroom, with the added bonus of that American boon, the basement – a very large area with what we would now call utility-room facilities and with plenty of space for children's activities. Our trunks and packing-cases took another two weeks to arrive, but meanwhile Joan performed her usual miracles of improvisation even in this completely new environment. Our neighbours were friendly and welcoming – Major Chuck Brown (Command Flight Safety Officer) and his wife Zona on one side, and Major and Mrs Benny Tack (a dental officer) on the other.

At the same time I was having a rapid handover from Gerry to my new job in the Command headquarters, a large imposing building painted a light green and known universally as 'the Kremlin'.

* * *

The Alaskan Command was the first of the joint or unified commands in the US armed forces, and was formed in 1947. Its mission (and all units in the US forces have a stated mission) was the defence of Alaska and the protection of the United States from attack through the polar regions and Alaska. The Commander-in-Chief (CINCAL) was always a USAF general officer, and in my time was Major-General Frank A. Armstrong, who had commanded heavy bombers in the UK during the Second World War. He and his staff, which included an Army brigadier-general as Chief of Staff and a US Navy captain as Deputy Chief of Staff, were housed in the same headquarters building as the Alaskan Air Command (AAC), the air component of Alaskan Command and the predominating one. The US Army Headquarters (USARAL) was at Fort Richardson, a few miles from Elmendorf, while the US Navy element (known as the Alaskan Sea Frontier) was based at Kodiak in the south.

AAC had a threefold mission, against the background of the Cold War: to give early warning of any attack on the Continental United States; to provide air defence for Alaska and the North-west Arctic approaches to the Continental USA; and to provide a launching platform, if necessary, for retaliatory Strategic Air Command bombers. AAC was also actively engaged in the support and operation of the western segment of the Distant Early Warning (DEW) Line, the chain of radars established along the Arctic coast to detect any air attack from the USSR. Various other functions included an air rescue service, support of polar weather reconnaissance, participation in annual Arctic manoeuvres, and support for polar research projects. The air defence role was carried out by the 10th Air Division (Defense) based at Elmendorf and operating two Northrop F-89D (Scorpion) squadrons and eight Aircraft Control and Warning (ACW) squadrons covering the southern half of Alaska; and by the 11th Air Division (Defense) at Ladd AFB close to Fairbanks in the centre of the Territory, with one F-89D squadron and ten ACW squadrons covering Alaska's northern half. Eielson AFB, twenty-six miles south of Fairbanks, had a three-mile runway from which to operate SAC aircraft, and was also the base for the 58th Weather Reconnaissance Squadron's daily weather flights with WB-29 (later WB-50) aircraft over the polar regions. Its controlling HQ, 7th Weather Group, was at Elmendorf, from which also operated the 71st Air Rescue Squadron with Piasecki H-21 helicopters and Grumman SA-16B (Albatross) amphibians (a second Air Rescue squadron operated from Ladd when I first arrived, but was later withdrawn, presumably for financial reasons). Both Elmendorf and Ladd housed Operations squadrons providing transport aircraft for the movement of men and materiel around the Territory, and in particular to remote radar sites; they used the old, reliable C-47 (Dakota), the C-119 (Boxcar), the H-21 helicopter and the ubiquitous de Havilland L-20 (Beaver), a small single-engined aircraft which put on skis in the winter and floats in the summer for true bush-flying.

All this perhaps tedious detail gives some idea of the many and various tasks of the Command – information I had to absorb quickly since I found that my job involved me with most of them. I worked in the Directorate of Operations and Training (OT) in the headquarters, with the job title 'Navigation, Reconnaissance and Rescue Officer', something like an RAF Command Navigation Officer but with several additional aspects. The first shock was that we worked in a large open office area with many desks fairly closely spaced, although the Director, Colonel Gray, had his own office – he was something of a character, very well disposed to the British since he had flown Mustangs with them in the Second World War, and very welcoming to me. My immediate supervisor was Major Steve Farris, a pilot (as, in fact, were all the OT staff officers) who was a West Pointer with a forthright personality and became a good friend. I discovered that, unlike the RAF system in which an established post must be filled by an officer of a specific rank, in the USAF a slot or space could be filled by someone one rank up or down; so, for instance, where ideally a major should report to a lieutenant-colonel who should report to a full ('bird') colonel, all three of these spaces could be filled by lieutenant-colonels, a situation which I experienced for a short period. With strong personalities, this could (and did) cause problems.

My immediate USAF colleagues were used to working with an exchange officer, and tempered the wind to the shorn lamb. However, since much of my work was done with units outside the headquarters, I spent a lot of time on the phone and had to cope with a variety of accents and the verbal shorthand invariably used for procedures and unit names. I soon learnt to modify my own accent and modes of speech to make myself fully understood, and also to adhere to USAF staff writing methods while trying to retain clarity and acceptable English (so much for all the work put into service writing at Bracknell).

As in most staff jobs at Command level, I was responsible for supervision ('monitoring' was the word used in my job description) of the work of formations down the chain of command. I was concerned with the adequacy and utilization of navigation aids and flight facilities (including instrument approach procedures); with search and rescue (SAR) policy and procedures, including the activities of the Command Joint SAR Center and Air Rescue units; with aeronautical charts and aeronautical information publications through the Aeronautical Chart and Information Office, Alaska; with all requests for air photography; and with the activities of the 7th Weather Group and its reconnaissance flights. At the end of the first year in post (1956), the job title was changed to 'Navigation Aids and Air Traffic Control Officer', the air photography requirement was removed, and responsibility for monitoring air traffic control facilities and procedures added. Of course, I had no formal air traffic control qualifications or training, but this work had really been part of the job from the beginning when I found that I was the Executive Secretary to the Air Defense Planning Board jointly established by AAC and the Fifth Region, Civil Aeronautics Administration (CAA). In the USA proper (variously called the Continental USA or the Zone of the Interior – more usually 'Zee Eye' in the vernacular), the air traffic control system was much more highly developed than in the UK; a network of airways with radio ranges and low-frequency radio beacons had been established from the 1930s, when civil aviation had developed nationwide, and during and since the Second World War there had been close liaison with military aviation in the provision of flight facilities. Since the overall airways and air traffic control systems in Alaska were the statutory responsibility of the Civil Aeronautics Administration, as in the Continental USA, the military – as the major users in the Territory – had to work closely with them, hence the joint CAA/AAC committee. All military flight facilities in Alaska were installed, operated and maintained by the Alaskan Airways and Air Communications (AACS) Service, which was administratively part of the USAF's Military Air Transport Service (MATS) but operationally controlled by Alaskan Air Command. This mixture of roles and responsibilities sounds like a potential disaster, but in fact I found that it worked well in practice once I had established personal contact with the individuals at CAA and AACS who could make things happen. I remember particularly Tom Walker, the operations planner of 5th Region CAA, with whom I established an immediate rapport, and who, luckily for me, remained in post for most of my tour; he had thirty years' service with CAA, so was knowledgeable and also unflappable – a sterling character.

My brief was to supervise the operational use of navaids and flight facilities, air traffic control procedures, airspace use, and instrument approach procedures in the Alaskan Air Command, and the first job was to become familiar with the appropriate regulations. I was not immediately impressed by the standard of staff work in the headquarters (a subject to which I will return), but I did find that the system of USAF regulations was well organized and efficient: the same pattern was followed from Headquarters USAF level down the formations to squadron level, and they were arranged in sections for the various broad subjects – 55 series for operations, 60 for flying and so on. I was responsible for keeping several AAC regulations (AACRs) current, including those dealing with the 7th Weather Group, the USAF Radar Advisory Service, Notices to Airmen, and Search and Rescue. Regulations were generally taken very seriously – 'If it isn't in the regulations you can't do it' – and we often received signals asking for waivers in specific circumstances so that common-sense action could be taken.

Work with the 7th Weather Group caused few problems: it had been flying almost daily weather reconnaissance flights in the polar regions for many years, and it had become a routine, though there were of course battles with the weather itself in the inhospitable Alaskan winters. I had very much more to do with the Rescue Group, particularly with the 71st Air Rescue Squadron at Elmendorf, operating on a continuous alert basis with five SA-16B amphibians and five SH-21B twin-rotor helicopters, and I had a close relationship with the Squadron Commander, first Colonel Stenglein and later Colonel Speer. Rescue incidents were comparatively numerous, from picking up hunters stranded in bad weather to incidents with civil aircraft; at that time the numbers of civil aircraft in Alaska per head of population were the highest in the world, mostly small aircraft on skis or floats flown by bush pilots, many of them kept at Lake Hood on the outskirts of Anchorage. Some of these pilots were rugged individualists, and they often flew off to some remote lake without telling anyone where they were going, let alone filing a flight plan; a lot of time, effort and money was wasted on looking for them when they failed to return. Conversely, incidents with military aircraft were few.

In the beginning I found the assimilation of new procedures – almost a new language – and the wide spread of responsibilities somewhat daunting, but my USAF colleagues were very supportive, and I consoled myself by remembering Gerry Daly's advice that I could always go out and fly. Rated (i.e. flying) officers in the USAF were required to keep themselves in practice, and there was usually someone out of the office and in the air; in fact, most of the officers in Operations and Training heartily disliked staff work and seemed to do as little of it as possible, mostly on the telephone. (They were not helped by the so-called filing system, which kept all correspondence loose in folders relating only to the current and past year, previous files having been disposed of, so that project histories were hard to come by. The Bracknell DS would have been appalled.)

A tradition had become established in the headquarters that the RAF exchange officer would act as navigator for the Commander AAC and also for the Joint Commander (CINCAL) when they used one of the two C-54 (Skymaster) aircraft at their disposal for official flights. These were four-engined transport aircraft well established in the USAF and with good performance and reliability. Nominally belonging to 5040th Operations Flight at Elmendorf, the C-54s were fitted up as VIP aircraft and were comfortable to fly in as passengers. The navigator was not so lucky, since the aircraft had no permanent navigation table or seating, and I had to pull down a folding table and use a loose stool to sit on; for some of the longer flights this was very tiring. I equipped myself with USAF flight plan and log forms, a copy of HO 249 (the American tables for precomputation of celestial observations), plus HO 211 altitude and azimuth tables and the Standard Operating Procedures for the navigation equipment carried by the C-54. This included Loran, a cloud-and-collision warning radar with a ground-mapping scope for the navigator, a radio compass (essential for airways flying), a drift meter, and an astro-compass. The compass system was the Pioneer Magnesyn, not unlike the RAF's DR compass but without any air position indicator; this was a blow – I would be back to manual air plots after some twelve years. I obtained a sextant but found it complicated and almost twice as heavy as the Mark 9 series, and I think I only used it on one flight.

My logbook tells me that I first flew (as navigator) a couple of weeks after I arrived, in one of the two VIP C-54s with Captain Dick Wolfersperger as pilot. He regularly flew these aircraft with one or other of the generals aboard, and was a very experienced, unflappable pilot; his quiet, almost taciturn, manner belied his sense of humour and his ability to cope efficiently with emergencies. I did a great deal of flying with him in Alaska and had tremendous confidence in him. On this occasion we took off early in the morning and flew to Nome via stops at Ladd and North-east Cape (an Aircraft Control and Warning site in the north). This was a routine flight to Dick, using normal airways procedures, which meant that I could concentrate on familiarizing myself with the aircraft and its navigation equipment without having to worry too much about the navigation. There were no VIPs, so it was a relaxed occasion; my memory of the flight is vague, but I must have been enthralled by the Alaskan terrain, of which we covered a great deal. Unfortunately our schedule required very short ground times, and I was unable to see much of our destinations except the operations block.

This was the first of many flights, mostly in Alaska, but some to Canada or the Continental USA, in some eight different types of aircraft, and I shall have more to say on this later. From the start I was made to feel welcome by those I flew with and was accepted as a professional among professionals. On the whole, flight safety was taken seriously, and we all carried personal survival kits as well as the aircraft survival equipment; like most people I included a hand-axe in my kit for obtaining firewood in case of a crash-landing in the bush, a contingency I was trained for when I did the Arctic Survival Course later; I still have the axe, and use it. Thankfully I was never personally involved in a flight emergency in Alaska.

*   *   *

Meanwhile, back at the ranch .... When the Dalys had departed, with due ceremony, we had already moved into our base quarters and the children had started at Mount Spurr School just across the road. It must have been an enormous readjustment for them: Jennifer seemed to settle in more or less happily with her motherly class teacher, but Susan came into conflict almost immediately with her teacher, who was an archetypical American young man with a crewcut and apparently little knowledge or interest in anything outside the USA; it must be said that Susan had something of an abrasive character herself, and she was very unhappy for her first few weeks. Eventually we had a chat with the head teacher, and Susan was moved to a class with someone more sympathetic in charge. In the USA, children did not start school until they were 6 years old, so I suppose Sue and Jenny had a small advantage – which they needed when it came to working in dollars and cents instead of pounds, shillings and pence, and in a new vocabulary and ethos; they cheerfully saluted the American flag every morning. Before we left Alaska Susan was able to sit the Moray House tests arranged for British children living outside the UK to equate to the 'Eleven Plus' examination, and she reached a standard which would enable her to go to a grammar school when we returned home. Mount Spurr School was very co-operative in this, and on the whole we felt that the children gained from the whole school experience at Elmendorf, and made many friends.

Once our heavy baggage had arrived, the house turned into a home, with some familiar pictures on the walls and our wedding-present brass candlesticks on the writing-desk (no fireplace or mantelpiece).

Joan also had to make a significant adjustment to her way of life: no local shops or deliveries, unfamiliar foodstuffs at the commissary (which was the base shopping centre for most food – meat, groceries, vegetables and so on). As Joan did not drive at that time, she had to depend on the kindness of neighbouring wives (and they *were* kind) for shopping.

Coming from an England which was only just emerging from post-war austerities – food rationing only ended in 1954 – we were struck by what seemed to us a more luxurious lifestyle (though the word had probably not been invented then). Also, pay in the USAF was comparatively substantially higher than in the RAF: our family had not lived extravagantly, but we had virtually no savings or other capital, and in fact I had had to borrow £300 from my father-in-law when we left for America to fund the purchase of the car and other items from the Dalys. However, RAF allowances for the posting to Alaska were not ungenerous, and after we had paid off our debt in the first three months we found ourselves comfortably off, with funds to spare at the end of the month for the first time in our married life. We bought a good single-lens reflex camera so that we could have a durable record of our Alaskan tour (and later an inexpensive 8 mm movie camera); as the first year went on we bought more suitable winter clothes for Joan and the girls; and we invested in a record player to start a modest collection of long-playing classical records – the LP had not yet fully caught on in the UK.

We had arrived at a good time of the year: as the weather grew warmer and sunnier and the snow receded (though never completely) on the Chugach mountains, we were enchanted with the rapid growth of grass and wild flowers which had lain dormant under the winter ice and snow. Between Elmendorf base and Fort Richardson, the Army headquarters a little to the east, was military territory on which we could drive unhindered and which was mostly open country with scrubby pine trees and the occasional small lake, like Six Mile, from which the L-20 Beaver aircraft were flown on floats in the summer. Between the trees flowered rafts of rosebay willowherb, called locally fireweed, and white and pink wild roses flowered everywhere. At Six Mile Lake there was a beaver dam, and swallows flew over the water (we identified them from our new bird book as purple martins); we saw the occasional moose and felt the occasional mosquitoes. Our favourite picnic spot was a small hidden lake fringed with trees and fireweed and bright with large yellow water lilies; we called it 'Susan's lake' because she found it by wandering up a tiny path off the dirt road. Later in the year we picked cranberries here, and Joan made jelly and put the rest in the freezing compartment of the fridge to make sauce for the Christmas turkey.

Another favourite outing was to the Matanuska Valley, not far from Anchorage, and opening into the Cook Inlet. One of the few fertile areas in the Territory, it had been settled since 1911 and now had a population of over 4,500 mostly engaged in farming, many of Scandinavian origin from Wisconsin and Michigan. There was extensive livestock and arable farming, with an annual fair which we visited and were amazed at the size and abundance of the fruit and vegetables on display; we remember seeing a huge cabbage entirely filling the roofrack of a small car. In this otherwise flat area rose a small hill known as the Bodenburg Butte, near which we usually found a picnic place and where there were trees other than the usual struggling pines, so that the striking autumn colours could be enjoyed. In the first June we drove down to the Kenai Peninsula, south of Anchorage, to stay at a log-cabin hotel ('Our Point of View') high above Kenai Lake; we travelled along the coast of the Turnagain Arm (where Captain Cook is said to have turned back when he could go no further) and down the Seward Highway, some of it blasted through rock where patches of ice still glistened. Picnicking on the way, we again marvelled at the profusion of flowering plants in this semi-wilderness. The lodge had been built on a high slope overlooking the lake, with a magnificent view of the mountains; the owners told us that the ice had run out of the lake only a few days previously with a tremendous roaring noise. On the mountain above us we watched wild Dall sheep through the binoculars and saw chickadees (like our titmice) in the trees nearby. The children enjoyed helping the Indian girl who worked in the lodge, and there was a large friendly collie to play with. Just before we left home Jenny had gashed her forehead on her metal bedside table and had had several stitches put in at the base hospital. She looked a little forlorn with a large dressing across her forehead, but soon perked up and enjoyed the holiday, as we all did. We drove down to Seward, the town at the southern end of the Kenai Peninsula, and although we enjoyed the drive (passing both Indian and Russian relics on the way) we were not too impressed by Seward itself (named, of course, for Abraham Lincoln's Secretary of State who had negotiated the purchase of Alaska from Russia). Later on in our tour we had at least one more holiday at 'Our Point of View', and always found the wonderful setting uplifting.

Gerry Daly had bequeathed me a fibreglass fishing rod and some tackle. I had done no fishing since my teens, but we spent a few days at a lodge at Wasilla Lake near Palmer (sleeping in a rather uncomfortable wooden shanty), and I tried my hand at lake fishing, hoping to catch lake trout: but not a bite did I get. However, we had a pleasant break and particularly remember walking one evening near the lake and looking at an enormous golden full moon through our newly purchased binoculars. Chuck Parker, a major who worked in our office and had spent some time flying with the RAF, promised to take me for some proper fishing. He and his family became great friends and we spent a weekend at 'Our Point of View' on Kenai Lake with them; whether it was this weekend or another I can't recall, but he and I drove off to the Kenai River, equipped with fishing and overnight camping gear, and packed into a remote spot after rainbow trout. We walked up through pine woods and disturbed a cow moose feeding in a shallow pool. The river itself was a green torrent, glacier-fed from the mountains and rushing over boulders and gravelly pools with a great clamour. We found a quieter stretch, and Chuck instructed me in the art of trout fishing using salmon eggs as bait. To my incredulous delight I hooked a small rainbow trout on my first inexpert cast, and we fished through the rest of the day to catch our legal limit, five fish each, eventually building a small fire and grilling them to eat with the bread we had brought. We sat round the fire and drank Scotch as the light faded, and then slept like logs until the morning. Chuck pointed out some bear sign on nearby trees, but after a little unfruitful fishing we saw no wild life as we walked back to the car, except for the same moose in the same spot. An unforgettable wilderness experience.

We tried a little salmon fishing too, but here I was not successful. But there was always plenty of salmon available in the season, and the family sometimes tired of it. When the salmon ran in Ship Creek near the base, one would see small boys wheeling their cycles back home with a salmon on the handlebars illegally caught by snagging with large hooks on a string.

There was a busy social life on the base, mostly informal parties with colleagues and neighbours, with some more formal occasions in the Officers' Club. We had frequent parties at home, and luckily were able to use our duty-free concessions to order the necessary drinks (usually Scotch, bourbon and gin) from the British Mission in Washington, ordering by the case – something we would have formerly regarded as enormous extravagance. We were delighted to see, when the cases arrived, that they bore the labels of the Acheson, Topeka and Santa Fe Railroad, a pleasingly exotic touch. The odd bachelor attending our parties would often bring along a container of frozen martinis; ice-cold, they tasted innocuous but had a lethal effect. Going to parties in the summer, we would often go home in broad daylight at midnight or one o'clock, but it was a different matter in the winter, when we would wear Arctic outer clothing and overboots for even a short walk.

Our daily domestic routine was adjusted so that we usually had soup and a sandwich at midday for the short lunch break, for which Sue and Jenny came home. Our evening meal would be around six o'clock, often preceded by a martini in our case and Seven-up for the girls. Joan baked her own bread, since we found the local bread too sweet and soft for our taste (oddly enough our American guests often preferred her bread), and she used the odd American recipe to vary her own well-tried dishes.

We soon contacted Jan's husband, Lieutenant Herb Guy of the 6981st Radar Group Mobile, and found him a delightful character. He came round to supper a few times before Jan arrived and they moved into a base quarter, when we saw quite a lot of them. Jan's mother, Mrs Joyce Waite, who had owned our cottage at Loosley Row, came over for a week or so during our first summer, and it was strange to renew our acquaintance in such circumstances. To us she had changed little, radiating charm and tartness in equal measure – we enjoyed meeting her again after nearly ten years, and she was a link with home and our past. In particular we remembered how kind she and her husband Arthur had been to a rather unsophisticated young couple.

Among the flying fraternity at Elmendorf the word was that it was the wives who did the Alaskan tour: husbands were often away flying or on courses for several days at a time, and the wives had to cope with the children and the chores, doubly depressing through the long and mostly dreary Alaskan winter with its short days and long nights. At these times I know that Joan felt a long way from home, and this was sadly underlined for us one day late in 1956 when I made an early-morning start for a flight to Seattle in one of the C-54s with General Armstrong. Flight plan completed, I was boarding the aircraft when someone from Base Operations handed me a signal repeating a cable which had been sent via the British Mission in Washington. It was from Joan's parents in Leeds and told us that her younger sister, Enid, had died the previous day. At this stage there was no way in which another navigator could be found at short notice, but the General delayed the flight for an hour and gave me his car in which to drive home and break the news to Joan, who was still in bed. It was a fearful shock for her, intensified by my inability to stay; she was used to my absence at difficult times, but this was particularly hard. Enid had gone into hospital for a minor operation but had died from an embolism on the operating table. We knew from the start that there was no way in which we could get back to the UK – later leave could have been obtained, but the cost of flying back home was beyond our means and no suitable military flights existed. I kissed Joan goodbye and went back to my job, leaving her to talk to her parents on the telephone and get what comfort she could. Service wives had to be tough.

The city of Anchorage, only a couple of miles from Elmendorf, was a place we visited frequently for shopping and sometimes for entertainment. It was laid out on the usual grid pattern, with 4th and 5th Avenues the main shopping streets, introducing us to meter parking. There was a department store – Northern Commercial – at which we bought mostly clothes; a good municipal library and a bookshop; and a good variety of small shops, banks and businesses. The Denali Theater showed up-to-date films, and we remember seeing those classics *The Lady Killers* and *High Society* before they were generally released. We had a favourite coffee shop where we dropped in for club sandwiches; nearby, most incongruously, was one of the original log cabins which had been part of the old town, still preserved and occupied. We have slides of Sue and Jenny standing in front of a shiny red fire engine at the fire station, and also in front of Alaska's first railway locomotive, ARR 1, which is preserved and on show at the railroad station. There was a TV and radio station, and several multi-storey buildings, including the Alaska Native Service hospital and an apartment block. Anchorage was billed as the fastest-growing city in America, not without reason: the 1940 census gave a population of 3,488, and in 1956 the estimate for the Anchorage area was 65,000.

One unexpected pleasure was that at Anchorage High School (out past Lake Hood with its many floatplanes) there was a splendid modern auditorium where concerts were held. The 1956 Anchorage Festival featured the Robert Shaw Chorale – one of the best-known choirs in the USA – singing classical, popular and folk music, and we went to two of their concerts; I still have several of their LP records autographed by Robert Shaw.

The other great annual event in Anchorage was the Fur Rendezvous, with sled dog races, Eskimo dancing and drumming, and other activities, including the crowning of a local beauty as the Fur Rendezvous Queen. We usually watched the start of the sled dog races from 4th Avenue, and were surprised to see what a motley collection of animals were hauling sledges – not pure-bred Huskies or Samoyeds, but mostly cross-bred dogs of one sort or another. The winner one year was an Alaskan Indian whose dog team was composed of almost all cross-breeds. I think that was the year when snow had to be brought in on trucks and spread on 4th Avenue for the races to start, as the roads had been well cleared, as usual, but there had been no further snowfall at the right time.

I have written at some length on our family and domestic background in Alaska since for us this was a life-changing (and in many ways life-enhancing) experience. The American way of life, although modified by the unusual circumstances in the Territory, was something entirely new to us (despite years of watching Hollywood films), and its advantages seemed to be equally balanced by the drawbacks. We found the average American to have a very insular attitude, and we missed what we perhaps snobbishly looked on as a cultured and educated environment, but at the same time we benefited tremendously from the kindness and hospitality of individual friends and colleagues, with some of whom we are still in touch and whom we remember with pleasure; a letter from one of these is on my desk at the moment. For our two small daughters it was certainly an unforgettable experience.

* * *

One of the first projects I was involved in was the support of the British Parachute Brigade Alaska Expedition. Contact had been made with AAC some months earlier, and Gerry Daly had been given the job of overseeing the USAF contribution. The four members of the team were all officers serving with the Parachute Brigade and led by Captain James Mills, who had climbed Ruwenzori in Africa and conceived the idea of the first British expedition to the Mount McKinley area. They were all in their twenties and experienced mountaineers and climbers, and the British Army had generously given them three months' leave with pay. Financially the project was planned on a shoestring: they had hoped to get free military air passages across the Atlantic, but these were not available and they had to pay for third-class passages on a Greek ship from Southampton to Quebec. Luckily they got an advance (£319) from Herbert Jenkins, the publisher, for a book to be written by Jimmy Mills; this duly appeared in 1961 under the title *Airborne to the Mountains*, with a foreword by Sir John Hunt, and it is an absorbing read.

The aim of the expedition was not to climb Mount McKinley but to explore the Traleika Glacier system and to carry out medical and physiological research (one of the team was a doctor), to collect geological specimens for the US Geological Survey, to take meteorological observations, and to test clothing, equipment and rations. Gerry had made provisional arrangements with Ladd Air Force Base, and I was able to confirm to Jimmy Mills in April 1956 that it was hoped to take the party to Minchumina (a small airfield about sixty miles north-west of McKinley) by Dakota, and then closer in to Kantishna by Beaver. If the spring break-up made landing conditions difficult, we would try and lay on a helicopter. Mills says in his book, 'I could hardly believe that on the basis of a single letter, this considerable assistance (which later on was to be greatly increased) could be given so easily by a foreign service to one officer in another!' Certainly I had nothing but enthusiastic co-operation from all the units concerned, plus what was more or less a free hand from HQ.

I flew up to Ladd early in May in a T-33A, the USAF's basic jet trainer, taking in Mount McKinley on the way – an awe-inspiring sight – and having a very productive meeting with the 11th Air Defense Division operations staff, Base operations, and Colonel Reichert commanding the 74th Air Rescue Squadron. Full support was promised, and I flew up again via T-bird to meet the expedition at Fairbanks International Airport on the evening of 22 May. They were four tired men, after travelling by train from Ottawa to Dawson Creek and then by air, courtesy of the RCAF, to Fairbanks via Whitehorse. We spent the night in the BOQ (Bachelor Officers' Quarters) at Ladd, and in the morning met the Base Operations Officer, Captain Harry Coile, and Colonel Reichert to discuss the airlift. The leg to Minchumina presented no problems, but anything further would have to be done by helicopter in present conditions. It was finally agreed that the team and their equipment would be taken in two lifts to the confluence of the Muldrow and Traleika glaciers, exactly where Jimmy Mills wanted to be put down, with Colonel Reichert giving rescue cover in the SA-16 amphibian. He also said that he would give the team a little radio set for contact and that they would fly over every three days to do this, even agreeing to drop mail from time to time. I could see that Mills and his companions were overwhelmed with all this support, and their thanks were heartfelt. I flew back to Elmendorf later that day (again via McKinley), content that we had done all we could for them and more.

The Para team had a briefing from the Arctic Survival Training School, met the National Park Superintendent, Grant Pearson, who gave the project his blessing, and were even given a short jet flight over the McKinley area. The following day they were successfully landed on the mountain, and their six-week expedition began; Jimmy Mills gives a gripping account of it in his book, writing frankly about the physical and mental problems they encountered as well as the practical difficulties of moving and climbing in the Traleika Glacier area, where the glacier itself was in an unstable state and riddled with shifting and dangerous crevasses. Their regular overflights and radio contacts were a blessing, although the USAF was puzzled by one of their requests: 'Can you get the Test scores?' This was relayed to me from Ladd, but although I explained its significance I was unable to help. I had hoped to overfly them myself and at least to meet them before they left, but other commitments prevented this. They were taken off at the due time by the 74th ARS helicopter, dirty, bewhiskered, smelly and exhausted, but they had achieved most of their aims, especially the study of the Muldrow/Traleika Glacier system, which added much to the state of knowledge of glacier movement. Jimmy wrote to me later from Germany, where he had been posted, to express his thanks and send on letters for all the people who had helped – 'The scale of help we received has amazed everyone.' His book is a fitting monument to this remarkable expedition, achieved with much determination and with negligible financial backing – their credit balance at the end of it was 64 cents.

*   *   *

All flying personnel in Alaska (and elsewhere in the USA if involved in Arctic flying) were required to undergo a course at the Arctic Survival Training School at Ladd AFB. Men on flying units naturally had the first priority, and it was not until February 1957 that I was detailed for the one-week course. This time I travelled up to Fairbanks on the Alaska Railroad, and thus saw something of the intervening country at rather closer quarters than from the air. Construction of the railroad started in 1915, with the line from Seward to Nenana (just south of Fairbanks) being completed in 1923 – an impressive engineering feat, with parts of the line as high as 2,200 feet in the McKinley Park area.

The course was about twenty strong, from majors to sergeants, and from all types of flying units. The NCO in charge, Master Sergeant Clemmonds, welcomed us and introduced our Field NCO, Sergeant Fredericks, who would be taking us out into the 'boondocks' for the practical part of the course. The School's main mission was to save lives by ensuring that aircrew would be in a position to survive in extreme Arctic conditions in emergencies; they also field-tested survival gear; trained survival instructors for flying bases; and provided a pool of survival experts who could be called on for help in rescue missions. I remembered that Scotty Heator, the head of the School, had met the Parachute Brigade team and given them a useful briefing.

The first three days were taken up by lectures and demonstrations, covering all aspects of Arctic survival from psychology – a very important factor – to crash procedures, geography and weather, health, survival kits and rations, fire making, and the use of tools and clothing. We were shown how to lay out emergency signals, how to live off the land, and how to make emergency shelters, including snow houses (one of which we made ourselves) and parachute tepees. Rudimentary snowshoes were fashioned from whippy birch and willow branches, and we practised using them in one of the training areas, struggling along with backpacks over deep snow. I was impressed by the knowledge, expertise and approach of the instructors, who all radiated confidence, competence and encouragement.

On the fourth day we were taken out to another training area in a remote spot with a few spindly birch and fir trees, dressed in our survival gear and carrying parachutes and survival equipment. We were then left to get on with survival for the next two days, having been organized into three-man crews (of one of which I was captain). We selected a camp site and set up our para-tepees using long poles cut from some of the few trees with our survival axes. A fire-pit was made in each tepee, and such firewood as was available was laboriously gathered and stacked. Our exertions kept our body temperatures up during the day, and we were fortunate that outside temperatures dropped no lower than 23° F (nine degrees of frost) and that the wind was light, with little wind-chill factor. We conscientiously set and marked snares to catch the odd rabbit, but as far as I recall we saw no signs of bird or beast in the area.

When the end of the short daylight came, we ate some of our survival rations (the high-energy bars were particularly nasty) and got into our sleeping bags around the small fire, with most of the smoke filtering through the gaps at the top of the para-tepee. My crew companions were Captain Hales and Sergeant Elliott: I cannot now remember what their flying jobs were, but we chatted comfortably for a while and then tried to sleep, rather a fitful sleep, never entirely warm despite our double underwear and outer survival clothing. I was wearing a long parka issued to me for trial purposes before I left the UK, with a hood fringed by wolverine fur, and I had often worn it for daily use over uniform; now it proved its worth in survival conditions.

Stiff and cold, but still in reasonable shape, we got up at daylight, tidied the camp, and set about constructing ground emergency signals to catch the attention of search aircraft, as we had been instructed. Each crew laid out its own signal, with the promise of an airdrop of extra rations for the best. The letters 'SOS' were tramped out in the snow and enhanced by brushwood or anything handy – our handaxes were perhaps the most useful tool in these conditions. Later in the day an H-21 chopper overflew the camp and, to the smug satisfaction of our crew, made the drop on our signal, though our pleasure was somewhat modified by the fact that most of the extra rations were high-energy bars. (I noticed at this stage that one or two other members of the course had cheated and were producing concealed chocolate.)

After one more night in our para-tepees we cleaned up the camp area and were taken back to Ladd by truck. Survival equipment was turned in, and the final session was a class critique in which we were given a chance to express our views and criticisms. With no exceptions it was felt that the course, apart from the new skills and experience gained, had greatly boosted morale and given us confidence that, if the worst happened, we would be in a much better position to survive. There were inevitably comments on particular aspects of the course, which the staff took in; my own feeling, which I did not voice for a variety of reasons, was that, excellent as the training was in most respects, we would perhaps have benefited from a longer period under survival conditions; having met several RAF aircrew who had undergone the Royal Canadian Air Force survival course, I knew that at least two weeks were spent out in the open, living off the land in Arctic conditions. Our two days were insignificant in comparison, but no doubt finance and the very large numbers of aircrew in Alaska had to be taken into account. Nevertheless, we received our end-of-course certificates with some pride and felt that we had gained a great deal from it.

*　*　*

Life and work in the Kremlin went on as usual between these occasional outside interests. Colonel Gray was replaced as our Operations and Training boss by Colonel Classen, a very different kettle of fish: a long-term Strategic Air Command man, he perhaps felt that Alaskan Air Command was not quite what he deserved. He had not served in the UK and his opinion of Limeys was not very high, as soon became obvious. He had a sardonic sarcastic humour which was not to everybody's taste, but we did rub along together eventually, once he recognized that I could do my job satisfactorily. He did not care for the fact that I was often away on longish flights, but since it was usually the Commander AAC or CINCAL who required my services he could hardly object. Later, Colonel Bob Baseler was appointed as his deputy – a very congenial character who became a friend, but (as I noted earlier) the USAF system of filling posts with a rank up or down could cause problems, and did in this case.

It was interesting to note the reaction of my USAF colleagues during and after the Suez débâcle of October/November 1956: the end of the affair was a humiliation for the British, but I received nothing but sympathy for the way in which our forces had to withdraw under US pressure – most people said forcefully that we should have gone ahead and finished Nasser off. Isolated as I was from public attitudes in the UK, it was heartening to get such uncompromising support.

But one of the best parts of the job, as I have said, was to be able to get out of the office and fly – not just to keep my hand in or to navigate for a general, but to visit other units and sites in Alaska with which my work was concerned. On another visit to Nome in north-west Alaska, I was able to stay overnight and see a little more of the area, flying up with Dick Wolfersperger in a C-54. We stayed at a small hotel in one of the main streets, some still with boardwalks like the set of a Western movie, with shops and saloons on either side. The hotel proprietress was bemoaning the temporary loss of her Eskimo carpenter, who did necessary repairs and made wooden furniture, all to a high standard. Apparently he would work for a few weeks until he got some money together, and then go on an enormous bender and be lost to the world for some time. Alcohol was a problem in the Inuit population, and I understand it still is.

The town had a population of about 2,000, about one-third native Eskimos, one-third white and the remainder of mixed blood. When the Gold Rush was at its height at the end of the nineteenth century, the population was around 15,000, much of it in tents. Enthusiasts still pan for gold in the area, but now such gold as still exists is extracted by unromantic gold dredges such as the one we went to see run by the US Smelting and Refining Company, where the work went on round the clock in the summer: an infinitesimal amount of gold was found compared with the tons of earth shifted, but the profits were presumably worth the expenditure. Certainly the dredging site and the noisy machinery hardly rated as tourist attractions, unlike the Eskimo craft shops in Nome, with their carved walrus ivory, fur garments and native art work. I bought a 'billekin', a gnome-like head carved from the tips of walrus tusks, and a tiny ivory goose; they still decorate our sitting room.

We had brought a group of Civil Air Patrol officers up to Nome in the C-54: the CAP is made up of part-time civilian flyers who can help out with various semi-military tasks such as search and rescue missions, using their own civil aircraft. They kindly asked us to a party in the evening, together with several local people, and this was in full swing when Major Weyer, a CAA man from the airport, but also a CAP officer, was called away to the telephone. An Eskimo skin boat – a umiak – with several people on board was overdue on a trip from King Island in the Bering Strait. Weyer proposed to go and look for them and asked if I would like to go along; naturally I jumped at the chance, and we were soon airborne in his Piper Pacer, a small tricycle-undercarriage aircraft. We took off at ten past eleven in fine weather over a fairly calm sea and did a visual search of the area between Nome and King Island, which was about eighty miles from Nome and some forty miles from the coast, with Siberia about a hundred miles to the west. Weyer was very familiar with the area, and as well as covering the direct sea route we searched along the coastline north-west of Nome, but found no sign of the umiak. When midnight came we were over broken ice near Port Clarence, and as it was only a few days past the summer solstice I was able to take a photograph of the midnight sun, just visible on the horizon. After nearly two hours, we gave up the search, landed at Nome and rejoined the party. I believe the umiak turned up safely the following day.

Some of the most enjoyable flying from Elmendorf was in L-20 floatplanes (Canadian-made de Havilland Beavers) from Six Mile Lake in the base area with Captain Chuck Bennett, another member of the Operations and Training Staff (although he seemed to spend a great deal of time in the summer out of the office, flying generals and other senior officers on hunting and fishing trips). One August day we took off from Six Mile and spent a couple of hours flying around the Anchorage area; it was a glorious day and I was able to take photographs of the base and the city of Anchorage. We flew over the Turnagain Arm area and over Lake George, said to be the world's only self-emptying lake: the advance of the Knik Glacier at the lower end of the sixteen-mile-long lake plugs up the outlet to the Knik River, the lake deepens, and by late summer the build-up of millions of gallons of water undermines the ice dam and eventually breaks up parts of the glacier and hurtles into the Knik River, part-emptying the lake. This had evidently happened not long before we flew over the lake, which was partially empty but with enormous house-sized blocks of ice still floating – an impressive sight which I photographed.

Not long after we arrived, the other RAF exchange officer at Elmendorf, Jimmy James, was replaced by Dave Vasse, also flying F-89Ds, and I was able to do some local flying with him in this (to my mind) rather cumbersome-looking jet. On one occasion we landed at Elmendorf and taxied into the squadron line-up of other F-89D aircraft; we clambered out of the cockpit and started to walk back to the operations block. We were wearing our RAF flying suits and carrying our bonedomes and parachutes, and were suddenly stopped by an armed airman patrolling the flight line. He had us up against the hangar wall with our hands in the air and kept us covered while he radioed for assistance; he had never heard of the RAF and evidently thought we could be Russian infiltrators, though what he made of our flying in via a USAF aircraft I cannot imagine. He was neither very bright nor very polite, but one of the operations officers came out and rescued us from what was, I suppose, an understandable Cold War situation. Joan recalls airmen walking past our married quarter, by the door of which appeared the legend 'Sq Ldr Cropper RAF', and speculating that this stood for 'Russian Air Force'.

There were other memorable flights within the Territory, one of which was in an SA-16 (Albatross) amphibian of the 71st Air Rescue Squadron, flown by the Squadron Commander, Colonel Stenglein, and practising jet-assisted take-offs (JATO) and water landings on Lake Skilak. With many lakes being surrounded by steep mountainsides, this was a necessary technique for getting airborne again after a landing, and the additional thrust when the JATO was operated was remarkable and exhilarating; again I was able to get both still and movie camera records. A winter flight in a H-21A helicopter was to test an air-droppable corner reflector which could be used to mark sites for radar pick-up from the air – a 'back-to-the-drawing-board' test, as the reflector would not stay upright in the deep snow. I remember another flight to a remote airfield at Tanacross between Anchorage and Fairbanks when we visited a missionary to the local Indians, being taken across a wide river full of break-up ice fragments in a canoe paddled by a young Indian boy. The missionary (David? Green) lived an isolated but evidently fulfilling life ministering both spiritually and medically to his flock.

Kodiak Island, at the northern end of the Aleutian Chain, was the headquarters of the US Navy in Alaska (known, rather dramatically, as the Alaskan Sea Frontier). I visited it once for a meeting on rescue business, and found it a desolate spot. The naval HQ was small, with few personnel, and they lived an isolated life in rugged and windswept terrain. The Aleutians themselves are virtually treeless, with volcanic mountainous terrain running in a long archipelago about 1,100 miles west into the Pacific. The USAF had had a base at Shemya until 1954, and the Navy had an air station and port at Adak which I also visited: if my memory serves, this was where there was a small enclosure with two very small fir trees which was labelled 'Adak National Forest'. Poor weather along the chain was more or less continuous, with low visibilities, turbulence, overcast skies, precipitation at all times, and icing in winter. No wonder the USAF pulled out.

These flights around the Territory alternated with occasional flights to the USA and Canada, in the latter to Whitehorse in the Yukon (where I was impressed to see a Mountie in full uniform in the room next to mine) and Edmonton, where the Hudson's Bay Company store seemed like an echo from the past. Our flights to the USA were invariably in one of the C-54s with a general aboard, with the first stop McChord Air Force Base at Seattle, a flight of seven or eight hours depending on the winds.

The route was along the coast of the panhandle, passing down the Alexander Archipelago, Queen Charlotte Sound and by Vancouver Island into Seattle, with navigation not too difficult (though the discomfort of the navigator's position, as I have said, was wearying). The weather was usually poor, and fixes were more often by radar than from sight of the ground. The radio compass was helpful, usually at the end of a long leg with a radio beacon available; I used Loran once or twice but, no doubt due to my own inexperience of the aid, did not find it very useful. The weather at Seattle was often poor, and we once spent two days there fogged in, with General Armstrong giving me a full briefing on American football as we watched TV in the Officers' Club at McChord. On one flight we went on to Davis-Monthan AFB near Tucson in Arizona, giving me a wonderful panorama of mostly mountainous American landscape over Oregon and Nevada.

The Stateside flight I have most reason to remember was to Burbank airport at Los Angeles, though I cannot now recall the object of it. One of the passengers was Lieutenant Pete Malatesta, a member of the Protocol staff at Alaskan Command HQ, who was no doubt acting as an aide to General Armstrong on this flight. We were chatting, probably on our stopover at McChord, and he told me that he had family in Los Angeles and was looking forward to visiting them; his aunt, he said, was Bob Hope's wife, and he offered to take me to see them as we had a free day in LA. I wasn't sure if he was pulling my leg, in the old-fashioned phrase, but on the evening we arrived in Burbank he told me that he had talked to Mrs Hope and she would be pleased to see me on the following afternoon, though unfortunately her husband was away touring. He also offered to take me on a tour of the Paramount studios in the morning, drove me there and introduced me to Bob Hope's brother, who was his manager. The studios covered a huge area, with some permanent sets varying from the usual Western cowtown to city streets and suburban houses. I was introduced to a very-good-looking lady as Mrs Someone who turned out to be Maureen O'Hara, and then taken to watch some filming in progress. The film was *The Buster Keaton Story*, and the great man himself was on the set. I shook his hand and had a few words with him; he looked older than his actual age, which was about 60 at the time, no doubt due to the very physical demands of many of the slapstick comedies he acted in when he was known as 'the Great Stone Face' because of his deadpan expression in the most extreme situations – he still had this when I met him. Though I had read about the problems of film making, I was impressed by the minute attention to detail in shooting a scene lasting a few seconds; the one I saw was repeated many times before the Director was satisfied.

In the afternoon Pete Malatesta dropped me at the Hope home on Moorpark in North Hollywood – the old-fashioned part, he told me, where the well-established stars lived, as distinct from Beverley Hills. It was a quiet area with wide avenues and well-separated houses; Bob Hope's was a long, low house with a touch of Spanish about it. Mrs Hope (Dolores) was a tall, dark, quietly dressed and quietly spoken lady who welcomed me with genuine warmth and introduced her four children, ranging in ages from about 8 to about 14 (all adopted, I believe). They were extremely pleasant and well behaved, and showed an interest in Alaska and flying. We spent a quiet afternoon chatting and listening to the LP record of *My Fair Lady*, a new release of the musical with the original cast which had opened in New York earlier in the year; I had not heard this before and much enjoyed it, buying the LP when I was back in Anchorage. Mrs Hope asked if I would like to go the Hollywood Bowl with them to a classical concert that evening – Marian Anderson would be singing. Of course I accepted the generous invitation, explaining, however, that I would have to leave half-way through the programme to get back to Burbank for a very early take-off the following morning. Mrs Hope quite understood this – apparently the Hopes had entertained many RAF cadets who had been stationed at Burbank for their flying training during the war. Before the concert we went to a small modest pizza restaurant where for the first time I ate a delicious pizza – the Hopes could hardly believe that this was the first I had ever tasted.

The Hollywood Bowl open-air auditorium was full to overflowing on a beautiful sunny evening; the orchestra was the Los Angeles Philharmonic under Eugene Ormandy, grouped on the stage with the unique shell-like covering. The opening item was one of Handel's Concerti Grossi, followed by Beethoven's Fifth Symphony – I marvelled at my luck. After two songs by Bizet, Marian Anderson sang 'Mon coeur s'ouvre à ta voix' ('Softly awakes my heart') from Saint-Saens' *Samson and Delilah* – a childhood favourite of mine, with the glorious contralto enhanced by the acoustics. At the interval I was loth to tear myself away, but after heartfelt thanks to Mrs Hope (she gave me a small gift for the children) I said goodbye to them all and took a cab back to Burbank. It was a memorable and unexpected episode.

The only other encounter with someone of note occurred when I was flying back to Elmendorf from the USA in a C-54 just before Christmas, with various entertainers for the troops and with Cardinal Spellman, then the head of the Catholic Church in the States, flying to visit the Catholic community in Alaska. Part of the flight was overnight, and as I walked up the aircraft back to the flight deck I passed through the area reserved for the Cardinal, with its own bunk. He was getting ready to go to bed, and I must be one of the few persons to have seen a cardinal in his long johns; he was not at all discomposed, and gave me a cheerful smile. At the end of the flight he talked pleasantly to the crew and gave us signed cards for our children – a shortish tubby man with a very friendly personality.

It was good to get back home after these long flights and days away from the family, and I usually had a feeling of guilt for leaving them to soldier on during my frequent absences; as I have written elsewhere, service wives have a hard row to hoe. On most occasions I was able to bring small presents back with me, and English food from Canada – marmalade, tea, Marmite, and chocolate – was much appreciated.

*   *   *

I have written little in this (or the last) chapter about navigation, and indeed in Alaska my main problems were concerned with rescue, air traffic control and flight facilities. But navigation aids were important in the Territory, especially for single-seat fighters, and I was interested to find on arrival that a TACAN programme (or program) was under way. I had encountered this system at Farnborough when Freddy Stringer and I had been working on fighter navigation aids, and since then it had become widely used in the USA, with numerous ground beacons and with receivers fitted in many fighter aircraft. Alaska was involved early on in the USAF-wide test phase of the system, with fifty AN/ARN-21 receivers fitted in aircraft and around nine mobile ground stations (AN/TRN-6) installed around the Territory by the Spring of 1955 (much smaller numbers than had originally been planned). There were problems with the installation and serviceability of the airborne sets, lack of standby equipment for the ground beacons, and a slowness on the part of pilots to adapt to this new system. By August 1955 there were seventeen ground stations and an additional eighty-four airborne sets, and the USAF Air Proving Ground Command was able to complete its test programme by February 1956. Its report concluded that TACAN was operationally suitable as a common system as long as dual ground equipment was used, but that further development was needed to improve its operational dependability.

This was roughly where I came in: the ground stations had been reduced to nine mobiles, but some three-quarters of air defence aircraft (F-89Ds at that time) were equipped with TACAN. We did all we could to encourage its use, but we found the squadrons somewhat apathetic, mainly because of general equipment unreliability and the availability of other familiar and proven navaids plus GCI control. Also, the Civil Aeronautics Administration did not recognize TACAN as an accepted navigation and air traffic control facility and had their own program for the installation of a VHF Omnirange (VOR) system throughout Alaska; unlike TACAN, these ground stations would not have a distance-measuring (and thus a fixing) facility. We recommended to HQ USAF that this CAA VOR program should be cancelled and that TACAN should become the common navigation system in Alaska. There followed a period of wheeling and dealing with CAA in which I was very much involved, culminating in word from Washington that the common system in Alaska was to be VORTAC, a combination of both VOR and TACAN, and that we in Alaskan Air Command were to work with CAA to establish it.

This we did, working closely with my friends Tom Walker and George McKean at 5th Region CAA.. By the beginning of 1958, we had six permanent TACAN ground stations (AN/URN-3) installed and operating (at sites including Elmendorf and Ladd), three more awaiting flight check, and four mobile stations eventually to be replaced by permanent ones. Four more were planned for 1959, with some preliminary plans for some five at more remote locations like Point Barrow.

The arrival of F-102 aircraft to replace the F-89Ds coincided with the installation of permanent ground stations in July 1957; since the single-seat F-102s were equipped only with TACAN (but later models), and the ground beacons now gave improved performance, the pilots' attitude to the system changed for the better, and they had much more confidence in its performance. By February 1958, some 130 AAC aircraft – nearly half of them F-102s – were TACAN-equipped, and they were able to use the system not only for navigation but for instrument approach to the main airfields. Most of the main operating areas in Alaska were covered, giving the pilot or navigator the ability to read off an accurate range and bearing from one dial in the cockpit and at a frequency (1,000 Mc/s) giving none of the reception problems of the old LF and MF radio ranges and beacons. My CAA colleagues and I were very satisfied with the final outcome.

* * *

In July 1957 there began what was known as the International Geophysical Year, inaugurated by a body known as the International Council of Scientific Unions, of which more than seventy nations were members. The purpose was the systematic study of the earth and its planetary environment, including oceanography and glaciology. The United States was particularly interested in the Arctic Ocean, and some years earlier had established an ice island between Alaska and the North Pole to study Arctic weather. It was now proposed to establish an ice island in the same area as part of the IGY programme, and the Alaskan Air Command was given the task of finding a suitable piece of ice floe on which a base could be established for scientific research – in particular the investigation of changes in the ice pack system with temperature variations and the effects on weather and climatic changes.

For once I was not involved at the beginning of this project, but I knew that reconnaissance was successful in finding a large floe area which seemed suitable for the task, that a Beaver had landed on skis, and that heavy equipment was to be dropped by C-124 to set up a basic camp. An Arctic specialist called Fritz Awe, who had worked on a previous ice island project, was in charge of construction, and towards the end of May 1957 had laid down an ice runway on the selected floe – now known as 'Ice

Station Alpha' – so that large aircraft could land and a more permanent camp could be set up.

A flag-raising ceremony to establish the camp was to take place on 21 May, with the Commander AAC, General Davies, to fly in on the first aircraft to use the runway and do the honours. As his usual navigator I was to fly with him in one of the C-54s, and afterwards to visit some DEW-Line bases.

We flew up to Point Barrow the day before; appropriately enough the pilot was Captain Burton Jenkins, who had made the first landing on skis on Ice Station Alpha. We stayed overnight in the Barrow hotel, a wooden structure with fairly primitive but adequate facilities, and took off for Alpha the following morning. Although there was coastal fog at Barrow, this cleared and we had sunshine and good visibility as we flew north over the ice-packed ocean. I had been given a position for Alpha, which was now between 80° and 81° north latitude, but was warned that this was likely to be inaccurate since the island was constantly moving. Luckily Alpha had now been equipped with a low-power, low-frequency beacon, and we were able to home on this for the last few miles; the island had indeed moved and was some thirty-five or thirty-six nautical miles from the position I had been given. It was quite a sight from the air – a large area of solid ice, with broken floes all round, and the new ice runway gleaming reassuringly. Jenkins landed perfectly, taxied gently to a halt, and General Davies stepped out to a welcoming party of the construction workers and USAF personnel, with their very basic accommodation – Jamesway huts, like small Nissen huts – in the background, along with a miscellany of heavy equipment which had been airdropped for the runway construction. This must have been a mammoth task with very basic facilities and below-zero temperatures.

General Davies's first ceremony was the planting of the American flag, pronouncing the ice station to be a 'going concern of the United States'. He then presented official commendations to the three men who made the first trial landing nearly two months previously: Captain Jenkins, the pilot; Fritz Awe, in charge of construction, a bulky figure in a fur cap and checked mackinaw jacket; and Chaplain Tom Cunningham, an Arctic specialist who was an adviser for the expedition and had helped in the early reconnaissance. We spent nearly two hours on Alpha, with the General talking to all those who had been involved in the establishment of the camp and the making of the runway. Later on in the day there would be further landings from C-124s with more equipment and personnel so that a permanent camp could be set up.

The three-and-a-half-hour flight back to Barrow was uneventful, and we spent a further two nights in this most northerly Alaskan settlement. I don't now remember why we spent a day on the ground there, but weather may have been the reason – just off-shore there was a more or less permanent fog belt which might have affected our next destination, Cape Parry on the DEW Line. So we had the opportunity for a look at Point Barrow, and an uninspiring place it was, with ramshackle wooden buildings housing the Eskimo (Inuit) population (about 600 at that time) who, although now having access to some modern food and facilities, mostly carried on their traditional way of life by hunting and fishing. Oddly enough, there was a Bureau of Mines coal project nearby which employed some Eskimos, but we saw no evidence of it. A few days earlier a skin boat had been lost off-shore with several people aboard, and the atmosphere was naturally not a happy one. We saw a hunting party returning with a large sled loaded with seals and king eider duck, so one or more families would have enough to eat for a while. A wooden church had been built in the village, mostly by the priest, Father Cunningham, whom we had just met on Alpha. With the summer temperatures above zero, all parts of the village were inches deep in mud and presented an unattractive sight; sled dogs were tethered outside most houses and barked fiercely as we walked past. There was a small village store as well as the hotel (whose sign proclaimed 'Top of the World Hotel, Point Barrow, Alaska'), but neither showed much sign of prosperity.

In the small graveyard there was one of the saddest sights I have ever seen: two small tombstones whose inscriptions showed that they covered the graves of two women from the South Seas who had married American whaler captains and had both died at this benighted spot. The memory haunts me yet.

Next morning we took off to fly eastwards along the northern coastline, crossing into Canada about half-way to Cape Parry, our destination. I had chosen not to use grid navigation, developed by Shawbury in the late 1940s for high-latitude navigation, to avoid difficulties caused by the rapid changes in longitude; I had only flown one training exercise in 1948 using this technique and did not feel competent to use it effectively. We were, however, flying mostly along the coastline and over a succession of radio beacons. One problem was the performance of the magnetic compass, which, although coupled to a gyro, tended to be erratic so close to the north magnetic pole; also, the magnetic variation changed rapidly from 29° to around 47° east over this leg. But with plenty of visual fixes on coastal features and DEW Line sites, plus frequent drift readings, we had no problems, and landed at Cape Parry – DEW Line station PIN – after a four-hour flight.

The main DEW Line stations were all built to the same design: an H-shaped building with the living and messing area in one leg and the technical site in the other, with a large radome adjoining, plus one or two dish aerials sited separately; the cross-piece of the H joined the two legs so that one could walk across without going outside – a very necessary facility in the long dark winters with exceptionally low temperatures. Both

Canadian and American flags flew over the site, but it was manned mostly by US servicemen and civilians, the latter no doubt well paid and all of them well fed and in reasonably comfortable accommodation; I don't recall the length of the tour of duty but believe it was of the order of six months. The servicemen were nominally Alaskan Air Command personnel, and it was to take a look at these that General Davies was visiting, though not on a formal inspection.

I occupied the room of an engineer who was away on leave, and was interested to note that the only books he had were technical publications and a few girlie magazines; however, there was a small cinema where some of the latest films were shown. I wandered up into the radome housing and found evidence of other spare-time activities – a polar bear skin pegged out on the floor to dry.

Ours was a one-night stay only, as the General was visiting another site further east at Cambridge Bay the following day. As we went out to the airstrip the following morning, I was surprised and pleased to see a civilian Avro Anson parked there (an early mark, by the look of it) and was told that it was a regular commuter from places in the North-West Territories like Yellowknife, and gave a very reliable service. We flew on to Cambridge Bay – DEW Line site CAM – where the General made another short visit, and then turned for home on a long, long leg across the barren lands of northern Canada, miles of small lakes, tundra, scrubby pine forests, and the occasional small settlement, often with an airstrip. We landed back at Elmendorf in the Alaskan twilight after a total of over ten hours in the air that day.

There was a sort of postscript to our flight to the ice island: the Command Historian, Dr Ira E. Chart, had come along with us especially to record for posterity the first landing on the runway, the raising of the US flag, and the presentation of commendations, taking an official photographer with him. He came to see me shortly after we had returned to Elmendorf, and asked if I had taken many photographs of the Alpha ceremonies, as he had seen me using my camera. It seemed that the USAF photographer's results were not satisfactory and could not be used. As it happened I had taken shots at each stage of the proceedings and was only too happy to let Dr Chart have copies, with which he was very pleased. So my photographs may still exist somewhere in the Alaskan archives – I was looking at my own slides the other day, and they are still in good condition.

As it happened, the last series of flights I was involved in before the end of our exchange tour was also along the DEW Line. It was in February 1958, and the Chief of the Air Staff of the Royal Canadian Air Force came to Ladd AFB to accompany the Commander-in-Chief Alaska, General Armstrong, on a tour of the DEW Line. Dick Wolfersperger was the pilot and I the navigator of one of the VIP C-54s, and we flew up to Ladd so

that the General could welcome the Air Marshal, who arrived in a de
Havilland Comet 2 recently acquired by the RCAF. General Armstrong
was offered a demonstration flight in the Comet – its first appearance in
Alaska – and we accompanied him into this beautiful four-jet aircraft,
smart in its RCAF livery. Alas, we sat in it for half an hour or so while the
crew tried unsuccessfully to start the engines, much to the chagrin and
embarrassment of the Canadians; no doubt very low air temperatures
were to blame, as figures of fifty degrees below zero were not uncommon
in the interior at that time of year. The disappointed party transferred to
the C-54 and flew to Point Barrow via the Aircraft Control and Warning
site at Cape Lisburne on the north-west coast above the Bering Straits and
facing Siberia – a desolate spot if ever there was one.

The intention was to visit the main DEW Line stations from Barrow to
Cambridge Bay, and this we did in the next few days, night-stopping at
Barrow and Cape Parry. Then on via Cambridge Bay to Hall Lake, on the
north-west coast of the Foxe Basin north of Hudson Bay, and finally to
Fort Churchill on the west side of Hudson Bay itself, where if I recall
correctly the RCAF chief was picked up for return to Ottawa. Navigation
was a little more demanding than on our DEW Line flights the preceding
May, with very short daylight hours and often poor visibility. Also, the
more easterly part of the route passed close to the magnetic pole, and
constant checks on true compass headings had to be made by astro-
compass; our ground-mapping radar was a great help since much of the
flight lay over the coastline and associated islands. I was making the
routine VHF position reports to the nearest DEW Line stations, and it was
amusing to hear the reaction from the ground controllers to an English
accent reporting from a USAF aircraft: some asked for a repeat.

Fort Churchill was an old settlement near the harbour where the
Churchill River flows into Hudson Bay, said to be the only harbour on the
west of the Bay for large vessels at any state of the tide, and dating from
around the end of the seventeenth century. I can recall little of it except a
cold and uncomfortable bunk for the night. We took off the following
morning for another long leg home to Elmendorf – 11 hours and 20
minutes says my logbook – and with the C-54's makeshift navigation table
and stool I was extremely tired by the time we landed. But it had been an
unique and valuable experience to see so much of Arctic North America
and to get a glimpse of what life was like for those guarding the northern
approaches at the height of the Cold War.

*   *   *

At the beginning of 1958 our thoughts were turning homeward again. I
received a posting notice from the Air Ministry via the Mission in
Washington for the job of Senior Navigation Lecturer at the RAF College

Cranwell. I had mixed feelings about this: although Cranwell might be looked on as a 'career posting', I knew little about the College, and, like most wartime aircrew who had stayed on to fly, our experience of the early post-war pilots who were Cranwell trained had not given us a very good impression of the system – we found them over-confident, if not arrogant, and not particularly competent in the air; this of course was a thoroughly prejudiced attitude based on a very small sample. Also I had not done any regular lecturing for some time and was not very keen on the idea of teaching basic navigation, with all the revision for me which that would entail. I consoled myself with the thought that flying should be available at Cranwell and that at least Lincolnshire would be in easy reach of our parents in Leeds.

The good news was that my replacement in Alaska had been named as 'Occ' Tarry, an old friend from my time at Waddington, a highly competent and dependable navigator with a dry sense of humour. His nickname went back to his training days when some minor navigational disaster had occurred which concerned an occult (a flashing beacon), and it had stuck ever since. We exchanged letters and I gave Occ a brief idea of what the job entailed. As a bachelor he would be living in the Bachelor Officers' Quarters, so would not need any of my furniture or effects; however, I offered to pass on our car to him at a reasonable figure, so reasonable that he wrote back and said 'It must be a heap!' I took a few photographs of it and sent them to him, after which he said he would have it. The same car was still being used by the exchange officer after him.

Our passage to Liverpool in RMS *Parthia*, another Cunarder, had been booked for 11 April from New York, and our advance baggage had to be dispatched by the beginning of March. We had collected many new possessions, including a large refrigerator, and we eventually packed up twelve containers to be forwarded to Cranwell, although we knew that we would not be going there immediately. The house looked a little empty when these had gone, but we 'made do' for the few weeks involved.

Work of various sorts, mostly in the office, continued unabated. I was at the same time trying to write a brief for Occ covering all the many and varied aspects of the job and referring him to all the contacts and references I thought might be helpful: I still have my draft copy of this – it ran to thirty pages plus appendices. Writing to me later in the year, Occ said, 'By frequent reference to what has become known as the RAF bible and by just getting up whenever I fell down, I first pulled in the slack rope and then began to lean my weight in the interests of AAC.'

One of the last projects in which I was involved was the airspace clearance for the Ballistic Missile Early Warning Station (BMEWS) planned to be established at Clear, Alaska, between Anchorage and Fairbanks, one of three sites – the other two being in Greenland and at Fylingdales in the UK. This was naturally a highly classified project, but we were given basic details and had to ensure that there would be minimum interference with civil and military aviation in the Territory and with the associated communications and navigation systems. This was done through the joint CAA/AAC Air Defense Planning Board, of which I was still a member, although no longer Executive Secretary after various reallocations of duties.

Major Doug Culver, who had worked closely with me in the Kremlin, had been posted back to the USA some time earlier, and he and his wife Lucy were now living in Charleston, South Carolina. They wrote to us suggesting that we stop off with them for a few days before we finally left the States, and after some complicated correspondence with the Mission in Washington I got agreement to take a few days' additional leave and to report to them after a detour to Charleston (the difference in air fares, of course, being paid by me). I pointed out that, unlike the majority of exchange officers, there was no chance of visiting other parts of the USA on leave, and that my family had been unable to leave Alaska for the full two years of the tour, with the full rigours of two Alaskan winters. This sob story seemed to work – the RAF administrative staff at Washington were in any case in no position to judge the conditions in Alaska since none of them had ever taken the trouble to visit us.

The last few weeks before our departure saw a round of farewell parties of various sorts: Occ Tarry arrived on 18 March, the same droll character as ever, and we had two weeks' hectic handover, interspersed with final domestic preparations, before the family – accompanied by a largish party of well-wishers – arrived at Anchorage International to board the plane for Seattle. It was an emotional occasion for all the family: for me our Alaskan tour had mostly been a busy, action-packed period but – as I wrote earlier – Joan and the children had had to make a new life with new friends, often in my absence, and cope with all the family problems in a very different environment. To quote my end-of-tour report to the Air Ministry,

> I feel most strongly that the present post could hardly provide a better cross-section of experience in USAF operations of all types, of problems of Arctic operations, and of airspace and air traffic problems in North America. ... Throughout my tour of duty I have been treated with the utmost friendliness and consideration by all ranks of the USAF with whom I have been associated. My wife and I have been shown the greatest possible kindness and have made many friends, and it has been a pleasure and a privilege to serve in the Alaskan Air Command.

Despite our longings for home, it was with genuine sadness that we said goodbye to our friends and to this fascinating country.

* * *

We were able to spend a day in Seattle – mostly shopping for clothes – before flying on to Charleston via Portland, Oregon, a night in Chicago and a short stop in Atlanta. Of Chicago we saw little except the hotel, Cafarello's; of Atlanta our main memory is of the segregation of blacks and whites at the airport, something we had not encountered before. We flew on a variety of airlines – Pacific Northern, Delta, and Eastern – and were well looked after, but we were all thankful to reach our destination and be taken home by Lucy and Doug to a pleasant single-storey modern house in a suburb of Charleston. We had arrived on a Friday, so Doug had time off and was able to take us around over the weekend.

We now saw a completely different America from the raw, mostly untamed vastness of Alaska. Charleston, the capital and seaport of South Carolina, was founded by the British in about 1670, and is a handsome city with buildings and houses in the old Southern architectural style. We had a walk round the centre and saw a variety of striking houses, including the Sword Gate House with an imposing set of entrance gates; Rainbow Row, in which each old house was painted a different colour; the Parish Church, with a classical portico and tall steeple, all in white; and the Antiquarian Society, also in the classical style. The place had a civilized atmosphere.

The country around Charleston had in the past been devoted to rice and cotton growing, and the Culvers took us to Middleton Plantation, a seventeenth-century estate restored and maintained in something like its original state (except, of course, for the plantations themselves). We drove along roads fringed with trees draped in Spanish moss, and as we approached Middleton there were small groups of black children dancing at the side of the road in the hope of a few pennies from the tourists. The old manager's house (William and Mary?), the cypress swamp, the azalea and camellia gardens, lawns grazed by sheep – we and the children (Mary Culver was about Jenny's age) found it all delightful. But my abiding memory of the place is of a group of black people, standing in a big, square boat at the edge of one of the small lakes and singing their hearts out. I wrote later,

My goodness, how they sang! It was just a natural outpouring of harmony, a gospel hymn whose words we couldn't distinguish, but whose sounds brought a lump to the throat and tears to the eye. Loud but unforced, straight from the heart, with the many parts seemingly blended by instinct, it was in direct contrast with the perfectly rehearsed and produced sound of the Robert Shaw Chorale. But elemental and unforgettable ....

On Sunday we went to church with the Culvers, who were committed Episcopalians (much later, Doug was ordained and became a Rural Dean in Wisconsin), and afterwards visited the Cypress Gardens, an large area of mangrove swamps planted with flowering bushes, where we were taken on a small boat through a maze of towering trees and black water; the boatman warned the children not to trail their hands in the water because of snakes. It was an eerie experience.

On the following day our hosts saw us off to Washington for a three-night stay. We were again booked into a family room at the Gralyn, and my first task was to report to the British Joint Services Mission. I had expected some sort of debriefing, but apart from settling a few administrative and travel details, no one seemed to be particularly interested, and we were soon free to enjoy a couple of days in the capital. The spring weather was good if not particularly warm, the cherry trees were mostly in blossom, and we visited all the places of interest: looking at the White House through the railings, walking down Constitution Avenue, admiring the Washington Memorial, and walking down to the Lincoln Memorial, where we were impressed by the massive Lincoln statue; on one day we picnicked in the park between the two memorials, and on another we had a seafood meal on the river front at a well-known restaurant where Sue and Jenny were amused by the waitresses tucking large bibs around diners' necks as they were served lobster.

All too soon it was time to take the train to New York to embark in the *Parthia* the following day, but we had time for a stroll up Fourth and Fifth Avenues and a little shopping. After so many days on the move it was a relief to take over our cabin and know that there was nothing to do for the next week but enjoy the Cunard lap of luxury. The weather was a little better than on our westward crossing, although on the second and third days out we did have strong winds, rough seas and a heavy swell; however, we did not suffer seasickness so badly as on the outward voyage, and there were several sunny days when we could enjoy walking the decks or sitting reading in the open air.

One of our fellow passengers was a Miss Ruth Mitchell, an American lady in her fifties or sixties. We fell into conversation, and knowing that I was in the RAF, she told me that she was General Billy Mitchell's sister. A US Army Air Corps officer between the wars, he was a vociferous proponent of strategic bombing policy, but at that time he was going against the flow and made enemies in both the Army and the Navy; he was eventually retired from the Army, and if I remember correctly, he did not live to see his ideas vindicated and taken up on a massive scale by the USAAF in the Second World War.

Miss Mitchell was a strong supporter of her brother and his ideas, and was still bitter about the treatment he had received from higher authority and about the fact that his proposals had eventually been seen as acceptable doctrine. She was an interesting, intelligent and articulate woman, and it was instructive to learn at (almost) first hand the background to a part of the history of air power.

We docked in Liverpool on the morning of 18 April, in time to catch the 11 a.m. train to Leeds with our mountain of hand-luggage; luckily porters and taxis were easier to come by in those days. The streets of Liverpool were something of a contrast to those of New York, and our pleasure at being back in our own country was somewhat damped by the sight of a slatternly woman pushing a mop around the filthy floor of the station cafeteria. But we were home at last and were given a heart-warming welcome by Joan's parents in Leeds, with whom we were to stay until ready to move to Cranwell.

*   *   *

This has been the longest chapter in this book so far, and I know that I could have written still more on our experiences in Alaska. With all its problems, we still regard it as a high point in our lives, and have vivid memories of the place and the people, assisted by our many photographs and cinefilms. We kept in touch with the Culvers for many years, and they visited us at our home in Yorkshire, as did Arlee and Cecil Walton, with whom we are still in touch and whom we visited in Ohio a few years ago. We will never forget the positive and practical kindnesses shown to us in that remarkable country.

CHAPTER FOURTEEN

Cranwell

It was strange to be back in Leeds, so familiar but such a contrast to our lives in the previous two years. The Clean Air Act had noticeably improved the atmosphere of the city; the ubiquitous trams were still running but had only a year or so of life before they were replaced by buses. (To our minds, Leeds was never the same again.) Much building was in progress, and the view from Joan's parents' house was no longer of fields with cows grazing, though such encroachments had been going on for some years.

I reported to the Air Ministry by telephone and was given fifty-six days' leave, to report to Cranwell on 18 June. The bad news was that a married quarter was unlikely to be available until September, and so we needed to find somewhere to live near the College until then. The first requirement was a car, and for the first time in our lives we had built up sufficient savings in the bank to be able to buy one without too much difficulty. Joan and I went down to Leeds a couple of days after we had returned home, and bought a Singer Hunter from a dealer in Albion Street, a smart two-year-old black saloon (most cars were black then). We had a short drive around the city with the salesman, and for the first and only time I automatically tried to drive on the right of the road after leaving a junction, luckily managing to pull over to the correct side and avoiding a collision with a horrified driver coming in the opposite direction.

It was delightful to drive up into the Dales again and see violets and primroses flowering in the trees alongside the lanes in Littondale, where thankfully little had changed, and we were able to picnic on Hawkswick pastures above the Skirfare as of old. We gave ourselves a short breathing space and then set about finding somewhere to live for a few months within reach of Cranwell. Despite my wartime postings in Lincolnshire and our time at Waddington and Scampton, we were not too familiar with the area around Sleaford, and I had never visited Cranwell. Sleaford was a small, pleasant market town about seventeen miles south of Lincoln and some three or four miles from the RAF College. The River Slea ran under the main street, and we remember thinking that the houses directly above the water would be able to fish from their windows. Neither Joan nor I can remember how it came about – presumably through an estate agent or the local press – but by the middle of May we had arranged to rent Homa House in Quadring, a small village in the fen country between Sleaford and Spalding: it was a square turn-of-the-century house, with four rooms downstairs, including a not very satisfactory kitchen and scullery, and three bedrooms upstairs with a bathroom. There was a garage and a sizeable garden with a summerhouse, which pleased Sue and Jenny, and the rent was very reasonable – the elderly owner, Mrs Almond, lived in the village and turned out to be very friendly. Our heavy baggage from Alaska was being held in the Technical Stores at Cranwell, and we arranged for a local firm to remove it to Quadring, where it was dumped in the garage and seemed like an immovable mountain when we arrived to take up residence. However, as always, we sorted ourselves out, and Joan had the place looking like a home in very short order. We secured places at the village school for the girls, knowing that it would only be for a month or two, and started negotiations for Susan to attend Sleaford Girls' High School from the autumn term. All too soon it was the middle of June and time for me to report to Cranwell.

* * *

Like the RAF Staff College, an Air Force cadet college was another proposal in Trenchard's 1919 paper, 'Scheme for the Permanent Organization of the Royal Air Force'. He had been pressed to make use of the existing Army and Navy colleges at Sandhurst, Woolwich and Dartmouth, but felt strongly that RAF cadets needed to be taught to fly during their training, if for no other reason than that the RAF should be seen as an independent service with its own specialized requirements.

Early in the First World War the infant Royal Naval Air Service had selected Cranwell as one of several air bases in eastern England, and by 1916 it had become the main RNAS training centre – a large airfield training air and ground staff, not only on aeroplanes but on kites, balloons and airships also. Despite its lack of permanent accommodation, Trenchard felt that this was a suitable site for a cadet college, with full flying facilities and in an acceptable location. His intention was to produce most of the RAF's permanently commissioned officers here – about half of the officer corps – with the rest being given Short Service Commissions. Accordingly about fifty cadets reported to Cranwell in February 1920, most of them direct entrants from school, but including two RN sub-lieutenants and fifteen midshipmen transferred from Dartmouth, accommodated in the wartime wooden huts. It was a two-year course of military, academic and practical subjects, with a modest amount of flying, probably less than sixty hours according to some authorities. Parents were expected to pay fees.

It was 1929 before the College had financial approval for a permanent building, and this was finally opened on 11 October 1934 by the Prince of Wales (later, and briefly, King Edward VIII), by which time cadets had already moved into the building. The *Shell Guide to Lincolnshire* (1965) says: 'The buildings, designed by Sir James Grey-West, in red brick dressed with stone, excellently planned with magnificent lawns, plantations and vistas, are like a 20th century version of Chelsea Hospital – owing to the influence of the late Sir Samuel Hoare (Lord Templewood), then Secretary of State for Air, and M.P. for Chelsea.' It is certainly an impressive building with its 140-foot tower bearing a revolving light which can be seen for miles around, and the circular lawn known as the Orange between the College entrance and the gates.

The Second World War brought changes, with the College as such closing and becoming a Service Flying Training School, one among many to meet the need for pilots, but whose trainees must have thought themselves fortunate to be posted to a comparatively civilized station like Cranwell. The RAF College reopened in October 1946 by absorbing the FTS based there, and for the next twenty years or so young men were again prepared for permanent commissions, mostly straight from school, gaining their pilots' wings after some 300 hours' flying on a two-and-a-half-to-three-year course. Not long before I joined the College staff the entries started to include a few navigators (not before time, since the declaration of 'equal careers' was in 1948) and cadets for the Equipment and Secretarial Branches. In the 1958 summer term there was a total of 258 flight cadets, made up of 191 pilots, thirty-one navigators and thirty-six equipment and secretarial.

A public road ran through the station from east to west, with the main College buildings, playing-fields and other sports facilities to the north, also the old hangars (one now a church), a range of wooden huts for instructional purposes, and across the old north airfield (grass, of course) the married quarters; there was also a primary school for service children. On the south were the College and unit HQ, the Commandant's residence, the junior cadets' mess and quarters, a gym and swimming-pool, and the main airfield with its concrete runways, hangars, control tower and modern flying facilities for pilot training. The College post office was housed in the last of the First World War huts, retained in use until 1960.

Although my posting notice had described my new job as 'Senior Navigation Lecturer', it had by now been retitled 'Senior Navigation Instructor' in recognition of the fact that it had responsibility for the training of some cadets as navigators, rather than heading an element of the Tutorial Wing purely for the purpose of teaching pilots navigation as just another subject. However, the accommodation had not substantially changed – a large wooden hut with an office for the SNI, one or two classrooms, and a staff room for the eight or so navigation instructors, sited to the north near the old hangars and quite a contrast to the imposing College building. I was to take over from Bill Pettifer, who had been a fellow student at the Staff College; I think that the handover must have been fairly short since I remember little of it, and my engagement diary at that time is mostly concerned with mundane personal administration problems – applying to live out and for married quarters, claiming 'disturbance' and removal allowances, arranging a medical, and so on.

I reported to my immediate boss, Wing Commander 'Dickie' Duckett, an Education Branch officer in charge of the Tutorial Wing, which covered all the academic subjects such as engineering, aeronautics, maths and physics. Navigation was slightly out of place now, since its syllabus included flying training, but the old arrangements remained and I was very happy to work for Dickie, who was a sterling character with a sense of humour; he and his wife Marjorie remained friends for life.

With a total of only thirty-one navigator cadets spread over several entries, the navigation staff was not overworked, as I remember, and I was only required to give the odd lecture from time to time. Our flying training was done via the Navigation Squadron based at Barkston Heath, a satellite airfield on Ermine Street about six miles south of Cranwell. My flying logbook shows that there were six Varsities, now the main RAF navigation training vehicle, and five Valetta 'flying classrooms', plus an Anson XIX, so we were not short of aircraft. They were run competently by Flight Lieutenant Joe Davidson, and often used for overseas and other visits by cadets and staff. I see that in my first two or three weeks I flew as an instructor in both Valetta and Varsity, gaining some initial but not particularly favourable impressions of the standard of navigator cadet. However, I had to bear in mind that, unlike students at the Air Navigation Schools, they were involved in a much wider education and a much less intensive flying programme. Moreover, like myself, most of them had hoped to be pilots and were perhaps not so strongly motivated. I reserved judgment.

Not long after my arrival I had a surprise visit in my office from the Commandant, Air Commodore Spotswood (who was to become Marshal of the Royal Air Force Sir Denis Spotswood, Chief of the Air Staff and finally Chief of the Defence Staff). He had the distinction of being the first post-war Commandant who was not an Old Cranwellian, and he had a distinguished wartime career. Tall and slim, with a bushy moustache (unusual for the time), he had an imposing presence, although I felt that he was never entirely at ease with himself. At that first unscheduled visit he was friendly and encouraging and patently interested in the training of the navigator cadets. He left me with a very favourable impression, reinforced at my formal arrival interview with him a little later.

By mid-July I had settled down into my new job, and found it a relief to be responsible mainly for one particular activity rather than the multiplicity of (usually unfamiliar) tasks in Alaska. It was pleasant to be back in the RAF atmosphere and among navigators again; we were somewhat removed from the mainstream of College affairs, but in many ways that was no bad thing – I was able to get on with my job without too much interference, and was also able to fly mostly as and when I liked. We had visits from Flying Training Command navigation staff officers (two of whom were old friends – Eric Lee and Eric Jee) and from the Navigation Instructor Examining Board to categorize two of my staff, Arthur Small and Barry Blakeley. All went well and I could see that not a lot had changed in the navigation training world.

At the end of July I had my first experience of a full-dress formal College occasion – the passing-out parade of No. 73 Entry, the senior entry of flight cadets, marking their graduation and commissioning as pilot officers. On the day before the parade, wings and individual prizes, including the Sword of Honour, were presented by Air Marshal Sir John Whitley, Air Member for Personnel, whose son was among those graduating. For the parade itself, the Reviewing Officer was General Lauris Norstad USAF, Supreme Allied Commander, Europe. The full three squadrons of the Cadet Wing, commanded by senior entry Senior Under Officers and Under Officers, were on parade in front of the College building and marched past in slow and quick time to the music of the College Band directed by Squadron Leader Bill Bangay, who had started his career as a trumpeter at Cranwell in 1920. I could now see the results of the emphasis placed on drill at Cranwell – the parade was immaculate, with orders precisely given and every manoeuvre carried out to perfection; I was immensely impressed. My only part in the event was to be one of the many spectators seated on the Orange and to host some official guests in the Officers' Mess afterwards. Since I had had virtually no contact with the senior entry I did not attend the graduation ball held in the College that evening.

No. 74 Entry, the first to include navigators (all four of them), now became senior entry and were working up to graduation in December. The term's programme for the navigator cadets included visits to Farnborough, the London Planetarium, London Radar and RAF Waddington, and an overseas navigation exercise to Malta in which I participated as an instructor – we staged at Orange in Provence and flew a day and a night navigation exercise from Luqa in Malta. We had at least one free day and were able to enjoy the Maltese sea and sunshine. Flying in pairs in the Varsities, the cadets acquitted themselves well and we were satisfied with their performance.

Since there was a long-standing prize and trophy for the most accomplished pilot in each entry, it was felt that an equivalent for the navigators should now be considered, and I opened negotiations with the Institute of Navigation and the Directorate of Navigation at the Air Ministry. There was a favourable reaction from Michael Richey, the ION Executive Secretary, and the Assistant Commandant, Group Captain Neil ('Nebby') Wheeler and I went down to London to visit the Institute and discuss the possibility. (I recall having to buy a trilby since I did not possess a decent hat to wear with my civilian suit). The mission was successful, and the Institute produced a modest trophy, in the appropriate shape of a radar dish, to go with a monetary prize from the Air Ministry – I cannot remember the amount – which was presented in due course to Senior Flight Cadet D.R.W. de Garis of 74 Entry as the Institute of Navigation Trophy and Air Ministry Prize for Navigators.

*   *   *

Living out at Quadring, we did not get much involved in the social life of the College, and were content to live a rural existence in Homa House for the time being. The village was small but had a post office and shop and a good butcher, and the girls were able to walk to the village school across the fields. We acquired a new dog: Joan had seen an orange roan cocker spaniel in the village, and through its owner was able to purchase one from a Miss Burridge near Bury St Edmunds, who was training two spaniels for showing but was willing to part with one, a six-month-old bitch who she said was a little nervous for show work, but affectionate. The dog was put on the train to Spalding and Joan went down on the bus to collect her; she was indeed nervous after the train journey in a box, and welcomed Joan as her saviour, and from that time on she was Joan's dog. Her kennel name was Cairnrua's Candour, and she became Candy – very much part of the family for many years – a pretty dog, slightly built, luckily house trained and very loving. We remember her with great pleasure.

Towards the end of July we took Susan for an interview for a place at Sleaford Girls' High School, then a grammar school with a good reputation, and she was accepted for the autumn term. That was one worry fewer: since coming back to the UK, Susan had been unsettled and difficult and had not taken to the village school, where she tended to gang up with the village boys. On one occasion – although this appeared to be on her own initiative – she let down the tyres of a tractor parked behind our house at a chicken farm; we made her go and apologize to the farmer and she was certainly contrite, although we could see trouble ahead. But we hoped that more demanding school work would keep her occupied and happier. Jennifer took life as it came, and enjoyed being at Homa House with its garden and the summerhouse to play in, and of course both girls were delighted to have a new playmate in Candy.

Inevitably the time came when a married quarter became available at Cranwell, to be vacated by one of my own instructors, Eric Williams, on posting. In many ways we would have liked to stay in Quadring, but accepted that we should be living on the job. The date set for our move was 2 September, with Susan to start school a week or so later and Jenny to go to the school at RAF Cranwell; the College term began at about the same time.

But first we took a few days' leave in the Dales, staying at the Bluebell Hotel at Kettlewell in Wharfedale, one of our favourite places. The weather was mostly kind, and we went to the top of the dale and over into Wensleydale, having a memorable Yorkshire high tea at Bolton Castle; then up the small but beautiful Littondale, and to Deepdale, an offshoot of Upper Wharfedale near Buckden, where the girls (and their father) plus the dog played in the fast-flowing moorland beck – an idyllic afternoon.

This pleasant interlude braced us for the move to Cranwell (which I calculate was the eleventh house move since we were married). The quarter was a standard post-war three-bedroomed house, with a garden which the previous occupant had found time to keep in good shape (unlike some of the furniture, which had been chewed by Eric Williams's bulldog). We looked out on to the old north airfield, which was handy for dog walking; I remember that the first time I took Candy out on the airfield I let her off the leash and she ran straight as an arrow back to Joan at home.

*   *   *

Back in the office all was busy, with preparations for the overseas training flight I have already mentioned, cadets from the new entry to interview, a visit from the RAF Staff College involving a Guest Night, staff visits from HQ Flying Training Command (Eric Jee again) and from the Air Ministry Establishments Committee to check on our manpower situation. After a week away on the flight to Malta, there were the arrangements for the new navigation trophy to sort out and the final examination papers for No. 76 Entry navigators to prepare. In common with many of the College senior instructors, I had been allocated a small number of flight cadets (not necessarily navigators) to whom I was to be a 'mentor' – someone who could talk to them on a personal basis, try and sort out any problems, and generally act *in loco parentis*. I found this of great interest and assistance, and I hope the arrangement was mutually helpful: these young men were mostly 18 to 20, having left school with two 'A' levels in the General Certificate of Education (if I remember correctly), and about sixty per cent of them at that time were from Headmasters' Conference schools (basically public schools) and the remainder from grammar schools, with a few ex-apprentices from RAF Halton. It was interesting to note the development from the junior to the senior entries, the latter being much more self-possessed and confident, although the occasional cadet might be weaker on the academic side but a promising aviator. They not unnaturally had a different approach from the young men with whom I trained, being career minded, and I remember being surprised to be asked by one newish cadet for the details of retirement pay – something I had never given a thought to at their age. On the whole I found these cadets interested in their work, keen to do well in their chosen career, and wryly tolerant of the necessarily strict discipline imposed on them.

By the beginning of October 1958 I had settled into my new job and was beginning to enjoy it. My own staff were a congenial bunch – all Staff Navigators, of course – and now that we were in quarters we were able to entertain and have most of them round for supper with their wives, if any. I was getting plenty of flying, both as instructor and navigator, including a flight to Jurby in the Isle of Man, to which I had not returned since observer training in 1943/4; the station was now involved in officer training, and we had a pleasant lunch there, enlivened by sharing reminiscences with an elderly mess waiter who had remained at Jurby since the war.

Was it Napoleon or Wellington who said, 'Always expect the unexpected'? Landing one October afternoon at Barkston Heath, I was given an urgent message to report to the Assistant Commandant immediately. As I drove back to Cranwell, my mind was running over the events of the last week or so in an effort to pin-point something I had or had not done which could have caused Group Captain Wheeler's displeasure. I was no wiser by the time I knocked on his door in the headquarters building, but was greeted with a smile and asked to sit down. He came to the point at once, saying that there was a problem with the recently appointed College Administrative Officer, who was about to depart, and that, having discussed it with the Air Ministry Personnel Branch and the Commandant, he would like me to take on the job. I could hardly believe my ears; I had held my substantive rank of squadron leader for only four years, and was not expecting promotion for some time. Now I was being offered the acting rank of wing commander in a post which, though it was not one I would have chosen, could be regarded as a career posting.

When I arrived at Cranwell, the College Administrative Officer had been Wing Commander Dick Kerby, an old friend from Staff College. I had had little to do with him directly but knew that his job was a busy and demanding one. He had departed on posting to Oslo as Air Attaché, and his replacement had only been in post a couple of weeks when he too departed; what the reasons were I never discovered, but evidently his face did not fit and he had to go. I was the lucky beneficiary.

Joan was as surprised and pleased as I was, although the pleasure was somewhat marred when I told her that the Assistant Commandant had felt that we should move to a larger senior officers' quarter. However, that would not be in the immediate future, and meanwhile I had to try and disengage from the Senior Navigation Instructor's duties – a replacement had not yet been named – and to take on my new job with no predecessor to brief me. I also needed to have my uniforms readjusted to my new rank and to invest in a more appropriate civilian wardrobe, since I was likely to be involved in many more formal occasions and had to be well turned out. (I recalled visiting the cadets' survival camp in the Cairngorms not long after I arrived at Cranwell; I was dressed in a sweater and Alaskan lumberjack's cap and was somewhat chagrined to see the Commandant and Asistant Commandant in trilbies and immaculate tweeds.)

I led a double life for the next few weeks between the navigation section and the College HQ, but was able to hand over temporarily to my senior instructor, Roy Staley, until a permanent replacement (Alec Barrell, a Spec N who had been working in the Air Ministry manning staff) arrived early in December. On one day I would be attending meetings in the College and the College HQ, and the next lecturing to navigator cadets on the Royal Aircraft Establishment preparatory to their visit to Farnborough, which I was now unable to join. I also had to miss a visit from the Specialist Navigation Course staff at Manby to talk about the latest navigation aids and the effects of high-speed flight on navigation instruments; I had particularly wanted to hear about the progress in inertial navigation and radio sextants, but now I had to put all that behind me for the time being. I reflected that I had been lucky so far in my career in that my new post was the first not concerned with navigation.

Finally I put up my new rank (still finding it hard to believe) and took over my office across the corridor from Group Captain Wheeler and close to the Commandant's office, his Personal Staff Officer and ADC, and the College Adjutant. Lower down the corridor was the College Records Officer, a civil servant who kept tabs on everything that was going on in the College, with the year's diary in wall charts around the office.

I cannot recall any formal list of duties for the College Administrative Officer, and in the absence of a predecessor I had to find out as I went along. I was certainly concerned with almost everything that went on in the College: I was President of the Mess Committee in the Cadets' Mess, President of Cadet Games, Chairman of the Cadet Activities Organization, was responsible for all visits to and from the College, and had oversight of the College programme for the current year and a year or two ahead. As far as games were concerned (athletics, cricket, swimming, rowing, tennis, modern pentathlon, rugby and probably a few more), there were officers in charge of each and I was only acting in a supervisory capacity, although I was expected to (and did) attend the more important fixtures. These included regular matches against Dartmouth (the Royal Naval College) and Sandhurst (the Royal Military Academy), either at home or away. As far as 'activities' were concerned, there seemed to be a College society for almost everything – gliding, canoeing, fine arts, aeromodelling, motoring, sailing, mountaineering come to mind – with many being carried on in the vacation periods and several overseas. Again, there was an officer in charge of each and I did not get too involved.

Being PMC of the Cadets' Mess – incorporated in the main College building and with a splendid dining-room overlooked by a minstrels' gallery – took up a great deal of my time, since all College formal functions – dining-in nights, guest nights, luncheons for visiting parties and notabilities – took place there. Luckily for me there was a permanent Mess Secretary, retired Group Captain 'Nutty' Nuttall, first commissioned in the RAF in 1922 and 'one of the old school', commanding the respect of the cadets and dealing with all day-to-day mess matters. We got on well together, and he taught me a great deal. The senior entry provided a Cadets' Mess Committee with a Cadet PMC who was a Senior Under Officer, and they made a substantial contribution to mess affairs; Nutty and I attended their meetings but only interfered when necessary – it was excellent experience for them. The Cadet PMC would normally preside at College dinner and guest nights – again excellent training – which were strictly formal affairs usually attended by the Commandant and/or Assistant Commandant and, of course, by me (staying until the last guest and senior officer had left).

The mess staff were all civilians and many had served at the College for twenty years and more, including the Head Porter and Head Batman; everything was well run, the formal functions usually went like clockwork, and the Mess always presented an immaculate appearance. I got into the habit of walking across for coffee most mornings, when one could meet the Squadron Commanders and Flight Commanders and settle minor problems; the College Librarian, John Tanner, and I would usually share the *Times* crossword.

The cadet body was divided into three Squadrons, A, B and C, each commanded by a squadron leader and each with two flights commanded by flight lieutenants. Each squadron had one cadet Senior Under Officer and three Under Officers, who were in command on all formal parades; I had been impressed by the standard of drill on the one passing-out parade I had seen, and now I was so much more involved with the College I was able to appreciate the hard work and sheer sweat that went into it, under the eagle eyes of the College flight sergeants, the College Warrant Officer, Mr Longhurst, and the Senior Ground Defence Instructor, Squadron Leader Fred Hudson. The College band added an extra dimension, playing under its Director of Music, Squadron Leader Bangay MBE, a great character who had started as a boy fitter at Cranwell in 1918 and remustered as a musician in 1920. In the same year he was the trumpeter on the first parade of the first entry at the RAF College, and recalled how some cadets were in Dartmouth naval rig and some in suits and bowler hats (the latter somewhat battered from initiation ceremonies). Apart from the war years, he was at Cranwell for all his service career – a total of thirty-four years at the College and forty-one years in all; no wonder he had some tales to tell.

I worked directly with Bill Bangay, and got to know him well until his retirement in April 1959, when he was presented with a splendid silver salver bearing the facsimile signatures of the twenty-nine Commandants and Assistant Commandants under whom he had served. He continued to live in the village and was given the honorary membership of the Officers' Mess in perpetuity. He was not only a unique character but an extremely competent musician, as one would expect. I recall a guest night which the Ambassador of a Middle East country was to attend; it was the custom to play the national anthem of our guests' countries, but in this case no copies of the music (if they existed) could be had. We persuaded one of the Ambassador's staff to hum the tune to Bill, and by that evening he had produced all the band parts and was congratulated on the performance by the Ambassador.

*   *   *

Early in 1959 the Croppers moved yet again, to a wing commander's quarter on the edge of the 'married patch'. Susan had started at Sleaford Girls' High School the preceding September, and travelled daily by bus from Cranwell; Jennifer had settled into the primary school on the camp. Our lives had changed in other ways: from the comparative seclusion of the navigation staff I had now been thrown in at the deep end of the social life of the College, one of the early results of which was that I had to re-equip myself with both new uniforms, including mess kit, and more formal civilian clothes for all the varied functions I was now involved in. I had not served on a 'normal' RAF station since Scampton in 1950, and an update was much needed. Joan's wardrobe was also augmented, including a sheepskin coat suitable for watching rugby on cold afternoons, and I seem to recall a 'little black dress' and some other evening clothes. There were functions in the College, drinks and dinner parties here and there, and entertaining at home, which Joan coped with in her usual efficient way, not materially helped by our civilian batman, Mr Bee, who was more of a liability than an asset. He did not seem to have had any training, although he had been in the job for some years, and was a hindrance rather than a help when officiating as waiter at parties: at one Sunday lunchtime drinks party in our house, he was heard to urge the Commandant to 'Go on, 'ave another one', receiving a quelling look in reply.

Family involvement did not stop at formal occasions and dinner parties: many weekends were taken up by sports and other activities, and Joan and the girls usually turned out to watch rugby matches against Dartmouth and Sandhurst, cheering Cranwell on from the touchline. In summer, cricket was played on the Orange in front of the College, and there were athletics meetings and beagle meets, and gymkhanas held by the College riding fraternity (Susan, like many young girls, liked the idea of ponies, but after a few sessions shovelling horse dung in the College stables lost her enthusiasm).

We also attended services from time to time in the College church, St Michael's, which had been converted from a pre-war hangar (and very successfully as far as the acoustics were concerned). As I have written, early in these memoirs, I claimed to be agnostic, but both Joan and I were brought up in the Church of England and had a respect and liking for the Anglican ritual. At the hangar church, with the College Band playing the music and our Chaplain, Len Ashton, giving his usual unstuffy sermon, it was an enjoyable occasion. The church was also the venue for classical concerts, and I recall at least two by the BBC Northern Orchestra under George Hurst, and a piano recital by Denis Matthews.

Jennifer seemed settled at the Cranwell primary school, but we were having difficulties with Susan, who, although academically bright, was rebellious and unhappy at Sleaford Girls' High School. We had messages from the headmistress complaining about Sue's behaviour, especially on the school bus, and finally a suggestion that she might be more suited to a boarding school. We knew only too well how difficult she could be ('naughty' is the word that springs to mind), but wanted to give her the best academic chances; at least two, and possibly three, more day schools would be on the cards in our movable lives, and reluctantly we discussed with her the possibility of boarding. To her credit she understood the advantages and was not against the idea. We surveyed the educational literature and came up with two possibilities, both with Church of England connections: St Elphin's in Derbyshire and Casterton, near Kirkby Lonsdale in Westmorland. We visited both and chose Casterton, being particularly struck by how happy and healthy the girls looked; also, the school was not too far from Leeds and Joan's parents if we should be posted an unreasonable distance away (or overseas, although that did not seem likely for our next posting). Much as we disliked the idea, the possibility of Jenny joining Sue at school at some later date did cross our minds.

The list of school clothes, uniforms (from Marshall and Snelgrove's in Leeds) and other equipment seemed never ending, but we eventually packed Susan's trunk and she went off to Casterton not too unwillingly, staying there for the next five years. There would undoubtedly be problems, but we liked the school and felt that we had chosen wisely.

* * *

Leafing through my 1959 engagement diary, it seems that there were few days not taken up with some College function, exchange visits in which I participated (Dartmouth, Sandhurst, Henlow, the French Ecole de l'Air at Salon-de-Provence) or visitors to the College. My logbook shows that I only managed forty-odd hours' flying that year – the smallest annual total for some time.

Much time was taken up by visitors of varying importance. On the first of April 1959 (the RAF's 41st birthday) we were honoured with a visit from the Prime Minister of the day, Harold Macmillan, accompanied by the Chief of the Air Staff, Marshal of the Royal Air Force Sir Dermot Boyle – a well-liked and effective CAS, and by the Under-Secretary of State for Air, George Ward, with the C-in-C of Flying Training Command, Air Marshal Constantine. This entailed a great deal of preparation, including a parade rehearsal at which 'Nebby' Wheeler, the Assistant Commandant, played the part of the PM, dressed in overcoat and bowler hat. The formal parade itself went off well, and Harold Macmillan appeared to be suitably impressed. Luncheon was in the College, and with our experienced and well-trained staff all went like clockwork. Although I sat at the top table, I regret to say that I do not remember a word of the no doubt sparkling conversation. Macmillan was geniality itself, and the CAS later congratulated the Commandant on a well-organized occasion.

A few days after this Group Captain Wheeler was posted away and replaced as Assistant Commandant by Group Captain 'Bob' Hodges; both of them were highly decorated wartime pilots (Group Captain Hodges had flown special-duties missions landing agents in enemy-occupied Europe), and both eventually became air marshals. I was sorry to see 'Nebby' Wheeler go: we had got on well together and he had given me a great deal of support when I was pitchforked into my College job. But 'Bob' Hodges was equally supportive, and he and his wife Elizabeth became good friends. He was a downright character with a strong sense of duty, and soon took over the reins with a capable hand. He liked to fly when he could, and took me with him on an Anson air test not long after he arrived, no doubt to see what sort of navigator I was.

At the end of July, 75 Entry passed out and the College nominally stood down for the summer recess; in fact most cadets were involved in various activities in various parts of the world, and the College staff were much concerned with these and with other duties which could only be done when the College was mostly unoccupied. I spent a few days with the Survival Camp in the Cairngorms, having broken in a pair of walking boots and done some walking on the north airfield. I flew up to Lossiemouth via Acklington in one of the Barkston Heath Valettas (being struck by the number of long empty beaches on the Northumberland coast on this Bank Holiday Monday), and joined the camp not far from Aviemore, which in those days was not the tourist playground it is now.

The tented accommodation was fairly comfortable for the staff, whereas the cadets had been distributed in small groups around what was virtually a wilderness area, and had to make their own shelters and cook their own food, as well as taking part in various strenuous exercises. I did join one of these, which involved climbing Cairn Gorm (4,084 feet); this in itself was not too difficult, as there were mostly established paths, but as I was carrying a heavy radio transmitter/receiver on my back it was hard going. I felt some satisfaction at having reached the summit, but was somewhat miffed to see the odd tourist party with small children who had also made the ascent. But the views were glorious and we got a good look at the reindeer herd grazing on the next mountain.

Flying back to Barkston Heath after a few days, I was able to snatch a weekend in Leeds with the family, and then it was back to Cranwell for the next excitement – a series of high-level NATO exercises, each with about 190 high-ranking officers from various countries and twenty exercise staff to accommodate, organize and entertain, which of course we could only do during the summer break. We had been planning this for some months: there were two connected exercises, codenamed 'Triumvirate' and 'Unison', each with two three-day sessions (including dinner nights). Triumvirate was mainly scene-setting by the exercise staff, while Unison involved further study and discussion. These sessions were highly classified, but if I remember correctly were mostly concerned with the NATO response to problems in the Middle East. The last session brought the most high-ranking NATO officers, and I well remember the official photograph being taken on the College steps, with Lord Mountbatten, then Chief of the Defence Staff, coming out in front of the assembled throng and saying: 'Right, all five-stars in the front row.' I was on the edge of the very back row, and I always regret that I did not obtain a print.

At the end of 1959, 76 Entry passed out, reviewed by General Festing, and work started on a fourth wing of the College building: it had always been the intention to add this to the other three wings, but the Second World War and later, perhaps, finance delayed the project. The work was finished the following year, using the same architectural style as the rest of the College, and the College Journal shows photographs of the Commandant, C Squadron Commander and a College flight sergeant breaking through to the new wing, which would eventually house a new D Squadron. Other new building projects in the pipeline included a new church, a new instructional block, a new Sergeants' Mess and Airmen's Club, a swimming-bath and gymnasium, and a new school for the children of serving personnel. I felt that many at Cranwell, like me, would miss the unique atmosphere of the old hangar church, but the structure was undoubtedly in decay and had to be replaced.

Other changes being planned were the replacement of the piston-engined Provost with jet Provost aircraft, to start in the autumn term of

1960, and beginning in January 1961 all entries would train exclusively on the JP from their fifth term; there would eventually be sixty to seventy JPs operating from Cranwell. Flying before the fifth term for pilots would be on the Chipmunk, on which they would solo, and cadets would in future be posted to an advanced flying training school after graduation. These plans entailed our satellite airfield at Barkston Heath being improved to jet standards, and the flying wing there would have to move temporarily to Spitalgate, with the navigation training squadron operating from Cranwell – a lucky break for the navigator cadets (whose numbers, incidentally, had not increased substantially).

As always, the arts were not neglected in the College programme, and we had a visit from Opera for All, who performed *The Barber of Seville* to a large and appreciative audience. Later there was an excellent performance of *The Mikado* by the College Choral and Dramatic Sections, with an augmented orchestra conducted by Flight Lieutenant Roy Davies, who had replaced Bill Bangay as Director of Music; I particularly remember the impressive singing and acting of the flight cadet who played the Mikado (John Nottingham was his name – I wonder what happened to him). I also recall hearing a rumpus outside in the College entrance hall during one of the intervals: when I went to investigate I found four hefty cadets sitting on a man lying on the floor. He turned out to be someone purporting to be an Air Training Corps officer temporarily staying in the College, but had been discovered removing valuables from rooms in the building. He was taken off to the Guardroom and presumably dealt with by the local police.

The great event of 1960 was a visit in July by the Queen, who had recently become Commandant-in-Chief of the College, to review the passing-out parade of 77 Entry and to present a new Queen's Colour. This naturally involved a great deal of planning and preparation, complicated as far as I was concerned by the Commandant's decision to hold a special parade for the Queen's Official Birthday on 21 June: all cadets were to be on parade, but, unusually, including the College Squadron and Flight Commanders, with the College Administrative Officer as parade commander. This caused some consternation, as the College officers rarely took part in parades and were hardly at the high standard expected from cadets, especially when swords were to be carried. In my case I had not been on any sort of formal parade since 1950, a ten-year gap which did not fill me with confidence. However, the College Senior Ground Defence Instructor, Squadron Leader Fred Hudson, with his staff, took us in hand and gave us daily drill sessions with swords until our proficiency satisfied him (if not us). As the parade commander I had to learn a seemingly endless string of drill commands for a parade which included an advance in review order and marching past in slow and quick time. The first and only rehearsal took place in front of the College, and all went well, but it was then decided that the station parade ground would be used, making further adjustments necessary. On the day there were no problems: the Commandant took the salute and there was an audience of station staff and families. The flight cadets' performance was immaculate as always, and I can still feel the sense of personal satisfaction in having had the honour of commanding the Royal Air Force College on a ceremonial parade.

Meanwhile the preparations for the Queen's visit on 25 July were going on all over the station and the College, and full advantage was taken of the opportunity to make improvements and redecorations.

The main College building was rarely anything but immaculate, with our experienced and capable domestic staff, but some retiring-rooms for HM had to be prepared, and elderly curtains replaced in the library, where the Queen would be receiving. The cadets had several parade rehearsals, and Flying Wing was busy practising the flypast and aerobatic display.

There was to be a formal luncheon in the College after the parade, the dedication of the Colour and some tree planting, and the Assistant Commandant told me that as PMC I would receive the Queen into the College when she came in preparatory to lunch. She would retire for a short break and then receive the College officers and their wives in the library; I would escort the Duke of Edinburgh to his retiring-room and then take him up to join the reception. How, I asked, would Joan fit into this arrangement? Bob Hodges looked disconcerted for a moment, but after consideration he said that he was very sorry but he didn't see how she could be presented: I would already have met HM and according to protocol I could hardly be presented a second time with my wife. I knew this would be a bitter pill for Joan to swallow, especially as several wives would be presented who had contributed very little to the life of the College; Joan had hosted guests, attended matches, given dinner parties and had senior cadets for informal drinks. As an ardent Royalist she was most upset that she would miss the chance of meeting the Queen; I naturally felt for her, and tried again to reverse the decision, but to no avail, and we had to accept the situation.

The great day came, and the Queen and the Duke of Edinburgh arrived in their red de Havilland Heron. Some 2,500 spectators were gathered on the Orange, and fervent prayers for fine weather were answered; the staging of the event in the wet-weather hangar was planned but would have been a nightmare to organize. HM took her position on the dais, and after a flypast by sixteen aircraft of the Advanced Flying Wing was received by a Royal Salute from the parade commanded by Senior Under Officer P.J. Kemp (Pat Kemp, who was later one of my co-pilots on No. 53 Squadron). She then inspected the three squadrons. After the march-past in slow and quick time, the old Queen's Colour was marched off for the last time to be laid up in the College Chapel, and the new Colour was marched on and presented by the Queen, who gave a short and appropriate address. She then presented the Sword of Honour to SUO Kemp and the Queen's Medal to SUO Bonnor (Norman Bonnor, a navigator who was later one of my students on the Specialist Navigation Course).

After some tree planting the Royal party came into the College, and I welcomed the Queen in the entrance hall, exchanging a gentle handshake and a smile. She then went off to her retiring-room with her lady-in-waiting, and I escorted Prince Philip to his before taking him up to the library, where the Queen was to meet College officers and their wives (with one exception!). The dining-room was full for luncheon, with the Commandant presiding, and I was at the foot of one of the long tables to act as 'Mr Vice' and propose the loyal toast; if I remember correctly, Joan was seated between the Commander-in-Chief of Fighter Command and the Captain of the Queen's Flight (of blessed memory).

The Commandant presented the Queen with a brooch, subscribed to by present and past members of the College, made by Garrard of platinum and diamonds in the form of the College badge.

After lunch we gathered in the entrance hall and watched as the Queen signed the visitors' book and the Royal party left the College building to inspect the Flying Wings and watch a display by the Vampire aerobatic team. They then departed in their Queen's Flight Heron, seen off by a gaggle of senior people, including the Under-Secretary of State for Air, George Ward, the Chief of the Air Staff, the C-in-C of Flying Training Command, and our Commandant. Joan watched the departure and was able to get a couple of photographs.

The Queen, who was 34 at the time, left a lasting impression of her personal beauty, simple dignity and sense of humour. It had been a memorable day, with everything going according to plan, and as the College Journal said, 'Two thousand four hundred and ninety spectators sat ... and watched the best Parade in living memory.' For the College officers and staff it was of course a great relief to have it all behind us and to feel that it had been a success. Normal College activities and visits went on for the rest of the summer but with a more relaxed feeling. I paid a short visit to the survival camp in the Cairngorms at the end of July, navigating a Varsity to Kinloss, and was finally able to take a couple of weeks' leave in August.

We had booked a cottage in the Dales for a couple of weeks – the first time we had tried this kind of holiday – and were looking forward to 'getting away from it all'. Susan was home from Casterton School and seemed to have settled there (if not happily, at least without too much complaint). We called at Joan's parents in Leeds on the way, and finally took over the Blacksmith's Cottage at Middlesmoor, a tiny village perched on a steep hill at the head of Nidderdale, with a pub, a church, a small village shop and little else except for stunning views down the dale and over Gouthwaite Reservoir, like a miniature Lake District. The living quarters of the cottage were on the first floor, reached by a set of stone steps, with the former blacksmith's shop down below. Spring water splashed into a stone horse-trough outside, but the indoor facilities were adequate and we settled down in anticipation of a relaxing holiday.

Joan and I certainly needed it after the demanding College programme, with rarely a day clear of some extra-curricular activity, including weekends. The preparation for the Royal visit had been hard work, but at least we had the satisfaction of knowing that it had all gone well. Also, my name had been in the 1 July promotion list as a substantive wing commander, and on the basis of this I had undertaken to serve to the age of 55 under the new career structure recently introduced (the former retiring age being 43 for squadron leaders and 45 for wing commanders). So I felt that my career was going well, and looked forward to at least another six months at Cranwell before the next posting, which I hoped would be a flying job.

We explored the area around Middlesmoor – which Joan and I already knew from our teenage days – and made expeditions to Ripon (shopping in the market-place and visiting the minster) and the local small town, Pateley Bridge, where we bought our food. Sue and I had a walk up on the moor to the massive Scar House Reservoir dam, built in the 1920s and '30s to bring water to Bradford, some thirty-odd miles away, and supplement supplies already piped from Angram Reservoir further up the moors and Gouthwaite below Middlesmoor – great Victorian/Edwardian enterprises. The Scar House workforce had reached 1,290, and a village was built to accommodate them; we inspected the site, now reduced to what archaeologists would call 'hut platforms', and thought it forlorn and a little eerie. Next day Jenny demanded to be taken on the same walk, and we repeated the exercise, to the accompaniment of the mournful noises of curlews and lapwings, and the song of larks.

Our idyll was rudely interrupted almost at the end of the holiday. A telegram was delivered from Cranwell instructing me to telephone the Commandant as soon as possible. When I did so, he told me that he had received a posting notice for me to be the Station Commander at RAF Gan (an island staging-post in the Indian Ocean Maldive Islands half-way between Aden and Singapore). As if this were not enough of a shock, the post was unaccompanied, and I was to report there in about three weeks' time. The Commandant was sympathetic, and said that he would see what he could do to give me a little more time; he added that it was undoubtedly a 'career posting' and that Joan could stay on in the quarter at Cranwell if she wished.

This was a blow to both of us; we had not expected another overseas posting so soon, and were indignant about the unreasonably short notice.

We hurried back to Cranwell, and I was called for an interview in the Air Secretary's department at the Air Ministry. I was seen by a placatory but implacable Air Commodore, who said he regretted the short notice but unforeseen circumstances required it. However, he agreed to put my posting date back to the end of September (it was now the end of August) when I explained that Joan did not wish to stay at Cranwell in my absence, and we would have to find somewhere else for the family to live. He said that the post was a challenging one and would be a great help to my career if I made a good job of it, and added that they would try and give me my choice of postings when I returned at the end of the twelve months' tour. I told his staff that I would like to command a flying squadron, preferably in Transport Command, and they said that they would see what they could do, words I received with a certain amount of scepticism.

I seem to remember that I walked across Whitehall to the Commonwealth Relations Office for a short briefing on the political situation in the Maldive Islands, which were under British protection at the time. It was a very basic briefing, but I was told that when I reached Gan the UK Political Representative would fill me in on the present situation and act as my political adviser.

The remaining few weeks at Cranwell were hectic: the normal College work had to go on, with the autumn term starting on 7 September; we had to find somewhere else to live; and I had to prepare a handover brief for my successor. Joan was determined not to remain as a grass widow at Cranwell, and she found an advertisement in the *Dalesman* magazine for a furnished cottage at Austwick, a village north of Settle, which would not be far from Leeds and also near to Casterton School, to which Jenny would probably go the following year. We made a quick visit back to Yorkshire and inspected the property – a three-bedroomed village house (next to the pub but overlooking the village green) with a sitting-room, dining-room, bathroom and kitchen, the latter being poky, slightly dark and damp and not very well equipped. The front door opened on to the village street, but there was a very small garden at the rear. The house had a long-term tenant, a widow, who was going to spend some time with her family in South Africa and was willing to sub-let to us for at least a year. Joan felt that she could cope with the cottage and its drawbacks, and we agreed the lease to begin towards the end of September at a reasonable rent. I was not entirely happy, but could see the advantages, and we had little time left to find anywhere else.

My replacement, Wing Commander Eric Brice, arrived on 12 September, and we had a rapid handover. His was an unusual appointment as he was a member of the Physical Fitness Branch, and we understood that he was being given wider experience in anticipation of his reaching senior rank in that small and specialized branch (in fact, he eventually became head of it as an air commodore some years later). He was a quick learner and a pleasant character, and I tried to make up for the short handover by preparing a comprehensive written brief, as I had done in Alaska. He wrote to me some months later, 'I found your brief admirable and I still look through it occasionally as a check-up. The Cropper systems remain, as well as your good name, amid everyone here. It is interesting to realize that this post, with its many facets, could be handed over effectively in four days together plus a good brief.' Another satisfied customer.

The remaining few days passed in a flash, with the house to be tidied up and our own possessions packed up ready for removal, Susan to be prepared for return to school, and innumerable little details to be sorted out. I was dined out in the College and said my farewells to the many people with whom I had worked. Joan and I went to the Commandant's residence to say goodbye to Anne Spotswood, but found she was ill in bed; however, she insisted on our going up to her, and kissed us both goodbye.

Finally, the inevitable removal van arrived and took away our own effects, some to store and some to Austwick, and we departed the following day to take over the cottage (which had no name, the address being merely The Green, Austwick).

We settled in as best we could, Joan promising herself that she would sort out the unsatisfactory kitchen. Once our own possessions were in place, the house looked more like home, Joan performing her usual magic as she had done so many times. We arranged for Jenny to go to the village school just up the road until she went to Casterton the following year, and after some sad farewells I drove back to Leeds where my brother-in-law (Joan's sister's widower) had offered to lay the car up until I returned. After saying goodbye to our respective parents I took the train back to Cranwell, was present at the 'marching out' inspection of our married quarter, and the following day went on to Lyneham, also by train. There was a day's delay at Lyneham ('if you've time to spare, travel by air'), but we eventually took off in a Britannia and flew via El Adem, Aden and Gan to RAF Changi in Singapore, where I was to spend a week being briefed at HQ Far East Air Force.

*   *   *

The two years at the RAF College had been a valuable experience, mostly enjoyable, and with the bonus of unexpected promotion and a change to a different and demanding job. It was good to be on a proper RAF station again after so many years away, although Cranwell was something special and unique in many respects. For the first time I had had a job unconnected with navigation, and undoubtedly this broadened my approach; on the whole I was converted to the Cranwell system of officer training and its carefully considered mix of general education, flying training and indoctrination into the RAF ethos of discipline tempered by individual encouragement. Facilities for sport and other leisure and cultural activities were unrivalled, and for me the opportunity of meeting so many people of distinction of one sort or another was a privilege and a pleasure. The RAF College has over the years changed and diversified, and is now a sort of university of the RAF, with a much wider brief; many of the cadets I knew have retired as air marshals, and I have some doubts as to the present graduates being of the same calibre. But old men often look at the past through rose-coloured spectacles.

CHAPTER FIFTEEN

'Cropper's Island'

D*aily Express*, 2 November 1960: 'CROPPER'S ISLAND. Wing Commander Eric W. Cropper, 37, of Leeds, is the new Commanding Officer of Gan, a tiny island in the Indian Ocean, but a vital link in the R.A.F.'s Far East route.'

In the twenty-first century, the Maldive Islands have become a holiday playground for Europeans and others. The brochures promise 'a taste of serenity as you visit the clear blue waters, ideal for scuba diving and snorkelling; discover the attractive coral reefs and white sandy beaches …'. The islands hang like a string of pearls in the map of the Indian Ocean from a point to the west of Sri Lanka, running south in a chain of nineteen coral atolls for some six hundred miles and ending just below the Equator. There are over twelve hundred islands, none of which is more than two miles long or nine feet above sea level. The total population is about a quarter of a million, with sixty-three thousand on Male, the islands' capital in the north of the group, where most of the tourist activity now takes place. Addu atoll is the most southerly atoll, just in the southern hemisphere, and Gan is the most southerly and the largest island of Addu.

In 1960 the Maldives were undiscovered by tourism. With little or no soil for agriculture, the Maldivians (Sunni Muslims) depended on fish, both to feed themselves and to trade with Ceylon (now Sri Lanka) and India for goods – Maldivian dried fish was well known as a delicacy. They built their own boats and ranged far and wide in the Indian Ocean.

The Maldivians had Indian and Sri Lankan origins, but had been influenced by Arab traders on routes to Malacca and China, and converted at an early date to Islam. In 1887 Britain, which of course ruled Ceylon at that time, made a protection agreement under which the internal government of the Maldives remained independent but the United Kingdom ran its foreign affairs. The islands had been under the autocratic rule of a Sultan for centuries, but in 1932 a constitutional Sultanate was established with an elected Sultan.

When war threatened in 1939, the British government was concerned about possible Japanese aggression in the Far East and Pacific, and in early

1940 flying-boat mooring and refuelling facilities were set up in Male atoll with the full co-operation of the Sultan. When the Japanese captured Dutch East Indies airfields, Allied shipping in the Indian Ocean was at risk and the Admiralty needed some safe haven between South Africa and the Far East. A reconnaissance of Addu atoll in the latter half of 1940 showed its suitability for fleet anchorages and as a flying-boat base, but reported that an enormous amount of work would be required. This was a massive understatement, and it took until 1942 to set up the base at Addu – known as Port T – with the facilities required (eventually including three compacted coral runways on Gan). Working conditions were atrocious, with mosquitoes, heat, swamps, and innumerable coconut palm trees to clear, at first few anti-malarial measures available, and scrub typhus endemic. Peter Doling (who was stationed at RAF Gan in the late 1960s) tells the full story in his monumental work *From Port T to RAF Gan* (Woodfield Publishing, 2003), and I am indebted to him for this very brief and basic account of Gan's history.

With the changing fortunes of the war in the Far East, it was decided in 1944 that Port T could be run down: this was a long-drawn-out process, and the last serviceman did not leave Addu atoll until the beginning of 1946, leaving the Adduans to try and recover their former frugal way of life, which had been torn apart by the construction and operation of the British base.

After a formal agreement with the United Kingdom in 1948, the Maldives became a republic in 1953 and a member of the Commonwealth, but the following year a Sultan was reinstated as an elected ruler. In the post-war period the Maldives suffered severe economic problems, and there were protracted negotiations with the UK, mostly through the High Commissioner in Ceylon, in attempts to attract aid, in particular with the Maldivian fishing industry. Britain had its own problems and was slow in giving any practical assistance. However, in the early 1950s the Air Ministry became concerned about the need for an independent air route across the Indian Ocean, and Addu atoll was considered to be a likely location, along with Diego Garcia and the Seychelles. Late in 1952 a survey of these three possibilities was made by a Sunderland flying-boat from the Far East Air Force (with Maldivian agreement for Addu atoll). The Seychelles were not thought to be suitable, and eventually Addu atoll became the choice. The Maldivian government agreed to the lease of Gan and other facilities in Addu atoll for thirty years from December 1956, receiving in return a direct grant of £100,000 and a grant of £750,000 to finance specific development projects over several years.

The saga of the development of RAF Gan is told in detail by Peter Doling in his book, from the arrival of a small advance party in January 1957 to the airfield becoming operational in January 1960. The practical problems were enormous: tropical heat and rain, extended supply lines, the housing

Raising the US flag on Ice Station Alpha on 21 May 1957.

Eric at Point Barrow in May 1957.

Ice Station Alpha. Capt Dick Wolfersperger centre with Fritz Awe, the camp boss, to the right.

DEW Line Station PIN.

A RCAF Comet 2 at Ladd AFB in February 1958.

Eric's family leaving Alaska from Anchorage in March 1958. Tom Walker of the Civil Aeronautics Administration is on the right.

Using the astrocompass in an RAF College Varsity on a training flight in September 1958.

The Queen's departure after her visit to the RAF College on 25 June 1960.

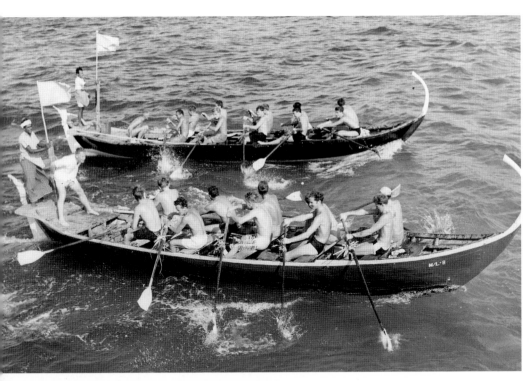

Dhoni race with RAF crews on Gan at Christmas 1960. *(Crown Copyright)*

Eric at the Maldivian children's party in station sick quarters on Gan in 1960. Tom Bucher, the Medical Officer is on the extreme right. *(Crown Copyright)*

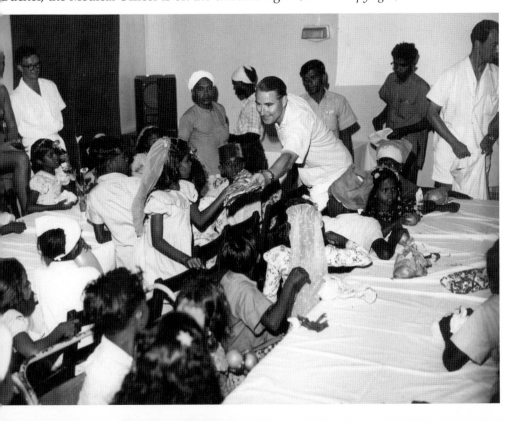

The visit of the Chief of the Defence Staff to RAF Gan in February 1961. Lord Mountbatten, the author and Afif Didi, President of the People's Council of Addu. *(Crown Copyright)*

The opening of the Gan steam laundry in December 1960. Bill Hart, Senior Equipment Officer and Mrs Grundy, the wife of AVM Grundy. *(Crown Copyright)*

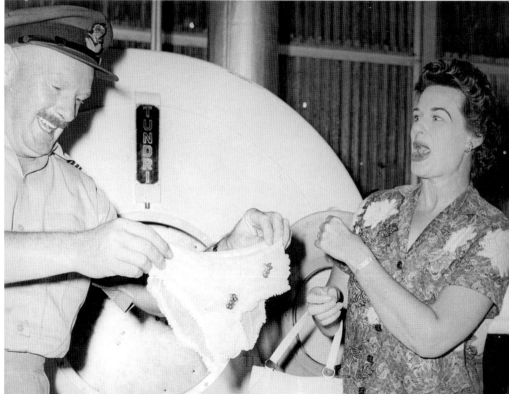

'Humphrey's Island', Dunidu, the residence of the UK's Political Representative, H Arthington-Davy, in Male Atoll in July 1961. *(Crown Copyright)*

Waiting for the boat to Male. Humphrey and Eric at Dunidu on the way to an audience with HE the Sultan of the Maldives in July 1961.

Visiting the Sultan of Male. L to R Humphrey, the author and The Sultan in the middle. *(Crown Copyright)*

The visit of the AOC, AVM Hobler, to Gan with the author in the Flight Planning Section. The map is centred on Gan. June 1961. *(Crown Copyright)*

Eric in his office at Gan.
(Crown Copyright)

The author holding the baby. Aircraft unserviceability sometimes left families stranded overnight on Gan.

No 101 NVGTR. REFRESHER COURSE.
F/L BROWN, F/L FLETCHER, F/L GOODMAN, F/L HANNEY, F/L LAING, F/L MARKS, F/L HUGHESNON.
F/L GATES, W/C CROPPER, F/L NEWMAN (C.C.), S/L CROUCHER, F/L STEWARTS..........

101 Navigator Refresher Course at RAF Topcliffe in 1961. *(Crown Copyright)*

A 53 Squadron Beverly at Nicosia in July 1962.

A normal working day at RAF Abingdon in 1963.

A Beverley of 53 Squadron at Kufra Oasis in January 1963.

The Kufra Beverley's crew L to R: author, AQM Thatcher, Signaller Mullins, AQM Dinnebier, Engineer Peto, Captain Bryan Lamb and co-pilot Tony Clark.

The presentation of flying badges to Air Quartermasters at RAF Abingdon. Eric at rear. L to R: Sgt Moore, Sgt Hardy, Gp Capt Sowrey, Sgt Neal and Sgt Slocombe. November 1963. *(Crown Copyright)*

AOC's inspection of 53 Squadron in June 1963. L to R: Gp Capt Sowrey, Eric and AVM Piper. *(Crown Copyright)*

Eric presenting Gp Capt Sowrey with the RAF Abingdon station plaque at the Station Commander's farewell guest night on 10 December 1964. *(Crown Copyright)*

The delivery of the first Andover to Abingdon on 21 December 1964. *(Crown Copyright)*

The No. 23 Specialist Navigation Course with the F-111 at General Dynamics at Fort Worth Texas in November 1965.

Eric and his wife Joan at Manby in 1966.

and feeding of the work force, the eventual removal of Adduans from the island with rehousing on the next island of Fedu, and all complicated by the internal political problems of the Maldives, in which the Adduans rebelled against what they saw as a harsh regime from the Maldivian government, with increased taxes and unpalatable edicts from Male. For a period the Adduans formed the United Suvadiva Republic, headed by Abdullah Afif Didi, the local headman, although relations with the British remained good and in general the work at Gan was not affected. Eventually they came to an agreement with Male, but the problems rumbled on for several years. Meanwhile the contract for building the runway had been awarded to Richard Costain Ltd, and though the work was delayed for various reasons, it was finally completed to the satisfaction of the RAF.

*   *   *

My first sight of Gan was from the air as we landed there to refuel on the way to Changi in Singapore. It was not a particularly encouraging prospect: Addu atoll was a heart-shaped group of coral islands, all green with palm trees except for Gan, with the 8,700-foot concrete runway running roughly east to west the full width of the island. Most of the vegetation had been cleared for construction, and the raw contrast with the other islands was marked. The accommodation and administrative buildings were grouped on the north-west corner, and all over the island other construction works appeared to be going on. When we had landed and taxied on to the large hardstanding where aircraft were refuelled, serviced, and repaired if necessary, we were met by the Station Commander, Michael Constable-Maxwell, who took me and one or two more senior officers (including the C-in-C of Fighter Command) off to his bungalow for the hour or so that the aircraft would be on the ground. He was a few years older than me and a highly decorated wartime fighter pilot with aristocratic connections, so could hardly have been more different from me in experience and background; however, he made me feel welcome and confided that a lot of his time seemed to be taken up meeting VIPs. After a drink we had a short tour of the island and met, very briefly, Humphrey Arthington-Davy, the UK Representative in the Maldives, and Afif Didi, the Atoll Representative, both of whom were welcoming and friendly. In a letter home I said about the station, 'I must say that things were rather better than I expected and I felt quite bucked when we left again.'

After a much-needed sleep in the Changi Transit Mess, I moved to the HQ Far East Air Force Officers' Mess – much more palatial – and checked on the HQ telephone directory for old friends and acquaintances, several of which I found. One had been a particular friend, both on the Specialist

Navigation Course at Shawbury and later at HQ Bomber Command – Ron Davis, who had transferred to the Equipment Branch and was a squadron leader staff officer in HQFEAF. He and his wife Rita were delighted when I got in touch with them, and were immeasurably helpful during the week I spent in Singapore, driving me around, introducing me to various useful people, and giving me a great deal of personal hospitality. They took me to a tailor who produced several items of tropical clothing in only a few days and at ridiculous prices, and generally hosted and shepherded me most generously.

I called on the C-in-C FEAF, Air Marshal Selway (soon to be Sir Anthony), and he was most encouraging and friendly, telling me to call on FEAF staff whenever I needed help, and also Air Vice-Marshal Grundy, the Air Officer i/c Administration, who would be my immediate superior as Air Officer Commanding various FEAF outstations. He was a jovial and expansive character who again pressed me to make use of his staff whenever necessary. I spent much of the working week touring the various HQ FEAF departments and picking people's brains, and I was impressed – as I continued to be throughout my time at Gan – by the readiness to give useful information and practical help when it was necessary.

I found Singapore itself not very attractive. I wrote to Joan, 'The traffic in Singapore is fantastic and frightening – much worse than London, and the Chinese seem to have no road sense at all. It's not too much of a place to look at either, and the sea front stinks to high heaven. A lot of the shops and offices are air-conditioned and it's like stepping into a refrigerator and then back into an oven when you go in and out.' However, I was taken to some pleasant restaurants and shops and hosted by various people, so the time passed quickly and I made some useful purchases (a record player and some classical records for one).

During my stay at Changi two Javelins arrived from Coltishall, having made a record-breaking flight non-stop from the UK using air refuelling. One of the navigators was Squadron Leader Bob Jefferies, who had been a College Squadron Commander at Cranwell, and as I was one of those who met the aircraft I was able to get a first-hand account from him: I forget the flight time but remember that Bob said that it was a hell of a long time to sit with a Javelin strapped to your bottom. They were due to fly back to Gan, so I would see them again.

Eventually, after saying goodbye to my various friends and new acquaintances (I took the Davises out to dinner – they had been a wonderful help throughout), I flew to Gan to take over from Michael Constable-Maxwell. He was to stay in post another week as the FEAF Commander-in-Chief was to pay his first official visit, and Michael felt – quite rightly – that he should do the honours. I was temporarily quartered in a transit block for people passing through or visiting who needed to stay the night; the room was air conditioned, but the permanent quarters on the station were not – we residents soon got used to it, and there was thus no unpleasant contrast between outdoor and indoor temperatures.

By this time Humphrey Arthington-Davy, the UK Political Representative in the Maldives, had left Gan and taken up residence on a tiny island (Dunidu) close to Male and to another island, Hulule, where a small airstrip had been built for his use if it should be necessary; he intended to pay regular visits to Gan, but this depended on the availability of lower-performance aircraft such as the RNZAF Bristol Freighters from Singapore which could land safely on the short strip. Michael C-M had in fact intended us to fly up to Hulule in a Valetta which was temporarily at Gan the day after I arrived, but a strong cross-wind was reported on the strip and the pilot decided not to go.

The week was busy as we went round the various sections on the station, meeting all the officers and some of the airmen, and discussing the daily round and its inevitable problems. For a small island there were a lot of people: a Royal Air Force complement of around 500; an Army Air Formation Signals troop twelve strong; around thirty-five UK civilians (Air Ministry Works Department twenty-five to thirty, NAAFI four, Met Office three); some 450 Pakistani contract workers, mostly semi-skilled – these numbers were reducing as the building projects developed; thirty Ceylonese NAAFI staff; one female British WVS worker; and up to 1,000 Maldivians employed in various unskilled jobs (they came in from other islands daily by boat). The RAF figures included a small detachment at Hittadu, an island on the north side of the atoll which housed a transmitter site, vital to our communications, which were via teleprinter only. This meant that no one from HQ FEAF (or anywhere else) could reach us by telephone or voice radio (a great boon in many ways), and in due course I became adept at drafting signals explaining why I had or had not done a particular task. It could hardly have been a more independent command.

As I have said, the single runway, built to very high standards, ran from one end of the island to the other, with a large hardstanding area – the Aircraft Servicing Platform, usually known as 'the pan' – alongside to the north-east, with the fuel tanks nearby carrying all types of aviation fuel plus diesel, which were topped up regularly from the refuelling jetty by visiting tankers, usually BP. The servicing and maintenance workshops were also close by. Approaches to each end of the runway were necessarily over the water, with the approach lighting built in the sea and serviced by boat. Two RTTLs (high-speed Rescue and Target-Towing Launches), plus a pinnace and various other small craft, were maintained in the Marine Craft Section, with its own jetty, and we normally had two Shackleton aircrraft and crews from 205 Squadron in Singapore on a rotating detachment standing by for rescue if required, since the routes between Aden and Singapore were almost all over the sea.

There were no hangars, and all aircraft refuelling and servicing had to be done on the pan, with the servicing crews working in either hot sunshine or torrential rain. The main job was to refuel and turn round the Transport Command Britannias and Comets: target turnround times were forty minutes for a Comet and ninety minutes for a Britannia. Passengers (mostly military personnel and families) were off-loaded for this short time and looked after in the Transit Mess; not infrequently there would be a servicing problem with an aircraft, and the crew and passengers had to stay overnight. This stretched our resources somewhat, but most people enjoyed their forced stay – I recall at least one such occasion when the island seemed to be full of mothers and babies. These scheduled aircraft came through every two or three days (except for times like the 1961 Kuwait emergency, when schedules were interrupted), and in addition we had a variety of odd aircraft passing through, such as V-bombers returning from trials at Woomera in Australia, military VIPs' personal aircraft, and special flights like the Javelin exercise I have already mentioned. So with the Shackleton detachments and regular visits from the RNZAF Bristol Freighters we always had plenty of work in hand, and it was a point of honour to achieve turnrounds in the shortest times compatible with aircraft safety. This was an important contributory factor to what I found to be high morale, plus the fact that we were all in the same boat doing a twelve-month unaccompanied tour.

In the north-west corner of the island were the messes and living quarters, all single-storey prefabricated buildings which were adequate if not luxurious – certainly an improvement on wartime Nissen huts. All had ceiling fans, but the only air-conditioned buildings were those where technical requirements demanded it, such as the Communications Centre, and the transit quarters. Station Sick Quarters had about twenty beds, with two medical officers (one qualified as a surgeon and the other as an anaesthetist), and on the whole the health of the service personnel was good; medical services were also provided for the Maldivians, and two Maldivian girls (Wadifa and Rosima, if I remember) acted as nurses for their own people. The administrative offices, including Station Headquarters, were between the living quarters and the servicing areas, and several building projects were nearing completion: a station cinema, church, a laundry, and a NAAFI bottling plant for making soft drinks.

The Air Ministry Works Department staff were kept busy, and I found the Principal Works Officer, Bob Lewis, efficient and congenial.

There was a great deal to assimilate as I was taken around by Michael C-M; not only was the daily routine fairly demanding, but the constant flow of senior officers and other VIPs passing through who had to be met by the Station Commander was an additional burden, although they were usually appreciative and gave little trouble. The relief when they departed was welcome, but often – and usually late at night – I would just have gone to bed to be awakened by a message to say that the aircraft had engine trouble and was coming back. On the credit side, many of our visitors were in a position to help our problems in various ways. For example, during our handover Group Captain Craven, the Station Commander at RAF Lyneham, whence the majority of our flights originated, passed through, expressed his appreciation of the way we handled his aircraft, and said that he would always be willing to help Gan in any way he could, particularly with mail problems and any special requirements which his aircraft could bring out. This was co-operation worth having, and was not unusual from those visitors in a position to give it.

The first official visit from the C-in-C FEAF, Air Marshal Selway, took place just before Michael C-M left, and went very well. I wrote to Joan,

The C-in-C arrived on Friday, accompanied by the FEAF Chief Engineer (i.e. Chief AMWD man), and his ADC. Almost the first thing on the programme was a visit to the next island, Fedu, in a dhoni (a native boat) laid on by Mr Afif Didi, the headman. These boats are about 40 feet long and shaped rather like the old Viking ships. Normally they are rowed by about eight men but they sail as well with an old-fashioned square sail. On Fedu we are building houses for those Maldivians who had to leave Gan when the airfield was built; we have completed about 150 out of 200 houses. The whole village was out to meet us – a most colourful sight, with small children in a variety of colours (one small boy wore a yellow jacket over pale violet trousers with a sort of violet mob-cap on his head). Some of the younger women were most beautiful, with great dark eyes – they wore this collar-work of gold and coloured threads and necklaces made of beaten gold and coins. ... We inspected the houses being built and then saw an exhibition or demonstration of handicrafts or rather native trades laid on for the occasion. There were copper and iron smiths (with small boys operating bellows fanning a charcoal fire), carpenters working with adzes and twist drills operated by ropes, children plaiting palm leaves, men showing fishing nets and gear, and women and girls making this remarkable collar-work. ... Then we went to the village headman's home for refreshment, which was coconuts – but new soft coconuts looking rather like turnips with a yellowy-green shell. A small hole was cut in the top and you drank the brimming coconut milk (actually clear as water) from it. ... When the juice is all gone (delicious) you scoop out the soft white flesh inside with a spoon.... We were then shown a boat-building team at work. They have no plans but just complete the thing by eye – really beautiful boats. We sailed back to Gan in one after a really enjoyable afternoon – the C-in-C enjoyed himself thoroughly.

Yesterday the C-in-C inspected most of the station – rather a gruelling morning, as it turned out hot – and then we went for a trip in the high speed launch in the afternoon. These boats are built to do a specific job – sea rescue – and to proceed at a high speed (up to 45 knots) and are not really pleasure craft. However, it was most enjoyable.

We had a successful guest night in the Officers' Mess (at which I wore my white tropical mess kit for the first time), and as well as welcoming Air Marshal Selway dined out several departing officers, including Michael. The following morning, after crossing the lagoon to Hitaddu in the pinnace (a much more dignified and comfortable vessel), the C-in-C inspected the transmitter site where some twenty-five RAF radio technicians lived permanently – the morale was very high and most of them preferred Hitaddu to Gan. The Air Marshal finally left Gan just before lunch, having expressed himself very satisfied with what he had seen and telling me to visit his HQ as frequently as I thought necessary.

Michael Maxwell departed a couple of days later, and though in some ways I was sorry to see him go it was a great relief to be in control and to start doing the job at last. I moved into the CO's bungalow, just across the road from the Officers' Mess and close to the shore, still fringed with a few palm trees. It was a modest building with a small sitting-room, a bedroom, a bathroom, and a small kitchen where the Maldivian servant worked; I dispensed with the previous servant, universally known as 'Idle Ali', and was provided with another (Ali Achmet) who seemed better and could hardly be worse. He would clean the place after a fashion and do a little laundry; all my meals were taken in the Mess.

The day after I took over was a busy one: we had the two Javelins returning from Singapore to the UK, three Valiant V-bombers going in the opposite direction, and the usual Comet and Britannia. Since a Bristol Freighter was going up to Hulule with freight for the UK Representative, I took the opportunity to go along (somewhat superfluously as second navigator) and see Humphrey's new abode. The Freighter was a real workhorse, like a flying furniture van, and noisy, smelly and uncomfortable with it. But the two-hour flight north over the islands was enchanting, the tiny islands in each atoll crowded with palms and fringed with white sand; in the clear blue waters large rays could often be seen swimming just outside the reefs, and few islands seemed to be inhabited. Male atoll was different, with the capital a sizeable town and the lagoon waters busy with various craft. We put down on the PSP (pierced steel planking) runway at Hulule, and I was taken in a boat to Humphrey's tiny island, Dunidu. He greeted me warmly and we had lunch in his bungalow (whose wall bore our Royal coat-of-arms), chatting generally about his domestic problems and discussing the political situation in the

Maldives: he was apparently on good terms with the Sultan and Prime Minister, but the uneasy stand-off between the Male government and the Adduans was no nearer resolution. Since we must retain the goodwill of the government but at the same time depended on the Adduans in various ways for the efficient running of RAF Gan, Humphrey advised me to maintain the strict neutrality we had so far shown in our relationship with both sides. He was an impressive character, highly intelligent and with a forthright manner, and had much experience in various parts of the Commonwealth, including the north-west frontier of pre-Partition India. I was grateful for his wise advice.

Back at Gan I was finding my feet and settling into some sort of a routine, as far as this was possible with sometimes unpredictable aircraft movements. From another letter home:

My day goes something like this. I usually wake up about 5.45, broad daylight, and lean up on my elbow to look out of my window and see several dhonis either sailing or rowing in from the other islands, with the crews sometimes singing. ... A steward comes across from the Mess with a cup of tea (undrinkable at first, but I'm getting used to it), and then I get up (exercising a lot of will power) at about 6.15. I wash or shower, shave and dress (KD shorts, shirt, stockings) and about this time Ali Achmet turns up, cleans my shoes (much too much polish) and collects the dhobi – laundry. Then I walk across to the Mess for breakfast. The food is a bit variable ... what I miss most is a nice cup of tea and nice bread and butter. I usually take 1 Paludrine and 2 salt tablets. ... Then off to my office in the Vanguard estate car, complete with flag, returning smart salutes from Pakistanis and Maldivians on the way. I have to park the car carefully outside SHQ to avoid getting a hot seat – very painful when wearing shorts – and then I start the day's work. Check my diary to see what's going on and who's arriving by what plane. Work through all the incoming signals and letters of the day. Deal with various bits of correspondence. See lots of people about various things – visiting officers, new officers, corporals who have rescued Pakistanis (drunk) from drowning, etc, etc. ... Depending on how the routine stuff goes I may go and see the Principal Works Officer, Bob Lewis, and look at progress on new buildings or decide what to do with old ones. New ones going up now are a station church (just completed), new cinema, new laundry, NAAFI shop, officers' quarters and other odd ones. We have plans to convert an old set of offices near the beach to a marine club where the sailors, canoers and fishermen can look after their boats and tackle, meet, etc. Every day we seem to complete something or start planning something new.

As a matter of course the Movements staff let me know if there is anybody important on planes (i.e. group captain or above), and if so, I meet them. Usually, people are making a flag-stop of 1–2 hours and I offer them the choice of a meal at the Transit Mess, a quiet drink at my house and/or a tour of the island. Seems to go down all right. Lunchtime (1 o'clock) comes as a great relief after six hours work and I drive down to the Mess. I usually linger with coffee afterwards and read a week-old 'Telegraph' or 'Observer' for a while. Then across to the house, strip and shower, and relax on my bed for up to an hour. … I have been out sailing twice, swimming once, and meeting aircraft several times. The swimming is wonderful but a bit scaring for a timid soul like me – Michael Maxwell bequeathed a face-mask to me, so I had a go. It was fascinating – lots of little striped fish all over the place, just like Hans Hass, and occasionally a bigger one. I saw a small Moray eel the other day near the shore and that rather put me off. The water is as clear as a bell and it's warmer in than out. Some of the coral formations look most odd, and you have to be careful not to scrape yourself on them.

Tea is about 4.30 in the Mess (just tea, toast and jam). This afternoon I have invited Mr Afif Didi, the chief Maldivian (really the President of the People's Council of Addu) to tea in my house to discuss with me and my Senior Technical Officer the question of our helping to set up a cinema for the Maldivians on Hitaddu island. In the afternoon, by the way, we just wear civilian shirts and shorts and sandals – I bought some in Changi that are quite suitable.

The dusk comes down very rapidly between 6 and 6.30, and there are some wonderful but brief sunsets. I change and shower in a very leisurely fashion. I'm finding that I definitely need a second shave every day before dinner, which is 7– 7.45. I usually appear in the bar at some time thereafter – there is often somebody visiting or passing through to talk to; if there isn't I have a game of snooker with Ted Churchill, my Senior Admin Officer, or anybody else who wants to play (I know all my officers now, and quite a bit about their personal backgrounds as well).

Usually, I try and drift away about 10–10.30 and go to bed. This is about the time when I feel a little low, as I switch the lights on in the empty house (not quite – the lizard scurries about on the ceiling) and get ready for bed. I have had one or two books from the library, so usually read a little while. If there is no cloud the stars blaze away through the fly-proofing on the window, the surf roars on the distant reef, and the waves pound the beach 20 yards away. The crickets sing, the lizards chirp like sparrows, and there's usually music from Radio Gan tinkling away on somebody's radio.

These rather rambling extracts, mostly written late at night, give some flavour of my daily life at Gan, although one day was rarely the same as the next. I was lucky in having officers who were almost all efficient, conscientious and congenial: Squadron Leader Ted Churchill, the SAdO and a former transport pilot, was shortly replaced by Johnny Johnson, an ex-fighter pilot, and I could rely on both to be my deputy and stand in for me when necessary. Flight Lieutenant Garry Weeks, the Adjutant, was well up to the job and I leaned on him heavily for many administrative and disciplinary matters. The Senior Technical Officer, a really key post at Gan, was Squadron Leader Gil Ridout, followed by Freddy Willgress, and both coped admirably with the technical problems that inevitably cropped up and had often to be solved by ingenious and unorthodox methods; the servicing crews, unlike the administrative staff who worked the 'normal' station hours of 7 a.m. to 1 p.m., worked a two-shift system of twelve hours each, and could be working through the night (often in heavy rain) if the aircraft schedules demanded it. We had an extremely popular Padre, the Reverend (Squadron Leader) Ted Cannan who, as an ex-Halton apprentice, was very well liked by the airmen and did a great deal of good on the station. It would take too long to enumerate all the officers and their qualities, but I will mention Flight Lieutenant Bill Batt, the Station Navigation Officer, who had been a sergeant navigation instructor at No. 5 Air Observers' School at Jurby when I was under training there and was now a very experienced navigator and a great help in flight planning for the transit aircraft. We all lived cheek by jowl in the Mess, got to know each other's tastes and foibles, and on the whole got on very well together.

*   *   *

Meanwhile, back at Austwick in the Craven dales, Joan was coping with a new life in a completely different environment: the cottage was next to the Gamecock Inn and looked across the green to the blacksmith's shop and the village stores, so was in the heart of this attractive village set in sweeping limestone country. She improved the kitchen as far as this was possible, and in due course tackled the owner (a grumpy and eccentric old man who ran a dilapidated shop further up the village) about the damp in the small back bedroom; after some time this was rectified, and Jenny was able to use it (redecorated) for hers.

The village also had a post office and a butcher's shop, and a fish van and the mobile library stopped once a week just outside the cottage, so most requirements were met. The market town of Settle was only a few miles away, with an adequate bus service, and the blacksmith doubled as a taxi driver when required, so at least Joan – who did not drive at that time – could get about. The village school was only a short walk away, and although Jennifer was not too happy there she knew that it would not be for long and that she would be joining Susan at Casterton the following year – a prospect I'm sure she regarded with mixed feelings. She and Joan got on well together and carved out a little niche for themselves in the village life; people were very kind and understanding, especially the two elderly ladies next door (both former nannies). In the usual village way the word had got round about Joan's circumstances, and there were many friendly overtures and offers of help. People met in the village stores run by the Hooles, and all sorts of village information were exchanged; Joan was invited to become a vice-president of the local British Legion, and she and Jenny went to several bring-and-buy sales. Susan at Casterton was near enough to get home for the occasional exeat, so they saw more of her than before. Our parents, too, visited from time to time, and Joan and Jenny would have the odd weekend in Leeds with her parents.

However she felt about the change in her life, Joan put a brave face on it in her letters to me, and, as always, coped admirably with the new situation. Indeed, she told me later that it had given her a new sense of confidence and satisfaction that she was able to handle things on her own. But both of us longed for the time when we should be together again.

*   *   *

Back at Gan, I took the opportunity to fly in one of the rescue standby Shackletons to make a mail drop for Humphrey at Hulule. The captain, Flight Lieutenant Elias, was kind enough to let me act as second navigator on the four-and-a-half-hour flight, so I was able to get some idea of the aircraft's navigation system. I had had a couple of short Shackleton flights from Kinloss when I was at Farnborough, but had forgotten how noisy the aircraft was – much more so than the Lancaster, from which it was developed. If I remember correctly, these 205 Squadron aircraft from Changi were Mark I Shackletons and had been in service for some time, so the airframes were comparatively old (although the type continued flying for at least another twenty years): the crews referred to them as 'fifty thousand rivets in close formation', and the long oversea flights they made in their maritime reconnaissance role must have been tiring. In the Far East, with no ground-based navigation systems such as Gee or Decca, navigation was largely back to the old Coastal Command systems with drifts and sun and star sights, although there was an excellent ground-mapping radar, API and Rebecca. There was one occasion when a Shackleton *en route* from Singapore to Gan got well off track to the south – probably due to a compass problem – and was heard by us calling very faintly on VHF at about the limit of its range; we were able to give them a steer, and they finally arrived after flying north for nearly an hour, short of fuel and very relieved.

The rest of October and most of November passed quickly, with a constant stream of visitors – VIPs, FEAF staff officers, and a succession of V-bombers (Valiants, Vulcans and Victors) passing through to or from Singapore or Australia on tests or exercises. One Valiant, with an Australian crew, suffered an undercarriage problem on landing and blocked the runway for an hour or so until we could drag it clear; luckily no other aircraft was expected. They were eventually stuck with us for a couple of weeks, as certain spares had to be flown out – sickening for them, but they appreciated our hospitality and on a later visit brought us a barrel of very special Australian claret, which we regarded with suspicion at first but found to be excellent – good enough to serve to Lord Mountbatten when he visited a few months later.

One visitor was my old boss from Richmond Terrace, now Air Chief Marshal Sir Theodore McEvoy and Air Secretary at the Air Ministry, responsible for officers' careers and postings. He first of all passed through on his way to Singapore and then returned some days later to stay for a weekend, relaxing and enjoying snorkelling. He was the same as ever – a delightful guest and no trouble – and expressed himself pleased with his short holiday.

I was now well into my stride and was able from time to time to take more physical exercise – swimming, sailing, tennis and even a game of cricket, more than I had done for some years. Alas, there was a price to pay. After a short swimming session I suffered an excruciating back pain: Tom Bucher, the MO, prescribed heat and massage and the usual painkillers, but nothing seemed to ease the pain, and after a couple of difficult days' work I had to take to my bed (reinforced with boards under the mattress). After another couple of days with no improvement, Tom decided that I needed more expert treatment and further rest, and shipped me off to Singapore on a stretcher in the next Comet. So I found myself in hospital for the first time in my life, in a ward in the RAF Hospital at Changi, where a small blue sleeping pill gave me the first night's sleep for some time. A slipped disc was diagnosed and bed rest prescribed, with physiotherapy after the first few days, but at first there seemed to be little discernible improvement. However, the other two or three officers in the ward were congenial, I had plenty to read, and I had many visitors, from the Davises to AVM Grundy. I was determined to get back to Gan in time for the dedication of the new station church by the Bishop to the Forces on 12 December, and had improved sufficiently for discharge from hospital as long as I used a stick for walking.

I flew back to Gan in the C-in-C's Hastings in the company of AVM and Mrs Grundy, Ross Campbell, the FEAF Chief (civil) Engineer and his wife, the three FEAF Assistant Chaplains-in-Chief, and Sally Grundy, aged 11. The Bishop to the Forces, the Right Reverend S.W. Betts, Lord Bishop of Maidstone, was what one might call the passenger-in-chief, and proved to be a professional charmer, but a sincere and pleasant one. After a ten-hour flight in the noisy Hastings we were glad to get a night's sleep before the rigours of the next day – the dedication of the new church, which was an impressive ceremony, with the Bishop knocking at the closed church door and being formally admitted by me for the dedication service. All went well, and our Padre, Ted Cannan, was delighted. Afterwards we had a reception in the Mess, followed by a dinner night with the ladies present – a welcome change from our normal all-masculine occasions. Dinner was enlivened – if that is the right word – by our Senior Equipment Officer, Flight Lieutenant Bill Hart, suffering severe stomach pains and being whipped off to Sick Quarters, where an appendectomy was performed by our two MOs, who impressed our Maldivian helpers by arriving in full mess kit. The operation was successful and Bill was flown back to the UK on the first available aircraft for recuperation. Luckily this event was the day after the official opening of the new station laundry (for which Bill Hart was responsible) by Mrs Grundy, and I have a photograph of Bill with Mrs Grundy putting the first garment through the laundry system – a pair of very exiguous ladies' panties.

One additional and unwelcome incident during the visit was that one of the high-speed rescue launches ran aground on the reef and took all night to dislodge; the damage could have been worse, and no one was hurt, but we would have to set up the inevitable Board of Enquiry. Unfortunately our Senior Marine Officer, Flight Lieutenant Mervyn Manson, was in charge of the vessel at the time and would obviously have to take some of the blame, conscentious and able as he was (all Marine Branch officers held a master's ticket). In due course the Enquiry was held, and if memory serves, Mervyn was formally given a reprimand, the lightest possible punishment; I hope it did not affect his future career.

The Marine Craft Section under his command was a busy little unit: apart from the maintenance of the rescue launches and pinnace they had a variety of small craft (including landing craft) to help with the job of unloading our regular merchantmen and tankers. Most of our supplies came via the Ben Line, a well-established line which operated all over the Indian Ocean, and our fuel tanks were resupplied mostly by BP and Dutch tankers. One refuelling incident was farcical but could have been disastrous: our Marine Craft airmen were busy on the fuel jetty coupling up the lines for an anchored Dutch tanker to start refuelling into our tank farm, when the fishing club's sampan *Suzy Wong*, manned by off-duty airmen, passed close to the jetty. The fishermen, seeing friends sweating on the jetty, shouted, 'Go on, get pumping!' The Dutch bridge officer on the tanker, hearing these shouts, in his turn shouted 'Pumpen!' to the tanker crew, who did just that, with the result that a substantial quantity of fuel was pumped into the lagoon before the error was realized. Luckily no serious pollution occurred, but there were some red faces both ashore and aboard.

These ship visits often provided a welcome change from the daily routine, as I was usually invited to take lunch or dinner aboard with the captain, who often had his wife with him, and we would also entertain the officers in the Mess; most of these small ships lived very well, and the small parties I would take with me thoroughly enjoyed the food and the pleasant company and talk. I remember one occasion when a party of ship's officers had spent an evening ashore with us and asked us to return aboard for a late drink; the ship's Chief Engineer was a very small Irishman with a very large thirst, and as we went aboard he missed his footing and fell off the ladder into the lagoon. Like a flash our Junior Equipment Officer, Ron Robertson, who was already aboard, dived off the rail and plucked him out, unharmed apart from the amount of sea water he had swallowed – quick thinking and a lucky escape.

Our sole resident female, Gwen Caton of the Women's Voluntary Service, usually accompanied these ship visits. I had been rather taken aback when I was told as I arrived at Gan that there was to be a WVS representative stationed there: no one at HQ FEAF had mentioned it and I had some misgivings about the presence of one woman among so many unaccompanied men. The Press gave this some publicity – headlines such as 'The only woman on the island' – but I need not have worried; Gwen, in her forties and an experienced welfare worker, gave no trouble and was able to help with many personnel problems, and most of our airmen liked and trusted her.

On the run-up to Christmas 1960 all sorts of activities were planned, and there was a very full programme, including a variety concert and pantomime, the Christmas draw and barbecue, judging of the various bars which sections had been allowed to set up for the occasion, a carnival with decorated floats, dhoni races, and the usual exchange visits to the various messes, plus of course a Carol Service on Christmas Eve and a Morning Service on Chistmas Day, both well attended. On the evening of Christmas Day the Queen's broadcast was relayed over Radio Gan, followed by a short message from me. I said, among other things,

Gan first functioned as a Royal Air Force staging post in January of this year. Since that time we have turned round some 630 aircraft and handled over 12,500 passengers and 1.5 million pounds of freight; we have turned a Comet round in 29 minutes and a Britannia in 40. In addition, the RAF Communications Centre, Gan, which commenced operations in April, has handled about 200,000 signals. These figures are interesting, but do not reveal one other extremely important fact: in the short time in which we have been operating we have built up, among transit crews and passengers, a remarkable reputation for efficiency and hospitality. Our Air Officer Commanding said recently that Gan is not one of the best staging posts in the Royal Air Force –

it is *the* best. I need hardly say how proud and pleased I am to command such a station and I would like to thank every one of you most sincerely for making it possible, by your cheerful hard work, for Gan to have earned such high praise in such a short time. [Perhaps a little on the pompous side, but it was well received.]

Writing to Joan about Christmas, I said,

Our special Hastings came in from Changi yesterday and brought us our last mail before Christmas. ... We started our Christmas break after duty yesterday (Friday) and it lasts till we start work again on Wednesday morning – quite a decent holiday. Of course, a lot of people will be working as usual, and we have a ship in on Boxing Day to start unloading on Tuesday. I went to three parties last night – the Air Formation Signals Troop (Army), the Marine Craft Section, and the Station Barbecue and Christmas Draw. The night before that it was the Station concert and pantomime, which was really very good, with two excellent bands, one dance band and one traditional jazz. The first engagement on Christmas Eve was at Hitaddu (variously spelt), our transmitter site on another island in the atoll. There are about 20 men there all the time; there is a daily run to and from Gan by the pinnace but most of the men prefer to stay on Hitaddu. Quite a party of us left in the pinnace at about 1030 – the OC Communications Centre, whose men they are, the Padre, the SWO and several others. It was a beautiful morning with the sea glassy as a millpond, and a hot sun.

The airmen had made a splendid bar in their communal room, with a built-in refrigerator, footrail and even 2 dummy beer handles labelled Mild and Bitter. We had a couple of beers with them, visited the chaps on duty, sang a carol, and then left at about 1215. On the way back we had a wonderful experience. In the middle of the lagoon we often see dolphins, and we saw some leaping in the distance. We altered course to get nearer and then suddenly we were in the middle of them – about a hundred, leaping right out of the water just at the side of the pinnace. As we put on speed a dozen or so crowded under the bows of the boat and raced a few inches in front. This went on for about 20 minutes, with the dolphins obviously thoroughly enjoying themselves.

Back at Gan ... at half-past two the billet bar competition started: every airman's block was allowed to build a bar, and I had to judge them and award a first, second and third prize (£10, £5, and £2). The catch is that the CO is expected to have a drink in each. Well, somehow I made it – there were 10 bars and I had a beer in each. Surprisingly enough, I was able to make a sensible assessment at the end, and I think the awards were popular. There were some really wonderful bars with really ingenious gadgets ... We finished about 5 o'clock, and all I wanted to do was sleep. All I could think of was that the Carol Service was at 8.30 and that I must be sober to read the lesson. What I completely forgot was that at 7.30 the Officers' Mess were having their Christmas Dinner. Anyway I tumbled into bed and slept like a log until awakened by the phone. I looked at my watch – 7.20, and Gil Ridout (the PMC) said, 'The chaps have gone into dinner, sir – are you coming?' Well, I was out of bed like a flash, had a cold shower, dressed and was over in the Mess by 7.30. Everybody cheered when I came in and I think several were surprised at my surfacing at all! However, dinner was good (no wine for Cropper, though) and I even made a short impromptu speech at the end. Then we went to church for a very pleasant service (9 lessons, 9 carols), with a packed congregation.

The last engagement of the day was at the Corporals' Club, where according to tradition the CO and other officers were induced to sing. ... By the way, nearly all our raffles, auctions, etc., this Christmas are in aid of Wireless for the Blind, and so far we have made nearly £150 from various methods. The SWO has been going round auctioning a pair of panties (pink lace) – the funny thing is, no matter how often they're sold, it's the same pair at the next auction.

About 1030 on Christmas morning we went up to the AMWD Senior Mess, where Bob Lewis, the Principal Works Officer, had made a very pleasant iced punch. We stayed there a little while and then came back to change into uniform and receive the Sergeants in our Mess. They spent the best part of an hour with us and then we went back to their Mess. Finally at one o'clock we all went over to the Airmen's Mess to serve their dinner. It all went very well – they had a jolly good meal with all the traditional things and seemed to be enjoying themselves. I signed about 100 menu cards and had quite a lot of fun. Finally, about 2.30 some of us went over to the Island Club – the Ceylonese NAAFI employees' club – and had one drink there. They had made a magnificent iced cake with a runway and model aeroplanes on it, and had been waiting for me to cut it. Gwen Caton and I did it together and they were very pleased.

I took to my bed again about 3.30 and slept till 5 pm when I got up and shaved, showered and dressed for church at 5.30. Then a party in the Church Club – no alcohol, thank goodness – with a high tea and games. ... I was able to sneak away early and had a good long sleep. I was called by 3 corporals bringing me early morning tea at 6.20, with the compliments of the Corporals' Club, then another cup at 7 from the airmen, and finally my usual cup from the Mess. After a Maldivian entertainment at the AMWD Senior Mess (a band of drums and bicycle bells, with singing and dancing) there was a crowded programme on Boxing Day afternoon, with 'the Station Carnival and Regatta'. First the Maldivian dhoni race – 6 crews all rowing like mad. Then the competition for decorated vehicles – the Fire Section took first prize with the fire truck bearing a life-size papier maché reindeer and fir tree. Then sailing races – there was a stiffish breeze and a choppy sea and it was quite exciting to watch; one crew capsized but righted the boat themselves. Then a round-the-island cycle race (standard service bikes only) and finally the big event – the RAF-manned dhoni race.

The Air Formation Signals Troop won this, as they've been putting in a lot of practice – as one airman put it, they've b—— all else to do. Anyway, it was great fun – there were cups and money prizes to present at the end and everybody seemed to be happy.

The last item on the programme was a party given by the staff of Station Sick Quarters, in the Sick Quarters itself – they had rigged up a bar (of course!) with a skull on top, and gin and whisky available from intravenous drip bottles. The party included a sit-down dinner, with Maldivian curry and other dishes. The SMO (newly arrived Squadron Leader Dennis Eastick) of course made a speech and yours truly replied.

I have quoted at some length from my contemporary account of the Gan Christmas festivities since it throws some light on the prevailing spirit and morale, which was high; I had the opportunity of talking to a wide cross-section of all ranks and was heartened by the friendliness and the enthusiasm.

As I have written earlier, there was a specific job to do, and most people were involved in it in one way or another. There was only one noticeable factor where a drop in morale occurred: at the end of someone's twelve-month tour, if a replacement was late arriving or return to the UK was delayed for some other reason, there would understandably be a visible decline in performance, and officers and NCOs recognized this and did their best to ease the situation. Otherwise most people enjoyed their work, did it cheerfully, and made the most of their spare time in sport and other activities, the opportunities for which were improving all the time.

After the Christmas break our routine was resumed, enlivened for me by the usual flow of VIPs and others, which included Ted Heath, then Lord Privy Seal, and John Profumo, Secretary of State for War, each of whom borrowed my swimming trunks and face mask and spent their flag-stop time in the water. I flew on two further Shackleton flights to Hulule to drop mail and generator spares for Humphrey A-D, and paid him a visit via Bristol Freighter. We had an informal visit from the C-in-C FEAF, who inspected the latest facilities (new cinema, laundry and church), went fishing, and seemed satisfied with everything. My old wartime Squadron

Commander from 103 Squadron, Eric Nelson (now an air commodore) passed through and shared some reminiscences, and our Senior Equipper (Bill Hart) returned from the UK after his convalescence from his appendectomy.

Bill's flight was a little later than scheduled, and we thought we would have a little fun at his expense. Bob Carden, the Provost Officer, met him off the aeroplane with two policemen and a serious expression. He showed Bill a signal purporting to be from HQ FEAF saying that Flt Lt Hart was to be apprehended for enquiry, being absent without leave. Bob then took him off to the Guardroom and got him to make a long statement before bringing him to me. I told him I was sorry but I'd have to put him in irons, and Garry the Adjutant arrived with a large ball and chain, when the penny dropped and Bill swore revenge. He had it too: he and the Padre cooked up a story about an airman who was asking permission to marry a Maldivian girl, which had me worried for an hour or two until I said I would interview the man concerned, when Bill arrived in my office in airman's uniform with a placard round his neck saying 'Just married'. This sort of unmalicious prank was possible – and appreciated – when the relationships were as good as they were throughout the station.

Towards the end of January we were told that the Chief of the Defence Staff, Earl Mountbatten of Burma, would be night-stopping on his way to the Far East the following month, and would like to see something of our operations. A short period of intense activity ensued, with some building projects completed ahead of time and the station generally cleaned up and tidied. I issued an administrative order to cover the visit programme, as I had done many times at Cranwell, and we prepared a suite of rooms for CDS and his entourage. We managed to get together a respectable guard of honour, commanded by Mervyn Manson, and give them some practice, and when AVM Grundy arrived from Singapore to greet CDS he brought the FEAF Band with him, so we were able to make it a reasonably ceremonial affair. Lord Mountbatten duly arrived on the evening of 10 February, was greeted by AVM Grundy and me, and inspected the guard of honour, on which he complimented us. We had laid on a dinner night in the Officers' Mess, and our Mess staff rose to the occasion and provided a very presentable meal (accompanied by our special Australian claret). Mountbatten was affability itself, and told us that when he had visited Gan in 1944 as Supreme Allied Commander, Far East Asia, his aircraft (a Mitchell bomber) had crash-landed on the crushed coral strip, but he and the crew were unharmed. After dinner I accompanied him to the Sergeants' Mess, where he turned on his not inconsiderable charm and had them eating out of his hand. As we left he said to me, among other things, 'I can see you have a happy ship here.' I was naturally very pleased.

The following morning we gave CDS a rapid tour of the station and a brief meeting with Mr Afif Didi. Mountbatten was naturally interested in the Marine Craft Section, and had a short trip in the lagoon in a rescue launch with AVM Grundy and me. It was waiting for us at the marine jetty, and as I accompanied CDS to go aboard I automatically stood back to let him cross the gangplank ahead of me. He stopped abruptly and asked, 'Are we leaving port?' I said we were, and he replied, 'In that case I board last.' I apologized for my ignorance of the finer points of naval etiquette, and I think he was more amused than otherwise. After our short voyage it was time for him to leave in his personal Comet, and we saw him off with relief. AVM Grundy also left shortly afterwards, saying that he thought everything had gone well, and in due course I had a letter from Mountbatten thanking me for 'the excellent arrangements for the visit' and the kindness and hospitality, and saying that he was most impressed by the very smart guard of honour. He concluded, 'It is clear that you have a very happy station at Gan, and I congratulate you very much.'

A few days later I got a seat on a Comet to Changi and spent a few days tackling various staff officers at HQ FEAF on some of our problems at Gan, bearing in mind the AOC's Inspection which was to take place later in the year; people were very co-operative, and I had many promises of help and plenty of helpful advice. As before, several old friends and acquaintances entertained me for drinks and meals: Ron Davis was a temporary bachelor as Rita had taken a break at home in UK, and he was hospitable and helpful as usual. I took one day off and did some shopping in Singapore, buying some gifts for Joan and the girls, and also visited the Tiger Balm Gardens, an astonishing gallimaufry of Chinese statues and temples built by the very prosperous makers of Tiger Balm ointment, apparently a sovereign remedy for almost every known ailment.

I flew back to Gan in AVM Grundy's Hastings, as he was going there to meet the naval C-in-C Far East Station, who was due to pay a formal visit in his flagship, HMS *Alert*; Admiral Sir David Luce had brought Lady Luce with him, and so Mrs Grundy accompanied the AOC. The purpose of the visit had originally been to have a conference with the naval and RAF Commanders from Aden, but they were unable to come (for which we at Gan were quietly thankful), and Sir David had decided to carry on with his visit as the ship was *en route* from Singapore. I wrote home,

HMS *Alert* arrived punctually … and I left in our high speed launch at 6.30 a.m. to meet her and pay the proper naval compliments. … Sir David Luce was charming and so was Lady Luce – I made my official call at 0900 and as I went over the side the Admiral received me, and the Captain (Commander Leathes), No. 1, and the officer of the watch were all smartly lined up with telescopes under arms to be introduced. I felt like a character in a Hornblower novel. I had a session with the Admiral in his cabin and then Commander Leathes took me to his own quarters (in what he called the mucky end of the ship). She was built as an anti-sub frigate and has to maintain that role as well as carry the C-in-C Far East Station.

I had a fairly large party to drinks at my house and then lunch in the Mess, and later in the afternoon there was tennis (the Admiral played and was first-class), and shooting and football matches (Gan won both). Then at about 6.30 p.m. all officers from Gan went aboard *Alert* for cocktails. The whole of the after deck was nicely organized and the whole thing was wonderfully civilized; the only things missing were our beautiful wives – the only ladies were Lady Luce, Mrs Grundy and Gwen Caton. The Grundys, Johnny Johnson and myself stayed on for dinner in the Admiral's cabin – echoes of Cranwell, a really well-organized pleasant dinner party with plenty of well-trained servants. I sat on Lady Luce's left and found her charming – completely unaffected, but interested in everything.

The Grundys left the following morning and Lady Luce went back with them to Singapore (having left her swimming costume in my bedroom ready for the next visit).

I took the Admiral on a tour of Gan and then he went aboard ready to up anchor. As soon as *Alert* was under way we also left the jetty in the high speed launch and ran alongside to pay compliments – I felt more like Hornblower than ever, standing up at the salute in a prominent place on the bridge, with the crew lined up, the RAF ensign streaming out in the breeze with my own flag at the masthead, the Royal Marines' band playing on *Alert*'s after deck, and all in glorious sunshine with a blue sea and white wakes foaming out behind. We escorted *Alert* right out of the lagoon and then when well out in the open sea we forged well ahead of her and turned back to do a high speed run alongside in farewell. ... Well, now I have finished boasting and we are back to normal routine for a while, thank goodness.

AVM Grundy had said that he would have no objection to my taking a mid-tour leave in UK if suitable 'indulgence' passages were available, so I started planning to go at the end of March for a fortnight. Events overtook these plans, as I received a signal from HQ FEAF saying that I was to go on a short course at HQ Bomber Command, concerned with Nuclear, Biological and Chemical (NBC) warfare for Station Commanders, on 17 April for four days. I felt guilty about going home and leaving Johnny to cope with all the pre-AOC's Inspections coming up, but he told me not to worry – he would be only too happy to run the show for a short while. Eventually I arrived at Lyneham on 1 April, hired a car and drove home to Austwick for a joyful reunion.

Oddly enough, I can remember little detail of those few weeks with the family in the village. I admired the improvements Joan had made to the cottage and was impressed by the way in which she had coped alone with many problems. Sue was home from school for part of the time, and we were all able to go to Leeds and see both sets of parents. It was strange but heart-warming to be back in the dales in the English spring, and we visited many of our favourite places. All too soon it was time to drive down to High Wycombe for the Bomber Command course, and I managed to get a few days back at Austwick before finally departing for Lyneham and the flights to Gan. I was happy to know that Joan and the girls seemed to be in good heart and to think that our remaining six months' separation would pass quickly. As usual, the big question was 'What next?'

Back at Gan, Johnny had dealt admirably with the usual succession of VIPs (including the C-in-C on his way to the UK to be knighted) and Lord Jellicoe, the Lords spokesman on defence, plus a succession of FEAF staff officers on pre-AOC's Inspections. The day I left Gan for the UK, he had had something of a shock when the Royal Fleet Auxiliary tanker *Wave Victor* arrived at almost no notice to be moored in the lagoon and left as a floating fuel tank with 1,500 tons of AVTUR for us and the Navy to use in emergency. The captain and crew made a perfunctory handover and then left on the first possible aircraft for the UK, with this rusting hulk sitting offshore with nobody aboard and apparently taking in water. The Senior Engineer Officer, now Freddy Willgress, and I spent a sweaty hour or so in the bowels of the ship to try and identify the leaks and see what action could be taken: these were in the engine-room section and seemed to be slow but steady. We found the bilge pumps, and Freddy hoped to get them working, but of course we had no marine engineer on Gan and no really expert knowledge. I sent an urgent signal to HQ FEAF outlining the problem and asking for some prompt assistance. After a few weeks a retired RFA bosun arrived and took charge, with a few Maldivian boatmen to help, and the *Wave Victor* became a fixture in the lagoon for some years, although in my time there were few refuellings.

Early in May we had some surprise visitors: a thirty-foot ketch came sailing into the lagoon quite unannounced, with an Australian couple, Dot and Blue Bradfield, aboard who were sailing round the world. They had built the boat themselves at their house in Fremantle, and had left Australia two and a half years earlier; as they had little money they had been stopping off and working here and there to keep themselves in funds for the next leg – they had spent a year in New Guinea. They were going on in a few days to the UK via the Seychelles, East Africa and the Mediterranean, and expected to fetch up in England about August 1962. They seemed to have no ties and were not worried about time. That sort of life certainly seemed to have its attractions (especially on Monday mornings about 6 o'clock) but of course they had had a very hard time of it on their big ocean crossings. They were a pleasant, homely, unaffected couple, and we were amused to see that they had a cat with them – it was first ashore. We were able to help them with a little work on the boat and with a few medical stores for their next leg. They gave us a slide show in the Mess about their travels, and also took some of us for a sail in *D'Vara*. They departed for the Seychelles after ten days or so, and I seem to recall that we heard from them once later on, but I had no further news of them.

Meanwhile we were working up to that annual but necessary bane of RAF stations, the AOC's Inspection. AVM Grundy had now been replaced by AVM Hobler, who was an unknown quantity and had not yet visited Gan. Over the last month or more we had had the usual succession of pre-AOC's Inspections by staff officers from HQFEAF, looking into all aspects of the work and organization of the station, and so far their comments had been mostly favourable. We managed to scrape together sufficient numbers of officers and airmen who would not be engaged on vital duties to form a respectable AOC's Parade, and I held a couple of rehearsals since drill was not an activity we usually indulged in. The FEAF Band arrived a few days before the inspection, and gave a concert at the AMWD Mess which was much appreciated.

In the middle of all this activity we received an urgent signal late one evening from the Governor of Mauritius, which lies nearly 2,000 miles south and west of Gan, to ask if we could airdrop some medical supplies to their nearby island of Rodrigues, where there was an enteric fever epidemic in which fourteen children had already died. We finally got one of the standby Shackletons off at about 2 o'clock the following morning with six containers packed with appropriate supplies and six spare containers as a back-up. They would overfly Rodrigues, which had no airstrip and was off the shipping lanes, and then land at the Mauritius airport, Plaisance, for refuelling and return. This was done successfully, and we had a signal from Mauritius saying, 'Deeply grateful'.

The AOC duly arrived for his Inspection and turned out to be a pleasant and somewhat avuncular character (hence his nickname, 'Daddy' Hobler). The formal parade was held in a respectable manner, with the aid of the FEAF Band, and culminated in the usual march-past and salute with me at the head of the troops. The AOC took the rather unusual step of addressing the assembled throng at the end of the parade and saying what a good show it was. Two days of inspection followed, at which no sinister problems appeared, and the final item on the programme was a Guest Night in the Officers' Mess, again with the FEAF Band playing – a very civilized touch. AVM Hobler boarded his Hastings at 8 a.m. the following day, having told me he was very pleased with the inspection and had no particular faults to find. However, as one might have expected, his aircraft was unserviceable, and he was with us again for the rest of the morning until he departed after lunch. He was no trouble, and we took him for a trip in the high-speed launch, which he said he much enjoyed. When he was gone we all heaved a sigh of relief, but in fact it had been a less trying experience than expected and something of a boost to morale.

*   *   *

We were now in June, and after the slight anti-climax of the AOC's Inspection, life continued with the usual succession of tankers, freighters, and transit aircraft, most with their complement of VIPs of one sort or another: the Commander-in-Chief of Bomber Command for one, Air Commodore Johnnie Jonhson, the former Battle of Britain ace now at Aden for another, and two old friends, Wing Commanders Ray Phillips (formerly flying with me in 'X' Flight at Scampton) and Danny Clare (a Spec N who had had my exchange post in Alaska some time before me). Johnnie Johnson arrived in a Victor on his way to Nairobi and stayed for a couple of days. He wrote afterwards, 'My dear Eric, Having got our Victor to 45,000 ft, levelled off, and slipped in the auto-pilot I thought I would drop you a line to thank you for a truly marvellous time on your Station. We all feel a 100% better than when we arrived from Karachi and it was good of you and your Staff to look after us so well – not always an easy thing to do when one has to cope with shoals of visiting firemen. As ever, Johnnie J.'

It's easy to see why he was so popular.

The middle of June was marked by local political difficulties. Early one morning Afif Didi came to see me and told me that there had been trouble at Huvadu on Suvadiva atoll just to the north of Addu. Some 'Male men' (presumably tax collectors from the Maldivian government) had been set upon by the local people and roughly handled. Would I take them at Gan, could they be sent back to Male, and could we airdrop a letter at Male for the Prime Minister? I promised to do what we could, organized a mail drop at Hulule (having put Humphrey Arthington-Davy in the picture) and in due course returned the 'Male men' – subdued but not badly hurt – by Bristol Freighter. Our sympathies tended to be with the local Maldivians, who received few facilities from Male but were still expected to pay taxes, but we had to maintain a strictly neutral position – we depended on the Maldivian government for our tenancy at Gan and on the Adduans for assistance in the running of the station. As it happened, Humphrey had arranged a formal audience for me with HE the Sultan only a couple of weeks after the Huvadu incident, and the Adjutant, Garry Weeks, and I flew up to Hulule, changed into formal tropical uniform (with swords and medals) and then went across to Male by boat.

Humphrey (in whites with a solar topee) advised that we should not discuss the trouble at Huvadu, and in fact the interview passed off very amicably with pleasantries and generalities, as might be expected; the Sultan was a small, apparently mild man who spoke adequate English and was very friendly, as were the Prime Minister and the Minister of Home Affairs, whom we also saw. When we left the palace we had a chat with the Mayor of Male, and in the afternoon attended a football match between the Male team and a team from Gan. I had to fly back to Gan that day as the C-in-C of Bomber Command was expected, but Humphrey said that he would come down in the near future and assess the situation.

This he did, bringing with him the Maldivian Deputy Home Minister, Mr N.T. Hassan Didi, who stayed a few days, had a tour of the station, and joined in talks with Afif. As I recall, he did not discuss the local politics with me, and in fact was generally uncommunicative, though polite. Humphrey told me that he was to go to Colombo in a few days with the Deputy Prime Minister, to have talks with the British High Commissioner, and suggested that I might like to go with him; I jumped at the chance, and we flew up to Katunayake airport in a FEAF Valetta and had two sessions with Sir Alexander Morley. My memory of the details of the talks is not very clear, but I said in a letter home,

> The present attempts (mostly by Humphrey) to bring about a reconciliation between the people of Addu atoll and the Male government have reached a critical stage, and the trick is to get both sides to give way a little on their respective positions without losing face. They are working towards this fairly successfully and hope to find a formula as the experts say.

This also applied to the people of Huvadu and Fua Malaku, and for the time being the so-called rebellion fizzled out and things went on much as usual in Addu atoll (until a later eruption when I had left).

I spent two nights in Colombo, staying with Group Captain George Rodney, the Air Adviser to the High Commissioner, but had little opportunity to see anything of the country. Driving from Katunayake to Colombo, about an hour's drive, there was all sorts of traffic on the road – cars of course, bicycles, rickshaws, innumerable bullock carts and even the odd elephant, looking quite at home in the traffic. From my bedroom there was a view of the local railway, with every train packed with passengers, who also were standing precariously on the footboards and sitting on the roof. What I saw of Colombo itself was not very attractive – an odd sprawling city looking very shabby and apparently with no big shopping centre. I was asked to two dinner parties by High Commission staff, and gained the impression that European and American business people were getting very impatient with the Ceylonese, who seemed to be taking all the money pouring into the country in aid but were not using it to the best advantage. For me it was a welcome break from Gan.

* * *

Back in the saddle, there was the usual bustle of transient VIPs, plus a freighter whose captain and officers were entertained as usual, with a reciprocal lunch on board. I had hardly cleared the work backlog when I was due to leave Gan for the C-in-C's annual conference in Singapore. This time I worked my passage on a 205 Squadron Shackleton returning from standby duty, helping out with the navigation on this ten-hour flight (under the nervous eye of a young flying officer navigator who no doubt expected me to operate with a quill pen and abacus).

I was booked in at the RAF Fairy Point Mess, a little way from the headquarters, and found it very comfortable and well run, with excellent food (in comparison with our usual fare at Gan). The C-in-C's conference, attended by all the Group and Station Commanders and the HQ branch heads, was illuminating for someone like me who was well set apart from the main stream, and I picked up a lot of interesting information which might or might not be useful to us at Gan more than a thousand miles away. The conference was followed by the usual guest night, which was entertaining and enjoyable. By now I had hosted many of the senior officers on their way through Gan, and was offered a great deal of reciprocal hospitality, including dinner and lunch at the Hoblers', the new AOC.

I went shopping with the Davises, who were kind and helpful as usual, and bought an eight-piece Noritake dinner set which would be boxed up and sent home from Singapore. In my round of the HQ staff I called in to the personnel office to see if there were any news of my posting yet, but drew a blank: however, I had heard informally from my replacement, Wing Commander Peter Ellis, in the UK that he expected to be arriving on 30 September – a couple of weeks later than I had hoped, but not to be helped.

After a pleasant – though not very relaxing – stay, I left Changi by Shackleton, and was again allowed to navigate for much of the eleven-hour flight, landing back at Gan in the dark. There was plenty of work waiting for me, a tanker in for our refuelling, our first naval vessel – a destroyer, HMS *Cassandra* – to refuel from RFA *Wave Victor*, and a farewell party for Padre Ted Cannan (replaced by Frank Price) to attend. I was delighted to receive, in the next few days, a signal from HQ FEAF saying: 'WG CDR E W CROPPER PROVISIONALLY APPOINTED BY AM TO COMMAND NO 53 SQN ABINGDON. AFTER NAVIGATION AND OPERATIONAL TRAINING HE WILL TAKE UP APPOINTMENT JUL 1962.' So the Air Secretary's department had kept their promise. No. 53 Squadron flew Blackburn Beverleys, at that time the largest aircraft in the RAF, a medium-range tactical transport, so this would be a complete change for me, and I looked forward to the posting with keen anticipation.

One spare-time activity I had been involved in for the past few months was a weekly broadcast on Radio Gan with a (mostly popular) classical music programme, on which I played a few records with a fairly relaxed commentary. The presenter was supposed to be anonymous, but I think most people knew who it was. My main problem was finding the time to select the records – some of my own and some from the record library kept by the Padre – and to write a suitable script that was not too highbrow. In those pre-Beatle days there was not the same slavish adherence to 'pop' music, and the programme did attract quite a few listeners: several people told me how much they enjoyed it, and 'Concert Hour' continued until I left the island.

* * *

At the beginning of August we received a signal from Mauritius asking if we could send an aircraft down for the presentation of a plaque to thank us and 205 Squadron for the medical airdrop at Rodrigues. HQ FEAF eventually gave permission for a standby Shackleton to be sent, and it was arranged that I should go, taking another officer from Gan and a few groundcrew airmen. The aircraft captain was Pilot Officer Roger Wellington, and he kindly agreed to my doing the outward flight as first navigator. Apart from the trips to and from Singapore in which I had been involved for some of the navigation, this was the first long-distance flight I had done for some time – 1,600 nautical miles over water and with few aids, luckily with the odd tiny island as checkpoints. I used the old and well-tried Coastal Command techniques: frequent drifts on the sea surface to establish track made good, and sun shots at regular intervals using pre-computed altitude and azimuth from Air Publication 3270, tables derived from the US Hydrographic Office Publication 349, which had virtually replaced the old Astronomical Navigation Tables (ANTs). As a bonus the moon was up and at a reasonable angle to the sun, and at the sun's meridian passage (its highest point, or midday) I was able to take – for the first time for me – a sun/moon fix which gave an acceptable most probable position. We picked up Rodrigues Island on the radar and made a few low passes in salute, and then set course for Mauritius and its civil airport, Plaisance, which we reached after a flight of nearly nine hours. We were taken to our hotel – with a very French flavour – and had a well-deserved good night's sleep.

Mauritius at that time was a British Crown colony, gaining its independence within the Commonwealth in 1968 and becoming a republic in 1992. It was at first a Dutch colony from 1638, but the French took possession in 1715 and stayed until it was taken by a British force in 1810 during the Napoleonic wars. The French influence was still very strong when we visited, and the wealth seemed to be in the hands of the old French families, with the economy largely based on sugar cane; there was a substantial Indian (i.e. from the sub-continent) population doing well in commerce. In the twenty-first century tourism has become big business, but in 1961 there was little evidence of it, and most of the indigenous population (speaking mostly Creole) were employed on the sugar plantations., which covered large areas of the island. We had seen these from the air when we arrived, and also the irregular white beaches and reefs, and once on the ground we were impressed with the dramatic shapes of the volcanic mountains, not very high but of striking appearance.

In the morning we had a walk around the local town, Curepipe, and then a pleasant informal lunch with the Governor, Sir Colville Deverell, at the residence – the Governor and his lady, his Secretary and wife, the Director of Civil Aviation and his wife, and a Red Cross nurse who had been at Rodrigues when we made the airdrop. I had the Shackleton captain, Roger Wellington, with me: I had hoped to bring our Senior Medical Officer, but he was unavailable. The plaque was presented to us, made by the Rodrigues islanders of polished wood with a map of the island carved thereon. It was apparently a rather poor island, with a population of about 35,000, and twenty-nine people had died in the epidemic; Miss Williams, the Red Cross nurse, said that only our airdrop had prevented many more deaths. The Governor told us that independence for Mauritius was on the way, and thought that this would be the beginning of the end for the French Mauritians, as most of the political influence was Indian or native Mauritian.

After lunch the DCA took us up to the northern end of the island to swim, through the cane fields and around the jagged mountains. After Gan the water semed to be bitingly cold, but it was bracing. Then we called on some friends of the DCA who had a beach bungalow, and since they were from Yorkshire, they gave us a first-class tea; he was the manager of a tobacco factory, and his family (including small children) made us very welcome. In the evening we had dinner with the local RN commander and the Chief of Police, and their wives, and went fairly early to bed.

We took off about 8.30 in the morning and did a very low-level flight over the island, with its beaches and weird mountains spectacular in the sunshine. We did a 'beat-up' of the beach bungalow we had visited the day before, with all the children waving madly, and then set course for home, another eight hours or so, during which I acted as second navigator. Back at Gan I found that the C-in-C FEAF was night-stopping on his way to a UK conference, but he was no trouble, and congratulated me on my posting before he went on his way. I cannot now remember what happened to the presentation plaque from Rodrigues, but I think that it remained with 205 Squadron, whose aircraft did most of the work. Since gaining independence, Mauritius has become another holiday paradise for those who can afford it, and tourism must now be a major source of revenue; no doubt it is a different place from the island we visited in 1961.

* * *

At home in Austwick Joan had organized a holiday for the girls and herself at a hotel in Whitby. They apparently enjoyed themselves, although Susan was in a difficult phase and not a great deal pleased her; however, her performance and behaviour at school seemed to have improved. Jenny was no doubt apprehensive of the fact that she would be going to Casterton in September, but the change of scene and the varied aspects of Whitby – the harbour, the old town and the abbey – were of interest and appeal. Joan took some splendid photographs with her new Japanese camera (especially of the traditional blessing of the fishing boats by the Bishop of Whitby) and sent them to me as transparencies. They had left Candy, our spaniel, with Joan's parents in Leeds, and spent a few days there before going home to Austwick – a pleasant break for them all.

* * *

I was now in the last month of my tour, with Peter Ellis arriving in Singapore for briefing on 18 September. The Maldivian political situation was quiet, not to say stagnant: I flew up to Hulule and had lunch in Humphrey's bungalow on Dunidu with the UK High Commissioner from Colombo. They had been in talks with the Maldivian government in Male in an attempt to resolve the stand-off with the Adduans, but with little success. Afif Didi was still adamant in his demand for greater autonomy, and our own government was reluctant to take any action which would affect the local relations with the Adduans (and therefore the effective working of RAF Gan). I had recently been invited to lunch by Afif in his house on Hitaddu, but it had been a social occasion and little had been said about the problems with Male; I took the opportunity to express our appreciation of the services rendered by the Adduans who worked on Gan, but was careful to avoid any suggestion of support for Afif's campaign for greater independence. Afif was an intelligent and courteous man, a graduate of Cairo University, and spoke excellent if formal English; like most Maldivians he was small and slight, with a hint of steel behind the gentle manner, and I judged that he would be a formidable political opponent.

The flow of transit aircraft continued unceasingly, seemingly with VIPs of some sort in each. We had the Imperial Defence College course of senior officers from all three services, luckily for a flagstop only; there were the three New Zealand Chiefs of Staff and their ladies, at varying times; our own C-in-C again; and a party of politicians from the Lords and the Commons, passing through twice (I wrote to Joan, 'Christopher Mayhew seemed about the livest wire there. They were an odd lot from portly peers to chaps looking like bookie's runners' – though I remember one congenial MP who was a left-wing ex-miner and enjoyed his drinks).

In the early hours of one morning a small Italian freighter, the MV *Ornella Prima*, bearing goods for the Maldivians, ran aground on the reef south of the island. We never discovered the precise cause, but there was some suggestion that the captain was asleep in his bunk and that the first officer, who was in command, was not entirely sober. Whatever happened, the ship was firmly fixed on the reef, and many efforts to get her off, including by means of a tow from a passing naval vessel, HMS *Lincoln*, were in vain After several days, by removing the cargo and waiting for a particularly high tide, the ship was floated off and apparently was not too damaged to be towed away by a tug after some minor repairs with assistance from our Marine Craft Section. I wonder what happened to the captain.

I had reached the stage in my twelve-month tour which I had sometimes deplored, if understood, in other end-of-tour people: not exactly a lack of interest, but a wish to be gone and (I hope mostly concealed) an impatience with the day-to-day problems with which I had to deal. However, the great day came when Peter Ellis arrived to take over and I realized that I was truly on the way. He was a tall, good-looking bachelor with a pleasant, sensible approach, and I took to him immediately. He had had a good briefing at HQ FEAF, as I had had, and showed a quick appreciation of the job and problems. It so happened that the day after he arrived a Valetta was scheduled to go to Hulule, so we took the opportunity of visiting Humphrey at Dunidu, and Peter had a good briefing on the political situation. My last few days passed in a whirl of farewell parties (from the Pakistani camp to the Corporals' Club to an Officers' Mess guest night), taking Peter around the various units and sections, and meeting the inevitable VIPs (including the Parliamentary group returning home). Two BOAC captains spent a night with us in preparation for a visit later in the year by Princess Alexandra, and expressed themselves satisfied with our facilities; I was happy not to have the organizing of that particular occasion. We also were invited to lunch aboard SS *Matra*, one of our regular freighters, and had the captain to dinner in the Mess. So our handover covered a great deal of ground, and Peter soon appreciated how much time was taken up by meeting people.

A farewell message was received from the C-in-C in response to one of mine, and said, 'Thank you for all your hard work and good luck with your squadron.' The AOC was a bit more expansive, and wrote, *inter alia*, 'Now that you are about to pack up and leave Gan I would like to tell you how very constructive your tour as C.O. has been and to thank you most sincerely for all you have done. Your devotion to duty in such a very mature way has been responsible for the very high reputation that Gan enjoys at present throughout the Service.' A little over the top, but very gratifying.

I had booked my passage home on one of the regular Britannias, whose captain had kindly agreed to take all my bags and boxes as well. I finally departed on 3 October, being towed to the aircraft on our new inflatable Zodiac inshore rescue craft, led by a piper and accompanied by a flotilla of bicycles, all ringing their bells. Now that the moment had come I had something of a lump in my throat as I waved farewell from the aircraft steps. Gan had been a unique and unforgettable experience: I had learnt so much and made so many friends, and I knew that I was unlikely to have such an independent command again, or to have such close relationships with my fellow officers and men.

* * *

The RAF continued to operate the Gan base until 1976, when the British withdrawal from the Far East made a staging-post redundant. Throughout most of this period there were difficulties and disagreements with the Maldivian government, making life difficult for successive station commanders and for the Adduans, who again revolted in 1963. Male wanted to arrest Afif Didi, who had to step down as atoll chief, but asked protection from the RAF; his wish for his family and himself to be taken to the Seychelles was granted, and this was done in September 1963 by HMS *Loch Lomond*. Afif was still on good terms with the Gan CO, and was given a pension by the British government.

Peter Doling recounts in his book the endless twists and turns of the British relationship with the Maldivian government. The Maldives became a special member of the Commonwealth of Nations in 1982, and a full member in 1985. An attempted coup in 1988 was foiled with the help of Indian Army paras, and the Maldives remain an elective republic. While coconuts and fish are still the main exports, along with shipping and copra, tourism is now big business. The threat of global warming increasing sea levels hangs over the Maldives, all of which are low lying (our highest point on Gan was nine feet above mean sea level), and it is difficult to see what practical steps could be taken if this threat became a reality.

As might have been expected, the Adduans suffered tremendous changes in their standard of living and way of life, which still have repercussions today. An attempt is being made to develop Gan as an airport and a tourist centre to compete with the developments in the northern atolls, but a great deal of financial suport will be needed if this is to be successful.

For me, the memories remain. I revisited the island in 1969 on my way to the Far East, and was struck by the way in which the tropical vegetation had returned, with most of the areas I remembered as waste land now green and flourishing. Rather than all the problems and tribulations, I recall the roar of the surf on the reef at night; swimming in a warm limpid sea with coloured fish all around; playing cut-throat Scrabble in the Mess in the evenings; sitting outside in the short dusk with Sputnik wheeling overhead and the flying foxes (fruit bats) coming home to roost; and the singing of the dhoni crews as they arrived for work in the early morning.

CHAPTER SIXTEEN

A Flying Command

After a long and weary journey from Lyneham via London and Leeds with all my boxes and bags, I eventually arrived back in Austwick, hardly believing that I was at last at home. Our laid-up car had been serviced and put on the road again by my kind brother-in-law, and I was able to drive it on the last leg accompanied by Joan, who had met me in Leeds for a joyful reunion. To complete the picture we were able to take Sue and Jenny out of school for part of the weekend and become a family again.

We needed to know what our immediate future would be, in particular so that we could let the main tenant of our cottage know how long we wanted to continue there. I rang the Air Secretary's department at the Air Ministry and was asked to go down for an interview almost immediately: back I went on the train to London via Leeds, and saw Wing Commander Tudor at Adastral House. I was to report to No. 1 Air Navigation School, Topcliffe, for No. 101 Navigation Refresher Course on 7 November for six weeks. I would then be on further leave until mid-February, when I was to join No. 25 Beverley Course at No. 242 Operational Conversion Unit at Thorney Island, on the south coast not far from Portsmouth, until 21 June, after which there would be a short Transport Support Course at Abingdon. I would finally be posted there on 16 July 1962 to take over No. 53 Squadron on 4 August.

Thorney Island could hardly have been further away from Austwick and the girls at school, but as Joan and I had been so long apart we felt that we must find somewhere to live near Thorney for the six months or so until we moved into a married quarter at Abingdon. As luck would have it, the Wing Commander i/c Administration at Thorney Island was Johnnie Whitlock, my old room-mate at Shawbury on the Specialist Navigation Course, and after a telephone conversation he kindly said he would do all he could to find us somewhere to live while I did the Beverley Course – married quarters were not normally available to students. With that we had to be content for the moment.

With the girls back at Casterton, Joan and I were free to take a short break away from Austwick, and we decided to take advantage of an invitation from Wing Commander Sanders, the current CO of No. 53 Squadron, to visit Abingdon and see the house we would eventually take over from him. We drove to Leeds and spent a night with Joan's parents, then on to Cranwell where we stayed with some old friends before pushing on to Abingdon, where we had lunch with Sandy and his wife and were shown round the OC 53 Squadron's ex-officio married quarter. RAF Abingdon had been built pre-war to house a group headquarters, and the houses designed for group captains were now mostly occupied by wing commanders: 4 Sycamore Close was a big house, rather like a barracks on the exterior (with traces of wartime camouflage paint still visible), but pleasant and comfortable inside, with seven bedrooms (including two for the servants), and a butler's pantry next to the large kitchen.

A small conservatory led into an extensive garden. Needless to say, there were no servants or butler, but the Sanders family had the services of a batwoman. This was certainly going to be a change after our small cottage at Austwick. Sandy was slightly older that I, with a wartime DFC and a forceful manner. He insisted that I pay a short visit with him to the Squadron HQ, despite my protestations that it was not appropriate at this particular time so far ahead of my posting. However, we went up to the Squadron – a fairly modern prefabricated building on the other side of the airfield, with a briefing room, a crew room, and various offices – and I met one or two of the officers and aircrew, all of whom were friendly and welcoming. We did not stay long, but my misgivings were not misplaced, as I had – some time later – a rather tart letter from the Station Commander, Group Captain Neil Cameron, expressing his displeasure that I had visited the squadron prematurely and without having the courtesy to report to him first. I could not but agree, and wrote to him apologizing and explaining the circumstances. It was not a good start, but the matter was never referred to again.

Joan and I continued our tour by visiting Kenilworth in Warwickshire and staying with some of her mother's family – great-aunts and cousins – who made us very welcome and took us around various local places of note: we remember Hidcote Manor, the bird gardens at Charlcote and, of course, Kenilworth Castle. It was a pleasant interlude and we spent a night with Joan's parents in Leeds before returning to Austwick.

The following weekend we picked up Sue and Jenny from school for an exeat, and I had a short interview with their Headmistress, Miss Staines ('Kitty'), who thought that Jenny was settling down but was not pleased with Sue's general behaviour; I promised to talk to her, which I did (with no very visible result). Jenny was not very happy during her first term, but made several friends – and one in particular who is still a close friend – and thereafter enjoyed her time at Casterton.

Leave finally came to an end and I reported to Topcliffe, betwen Ripon and Thirsk, early in November to start the Navigation Refresher Course, living in mess during the week but driving home to Austwick for most weekends, a forty-five-minute drive. Topcliffe was a pre-war station with mostly permanent buildings and comfortable accommodation, and its main task was basic navigator training; the refresher course was designed for navigators returning to flying after ground jobs, and used the ANS facilities and aircraft – the Varsity, with which I was already familiar, and the Valetta Flying Classroom, which could carry up to six students and was fitted with six astrodomes and navigation positions. There were about a dozen navigators on the course, of various seniorities and experience; the Course Commander was Flight Lieutenant Newman, who taught navigation methods and maps and charts, and there were separate instructors for airmanship, instruments and compasses, astro-navigation, radio and radar, and meteorology. I was interested to note that these subjects were mostly covered at the standard of the old Staff Navigator Course which I had taken nearly twenty years before, except that spherical trigonometry was not taught and that the astro-navigation was of a more up-to-date and practical nature. We started with the inevitable ground school, which was hard work, especially as I was the senior student with Staff Navigator and Spec N qualifications, and had to make a respectable showing. I was lucky that in my last few jobs I had been able to keep my hand in to some extent, even at Gan with some Shackleton experience.

The flying phase started with a Varsity day cross-country, and continued with a night exercise in the Valetta in which we used the Periscopic Sextant Mark 2 with pre-computation techniques, selecting the appropriate celestial bodies and working out their azimuths and altitudes before flight, using the AP 3270 tables, for selected positions and times on the route to be flown. By setting these on the periscopic sextant at the appropriate time, the chosen body should appear in view, and its altitude could then be measured against the bubble reference. This system worked well providing that the aircraft was somewhere near the expected position at the preselected time, and I found that it gave me greater confidence in astro-navigation than the old-fashioned method of making the calculations in flight and searching for the target body with the Mark 9 sextant (which, incidentally, we brushed up on at the same time). As it happened, the periscopic sextant was not in use on the Beverley squadrons, and I was unable to use it for some years.

After two more day cross-countries in the Varsity, by which time it was mid-December, we had the pleasure of an overseas flight to Malta via Orange in the south of France, helpfully planned so that we had a pleasant weekend between the outward and return flights. The captain of my aircraft was Group Captain Stubbs, the Topcliffe Station Commander, and we got on well together, with no flight problems. That was virtually the end of the course, with some thirty-five flying hours, except for the final examinations, which, though not making any concessions, did not present too much difficulty. One aspect of the course I found particularly helpful was that the airmanship syllabus included much information on current air traffic systems, flight information documents, and the survival and rescue organization, most of which I had picked up over the last few years but which was constantly expanding and changing. On dead-reckoning navigation procedures I was amused to see that, some seven years after I chaired the (not very constructive) Institute of Navigation working party on DR error, the RAF was still working on a figure of eight nautical miles per hour since the last reliable fix; however, with a nod in the direction of vastly improved aircraft performance, the figure for speeds between .65 Mach and .85 Mach was said to be 20 nmph. So a most probable position was still not something to be relied upon.

Successfully refreshed navigationally (and personally), I left Topcliffe on 20 December and returned to Austwick for Christmas with the family. We spent a few days in Leeds after Christmas, taking the girls to the pantomime at the Grand Theatre, which they much enjoyed. The day before they returned to school we had a telephone call from Johnnie Whitlock at Thorney Island to say that he had found a small modern furnished bungalow available for rent on Hayling Island which he thought would be suitable for us for six months or so. We made a swift decision, and I sent off a deposit to the owner the same day: the next three weeks were a whirl of packing, telephoning, and making all the necessary arrangements, but on 9 February we moved into Sea Haze, The Glade, Hayling Island, a small three-bedroomed bungalow only a five-minute walk from the sea, and from which we could see ships passing in the Solent. The owners, the Treptes, lived in a similar bungalow next door on this small modern housing development – we got on well with them and they were very helpful. Some of our own furniture and effects had had to go into store, but as usual Joan soon had the place feeling like home.

Hayling Island – no longer a true island since the road south from Havant bridges the sea at Langstone Harbour – had Chichester Harbour and Thorney Island to the east and Portsmouth a few miles to the west. It depended heavily on tourist trade in the summer, with much new building and a small holiday camp near the south coast, but in the winter months it was quiet and there were pleasant walks along the beach which we (and our spaniel) much enjoyed. It was only a few miles to the South Downs country with its sheep walks and sweeping views.

* * *

Work started within a few days, and I reported to the ground school at No. 242 Operational Conversion Unit at Thorney Island, a similar but smaller peninsula about eight or nine miles from Hayling, with much of the area taken up by the airfield and its buildings. Thorney was another pre-war station, which had been the home of an air navigation school before switching to Beverley conversion. The Beverley was a remarkable and unique aircraft: many years later I wrote a semi-humorous article about it which attempted to summarize its qualities, and it is perhaps worth quoting from this. I wrote,

'It'll never replace the aeroplane' was one comment when the Blackburn Beverley went into service with RAF Transport Command in 1955. Similar humorous or incredulous comments followed this aircraft wherever it flew. One American pilot, taxiing behind a Beverley, was asked by Air Traffic Control: 'Do you see the Beverley ahead of you?' He replied: 'I see it but I don't believe it.' The captain of a jetliner called up a Beverley captain and said: 'Did you make it yourself?' At this time this was the biggest aircraft ever flown by the RAF: it had a wingspan of 162 feet, a length just short of 100 feet, and a height of 38 feet 5 inches to the top of the twin fins. The freight bay measured 10 by 10 by 40 feet and looked like a metal box, and there was a massive fixed undercarriage, almost unheard of for a large aircraft at the time. With its four Bristol Centaurus piston engines, it had a cruising speed of 155 mph, slower than wartime bombers. It was described as bizarre, ugly and ungainly, and a lot of other uncomplimentary terms, some unprintable. But the crews who flew it developed a respect and liking for this seemingly old-fashioned aeroplane, which could do jobs that no other could do at the time. It was designed as a rugged, heavy-lift, short-range vehicle, and it was ideal for that particular role. Unfortunately, it was not always used as it should have been, and crews often found themselves flying on long-range trips where little payload could be carried and several stages had to be flown to get to where it was needed. But on operations in support of the Army, its proper role, the Beverley came into its own. For trooping, 94 fully equpped troops could be carried, or 70 for parachuting. For casualty evacuations 48 stretchers could be taken in the freight bay and 34 sitting cases with two attendants in the boom, the upper part of the fuselage. Typical freight loads were two complete Sycamore helicopters, a Hunter fighter with the wings removed, and many types of Army vehicles – Scout cars, personnel carriers, guns and trailers, Land Rovers and so on. Beverley squadrons were stationed in the the Far and Middle East, and would take these loads into short dirt strips in the jungle and in the desert: the aircraft could land in about 500 yards and take off in just over

300. The chaps who designed the engines and the undercarriage were not so daft after all: the ability to go into reverse thrust on landing, and the punishment the landing-gear would take, enabled the aircraft to use hastily prepared strips that no other type would look at. They could touch down, usually in a cloud of dust, disgorge the vehicles and troops down the rear ramps, and then reverse back to the start of the strip to make a quick take-off.

All this expertise lay well into the future as we started to learn about the Beverley at Thorney. I was crewed with Flight Lieutenant Chris Lansdell, who already had Transport Command experience and was an excellent pilot, with whom I got on well. However, there were a few weeks of ground school to undergo first, and in the navigation aspects there was much repetition of the subjects covered in the refresher course I had just done. On the other hand, some time was devoted to the particular requirements of Transport Command – route flying around the world, the use of the airways system, and the capabilities of the Beverley. We were introduced to Transport Command Air Staff Instructions, the sort of 'bible' which reminded me of USAF regulations ('If it isn't in the regulations you don't do it.'), and purported to cover all aspects of transport flying. There was also much emphasis on airmanship, survival and rescue, and the care of passengers, all of which I found helpful. World climatology was also covered in a very thorough fashion.

We finally started the flying phase in April with the inevitable circuits and landings and local flying. The sheer size of the aircraft was daunting: the crew entrance was up a nearly vertical ten-foot ladder to the flight deck, which was somewhat hazardous for the navigator, usually encumbered with navigation bag and sextant, but at least we did not have to carry parachutes, as these were not normally worn for flights other than paradropping; this was the first time I had flown as crew without parachutes, and I viewed this with mixed feelings. The standard crew was a pilot captain, a co-pilot, an engineer, a signaller, a navigator, and one or two air quartermasters, though we did not always carry AQMs on training flights; at this period the NCO quartermasters were not classed as aircrew, but theirs was a very important job, especially in the Beverley, which could carry such varied cargoes needing careful loading and weighing, apart from passenger care. AQMs were given aircrew status in the next year or so.

The flight deck was fairly spacious: the engineer sat behind the co-pilot, and the navigator's position faced forward on the port side with a large plotting table and a comfortable seat back-to-back with that of the signaller, a convenient arrangement. There was nothing new to me in the navigation equipment: Gee Mark 3 (the miniaturized version with automatic readouts); Rebecca Mark 4; the GEC radio compass (ARI 5428) on which Freddy Stringer and I had worked at Farnborough; the standard G4B gyro-magnetic compass and air position indicator; the Mark 2 drift recorder, old fashioned but useful and reliable; and the Mark 9B sextant, another old standby, as was the Mark 2 astro-compass – the astrodome was just overhead. There was no ground-mapping radar, but the pilot had a cloud and collision warning radar screen in the cockpit (known colloquially as the 'cloud-and-clonk') with which some ground features could occasionally be identified. The radio compass was essential for airways flying, which depended on radio beacons at each turning point and was also used with a standard let-down procedure in poor weather. Altogether there was little change from systems in use ten or fifteen years earlier, although I found that the Transport Command requirements for navigational activity and log keeping during route flying were more stringent than anything I had experienced previously – unsurprisingly, since we could be required to operate anywhere in the world with passengers and valuable freight.

Chris progressed to flying solo both day and night, and after a great deal of local flying, including radio compass let-downs, we flew a couple of cross-country flights, the first one 'screened' (with instructors) and the second solo; I enjoyed navigating the Beverley, and soon felt at home in the navigator's position. On the whole the Beverley had a good safety record, but there was one serious accident on our course. In his book *Blackburn Beverley* (1990), Bill Overton referred to the problems of local flying at Thorney, a residential and holiday area with

> many prominent people, such as retired Admirals, Generals and the like. These people objected strongly to the night-flying and its attendant noise … and many irate letters appeared in the local press. … Matters came to a head in May 1962, when XL 132 suffered an uncontrollable engine fire. The engine, with an overspeeding propeller, wrenched itself from its mountings and fell on to someone's property in the village of Bosham. This aroused such a public outcry that night-flying training at Thorney Island was virtually forbidden from then on and a system was implemented whereby the night-flying was done overseas, usually at Idris, El Adem or Luqa.

What Overton does not say is that the aircraft came down in the sea and that crew members were killed, including the navigator. This cast something of a blight on the station, and on our course in particular.

However, we had virtually finished our night-flying, and were cleared to go 'down the route' to Luqa in Malta, directly on the way out and via Orange in the south of France on return for refuelling. This was the standard route to the Mediterranean and the Middle East for the Beverley force, and I came to know it well in the following years. I alternated as first navigator, and for the first time used the specially printed airways charts with the standard routes already drawn; flying across the Med south of Sicily we were back to old-fashioned navigation using astro-compass bearings from Sicilian landmarks and drifts from the sea surface.

After a pleasant free day in Malta we took off for Orange, and for some reason (aircraft serviceability?) stayed overnight there at a hotel in the town. We had several trainee AQMs on board for flying experience and we were all accommodated in the same place. I was awakened very early the following morning by the aircraft captain, Flight Lieutenant Henry, who told me that the flight engineer had stabbed one of the AQMs (or was it the other way round?); the French police were here and could I come? Since I was the senior officer on the flight I had no option, and roused myself from a stupor not unconnected with the excellent after-dinner cognac of the night before. There was a fair amount of blood but no serious injury, as I recall, and I never did find out exactly how and why, although I know that some of the AQMs were female (destined for the Comet squadrons) and that this was not entirely irrelevant. The police wanted to arrest the culprit, but I summoned up my rudimentary French and persuaded them that as no French citizen was involved and we were a military organization we could deal with this under British military law. I put the NCO concerned under close arrest (the victim had been taken to hospital), and we flew back to Thorney that day. Evidently life in Transport Command was going to be full of incident.

The course came to an end in mid-June with a night cross-country, and the next and final step in our Beverley conversion was a four-week course at the Transport Support Element at Abingdon, a small unit commanded by Squadron Leader Paul Mayall, whose job was to teach newly qualified crews the techniques of their tasks in the transport support role – paratrooping and supply dropping, the latter concerning basically the One-Ton Container and the Medium Stressed Platform Mark 1, from which a variety of military loads could be dropped. The Beverley could carry seventy paratroops plus dispatchers in the freight bay on the lower deck, and thirty in the rear fuselage on the upper deck; heavy dropping-platforms up to 30,000 lb could be carried in the freight bay, typical loads being two 7,000 lb platforms, or one 7,000 lb platform and one 1-ton truck platform, or four 6,000 lb supply dropping-platforms, or one large heavy-equipment dropping-platform. So the aircraft was very versatile in the Army support role, and the AQMs needed to be well versed in all these varied types of drop loads. The flight engineer had to be precise in his fuel calculations, as with heavy loads the range of the Beverley was very much reduced, especially at the low altitudes required for some drops. The aircraft captain had a great deal to remember apart from loading and fuel problems: the aircraft would be handled differently during and after the drop, depending on the type of load, and had to be flown accurately up to the aiming-point and leaving the dropping-zone (DZ). Hang-ups had also to be kept in mind.

The navigator's job, apart from finding the DZ, often at low level, was to direct the aircraft to the release-point, having worked out where this was by the use of Calculated Air Release Point (CARP) tables, taking into account the estimated wind velocity over the DZ and the type of load. The dropping-point would normally be marked in one or more of a variety of ways, usually the responsibility of the Army, and could be a simple T marker, recognition letters, smoke or flares, or in rare cases a radio beacon. The navigator had to clamber down from the flight deck to the freight bay and into the supply aimer's position under the nose, rather like the bomb aimer's station in a bomber aircraft; having worked out the release-point, he would guide the captain to it by the traditional 'Left left' or 'Right' method, having told him 'Five minutes to go' at the appropriate time and checked with the AQM. The navigator had control of the signal lights via a supply aimer's panel, and he would switch (and call) 'Red on' five seconds before the release-point, and then 'Green on' over the release-point – the signal to drop, at which the AQM and/or dispatchers would release the load or start the drop of paratroops. There were various emergency drills for hang-ups, but this in essence was the procedure. There was a great deal for captain, AQM and navigator to remember, but once we were familiar with the drills I found it the most enjoyable part of Beverley flying, and rewarding when everything went well.

With TSE we practised supply drops at nearby Watchfield and paratroop dropping at Weston-on-the-Green, another small airfield close to Abingdon. The final flight was a short low-level cross-country, always enjoyable, with simulated paratroop dropping at Weston. We were now a qualified Beverley crew in the Medium Range Transport Force. Chris and I were very pleased with ourselves, as were the rest of the crew, and I was delighted that he was also to be posted to 53 Squadron. It had been a long haul since I started the refresher course in the previous November, but at least I now felt more confident of taking over the squadron with a substantially increased knowledge of its role, technical capabilities and problems.

We were now at the height of the Cold War. The previous year (1961) had seen the 'Bay of Pigs' crisis and the construction of the Berlin Wall, with the Cuban missile crisis ending in October 1962. The RAF's V-Force provided the British nuclear deterrent until the Navy's Polaris submarines became operational some years later. The role of the Medium Range Transport Force (later designated Tactical Transport (Medium Range)) was to provide strategic mobility and tactical flexibility for the Army's strategic reserve units, taking heavy-lift loads and troops to forward airstrips or delivering them by parachute to areas with no suitable landing places, helping to keep the peace in the many British territories still scattered around the world. The Beverley squadrons also had a contribution to make to the nuclear deterrent, providing tactical flexibility to Bomber Command if there should be a need to move V-bomber squadrons at short notice away from their known bases.

The Strategic Transport role of Transport Command was still being built up in the Comet and Britannia squadrons (with the Belfasts to follow later), and often required assistance from the MRT force's Hastings, Beverleys and Argosies. As I've written earlier, this meant that the Beverleys in particular had frequently to be employed on tasks for which they were not specifically designed, carrying such loads as mobile radar stations (with trucks which no other aircraft could carry) and troops to overseas bases, requiring frequent refuelling stops. Beverley crews spent a great deal of time away from base and had to be prepared to depart at short notice, and sometimes to operate under field conditions at remote airstrips and in varied climates.

This was the force I was now joining, and in the next three years I would experience every facet of Beverley operations. When I reported to 53 Squadron I had an immediate taste of route flying: there were still a few weeks until my formal takeover date, and I had the opportunity to fly to Cyprus and back. I cannot recall what the payload was, but we refuelled as usual at Orange and Luqa in Malta before going on to El Adem in North Africa, and finally to Nicosia in Cyprus, returning via the same airfields, a total of over thirty hours' flying, for all of which I was first (and only) navigator. This was invaluable experience, especially as I was crewed with one of the squadron's most experienced captains, Flight Lieutenant Bryan Lamb. He was not only an excellent pilot but a congenial character with an irrepressible sense of humour, who became a good friend; we are still in touch. He was a bachelor at that time, and we found several common interests and a bond in our knowledge of Leeds, at whose university he had taken his (English?) degree (and finding a holiday job as a tram conductor on routes I knew well).

* * *

Joan had settled in to the bungalow on Hayling Island, taking the dog for daily walks on the beach, but it must have been an uneasy time for her, knowing that we should shortly be moving to Abingdon. Sue and Jenny came home for the summer holidays, taking the long train journey down from the north and being met in London, and I think they enjoyed the novelty of living by the seaside and having the odd picnic on the beach. I had started taking over the squadron by this time, and was unable to go home as frequently as I would have liked – I remember that one weekend was taken up by the annual Open Day at Abingdon, in which I flew in a close formation of four Beverleys – an exciting experience. However, I managed a few days off, but it was soon time to take over our married quarter at Abingdon, moving in in mid-August. Joan had already seen the house when we visited the Sanders family early in the year, but it must have been a surprise to the girls to move into the biggest house we had ever had. I was thankful that they were there to help Joan settle in when the rest of our effects arrived; as usual I was tied up with duties of various sorts, and was also trying to fly as much as I could. Joan was soon involved in the social round of giving and attending dinner parties, sherry mornings, and so on, and getting to know the squadron wives (and their problems).

*　*　*

RAF Abingdon was established in 1932 as a permanent station, and during the Second World War it became an Operational Training Unit for heavy bombers, transferring in 1946 to Transport Command and operating Dakota short-range transport aircraft, then replaced by Avro Yorks which took part in the 1948 Berlin airlift. For a short time it was the home base of the Overseas Ferry Unit, accepting Sabre jet fighters presented to the Royal Air Force by the people of Canada and flown across the Atlantic via Greenland and Iceland. Now, in addition to the two MRT Beverley squadrons, 47 and 53, Abingdon housed No. 1 Parachute Training School, which began life in 1940 at RAF Ringway, near Manchester, and trained all the parachutists of the British Army. After the war No. 1 PTS moved briefly to Upper Heyford near Oxford, and then to Abingdon in 1950. The jumping towers and the captive balloon used for practice descents were prominent on the Abingdon skyline, and descents from aircraft were made at Weston-on-the Green, a nearby grass airfield. The small Transport Support Element gave air support to No. 1 PTS, and the Transport Command Air Movement Development Unit was researching the problems of transporting heavy freight and of large air movements generally. The station operated on the usual three-wing system – a Transport Wing containing the flying elements, plus Technical and Administrative Wings – and was a busy place with a high air movement rate.

I assumed command of 53 Squadron on 4 August, having by this time got to know most of the captains and crews, and become familiar with the daily routine (if there could be said to be such a thing with the varied and sometimes short-notice tasks and training requirements imposed by 38 Group, our governing formation under Transport Command). Although there were two Flight Commanders, neither was actually in command of a flight in the disciplinary sense. Squadron Leader Maurice Wells was Flight Commander (Training) and Squadron Leader Cheshire ('Ches') Flight Commander (Operations); these titles speak for themselves. There were leaders for each aircrew category, and most members of the squadron had a secondary duty such as i/c sports, entertainments, or rescue and survival. The Adjutant was a very quiet and efficient warrant officer, who looked after all squadron files and records, as well as being a sort of secretary to the CO.

The squadron had a long history of working with the Army. No. 53 (Army Co-operation) Squadron first formed at Catterick aerodrome in 1916, flying the BE2 Artillery Observation aircraft and later with RE8s, spending the rest of the First World War in France, and also carrying out close support tasks using bombs and guns against enemy troops. The squadron disbanded a year after the war ended, and did not form again until June 1937, when it was equipped with Hector close support aircraft at Farnborough, later replaced by Blenheims and deployed to France a fortnight after the Second World War started in 1939. Its job was tactical reconnaissance until the withdrawal from France in May 1940, when it returned to the UK and operated from Detling in Kent, carrying out reconnaissance and bombing missions over Dunkirk and other French ports, and later convoy protection. The Blenheims were replaced by Hudsons in the maritime role, attacking U-boats and enemy shipping in the Western Approaches, operating from St Eval in Cornwall. With U-boat activity increasing in the western Atlantic, the squadron moved to Quonset in the USA, and later to Trinidad, to assist the US Navy in its attacks on U-boats, which up to then (1942) had had little opposition. Back at St Eval, the squadron was re-equipped with Whitleys for a short time, and then its first four-engined aircraft, the Liberator, with greater range and capability. Carrying on the U-boat campaign, the squadron sank at least five U-boats, finishing the war at Reykjavik in Iceland on convoy protection, and returning to the UK when the war ended.

Now in the transport role, first with Dakotas and then with the Hastings, the squadron operated mainly in Europe, and took part in the Berlin airlift in 1949. Flying from Topcliffe and then Netheravon, the squadron extended its role to transport support as well as route flying to the Middle East, culminating in troop- and supply-dropping missions from Cyprus to the Canal Zone in the ill-fated attack on Egypt in 1956. Finally, the move to Abingdon was made in 1957 to convert to the Beverley. Looking back over its chequered history, it seems that few squadrons could have made so many changes of location, aircraft and role, but of course this was not unusual in the period from just before the Second World War to the years immediately following. The Royal Air Force was changing all the time throughout its short history as aviation technology and the political situation developed.

Most of the captains and crews when I took over had many flying hours on the Beverley, and had grown to like the aircraft and appreciate its unique qualities. Ches Cheshire, who was also a navigator, was an old hand who gave me plenty of advice; Maurice Wells was a very different character who had spent most of his career on fighter aircraft and had recently converted from the Swift to the Beverley – a very unusual career change. But he was an intelligent and conscientious Flight Commander, if a little reserved, and I grew to like him, as, I think, did the crews. The least experienced crew members were the co-pilots, mostly young, in their first operational job and aspiring to become captains eventually. Co-pilot training included local flying with two co-pilots in charge without the supervision of a captain, and I often acted as navigator on these flights, keeping a low profile but able to assess their capabilities as well as practising my own radio compass and Rebecca let-down procedures.

I had only been in the saddle for a few weeks when a major MRT exercise took place codenamed 'Fallex', a major drop of troops and Army equipment based on an airfield in northern Greece called Larissa. I left Abingdon in one of ten Beverleys (on the same day that Jenny and Sue returned to school) and flew to Larissa via Orange and Luqa. We were under canvas, in somewhat primitive conditions, together with a force of twenty Hastings aircraft, altogether a large contingent to feed and house. When my father, an old Salonika hand from the Great War, had heard that we were going to Larissa towards the end of September, he had said, 'Well, I wish you luck – that's the rainy season.' I told him not to worry as our Met men had said conditions would be all right. I recalled this conversation when, on the first or second night at Larissa, the heavens opened and the camp was extensively flooded. I spent most of the night sitting on the back of a folding chair with my feet on the seat just above the level of the water in the tent. I still have the 8 mm movie film I took the following day, showing the squalor and desolation, with soaked and sagging tents, lakes of mud, and people forlornly picking their way through the mess. Luckily we had a day or two to spare before the first drop, and somehow a modicum of order was restored, some aircrew going back to their Beverleys to sleep. We had a day of extensive briefing for the large-scale exercise, with much use of all the (to me) new terms and acronyms for the complicated control system: I remember one AQM saying as we walked out of the briefing room, 'ATOCs, FETOCs, BASOCs – personally I wear blue socks.'

This must have been one of the last large-scale drops in the history of transport support – thirty aircraft dropping troops and (in our case) medium-stress platforms over the DZ, followed by a similar exercise the following day. The weather was now acceptable, and all went well as far as I remember. We had a free day afterwards, and celebrated in one of the local tavernas in Larissa town, to the amusement of the locals. We flew back to Abingdon via the now familiar route, and a few days later had a similar exercise, with only three Beverleys and eight Hastings, based at Gütersloh in West Germany.

*   *   *

At home we had by now settled into some sort of routine, although my own movements were likely to be different day to day. On days when I was not on exercise or 'down the route' – these were not very frequent – the MT section would drop off my Land Rover at the house and I would drive up to 'Sleepy Hollow', the station nickname for 53 Squadron HQ. Here I would run over the day's flying programme with the Flight Commanders, allocate various duties, and deal with the day's correspondence and any personnel problems. Finding the number of crews and aircraft required for stipulated tasks was never easy: if one crew member was not available (sickness, leave or in some cases playing rugby for the RAF), or one or more aircraft were unserviceable – the Bristol Centaurus 173 engine was notably unreliable, and was later replaced by the 175 – it was not always possible to meet all commitments. There was usually at least one aircraft 'down the route', and we had to keep two aircraft and crews on continual standby for Operation Clipkey in case unforecast movements by Bomber Command squadrons required short-notice transport back-up. Daily flying training was of course continuous, and I would get airborne whenever possible, even if only on local 'circuits and bumps'; this would often entail night-flying if I could not get away during the day.

Joan meanwhile had a largeish house to cope with; our batwoman was not a great help, but better than nothing. Shopping was either at the station NAAFI or in Abingdon town, a mile or so away, which meant a bus journey, as Joan did not drive at this time. As I have said, she was soon involved in coffee and sherry parties with other wives, and we were both frequently asked to dinner or drinks as well as giving our own parties. We gave dinner parties regularly, and Joan produced some splendid meals single handed. We usually dined at the Station Commander's when some VIP was being entertained, and by now we were on good terms with Neil and Mrs Cameron – he had been on the directing staff at Bracknell in our time there. He was a well-decorated Battle of Britain pilot, and later became Chief of the Air Staff and Chief of the Defence Staff (a future I should never have thought likely for him). Our particular friends were Jerry Barr, the CO of 47 Squadron, and his wife Tommy, with whom we hit it off immediately; we would have informal meals in each other's houses, and often went out to a local pub for an evening (though pub cuisine was not very enterprising in those days). We were able to discuss similar problems of squadron life and always enjoyed each others' company. What Joan and I particularly liked was having some of our squadron bachelors – Maurice Wells, Bryan Lamb, Hugh Crawley and others – for supper on our knees (spaghetti bolognese or an Italian-American dish called Jo Mazzotti with pork and beans, noodles and other ingredients, which was Joan's speciality and a general favourite) with plenty of beer and with pontoon or some other harmless game to follow;

we learnt much about what was going on off the record in the squadron, and the state of its morale, which was in fact usually very good. Other good friends were the Church of England Padre, Harry Phair, and his wife Esther; as a bonus they had two daughters of similar ages to Sue and Jenny.

Such social life was always liable to be interrupted by short-notice flying tasks or other duties. The wing commanders on the station (and the Station Commander) took it in turns to be Duty Commander, which came round every five weeks at that time, and involved being available twenty-four hours a day and coping with any unexpected problems that arose, operational or otherwise. I remember one Sunday, when we were having a pre-lunch sherry party at home, that there was an enormous explosion nearby, and as Duty Commander I had an immediate call from the Station Duty Officer to say that the captive balloon used by No. 1 PTS had exploded, possibly through some sort of surface friction. I went up to the site and found that, although there was extensive damage to the wooden hut used as the duty crew's living accommodation, there were no serious injuries. Unfortunately some of the local houses had broken windows from the blast, and having put an official inquiry in motion I returned to the sherry party, announcing that 'The balloon's gone up!'

Life was not all duty, however, and we would occasionally have a picnic up on the Berkshire Downs or visit Cirencester or Cheltenham, pleasant towns not too far away. We would also visit the theatre in Oxford (two for the price of one on Monday nights), and I remember seeing *The Tempest* with Alastair Sim at the New Theatre, and *Iolanthe* at the Playhouse. I was fortunate enough to be able to attend some sessions of weekend courses organized for serving officers by Oxford University Delegacy for Extra-Mural Studies on the general theme 'Recent Developments in the Sciences', based at St Catherine's College, although the lecture venues included the Clarendon Laboratory and Engineering Laboratory as well as the University Observatory. Subjects included astrophysics and cosmology, metallurgy, recent engineering developments and others, all given by leaders in their particular fields. Some aspects were obviously over my head, but it was fascinating to be in an academic atmosphere and to hear of the advanced work going on in these fields. Inevitably I had to cancel my attendance at some of the sessions when duties intervened, but it was a valuable insight.

Our lives became closely interwoven with those of the squadron personnel, whose personal and family problems were often as important to us as their professional performance – indeed the two were interdependent. There seemed to be a spate of weddings, mostly of young co-pilots and often to WRAF officers on the station (but later including Bryan Lamb, that confirmed bachelor). Towards the end of 1962, Chris Lansdell (my former pilot at Thorney Island and now a captain on the squadron) had a serious car accident and was taken to hospital on the dangerously ill list. His young wife José, who was pregnant and had a small boy, Timothy, lived off the station and did not drive, and we thought it best to bring her home to stay with us until the situation improved. They were delightful guests and stayed until a married quarter on the station became available and they were able to move in not long before Chris came out of hospital; he was unfit to fly, but we found him a job in the Station Operations Section for the time being. Joan was godmother to their new baby. (Chris and José now live in France and we hear from them every Christmas).

In December of that year Group Captain Cameron was replaced by Group Captain (Freddie) Sowrey, another former fighter pilot, and recently converted on to the Beverley. He was a punctilious and conscientious Station Commander, flying when he could, and we came to like him and his wife Anne very much.

About this time there was an airborne assault exercise in the south of France for which we provided five Beverleys and RAF Colerne eight Hastings. I was designated Force Commander, which entailed briefing the crews, monitoring the drop from the air, and altering timing and tactics if necessary. The Beverleys, based at Perpignan, dropped a total of one hundred troops and five medium-stressed platforms with vehicles and equipment, and the whole exercise was carried out with few problems. While at Perpignan we had a free day and were taken in a coach down the Roussillon coast close to the Spanish border, with a splendid seafood lunch at a small fishing village. But what I remember chiefly about the exercise was flying at low level over deeply rural France, and glimpsing villages and farmsteads which had probably not changed in more than a hundred years. Maurice Wells was the captain of the aircraft I was flying in, and I acted as navigator on the way back via Toulouse; the whole exercise was valuable experience for me.

The winter of 1962/3 was one of the worst in this country for many years, probably as far back as 1946/7. During the height of the snow the runways had to be cleared daily, as had the aircraft, and in the tactical transport force the Argosies and Hastings were unable to operate for some weeks, but the Beverleys managed to keep flying, giving us a gratifying glow of one-upmanship. Farmers in the west country were particularly hard hit, being unable to feed hill sheep, and Bryan Lamb and Hugh Crawley did at least one flight each in atrocious weather conditions dropping hay bales over the moors at very low level; the freight bays retained the odour of hay for days afterwards. The local bird life was badly affected – at the end of the winter we found the emaciated corpses of a pair of woodpigeons in our garden hedge, a most pathetic sight.

Christmas festivities went ahead as usual, with the traditional Christmas dinner served in the Airmen's Mess by the officers and senior NCOs. Sue and Jenny came home for the holidays and there were various formal and informal parties despite the hard weather. Their long train journey from and to school must have been a cold and tiring one. I was lucky enough to get away to the sun for a few days in January when I flew with Bryan Lamb via Orange in southern France, Luqa (Malta) and El Adem, Libya, to Kufra Oasis in the centre of the Libyan Desert; we were taking a load of fuel drums for a desert exercise by the 2nd Battalion Greenjackets. The oasis was some three hours' flying from El Adem, mostly over featureless terrain with few navigational aids, and as navigator I was relieved when it showed up ahead more or less on ETA. The airstrip was fairly basic but no problem for the Beverley; Kufra itself was a large cultivated area with a population of several thousand, mostly Senussi Muslims, and in the Second World War had been an important part of lines of communication, at first for the Italians but then captured by the Free French forces and occupied for the Allies. This large green area with trees, crops and dwellings was a surprising sight in the middle of the vast barren desert, and we would have liked to take a closer look, but were scheduled for less than two hours on the ground. Back in wintry Berkshire, a day late because of unserviceability, I found that at home we were having problems with our water supply because of frozen pipes in the roof; we were having a dinner party that evening with the Sowreys and another couple, but Joan was coping valiantly as usual. As we dressed for dinner, two Works Department workmen were unfreezing the pipes with a blowtorch, and as one inadvertently scorched the other we could hear the ensuing oaths above our heads. It was a successful evening, but I was glad to get to bed that night.

*   *   *

That Easter (1963) the family took advantage of the Transport Command 'indulgence passage' scheme, whereby families could use seats in route aircraft if and when they were available, taking the chance that similar seats could be used on the return journey. We flew to that now familiar staging post, Orange, in one of our squadron aircraft; the OC RAF Detachment at the airfield had arranged accommodation at the Hotel Terminus at the railway station, hardly luxurious, but adequate, and on the edge of the town of Orange. This was a place of great antiquity, with a surprisingly well-preserved Roman amphitheatre and a splendid Roman triumphal arch, which was the prototype of the Arc de Triomphe in Paris. It was set in beautiful countryside with orchards, lavender fields, vineyards and small farms. It so happened that one of the RAF Detachment officers was Flight Lieutenant Louis Maisonpierre, who, although British, was of French origin, as his name suggests, and spoke idiomatic French; he knew the area well and took us out to a small vineyard where we were entertained in the farmhouse home of the owner (with a fire of vine cuttings blazing on the hearth), and then taken to the 'cave', where we selected a bottle of Côtes du Rhône, vintage 1949 (Jenny's birth year). Louis was greatly helpful in many ways, and we eventually reciprocated by transporting his piano by Beverley when he was posted back to the UK.

Orange was a pleasant town, and we would usually have a picnic lunch in a small park – La Colline – having bought baguettes, pâté and cakes. For dinner we found a small back-street restaurant called Le Bec Fin, family-run and with excellent food at reasonable prices, grandmère behind the till and small grandson running out for fresh bread; the clientele were invariably all French, and we thoroughly enjoyed the atmosphere. On a couple of days we got a bus to Vaison-la-Romaine, a small town in the foothills of the Alpilles (the little alps) with Mont Ventoux in the background – another ancient town with a Roman bridge and old men playing boules in the square. Since Avignon was only a few miles from Orange we took a train there and stayed in a small hotel for two or three days, visiting all the usual tourist attractions – the 'pont', of course, the Palais des Papes and the old castle at Villeneuve across the Rhône. On one memorable day we had an all-day coach tour which took us to Daudet's mill, the hill village of Les Baux, Montmajour abbey, and finally to Arles via the Camargue and Tarascon, a comprehensive if brief taste of Provence.

This enjoyable holiday had an unpleasant ending: on the day we expected to be picked up again by a 53 Squadron Beverley, the RAF Detachment had a signal saying that the aircraft had crashed at El Adem. Few details were available except that there had been casualties. We had to wait impatiently for another couple of days before a Beverley returning from a route trip was able to fit us in. Back at Abingdon I found that the acting Squadron Commander, Ches, had flown out to El Adem, and the details of the incident became clear. The aircraft had been on a night low-level cross-country exercise from Idris to El Adem and had crashed short of the runway while starting an overshoot in very poor visibility. The AQM and a ground crew member had been killed, and two other crew members were seriously injured and had been flown to hospital in Cyprus.

Joan and I visited the families involved and did our best to comfort the wife of the AQM, who had been an experienced and valued member of Bryan Lamb's crew flying temporarily on this exercise.

The morale in the squadron was naturally affected by this incident, but training and overseas flights and exercises continued unabated, as did the flow of VIP visitors to the station, for whom various arrangements had to be made, including miniature flying displays. But a greater blow was about to fall: for some time we had heard rumours that the squadron was to re-equip with the Short Belfast, a large transport aircraft under development. However, Group Captain Sowrey called me in one day in May and told me that 53 was to disband temporarily before re-equipping at some unspecified date, and the aircraft and personnel were to form part of an expanded 47 Squadron at Abingdon. Since Jerry Barr, the OC 47, was due for posting and I had served less than a year with 53, I would take command of the new 47 Squadron. This was a shock, but my situation could have been worse, and Jerry and I got together to work out the details of the reorganization. We decided that the larger 47 Squadron should operate in two flights, with 'A' Flight formed from the old 47 Squadron crews and 'B' Flight from 53 Squadron; the Flight Commanders would have disciplinary powers and the crews would remain in their present headquarters and dispersals. It was also agreed that first-line servicing, hitherto provided centrally by Technical Wing, should come directly under the new squadron.

Jerry and I also worked out details of a ceremonial parade in which the two squadrons would march on separately, Jerry would hand over to me, and the two separate bodies would close up together and march past the Station Commander as one squadron. We were able to time this for the day after the annual AOC's Inspection and Parade so that the participants had had some drill practice and did not disgrace us. So the amalgamation parade took place on 28 June 1963, in a hangar because of poor weather, and with families as guests and both squadrons' silver on display. All went well and there were appropriate refreshments afterwards.

No. 53 Squadron's silver was sent to RAF Benson as the next expected home of the squadron, and various files and historical records were sent to the Air Historical Branch at the Air Ministry. In the event the squadron did not re-form until the end of 1965, and at Brize Norton instead of Benson. There had been several development problems with the aircraft, and the first one was delivered in January 1966, flown by Shorts' Chief Test Pilot, my old Farnborough colleague Tich Tayler. No. 53 continued with the Belfast, but was finally disbanded in September 1976.

No. 47 Squadron had an equally long and distinguished history: formed at Beverley in 1916 for the defence of Hull against raiding German airships, it ended the First World War in Greece. After the war it was stationed at Khartoum with DH9As for some fourteen years, hence the squadron's crest with a crane and the motto *Nili Nomen Roboris Omen* (roughly 'The name of the Nile is an omen of our strength'). The Second World War was spent mainly overseas, in the Middle East, Italy and the Far East, flying Wellesleys and then Beaufighters. It returned home and was disbanded in 1946, to be re-formed six months later and equipped with Halifax 9s in Transport Command, and then the Hastings with which it took part in the Berlin airlift. The squadron moved to Abingdon in 1953 to be the first re-equipped with the Beverley, and in 1955 it received 'The Standard', an honour created by King George VI to mark the 25th anniversary of the RAF in 1943, and only presented to squadrons of twenty-five years' standing or with a history of 'specially outstanding operations'.

We settled into our reorganization without too much difficulty. The rivalry between the two squadrons had always been friendly, and my close ties with Jerry Barr had helped. Ches Cheshire had come to the end of his tour and was replaced by Squadron Leader Derek Grubb, a very experienced Beverley hand who had headed the Wing Flying Staff on the station, responsible for overall flying and training standards; he became OC 'B' Flight. One of the old 47 Squadron Flight Commanders had also been posted, and the remaining one, Roy Daysh, who was a navigator, remained as OC 'A' Flight. I was very happy with both, and relieved that Derek, who was a forthright, no-nonsense character, had the experience and standing to keep the crews well up to scratch.

It was a busy summer, with a succession of overseas exercises. I tried to fly as much as possible with the old 47 Squadron crews, and since we were one wing commander short on the station, the Duty Commander week came round more often; as I was the senior wing commander I also stood in for the Station Commander when he was absent. The family did manage a week's break at Kettlewell in the Dales, a much-needed relaxation pleasantly completed by a few days with Joan's parents in Leeds. Then it was back to work, in particular the preparations for the station's Battle of Britain 'At Home' day on 14 September, an annual event attended by the public, for which a demonstration of transport support flying was given, followed by a formation flypast, all of which required several rehearsals. I flew on some of the rehearsals, which included paradrops and short-field landings with troops on the airfield, and I also took part in the paradrop on the day and the four-aircraft formation display. I still have an 8 mm movie I took on the formation flypast in the No. 4 aircraft, piloted by Ian Wines, and the sight of these four great machines in close formation must have been impressive from the ground – it was certainly impressive from the air. On the day after, Battle of Britain Sunday, there was a civic service in Abingdon, followed by sherry in the Mayor's Parlour. There was a good and close relationship between the RAF station and the town (the Station Commander was a governor of the local primary school), with many shared social occasions, and the Mayor was usually invited to Mess functions.

At the end of September came the annual large-scale tactical transport exercise, this year codenamed 'Triplex West', and involving the move of a Brigade Group out to Libya and further support exercises based on El Adem with Beverleys and Argosies participating. Joint Force HQ was in a tented camp at El Adem. As the Beverley detachment commander, I had a tent to myself, but watched with some envy the young Army captain in the next-door tent whose soldier servant brought him a cup of tea before breakfast, laid out his clothes and kept his kit clean. The RAF had still not got to grips with al fresco living, and the food in the mess tent was only just acceptable. Our main job was supplying the Army at outlying desert strips, and the pace was fast and furious, coping with crew availability and aircraft serviceability in the very hot, dusty atmosphere. I found my tent too far from the operations and briefing complex, and eventually moved my camp-bed down to a hangar close to the airfield, sleeping (when it was possible) alongside the Argosy detachment commander, Wing Commander Arthur Munday. I flew whenever I could, and recall one evening when there was still one sortie to complete and no navigator was available; I had been on my feet all day and was dog-tired, but as this was a short half-hour flight I wearily climbed aboard and sat half asleep at the navigation desk. The flight was a resupply to the Bomba strip close by, and did not really need a navigator, but the regulations had to be observed. We returned to Abingdon after nearly two weeks and had a free Sunday to recuperate.

At Christmas 1963 we were on standby for a task to move an armoured unit from Libya to Cyprus because of civil unrest in the island. I left Lyneham on Boxing Day for Benina as a passenger in a Britannia (one of the 'shiny fleet', as our Beverley crews called the Comets and Britannias) to prepare the way for a Beverley detachment to do this job. I was based in an old control tower at Benina, and ran the operation from here (sleeping when possible on a camp-bed under the stairs). We completed the task in two or three days, and as at El Adem in the September exercise, I was exhausted. The local Army base commander bore me off to his house and I had my first decent meal since Christmas dinner, preceded by a welcome shower. As a bonus the Colonel's small boy played the recorder to me, and I slept the sleep of the dead in a decent bed, returning to Abingdon in one of my own aircraft the following day.

The squadron had a similar task at the end of January, and I flew out to Cyprus (again via the 'shiny fleet') to supervise the other end of the operation. As I came off the aircraft in Nicosia at 7 a.m. I had an urgent message saying that a helicopter was waiting to fly me to Episkopi, the joint British Forces HQ, where the Senior Air Staff Officer wanted to see me. This sounded ominous to me, and I took the helicopter with some forebodings. As it happened, the Sycamore was from 103 Squadron, my old wartime operational squadron, and I told the pilot that the last time I flew with 103 was nearly twenty years before; he was not particularly impressed, probably regarding me as another old fogey. The interview with the SASO at Episkopi was something of an anti-climax: the King of Jordan had presented two polo ponies to the commanding general in Cyprus, and I was asked to provide a Beverley to fly to Amman and bring them back. As it happened, Squadron Leader Grubb was one of the captains on the 47 Squadron detachment, and we arranged for him to do the job. No doubt the AQM had some problems preparing the freight bay, but the task was completed without incident. I flew back to the UK with Derek, and he told me that, having consulted TC Air Staff Instructions on the carriage of livestock, he asked the grooms who travelled with the horses if they had a humane killer with them. 'Oh yes, sir', they replied, each flourishing a sharp knife.

I arrived back at Abingdon to find that I was the acting Station Commander, as Group Captain Sowrey was away on a ten-day course, and that I would be Duty Commander for the week after that. So the months progressed with a seemingly unending stream of VIP visitors, overseas exercises, local flying training, and the social round. There was one day of light relief when I was invited to be on the flight deck of a BEA Vanguard on a routine daily flight between Heathrow and Manchester, to see how the airlines operated. It was a fascinating glimpse of a different world, where captain and co-pilot had apparently been flying together for years, and apart from routine check lists no conversation was required, and the flight went like clockwork. No doubt there could be problems and emergencies, but this flight and the return went remarkably smoothly.

At about this time Bryan Lamb, who had been posted away to command a small airfield in the Aden area, returned to Abingdon on the Wing Flying Staff as a squadron leader. It was good to see him back and to hear of his adventures in an outpost of the Empire in the remote South Arabian hinterland. Roy Daysh was posted away and was succeeded as 'A' Flight Commander by Squadron Leader Paddy King, a larger than life character and an experienced Beverley pilot. Our old 53 Squadron HQ building had undergone refurbishment, during which time we worked temporarily from the former 47 Squadron HQ, until we could move into the new accommodation in April: there was little basic change, but we had a new briefing room and the place had generally been repaired and smartened up.

*　*　*

In mid-April I took some much needed leave and managed to arrange an indulgence passage for the family to Malta. We stayed in the RAF Luqa Transit Mess, which, though basic, was adequate, and hired a small car to get around. It was a great pleasure for me to show Joan and the girls around the island with which I was now familiar, and Luqa was a useful central base from which to see the main tourist delights – Valletta with its shops and Grand Harbour and impressive public buildings of the ubiquitous local stone; the delightful Buskett (or Boschetto) Gardens; the splendidly domed church at Mosta; Paradise Bay for swimming; Marsaxlokk harbour with its colourful boats; and the ancient capital city of Mdina, with its still, cloistered atmosphere. We found quiet places to picnic, away from the coast and main roads, and often near prehistoric sites. Joan was entranced to see orange and lemon trees with fruit and flowers, and Sue and Jenny enjoyed the sea bathing in the pleasant weather. We called on some old friends from Farnborough days who had a flat in Sliema, the Howard Murleys, and discovered a delightful small seafood restaurant for our evening meal. It was a totally relaxing few days, and we flew back to Abingdon much refreshed. I still had a few days' leave left, and we took the girls back to school via Leeds, spending a pleasant weekend with Joan's parents.

*   *   *

During the summer of 1964 I was given advance notice of my next posting, as Directing Staff Navigation at the RAF College of Air Warfare at Manby, with the main job of overseeing Specialist and Staff Navigation training. I suppose that with my background this was a logical move, and at least it was still a flying post. I was required at Manby in November, and my replacement at 47 Squadron would be Wing Commander Doug Chandler, ex-OC Admin at RAF Tengah in Singapore, and due to finish his Beverley training at the end of September. In August I flew up to Manby for a day and spent some time with the current DS Nav, Pinky Grocott, to get some idea of the job. However, all was to be changed: there was evidently some hold-up in the postings chain, and the post at Manby would not now be available until well into the following year, although my posting still stood. As it happened, the OC Flying Wing at Abingdon, Ken Johnson, was just finishing his tour of duty, and I was appointed to the post when I handed over 47 Squadron to Doug Chandler on 23 October.

I look back on my commands of 53 and 47 Squadrons as a high point in my career. The disbandment of 53 had come as a blow, but I had been extremely fortunate that the command of 47 Squadron came up at the same time, and even more fortunate that I was able to carry on in a flying post at Abingdon when my posting to Manby was delayed. I had had valuable experience, had worked and flown with some very capable people, and had made many friends. There were the usual farewell parties, but it was comforting to know, as I handed over to Doug Chandler, that I would be working and flying with many of the same people and putting my recent experience to good use.

*   *   *

Between jobs we were able to take a week's leave, and spent a few quiet days in Leeds. I had arranged to see the recently appointed headmistress at Casterton, Miss Willson, mainly to discuss Susan's progress: she had just turned eighteen and was preparing for 'A' level exams, taking maths, physics and chemistry, a formidable trio. I felt that Casterton, still a slightly old-fashioned girls' school, was not too well equipped to teach physics and chemistry, although Miss Willson made it clear that while she thought

Susan capable of passing, her attitude to her studies and her general behaviour were unsatisfactory. Later in the year we took Sue down to Brighton to visit the University of Sussex where she hoped to get a place, but in the event the only 'A' level she passed was maths; she was adamant that she did not want to go on studying towards a university place, and so left Casterton the following summer just after we moved to Manby. Meanwhile Jenny was happy at school and working towards her 'O' levels.

*   *   *

Back at Abingdon I moved into my new office on the ground floor of the old control tower with a comprehensive view of the airfield; a new up-to-date tower had been built a few years previously on the other side of the airfield, and the old building housed the Operations Centre, a self-briefing room, and the office of the OC Technical Wing, which was next to mine – a very useful arrangement, as we were continually consulting. George Crabb was an old acquaintance from HQ Far East Air Force, and we got on well together. My new job encompassed a variety of functions: Air Traffic Control and the care of the airfield generally; the Air Movements Squadron, overseeing the loading and reception of passengers and freight, and also the Air Movements Training School and the Air Movements Development Unit; Operations, coping with and recording the various tasks allotted by HQ 38 Group, our parent group under Transport Command; and the Wing Flying Staff, responsible for checking aircrew flying standards and training. The Wing Flying Staff was headed by Bryan Lamb, with whom it was a pleasure to work again (he had recently got married, and we had attended the wedding in a delightful little country church near Letchworth).

We were also about to acquire a new flying unit at Abingdon – the Andover Conversion Flight under Squadron Leader Ross, eventually with four aircraft, the first arriving just before Christmas 1964. The Andover C1 was a development of the Avro 748, a medium-sized twin turbo-prop passenger aircraft. Its RAF role was tactical transport, intended to replace the Beverley (it could carry forty-four troops and up to 14,000 lb of freight, so it fell somewhat short of this requirement). The job of the flight at Abingdon was to train pilots and crew who would take on the operational conversion training needed before squadrons could be formed; in due course the type came into service in 1966 with 46 Squadron at Benson, and in 1967 it replaced the Beverleys of 84 Squadron in Aden. The Andover remained in service until 1975, both in the UK and overseas; the CC2 was a passenger version, and three of them did stalwart service in the Queen's Flight until 1989, while the E3 was designed and used for special duties in Signals Command till as late as the 1990s.

As it happened, the Andover was the first aircraft I flew in as OC Flying, and I found it a pleasant change after the noisy Beverley, though I felt that it could never do all the jobs that that maid-of-all-work could tackle, with its enormous freight bay. The navigation equipment was similar to that of the Beverley, and I made several flights as second navigator, including a route trip to the south of France and back. We had many visitors to see the aircraft and discuss its performance and problems, and Squadron Leader Ross coped admirably and capably with the conversion programme.

December 1964 also saw the departure of Group Captain Sowrey as Station Commander, to be a student at the Imperial Defence College and to be replaced by Group Captain L.G.P. Martin. Freddie Sowrey had been a popular and hard-working CO, and in my speech at his dining-out in the mess (attended by the Mayor and other local dignitaries) I said,

> I would like to pay tribute to the way in which you have pushed the efficiency and prestige of RAF Abingdon to its present high level. You have worked harder and longer than any one man on this station and little has happened of which you were not aware. In a very turbulent period you have always kept the interests of your officers and men and their wives and children at heart, and you have managed to retain some sense of humour in such situations as the cold waters of Poole Harbour, the sands of Tobruk, and the dreaded night haunts of Berlin. This occasion cannot pass without my mentioning in all sincerity the hard work and unstinting service given by Mrs Sowrey to all kinds of station activities, to local charities and church affairs, and particularly to the welfare of the wives and families of this station.

This may seem like fulsome praise, but it was well deserved and we were all sorry to see the Sowreys depart. Freddie, as was not unexpected by those who worked with and for him, became an air marshal and Sir Frederick Sowrey.

Group Captain Martin was a very different character, but pleasant and equable to work for. If I remember correctly he had little experience in Transport Command (although he had of course converted to the Beverley), and leaned heavily on me as the senior wing commander with more than two years' experience on the station and in the transport support role. He flew whenever he could, but the demands of the job made this difficult: as 1965 began it seemed that we started an unending stream of visitors to Abingdon, from the AOC 38 Group, the C-in-C Transport Command, the Chief of the Air Staff with the appropriate Permanent Under-Secretary, to the Chief Constable, various senior staff college courses including that of the German Armed Forces, the Commander of the Army's 3 Division with whom we worked, and a variety of schools and cadet organizations. Most needed meeting and greeting, briefing and entertainment, and for some we laid on a flying display showing our main roles. I was inevitably involved in most of these, especially the briefing and the flying display. We evolved a short (15–20 minutes) programme portraying our main support roles: there would be a paradrop of troops from, say, 700 feet, followed by another Beverley making a very short landing, with troops and vehicles emerging from the freight bay and the aircraft backing-up for a quick take-off, a heavy-container drop and finally a spectacular high-level demonstration by the Parachute Training School of delayed drops from perhaps 10,000 feet, with the PTS team linking up and breaking away before finally landing on the DZ with coloured flares issuing from their boots. I would control these displays from the Air Traffic Control mobile caravan somewhere on the airfield; depending on the wind and weather conditions, which affected each item differently, we aimed for a continuous show, and this was sometimes difficult to achieve – I recall asking Hugh Crawley, on finals for a short landing, to go round again because the previous item had taken longer than scheduled. With, for example, CAS and the C-in-C watching, we needed luck as well as skill and judgment, and luckily we had no serious problems, but it was always a relief to have these displays behind us.

*   *   *

In April, with the girls home from school, we managed to get away for a week to Devon, staying in a caravan belonging to George Crabb in the grounds of a hotel at Woolacombe. The weather was chilly and wet and the caravan was not really a success, but we enjoyed the North Devon coast and countryside, and particularly liked Barnstaple with its market and quays. It was good to be together again as a family and for Joan and me to be away from the never-ending commitments at Abingdon; Joan was heavily involved with the Wives' Club and the round of entertaining and visitors, and having time to ourselves with Sue and Jenny (and our spaniel Candy) was an unlooked-for bonus.

*   *   *

Being acting Station Commander was not always onerous. During a couple of weeks in May when Group Captain Martin was away on leave in Malta, one pleasant duty was attending the BBC TV International Balloon Race at Stanton Harcourt near Oxford, the first time such an event had taken place. Ballooning was becoming popular though still not very common: there were at least six entrants from various countries, including one from the RAF which the Parachute Training School was operating. The OC PTS, Gerry Turnbull, was a keen balloonist and held one of the first, if not the first, balloon instructor's tickets; he was very much in evidence, and boarded the RAF's entry, marked CARD 1 in remembrance of RAF Cardington's long history of balloons and dirigibles, its comparatively drab colouring in contrast with the flamboyant colours of the other entries. It was a fine sunny day and the balloons made a splendid sight as they soared away at the start, filmed by the BBC. I cannot now remember which entry was the winning one, but it was an enjoyable experience and Joan and I took plenty of photographs and movies, which we still have.

More humdrum activities were the usual pre-AOC's Inspections, when the various staff officers from HQ 38 Group visited to look at those station activities with which they were concerned, culminating in the formal AOC's Inspection itself, with a Station Parade (preceded by several tedious rehearsals). Throughout this busy period I was conscious that I ought to be making some sort of preparation or study for taking up my new job at Manby later in the summer. This was just not practicable, although I had managed to visit the SBAC Show at Farnborough the previous September to look at the Hawker Siddeley 125 which, as the Dominie, was to become a navigation trainer for the RAF and replace the Manby Canberras as the main aircraft for the Staff and Specialist Navigation Courses. It was basically a private jet for business concerns, but was to be fitted with two navigation desks and some of the latest navigation kit for its new job: I was suitably impressed.

In mid-May the title of Flying Wing was changed to Operations Wing, which I suppose was more appropriate to all the various functions. Flying hours were difficult for me to fit in, but I did manage to fly one exercise as so-called Stream Commander for a night drop, although the stream concerned dwindled to two Beverleys and one Argosy by the time of the exercise, which was in any event abortive because of unforecast low cloud over the DZ; this turned out to be my last flight at Abingdon. An unexpected and short-notice task was to be President of a Board of Inquiry into a parachuting accident in which a young soldier had been killed; another member of the Board was Major Larry Orpen-Smellie of 3 Para, so at least I had some appropriate expertise on hand. We had of course to view the scene of the drop on the Brecon Beacons, and the body of the unfortunate young man, but the results were virtually inconclusive: he had operated neither his main nor emergency parachute, and presumably had suffered a blackout or heart failure. This took me away from Abingdon for several days which I could ill afford, but it was an illuminating if not very cheerful experience.

Early in July Wing Commander Peter Thomson arrived to start his takeover as OC Operations Wing, having just completed his Beverley Course. He was pleasant and co-operative, and I could see that the job would be in good hands. On the second day of our handover there was a tragic accident: a Hastings from Colerne had dropped in to pick up a party of AQMs, male and female, who were being given air experience as part of their training. The aircraft took off from Abingdon but crashed locally. Peter and I were in the Operations Section at the time, and immediately set up an incident control as reports kept coming in; men were required to search for survivors, and our Station Fire Section sent at least one vehicle, but no one aboard survived. The Station Commander visited the scene as I stayed in Operations to co-ordinate the necessary activity, and it was a distressing experience. We later attended funerals at RAF Colerne, and there was a shadow over both stations for a while.

But life must go on, and the day after the accident we had a scheduled visit from the Permanent Under-Secretary (RAF), Sir Martin Flett, from the Ministry of Defence (which had recently replaced the three separate Armed Forces ministries), accompanied by our C-in-C. The visit was short, but we laid on the usual flying display and briefed the PUS on our role and activities; all seemed to go well.

This was virtually my last task at Abingdon: the odd farewell party was overshadowed by the Colerne funerals, and I was required a little early at Manby to take part in a special Arctic flight for the Spec N Course to study the performance of gyro systems at high latitude. This was done in a Britannia from Lyneham, provided by Transport Command, and we spent a night at Sondrestrom in Greenland before flying back to Lyneham, whence I returned to Abingdon to help Joan oversee the removal of our furniture and effects from our house – which took place on our twentieth wedding anniversary – and drive up to Manby. 'Marching out' from our large and comfortable quarter was a wrench after three years, as was leaving the station at which I had served for the longest tour so far in my service career.

Looking back over this correspondingly long chapter, I can recall so many characters who went to make up this most rewarding of experiences but whom I have not mentioned: 'Manny' Mercer, the oldest AQM in the RAF who had to retire from 53 Squadron with serious illness but was specially awarded the coveted QM flying badge before he died; Flying Officer 'Basher' Noor, of Pakistani origin, who was a popular Signals Leader on 53 (on being asked if a party he was giving was 'stag', he replied, 'Oh no, man: best English beef'); Major 'Bonzo' von Haven, our USAF exchange officer on 47 Squadron, laconic and imperturbable; Hamish Raynham, a young but already eccentric co-pilot, who was later awarded the AFC and whom I met in 1971 in Oman flying for the Sultan's Air Force. Another co-pilot, David Jenkins, married Thea Rimmer of the WRAF (a charming girl who looked after our spaniel occasionally and of whom we became very fond) in Southport, her home town, and we were made welcome by her family for the wedding; we are still in touch. There were our friends and neighbours, Margaret and Alan Johnson, with four delightful small children: Alan was a doctor and keen parachutist and later became an air vice-marshal. We had a postcard from them the other day from their retirement travels around the world.

Joan had also been busy at Abingdon, and worked very hard to keep the house going and support me in my jobs. She had problems with unhappy wives, but had also made some good friends, and had certainly presided over some notable social occasions. I could not have coped without her – a constant refrain throughout our married life.

CHAPTER SEVENTEEN

From Navigation to Aerosystems

The RAF College of Air Warfare, formed at the beginning of 1961, developed from the RAF Flying College with which I had become so familiar during my time at the Air Ministry in 1953/4. Manby was opened in 1938 as an Air Armament Training School, and remained associated with air weapons during the war and the immediate post-war period (in 1944 it became the Empire Air Armament School). It was a pleasant, permanent station about three miles from Louth, a small and friendly market town in North-east Lincolnshire amid wolds country.

The senior course at the College was the Air Warfare Course, of six months' duration, to give senior General Duties branch officers (mostly wing commanders, with the odd group captain, and including students from the Navy, the Royal Canadian Air Force, the Royal Australian Air Force and the US Air Force) a comprehensive knowledge of air operations to fit them for senior air staff and command appointments. The Specialist Navigation Course, still twelve months long, continued a long unbroken line and was now at No. 23 Course; its aim was unchanged – to produce General Duties officers of flight lieutenant and squadron leader rank, mostly navigators but with the occasional pilot, to fill staff and research and development posts concerned with navigation and related matters. The syllabus had developed over the years to place more emphasis on air operations, but still had an initial academic phase. Officers from the Commonwealth air forces and the USAF had places on the course. The three-month Staff Navigation Course was still geared to training navigation instructors and filling junior staff appointments, and though developed in line with modern navigation systems had not changed basically.

Other activities at Manby included the School of Refresher Flying for pilots who were returning to flying duties after varying periods away, or changing roles. Jet Provosts operated from Manby for this purpose, and also Varsities flying from the satellite airfield of Strubby, a few miles to the south-east; Canberras used for the Staff N and Spec N Courses were in the process of being replaced by Dominies. There was a twelve-week Weapons Employment Course for General Duties officers in the rank of squadron leader and flight lieutenant, continuing Manby's long connection with weapons training, and the College also held a large number of briefing periods for senior officers of all three services over a few days or a working week to put across the contemporary roles and equipment of the RAF, the employment of air weapons, electronic warfare, and developments associated with space. The College's 'Royal Air Force Aerospace Briefing Team', formed in 1962, gave many Aerospace presentations throughout the UK to military colleges, professional bodies and universities.

The College had Group status within Flying Training Command, with the Commandant – an air commodore – reporting directly to the Air Officer Commanding-in-Chief. A group captain Station Commander was responsible for the administration of Manby and Strubby, and commanded the School of Refresher Flying, while a group captain Assistant Commandant oversaw all College courses via a number of directing staff groups – Operational Studies, Navigation, Weapons and others. Two wing commanders on the Directing Staff each led one of two syndicates of the Air Warfare Course and were directly responsible to the Assistant Commandant. The Operational Studies Section had grown out of the special group set up (as I recorded in an earlier chapter) by the Empire Air Navigation School's Investigation Wing at Shawbury to study each operational command's navigation techniques. It transferred to the RAF Flying College in 1949 with the Spec N Course, and gradually developed to look at all operational flying techniques and requirements in the RAF, acquiring knowledge and expertise which was used by all courses at the College of Air Warfare and many outside organizations – a very significant asset.

* * *

Our move from Abingdon to Manby – delayed partly by the funerals for the Hastings crash victims at Colerne and partly by my hurried visit to Manby to take part in the polar flight – seemed to be a fragmented business, but we finally 'marched out' with regret from our spacious quarter at Abingdon and drove to Manby the same day. Our new house had the inauspicious address of 1 Venom Road; roads on the station had been named, not unreasonably, after notable RAF aircraft, but some insensitive person had included the Vampire and Venom, with predictable but unsuitable results.

Wing Commander Grocott (always known as 'Pinky'), from whom I was to take over as Directing Staff Navigation, had campaigned for some time to have an ex-officio married quarter for DS Nav, and had succeeded – too late for him to reap the benefit – with 1 Venom Road. It was a pre-war four-bedroomed house with a sizeable garden and a garage, and we came to like it more than any other house we had lived in – comfortable and manageable. We had just two days to sort ourselves out there before Sue and Jenny arrived from school by train to Grimsby, with our new home no doubt an unsettling change for them after our three years at Abingdon.

Susan was awaiting her 'A' level results, and when they arrived was devastated to find that she had passed only one subject, mathematics, and could not therefore take up a university place. The situation was not helped by Casterton School, who expressed no sympathy or suggestions as to what she should do next. We urged her to do some further study and retake the examinations, but she was adamant that she had had enough of school and academic work, and would stay at home and look for a job. Nothing we said could change her mind, and after one or two local part-time jobs for pocket money she eventually found a clerical post in the Education Section at RAF Manby, which at least kept her occupied and at home. She had one or two unsuitable boyfriends, but later met a student on the Staff Navigation Course who seemed to be an acceptable character.

Jenny had at least another year to go at Casterton before her GCE 'O' levels, but was not particularly academically inclined and showed no great interest in going on to university. But she was happy at school, with many friends (some of whom she still has), and it was a pleasure to have her at home for a few weeks.

* * *

On the following Monday morning I walked across to the College building, set amid trees behind the Officers' Mess. My takeover from Pinky Grocott was to be somewhat longer than was usual, mainly because he had arranged – as his farewell flourish – to accompany the annual Spec N tour of the USA and Canada scheduled for three weeks beginning in mid-November. I reported to the Assistant Commandant, Group Captain Holmes, who was to be my immediate boss and whom I remembered well as the co-pilot on the flight I made to West Africa with AVM McEvoy in 1954. We got on well, and I found that he left DS Nav to do his job with little interference. I also made my number with the Commandant, Air Commodore John Topham, a well-decorated wartime pilot with a jovial manner who controlled with a light rein but kept well abreast of what was going on in the College and all its ramifications.

Sitting in with Pinky I soon realized that I had a lot of catching-up to do, having spent some years away from the major technical developments in navigation systems, such as those with which the V-bomber force was equipped and those being developed at Farnborough and Boscombe Down. The current Spec N Course was at the stage where they were studying the work and techniques of the operational commands and also current research and development in navigation aids, involving visits to appropriate RAF stations and to scientific establishments and the aircraft industry. In my first week I visited Ferranti in Manchester and the Decca Navigator Company at Gatwick, meeting some old acquaintances – Bob Findlater, who had been a colleague at HQ Bomber Command in 1948 and was now working on navigation systems for Ferranti, and Harvey Schwartz at Decca with whom I had worked when I was at Farnborough.

Although I gained some benefit from these visits, which had been programmed for some time, I really should not have spared the time away from the College, where I was getting to grips with the varied responsibilities of my new job. The most important of these was probably the oversight of the Specialist Navigation Course: the day-to-day running of the course was done – very competently as far as I could see – by two squadron leaders, Moe Gates on exchange from the Royal Canadian Air Force, and Dick Tomlin, both, of course, Spec N graduates. (Dick's tour of duty was up before the end of the year and he was replaced by Mike Banfield). They planned, programmed and supervised the year-long course, getting to know the twenty or so students well, and holding (or tapping) their hands when necessary. Since the first half of the course was mainly devoted to academic work (maths, physics, electronics and so on) they were able to spend time making the detailed arrangements necessary for the numerous visits – in the UK, Europe, USA and Canada – in the second half, a time-consuming and sometimes frustrating occupation, along with organizing visiting speakers. At the same time they planned the flying programme – in the process of switching from Canberras to Dominies – and had to keep themselves in flying practice. It was a busy and demanding job: their office adjoined mine, so I was able to keep in close touch with what they were doing. In particular, I came to like and respect Moe Gates, who was knowledgeable, hard working, and unflappable, but with an active sense of humour: he and his wife Francie became good friends.

Squadron Leader Tony Tye was in charge of the Staff Navigation Course, which I was interested to see was as intensive as ever and began, just as in 1944, with mathematics – logarithms, plane trigonometry and spherical trigonometry, the latter evidently still valid in this electronic age. Under the title 'Avionics' they went on to study radio theory and its application before moving on to look at current navigation techniques and systems which they could then practise in the air. They were also given tuition in instructional methods and the evaluation of navigators' capabilities. So the course was fundamentally the same as it had been twenty years earlier, if slightly more rigorous and exacting.

Another group under the control of DS Nav was known as Applied Navigation, run by Squadron Leader John Preston, whose task was to oversee the flying phases of the Specialist and Staff Navigation Courses – briefings on the aircraft and the exercises which they designed to accompany the classroom instruction on systems and operational techniques, including some experience of research and development methods for the Spec N Course. John was a particularly capable officer, and again became a friend with whom I am still in touch.

A Royal Australian Air Force exchange officer, Squadron Leader Pete Kennedy (later replaced by Frank Lonie, also from the RAAF) headed a group known as 'Guidance', which provided instruction to both navigation courses (and the Air Warfare and Weapons courses on occasion) on navigation and guidance systems in current use and under development – a busy and highly technical function.

There were two further functions which completed the list of those under my supervision. One was the Flying Training Command Navigation Instructors' Examining Board, responsible for categorizing all navigation instructors in the command to ensure acceptable levels of performance; their remit included our instructors at Manby, but they spent much of their time (as we had done in Bomber Command's 'X' Flight in 1950) working at other stations in the command, mostly the Air Navigation Schools. So the unit was more or less self-contained, under the command of Squadron Leader Jack Towler, large, cheerful and capable.

Finally there was a small cell working on the rewriting, updating and production of the RAF Navigation Manual, Air Publication 1234, now in five volumes, as I recorded when I wrote of my work at the Air Ministry, which had included some oversight of this publication. As navigation techniques changed and new instruments and equipment became available – a process which had speeded up enormously of late years – so the manual had to be kept abreast of developments, which included the introduction of new electronic aids and airborne computers; at the time many of these systems were security classified, and at least one of the volumes was rated secret. I took an interest in this work to the extent that my other responsibilities allowed, and was able to do a little proofreading, but the navigation manual section really ran itself without interference from me.

So there was plenty of work on hand, especially as I had arrived during the stage of the Spec N Course mostly given up to visits around the country, some of which I accompanied; as well as Ferranti and Decca, already mentioned, I recall going to the Royal Radar Establishment at Malvern and to the Ballistic Missile Early Warning Station at Fylingdales, learning all the time. After a couple of weeks of dual control, Pinky Grocott departed with other fish to fry before he was due to rejoin us for the Spec N North American tour in November.

At the same time I was trying to refamiliarize myself with the Canberra, and after undergoing a decompression test at the Aeromedical Training Centre at North Luffenham made several flights, mostly sitting in the right-hand seat with students working away in the back. In my first few weeks at Manby there was a flight to Cyprus, and after the long tiring legs in the Beverley it was a pleasure to reach Luqa in Malta in three hours (at about 450 knots and 45,000 feet) and Akrotiri in Cyprus in another two and a half, with the added pleasure of a weekend in the sun (a somewhat guilty one, as Joan was still working away to sort out our new quarter). While enjoying the high performance of the Canberra, I found – as I had done at Bassingbourn in 1956 – the cockpit space restricted compared with an aircraft like the Beverley, although it was certainly more pleasant to fly in a front seat than tucked away in the navigator's position with little outside vision (and a higher workload!).

*   *   *

These first few weeks at Manby reinforced the knowledge I had had when I arrived that I had been out of the mainstream of navigational development for too long. In the post-graduate courses I was now responsible for, not only had the academic and theoretical content moved on, but the studies of the techniques of the operational commands now included a whole range of new navigational systems, some based on developments of existing equipment and some on entirely new concepts.

The V-bomber force, starting with the Valiant, then the Vulcan, and finally the Victor, carried the latest development of ground-mapping radar, H2S Mk 9, coupled with the navigation and bombing computer (NBC); to the best of my recollection these two systems were combined and cross-referenced using analogue computing techniques, as the use of digital computers was still in its infancy, but this was symptomatic of a growing tendency for the integration of different navigation systems to give more accurate results. Particularly in civil aviation, the use of VHF omni-range (VOR) and distance-measuring equipment (DME) was now more or less standard, and I recalled that when I was at Farnborough there had been much debate in the aviation world about the use of VOR/DME as the basic navigation aid. By 1965, the RAF had installed VOR receivers in all long- and medium-range transport and some training aircraft, and there was good VOR coverage from ground beacons in most of western Europe and, of course, the USA.

Interestingly enough to me, TACAN (the 1,000 megacycle system providing distance and bearing information in one receiver, with which I had been concerned at RAE and again in Alaska) was also being widely used, with twenty ground beacons in the UK (at May 1965) and others sited in western Europe, and the current RAF policy was to install TACAN in all NATO-assigned aircraft, and all maritime, long-range transport, and fighter aircraft plus some training aircraft. The Decca Navigator system was still going strong, with eight civil Decca chains in Europe and others elsewhere in the world, including the USA and the Middle and Far East. RAF policy was to fit the system to all NATO-assigned Canberras, to transport support aircraft (not the Beverley!), communications and calibration aircraft, and most helicopters stationed in the UK and Germany.

A development from Decca was Dectra (Decca track and range), also a low-frequency system designed mainly for long air routes such as the north Atlantic, for which an experimental three-station Dectra chain had been operating since May 1957. Using a similar phase comparison principle to Decca, the aircraft equipment gave ranging and tracking information on both meters and a flight log chart; there were still some problems with lane identification and accuracy, but these were expected to to be reduced with the introduction of new ground stations in 1966. As with all low-frequency systems, Dectra was susceptible to precipitation static, and on this account the RAF was not likely to make much use of it.

Another development of an existing system was Loran C, following the original long-range navigation system now known as Loran A, of which I had had some experience at Farnborough and again in Alaska, and which now had a network of ground-station chains on the USA seaboard, in the north Atlantic area, and in the Pacific; Loran A was now fitted in all RAF maritime aircraft and some long-range transport aircraft. Loran C was also a hyperbolic fixing system, but operated on a low-frequency band of 100 kilocycles; it too had been developed in the USA and was under the sponsorship of the US Coastguard. Since the first airborne receiver was flown experimentally in 1950, a few transistorized semi-automatic receivers had been produced by the Sperry Gyroscope Company, eventually followed by fully automatic models for military use, and finally with a fully automatic micro-miniaturized version receving both Loran A and Loran C. Again, as an LF system, reception and accuracy depended on the atmospheric conditions, affected not only by the time of day but by the time of year, being unusable during twilight periods; range varied from 800 to 1,300 nm. However, there were six Loran C chains in operation, three in the Pacific and three in the Atlantic/Mediterranean area, with more stations being built. An International Civil Aviation Organization (ICAO) conference to be held in November 1965 was to decide whether to adopt Loran A or Loran A/C as the recommended long-range navigation aid, and if this was the case the RAF intended to fit this aid more widely in long-range aircraft.

Automatic dead-reckoning systems were also being developed, and the Dominie aircraft was fitted with the GPI Mk 4, still using analogue computing principles but capable of accepting data such as track and groundspeed from other navigation sources, and displaying computed ground positions in latitude and longitude to a much greater accuracy than the old GPI Mk 1 we used in the later marks of Lancaster.

Finally, in this catalogue of systems developed from existing equipment, there was the periscopic sextant (also available in the Dominie), which could be fitted in a pressurized cabin and was simpler to operate and more accurate than the old Mark 9 series. Combined with the steadier platform of the jet aircraft, with less vibration, and the fact that the operating altitude was normally above cloud cover, pre-computed sights with the periscopic sextant at last made astro-navigation substantially more viable than before, although paradoxically the existence of new navigation systems made it less essential.

Of these new systems, Doppler navigation had now been in use for some years and was also fitted in the Dominie. The principle on which this aid was based had been known for over a hundred years: Christian Johann Doppler, a celebrated Austrian scientist, pronounced in 1842 that the pitch of a sound is changed if the object emitting it is moving relative to the observer (as when we are passed by a railway train moving at speed). Using this principle, the speed of an aircraft over the ground can be measured when emitting and receiving radio waves, and receiver/transmitters were designed also to measure drift, both with good accuracy. Doppler navigation systems were now well established, and fitted in a variety of RAF and civil aircraft.

Inertial navigation (IN) systems were also being developed for manned aircraft, missiles and ships, again using well-established scientific principles which could now be put into practice using modern instrument-making and engineering techniques to produce more reliable and accurate gyroscopes, accelerometers and electronic processing. In simple terms (or as simple as I can make them), velocity is the rate of change of position, and acceleration is the rate of change of velocity; an accelerometer is a mass suspended on springs within a housing firmly attached to a craft, and the inertia of the mass causes it to remain stationary while any acceleration of the craft tends to displace the housing relative to the mass. The forces required to nullify the relative motion of the mass and the housing (in three directions fixed by gyroscopes) can be measured electrically, with signals directly related to the forces and to the accelerations (for the latter, Newton's Second Law of Motion applies – 'the rate of change of momentum is directly proportional to the force and takes place in the direction of the force': another use of standard scientific rules). Electronic circuitry performs the necessary integrations of accelerations to provide distances and directions in three dimensions through which the craft has moved from its original position. (For this basic explanation of IN I must acknowledge a debt to the *Encyclopedia Britannica*, which provides about as intelligible a description as I can find.) Errors of the system were cumulative over time, but more than acceptable in comparision with other systems. In 1965 IN was not in general use but was being developed with many military applications in mind.

The search for a universal worldwide navigation system had led to yet another low-frequency (and therefore long-range) development – Omega, an experimental continuous wave phase comparison system originally for the US Navy. In 1965, this had four ground transmitters: in the Panama Canal Zone, in Hawaii, near New York, and in Wales, operating at between 10 and 14 kilocycles. Ranges were expected to be 7,000–8000 nm over sea, and 5,000–7,000 nm over land, depending as always with these frequencies on atmospheric conditions. Accuracy was forecast as 2 nm in daylight and 10 nm at night, both at a range of 5,000 nm, but (as with Dectra) the system would not be usable in the twilight period or during heavy precipitation static. Experimentation was still proceeding, but I note that as late as 1970 Freddy Stringer, my old partner at RAE, was still expressing doubts as to the reliability of Omega as a worldwide system unless cross-referenced with another navigation aid.

The periscopic sextant, mentioned above, was not the only development in the astronomical field: automatic astronomical navigation (auto-astro) was being worked on by various bodies, including the Instrument and Photographic Department at RAE Farnborough, and there were requirements for the guidance of missiles as well as manned aircraft. The development of photo-sensitive devices, monitored by computers, was making possible the automatic tracking of two or more stars to give continuous position information; definition of the vertical was a vital requirement, and was being provided by inertial systems, and daylight star tracking was also being developed. An all-weather radio sextant, automatically following the sun, had already been successfully operated at sea as early as the1950s.

But perhaps the most significant development, though still in its infancy in 1965, was satellite navigation. Artificial earth satellites were first launched in late 1957 in the USA, and scientists from the John Hopkins University, later monitoring the radio signals from the satellites, discovered that by measuring the Doppler shift in the signals they could determine all the parameters of the satellite orbit – a complex calculation for which a digital computer was necessary. Further work at John Hopkins observed that if it is possible to do the difficult job of determining the orbit from a single passage, it should be easier and more accurate to do the opposite – to use the same data to locate the ground observing station. This led to the Transit system, with a satellite launched in the early 1960s by the US Navy, and circling the earth about every ninety minutes in polar orbits some 600 miles high, with five tracking stations measuring the Doppler shift on the satellite and transmitting this information to a computing centre at John Hopkins University. Transit was accurate to about 180 yards, but was not suitable for aircraft use, as any sudden and unexpected change in the receiver's velocity modified the Doppler shift trace and led to position errors. Much work was going on in this field, but it would be another eight years or so before a viable satellite navigation system – global positioning system (GPS) – was launched by the US Department of Defense, followed by the Navstar satellites in 1978 with continuous worldwide coverage giving latitude and longitude within about 30 feet. Commercial pressures eventually resulted in the tiny handheld satnavs that almost anyone can now afford to buy (though sensible use of them is another matter). The John Hopkins team which originally discovered how to measure satellite orbits could never have guessed what the next forty years would bring.

Looking back over this rapid and somewhat sketchy summary of what had been developing in the navigation world, I see that the word 'system' is used again and again. The *Concise Oxford Dictionary* defines it, *inter alia*, as 'a complex whole; a set of connected things or parts', and this well describes what was now being developed – not stand-alone aids but a mix of different items put together to give improved reliability and accuracy, or mutual monitoring. This was, of course, not just in the sphere of navigation: the aircraft industry in general was trying to design military aircraft with their flying controls, their guidance equipment and their weapons all contributing to the operational requirement, in contrast with past designs which tended to concentrate on the aircraft's flying performance and then consider what equipment or weapons it needed. The ill-fated TSR2 project was an example of the systems approach, and it was a blow to the aircraft industry (and the RAF) when political and financial considerations caused it to be cancelled by the incoming Labour government in April 1965. It was intended as a replacement for the Canberra, so this stalwart and versatile aircraft had to be retained; in fact, the last Canberra was only withdrawn from service in 2006. The proposed replacements – the F4 Phantom and the F-111 – excellent American aircraft though they were, had to be partly redesigned and re-equipped to meet British requirements (although the F-111 never materialized in the UK) at great cost, not only in money but to the 'system' concept.

My first couple of months at Manby were enough to show me how little I had been involved in what might be called the navigation world in the previous ten years, and how much I had to learn, and quickly. Luckily, in the first few weeks I was able to visit Farnborough, the Royal Radar Establishment at Malvern, Ferranti, Decca, the British Aircraft Corporation (Bristol), Boscombe Down, and even the BMEWS site at Fylingdales, and so absorb a great deal of information on what was now going on. There were also several visiting lecturers for the Air Warfare Course at Manby, plus a one-day course there on space developments, all of which susbstantially increased my knowledge of current work on aviation systems (that word again!).

*   *   *

Looking at my diary for the last few months of 1965, it shows a constant stream of visits, meetings, visiting lecturers and staff officers (with the accompanying social obligations), plus a little Canberra flying when I could fit it in. More or less settled in at home, and with Sue in some sort of work and Jenny back at school, Joan became involved – not entirely voluntarily – in running the Station Thrift Shop and Wives' Club and entertaining at home with the usual sherry mornings and dinner parties. Very few officers' wives had a job in those days, and in particular those of senior officers were expected to give time to welfare and other activities: it could be hard work but was sometimes rewarding (and sometimes frustrating).

Not long after I had arrived we (the navigation staff) had a meeting to discuss the current Staff Navigation Course and Spec N Course programmes and syllabus – an ongoing review usually held a couple of times a year. I see from the notes I took that there was pressure for the introduction of information theory (IT) into the Staff n syllabus; this subject was in its infancy at the time and would mainly be concerned with the theory of computers and their uses. The maths and physics syllabus was felt to be satisfactory, though I pressed for some more practical applications of statistics to be included; I was amused to see that spherical trigonometry was still taught, but at the fairly basic level thought to be necessary for a complete understanding of astro and maps and charts. It was agreed that the ancient Astrograph Mk 2 could be deleted from the syllabus (I was surprised to see it still taught), and we discussed the changes needed to the flying exercises with the coming introduction of the Dominie.

We also looked at the following year's programme for No. 24 Spec N Course, and decided that, with extra hours needed for teaching guidance and control systems, there would have to be some cut in private study time and probably in the traditional Wednesday afternoon games sessions. It was interesting to me to see how the emphasis of the syllabus had shifted from theoretical navigation subjects (although the maths, physics, and statistics were more rigorous than ever) to the practices and requirements of the operational commands and to the systems approach. Again the flying programme was being reviewed with the advent of the Dominie, and emphasis would be put on techniques of evaluation and experimentation in navigation systems. With the two Spec N squadron leaders, Moe Gates and Mike Banfield, working on this, I was content to leave them to it on the lines we had discussed and which Pinky Grocott had earlier laid down.

I wrote earlier in this chapter that the aim of the Spec N Course was largely unchanged, but it might be useful to quote the official statement on this subject as published in 1965: 'To train General Duties officers for the more responsible appointments associated with:

(a) The formulation and progressing of operational requirements.
(b) The development of navigation and weapons techniques and tactics in the operational commands.
(c) Navigation policy, training and operating standards in the Royal Air Force.
(d) Research and development programmes.'

This was a fairly wide brief, and normally a new syllabus was written for each course. A preliminary study phase of twenty-two weeks gave students a thorough grounding in maths (including statistics), physics, aerodynamics, electronics and guidance, and was followed by a twenty-seven-week operational studies phase covering the present and future environment of each command in turn, with emphasis on the equipment, techniques and problems in the navigation and weapons field. Students were given individual and syndicate tasks designed to bring out the principles and problems of operations and weapons system employment and selection. The major individual task was the personal project, a thesis on a major navigation or weapons system topic: typical titles were 'Self-Contained Navigation Systems – The Choice', 'Analogue versus Digital Computers in Modern Navigation and Weapons Systems' and 'The Underwater Detection and Location of Submarines'. Other individual tasks required the study of relevant technical literature to provide a brief on a new system and answer a number of searching questions. Syndicate tasks were designed to focus on the navigation and weapons aspects of strategic nuclear operations (the Cold War, of course was still all pervasive), tactical support operations and conventional attacks in a limited war setting, plus the framing of an operational requirement for a future aircraft.

Visiting lecturers from the Ministries of Aviation and Defence, the operational commands and the aviation industry talked about their particular programmes and problems, and there were visits to operational and training units, R&D establishments, and companies manufacturing navigation and weapons equipment for the RAF. These visits were no doubt a relief from the day-to-day grind, but detailed reports were required, and concentration had to be maintained (I still have my own notes from some of these visits, and am amazed at the amount of detailed information we collected). The students, all experienced navigators or pilots, logged about fifty Canberra hours during the course, and were also able to fly in some operational aircraft such as V-bombers. The Britannia flight to the North Pole that I had joined shortly before leaving Abingdon was an exercise to monitor development-batch gyros which were loaned (plus precision gyros, twin-gyro platforms, and Loran A/C equipment) by British and American manufacturers – a valuable experience for the students.

Of the twenty-three students on No. 23 Course there was one RAF squadron leader, eighteen RAF flight lieutenants, one RN lieutenant, one USAF captain, one Royal Australian Air Force squadron leader (who was the senior student) and one RAAF flight lieutenant. Just under half of these were eventually posted to research and development posts, three to the College of Air Warfare staff (including Squadron Leader Frank Lonie as head of my Guidance Section), and the rest to a variety of staff jobs. They were a conscientious, hard-working lot but quite able to let their hair down and enjoy themselves when the occasions arose.

The three-week tour of Canada and the USA in November/December was undoubtedly the highlight of the course. Its origins went back some years to exchange visits between the Spec N Course and its RCAF and USAF equivalents to discuss navigation methods and training, which were gradually widened to take in R&D establishments and companies working on navigation and weapons systems. As can be imagined, the tour required a great deal of planning and preparation, mainly done by the two Spec N squadron leaders. In this particular year planning was complicated by the fact that at a late stage Transport Command was unable to provide an aircraft to cover the whole tour, although it was able to take us the first leg to Ottawa in a Britannia via Gander. Internal flights in North America were to be by various civil airlines, with the flight home from New York, the last stop, still to be booked when we left. The Commandant, Air Commodore Topham, was to lead the party, which also included representatives from the MOD, Ministry of Aviation, and Flying Training Command (the latter being the Command Navigation Officer, Wing Commander Jack Midwood, something of a character – a professional Yorkshireman – with whom I happily shared a room for most of the tour).

We arrived in Ottawa after a long haul from Lyneham, stopping for an hour at Gander in Newfoundland. To us it was late evening, but in Ottawa only mid-afternoon, and after sorting our rooms out in the Lord Elgin Hotel there was time for an impromptu party before going off to a more formal one hosted by the Air Adviser to the British Defence Liaison Staff, Air Commodore Plumtree – a very enjoyable function – but the older members of the party were only too happy to roll into bed later. Fortunately the following day was a Sunday, and we were able to see something of Ottawa, a handsome if rather staid city, we thought, but with magnificent views from the tower of the Parliament building, looking over the River Ottawa to rolling hills, with log rafts being floated down the wide river.

Our first scheduled visit was to Computing Devices of Canada, a company specializing in the manufacture of automatic dead-reckoning equipment, topographical display units and head-up displays (the latter then becoming required equipment in fighter cockpits, so that pilots would not have to look down continuously at their instrument panel). We were particularly interested in their work on an integrated navigation and weapons system for long-range maritime aircraft, for which the RCAF had a requirement in view of Canada's long Atlantic seaboard, and were impressed by CDC's expertise and by its future plans for projects in this field.

The next day saw a visit to HQ Canadian Joint Forces, where again the maritime problems were high on the agenda, with assessments of the Cold War submarine threat and the forces available and required in the future to deal with it. The presentations and discussions also covered future transport, strike and navigation training aircraft for the RCAF, and we came away with the impression that the Canadians were tackling their operational requirements with a rather more direct and down-to-earth attitude than our own MOD and MOA.

In the afternoon we flew on by Air Canada to Winnipeg, where the Canadian winter had arrived and snow lay on the ground. We were visiting the RCAF Central Navigation School, the home of the RCAF Aerospace Systems Course (called the Specialist Navigation Course until 1963) whose director was, as it happened, a RAF Spec N graduate on exchange with the RCAF, Squadron Leader Dave MacArthur. We discussed the role of CNS – very similar to that of our old Empire Air Navigation School – and the present Aerospace Systems Course syllabus, which was developing in very much the same way as our Spec N Course, and agreed that we in the RAF would have to look carefully at its title. There was a look at the next generation of basic navigation and applied weapons system training aircraft, and again we had the feeling that the RCAF, with probably more limited resources than in the UK, was approaching the future sensibly and practically. (We noted with some amusement that the RCAF Station Commander at snow-covered Winnipeg was appropriately named Group Captain Christmas.)

Flying via a brief stopover in Vancouver, there could hardly have been a greater contrast than with our next stop, Sacramento in California, with a pleasant temperature and wall-to-wall sunshine; the state capital is an attractive city with parks and green spaces and a particularly impressive State Capitol building. We left by bus for Mather Air Force Base, where we were accommodated in the Bachelor Officers' Quarters (BOQs). Mather was a long-established military airfield, opening in 1918 as a pilot training school, and was now the centre for USAF bombing, navigation and electronic warfare training for the B52 and B58 aircraft of Strategic Air Command, with the 320th Bomb Wing of SAC as a lodger unit. A course similar to the RAF Spec N Course had been held here some years previously (hence the regular visits from Manby) but had been replaced by degree courses at the Air Force Institute of Technology and the Massachusetts Institute of Technology (MIT). We were given presentations on the mission and facilities of the base and on navigation training at all levels in the USAF; there was also a briefing on SAC operations.

It was now some seven years since I had left Alaska, and it was strange but familiar to be back in the USAF atmosphere and find myself automatically reverting to American speech locutions; the RAF Spec N exchange officer here, Flight Lieutenant Dave Chrispin, seemed to be enjoying his job as much as I had mine. A guest night was laid on for us in the Officers' Club, and it must have been attended by up to 200 people, with two MCs regulating the proceedings via amplifiers and background music. During some past visit we had injudiciously presented Mather with a yard of ale, and it had now become a 'tradition' for a drinking contest to be held with the visitors – I forget who the unfortunate Manby representative was on this occasion, but I know that I had to uphold the honour of the RAF on a later visit, not an experience I wanted to repeat.

There were a few thick heads in the morning: on all our North American visits the students, mostly in their late twenties, took full advantage of the hospitality on offer (and it was usually generous) and also sought their own pleasures in the various cities. At the same time they managed to absorb most of the detailed technical and other information that we were given, and took a full part in the discussions; I noted that nearly all of them took detailed notes, as I did (still on my steep learning curve). At each place on our itinerary a small group of students was tasked with producing a full report, which would eventually be used towards the final official report on the tour, a widely circulated and (we liked to think) eagerly awaited document.

The next port of call was Los Angeles, but since a weekend intervened we had cunningly arranged a night stop in San Francisco, only a short distance – as distances went in the USA – from Sacramento. We were accommodated in the Marines Memorial Hotel, reserved for 'veterans' (as all ex-servicemen were known in the States and are now known in the UK), comfortable, inexpensive and central. San Francisco is a fascinating and idiosyncratic city, with its cable cars running up and down the steep streets, the Golden Gate and Oakland bridges, Fisherman's Wharf, and other places of interest we had too little time to take in on this short visit. We had a drink at the Top o' the Mark, going up the many floors in the vertiginous elevator on the outside of the building, and Jack Midwood and I had tea in some Chinese tea gardens overlooking the Golden Gate bridge. It was the period of the flower people, peaceniks and hippies, and I remember that the streets seemed to be full of long-haired young people of indeterminate sex, often with guitars slung over their shoulders.

We were reluctant to move on, and found LA to be characterless by comparison – 'nineteen suburbs in search of a metropolis', to quote the old tag. In any event we had little time for sight-seeing, but some of the students found their way to night-spots such as the Body Shop and the

Pink Pussy Cat. But our purpose was to visit the Autonetics Division of North American Aviation, and also Litton Industries, both firms heavily involved in the development of inertial navigation and associated systems.

Autonetics was working on a series of lightweight precision IN equipments and hybrid navigation systems, and also micro-miniaturized terrain-following radars, attack radars and indeed multi-purpose airborne radars. Most of these were at an early stage of development, as was work on the use of digital computers and data systems, for missiles as well as manned aircraft. R&D was also in progress on the use of lasers for aviation systems, one of the latest technical developments which seemed to have great potential in several fields. Litton was working on similar lines, but with a particular interest in low-cost IN and in hybrid navigation systems such as stellar/IN, Doppler/IN, Loran C/IN and even stellar/Loran C/Doppler/IN – ways of reducing navigational errors and reliability by continual cross-referencing. They were also involved in developing pilot and navigation cockpit displays and weapons-release computers for strike aircraft. The scientists involved in this work who talked to us gave us some valuable information, much of it highly security classified, and the discussions were wide ranging and productive. These two visits made us realize how much effort and finance the USA was able to put into this work compared with the reducing resources at home.

The knowledge gained from Autonetics and Litton was reinforced by our next visit, to the USAF Central Inertial Guidance Test Facility and the Inertial Navigation Development Detachment at Holloman AFB, some eighty miles north of El Paso, New Mexico (where on a brief overnight stop we also gained a little experience of Mexican food and tequila). Holloman was engaged in ground and flight testing of IN components and systems and hybrid navigation and weapons equipment, so we were able to get a feel for the user's approach and some knowledge of its test facilities.

From El Paso we flew to Fort Worth in Texas, where we stayed in the Western Hills Motel. We had arrived the day before Thanksgiving, which we accordingly took as a day off, and were given an extended coach tour of Fort Worth and the neighbouring city of Dallas ('Big D'). Fort Worth was originally an outpost in Indian country, later a trading-post, and was now the leading railroad and trading centre for the large stock-raising, oil-producing and farming region of Tarrant County, a wealthy place, as evidenced by some of the luxurious (not to say ostentatious) homes we were driven past. We were also taken to one of those archetypal American events, a football game, complete with marching band, drum-majorettes, stetson-wearing spectators, and hot dogs on sale: one of the teams was from the Southern Methodist University at Dallas. I had seen the game on television, but it was instructional (and exciting) to watch it in the flesh, so to speak, with explanatory comments from our hosts from General

Dynamics. Some of us were also kindly entertained to dinner at a very up-market country club with its golf course and other sporting facilities – a glimpse of the high life as lived in Texas.

General Dynamics was producing the F-111 'swing wing' fighter aircraft which at that time our MOD was considering as a replacement for the cancelled TSR-2, and we spent a day with the company looking at the aircraft itself – a very forward-looking design for the time – and its navigation and weapons systems. If I remember correctly, the Chief Test Pilot, Doc Witchell (who had taken a prominent part in the hospitality we had already received) gave a comprehensive presentation on the aircraft, its performance and flight profile, and impressed us as a very competent, down-to-earth operator. (We were able to return some of his generous hospitality when he visited Manby the following year). We also studied the navigation and weapons system in the F-111, which included a forward-looking radar and a terrain-following radar, and were given details of the procedures developed for system alignment, pre-flight checks, and in-flight navigation. This was a valuable and instructive visit, involving as it did some real hardware and enthusiastic aviators.

Wright-Patterson AFB, near Dayton, Ohio, was the next place on our itinerary, an important and historic base with two airfields – Wright after the immortal brothers, and Patterson after a First World War test pilot. Its function was something like that of our own Aeroplane and Armament Experimental Establishment at Boscombe Down, and we were there to spend a day with the Avionics Laboratory, where we discussed future trends in inertial and hybrid navigation systems, including IN/Loran C/Loran D and IN/satellite systems, with a look at astro-inertial systems. Work was also going on in the future application of lasers for airborne use, airborne passive and active reconnaissance systems, and future Doppler developments – all still at the early experimental stage, but a fascinating glimpse of the future.

Our programme was tight here, and there was no time for local exploration before we were on our way again to Washington DC, where we stayed in a hotel in Connecticut Avenue in the embassy area.

We were there for a briefing from the US Air Force Systems Command at Andrews AFB, which gave us an overview of the strike aircraft weapons systems planned for the next decade, a long-term projection pulling together the various strands of R&D work we had been hearing about elsewhere – aircraft performances, crew composition, flight profiles, navigation and weapons systems, and weapons delivery methods, including nuclear, with a look at proposed transport aircraft and a review of Loran C/D and Omega programmes. There was a great deal of valuable information to assimilate (mostly security classified), and I took copious notes myself while the majority of the students were also scribbling away furiously.

Our final stop was New York, with an early start getting us to John F. Kennedy Airport mid-morning on 1 December. Our accommodation was in the Governor Clinton Hotel opposite Penn Station (which did not seem to have changed since I stayed there with the family in 1956 and 1958 on our way out to and back from Alaska). We were visiting the Kearfott Division of General Precision Inc., specializing in guidance equipments and particularly inertial navigation, periscopic sextants, automatic star trackers and hybrid navigation systems. The company was based in Little Falls, New Jersey, and on the coach journey there we were able to see some of what passed for countryside in the area, where the fall colours were still visible. The members of the Kearfott team who talked to us were again enthusiastic and knowledgeable, especially on gyro development in the precision and low-cost fields, and dealt thoroughly with their work on IN and their proposals for the navigation and control systems for the supersonic transport aircraft now being considered in the USA (no doubt spurred on by the Anglo-French Concorde project now at an advanced level of development). Hybrid navigation and Doppler projects were also covered, and we came away with a great deal more information and ideas to add to those already assimilated

In the short time we had in New York we were able to do a little sight-seeing, and I still have a few slides taken in the city among the 'stone canyons' of Fifth Avenue and other places, including Chinatown. Since Christmas was coming up, a great deal of shopping was done, and when we arrived at JFK for the return flight several members of the party were laden with large teddy bears, other toys, beribboned boxes, and in one or two cases new sets of golf clubs (made in Japan and then comparatively inexpensive). We flew in a British VC-10, and it was pleasant to be in the home atmosphere again. Leaving in the evening and flying east it was a short night: as the dawn came up and the air hostesses drew curtains, the faint sound of 'Reveille' came from the rear of the aircraft, played by Eric Eatwell, our naval student, who had bought a toy trumpet for his children.

Flying back to Manby via Northolt, it was a great relief to be home again after a demanding but immensely rewarding three weeks touring North America. For me it was a much-needed education in the latest and future work in the navigation field, and a recognition that 'systems' were the future rather than the old personal and partly intuitive skills of the individual navigator. I have written at some length about this experience since it encapsulates the great changes under way in the aviation world, and also underlines the contrast between the US and British research and development programmes – the latter not quite a shadow of its former self as I had known it at Farnborough, but gradually being reduced in scope and finance, as demonstrated by the TSR2 fiasco, while in the USA many military establishments, universities and commercial companies were being given sufficient funds to carry out a variety of overlapping programmes. We had, of course, realized that many of the commercial firms we visited were hoping to sell aircraft or equipment to the UK, but the people who had briefed us were not salesmen, and their technical knowhow and general enthusiasm for their projects was evident. It has been of great interest to see in the last few years, in conflicts in various parts of the parts of the globe, how many of the projects which seemed visionary in the 1960s are now in general use in the RAF and USAF.

*   *   *

Back at Manby the run-up to Christmas was starting, and No. 23 Spec N Course was finishing, so there were many celebrations of various sorts. But work had to go on, and the two Spec N squadron leaders, Moe Gates and Dick Tomlin, were busy preparing the voluminous report on the North American tour while Dick was handing over to Mike Banfield, who had just arrived. All the end-of-course results and reports had to be completed and each departing student interviewed. The grading for the course results still employed the A1/A2/B1/B2 system which, though now somewhat archaic, was keenly watched by the students. I had one unpleasant interview with a student who had probably been the best of the course academically and technically and reached A1 standard in all examinations and in his personal projects, but was a difficult personality who found it hard to interact with and make allowances for others not quite so gifted. A small proportion of the marks awarded was at the discretion of the directing staff and based on personal qualities, and in this case our judgment brought the overall result down to A2 level; our feeling was that, as a staff officer or a member of a research and development team, a graduate of the course should be able to work well with others, and this was certainly not the case. The student naturally felt aggrieved by this downgrading, but we hoped that with hindsight he might come to accept that it was in his own interests.

With the Christmas period over, and the arrival of new courses – Air Warfare, Spec N, and Staff n – dealt with, it was time to start converting to our new aircraft, the Dominie, the first of five of which was to arrive in February 1966, the type having already been introduced to the Air Navigation Schools. Deriving from the Scots for schoolmaster, the name echoed an earlier version developed in 1939 for the RAF from the de Havilland Dragon Rapide biplane (still in use at Farnborough in my time) and used as a radio and navigation trainer. The new Dominie T Mk 1 was a military version of the Hawker-Siddeley 125 private jet, twin-engined, 42 feet long and with a 47-foot wingspan. Its external appearance was very elegant, with clean lines – and it's an old aviators' maxim that a good-looking aircraft will have a good performance. The pressurized cabin had seating for two pilots, two student navigators, an instructor and a spare crew member, with the two students in rear-facing seats with plenty of working space and stowage and a well-designed console for the various navigation aids and instruments. These included the Marconi AD 260 VHF omni-range (VOR)/instrument landing system (ILS); two AD 722 radio compass systems (remembering our work at RAE I was interested to note that the loop aerials were fully suppressed, with one sense aerial externally mounted and the other a suppressed plate aerial, as in our prototype Viscount experiments); an Ekco E 190 weather radar with a ground-mapping facility displayed on the students' console; a Decca Doppler 62 system showing drift, groundspeed and distance gone; a Decca Mk 1(air) navigator with a decometer display on the students' console and a flight log for the pilots. The compass system was a Sperry CL-11, a high-accuracy gyro-magnetic type with latitude/longitude and deviation correctors, also feeding two ground position indicators (GPIs) Mk 4A – one for each student – which would display continuous ground position. A periscopic sextant could be mounted with 360 degrees of vision and near the aircraft's centre of gravity to reduce acceleration errors to the minimum. I couldn't help comparing this array of equipment with our old training Ansons some twenty-odd years earlier, with their magnetic compass, astro-compass, drift recorder, loop aerial, and the Mark 1 eyeball – a different era entirely.

Cruising at between 30,000 and 38,000 feet at around a true airspeed of 400 knots, the aircraft had a range of some 900 to 1,200 nautical miles, which could be stretched to about 1,230 nm at 38,000 feet and a lower airspeed of 350 knots. As with all turbo-jets, the lower the altitude the shorter the range, and I recall that on one flight from Orange in the south of France to Gibraltar the French air traffic controllers, whether from bloody-mindedness (not unusual) or inefficiency, kept us at a lower altitude for so long that we had to drop in to Palma airport in Majorca to refuel; I remember it well since we were parked next to a restored Second World War Mustang fighter and near to a three-engined German Ju 52 transport aircraft – also a relic of WW2 – which was evidently still in service.

John Preston, in charge of the Applied Navigation Section, had organized a very helpful Dominie ground school for which I still have the notes I took, covering in some detail the aircraft performance, its electrical and other systems, and the use of the navigation aids. I also have the logs and charts for most of the Dominie flights I did – some eighty-odd hours – and they bring back the enjoyment of flying in this quiet, comfortable and efficient aircraft. As I have said elsewhere, it was only in the Dominie that astro-navigation, with the periscopic sextant and a steady platform, became a pleasure rather than a pain as far as I was concerned. I notice from the 2006 RAF Handbook that the Dominie T Mk 1 is still in use at the RAF College Cranwell for training purposes more than forty years after its introduction – a remarkable record.

*   *   *

Leafing through my engagement diaries for the years we were at Manby, I am amazed at the way in which they are filled with non-stop activities of varying kinds: visiting lecturers, who might be very senior officers from the operational commands or the ministries or scientists from industry or research, had to be hosted – lunch or dinner in the Mess or in some cases at home; welcomes and introductory talks to newly arrived courses; farewells to courses or staff (for the latter usually a lunchtime 'tankard party' at which an engraved tankard would be presented); and meetings in London or elsewhere. All this had to be fitted in with normal day-to-day work and a flying programme which as usual would be subject to the weather and unserviceability. The latter half of the year would be largely taken up with Spec N Course visits within the UK, in Europe and finally in North America.

At the same time family life had to go on, and Joan was much involved in social entertainment and in work for the Wives' Club and Thrift Shop. After the summer of 1966 we were a complete family again, with Jenny leaving school and eventually starting a business studies course at Grimsby College. In the spring of 1966 we had a holiday in a cottage at Ashkirk in the Scottish Borders – wonderful country but indifferent accommodation. This led us to consider caravanning, and after a trial weekend in a hired van we bought a Sprite Musketeer four-berth caravan and headed for the coast. There is a slightly snobbish view of caravanning, of unsightly vehicles cluttering up the roads, but we found it an enjoyable and useful way of taking holidays – self-sufficient and flexible and particularly convenient in service life when leave dates could not be depended on (although Manby's year did include programmed breaks which were usually available for leave).

Both Joan and Jennifer took driving lessons at Manby, and when they had passed their tests we bought an elderly Morris 1000 from Ray Phillips, who had been one of our pilots on the Bomber Command 'X' Flight and was now on the College Directing Staff. It was a reliable vehicle which gave us good service for several years, and certainly gave Joan some independence when I was not available; she turned out to be an excellent driver and enjoyed her little car.

Susan left home to take up a job in financial services in the London area. She had by now found a new boyfriend, a young pilot stationed at Manby: she had always said, 'I shan't marry into the RAF and shall certainly not marry a pilot.' However, they became engaged and did marry later.

*   *   *

Moe Gates was posted back to Canada and replaced by Doug Stonehouse, another RCAF exchange officer. We missed Moe and Francie, who had been good friends, and we are in touch with them regularly; Moe became a colonel in the reconstituted Canadian Armed Forces, and we visited them in Ontario not long before he retired. Moe has been active with Canada's air museum and has also jointly written two books with the stories of Canadian air navigators – for me a gripping read. As I write I have just received a Christmas card from him with news of his family and their latest doings.

Summer 1966 saw a new Commandant at Manby – Air Commodore C.B. Brown, universally known as 'Cyclops', since he had lost an eye in an early flying accident as a sergeant-pilot, and wore a black eye-patch. He had had something of a struggle to be graded fit for flying again, but had shown that he was an exceptional pilot, and indeed had qualified as a test pilot at ETPS. He was an engaging character, interested in everything that was going on at the College, and I was soon flying with him in the Dominie and briefing him on our various navigation activities.

One of my duties was to give the first navigation lecture to the Air Warfare Course. Talking to a bunch of senior General Duties officers, usually including an American and some Commonwealth representatives, I had to steer a careful course between assuming that they knew a great deal about the subject (which many of them did) and that they were not so well informed. It was a very general talk, harking back to the beginnings of air navigation – when pilots in the early days flew low over railway stations to read the name on the platform – through the developments in the Second World War and concluding with a review of the latest navigation systems and their future application. The lecture was illustrated by slides and was usually received with interest and many pertinent questions (although as it was frequently scheduled for the immediate post-lunch period, some of the older students could occasionally be detected nodding off).

An occasional variation on the Staff Navigation Course was the Pilot Navigation Instructors' Course, designed specifically for Fighter Command, whose Station Navigation Officers and navigation instructors at operational conversion units were usually pilots and mostly dealing with single-seat aircraft where the navigation problems were a little different. While normally operating under ground control interception (GCI) radar stations, there were occasions when fighter pilots needed to navigate themselves, and indeed this was encouraged, especially when new aids such as TACAN became available and when GCI units had to cope with larger numbers of aircraft. The PNI Course, slightly shorter than the Staff n Course, refreshed pilots' basic navigation theory, including such necessary subjects as compass swinging and maps and charts, and concentrated on single-seat navigation techniques. We found that, although many of the students were reluctant to be put on the course, they found it of great benefit and were usually enthusiastic in their end-of-course critiques.

My main preoccupation was of course with the Specialist Navigation Course, and when I had arrived at Manby it had already been decided that the course title was to be changed and that No. 25 Course in 1967 would be the last Spec N Course so named. This was a regrettable break with the course's long history back to 1920 (when it was known as the Long Navigation Course), but the face of navigation and aircraft performance had developed so rapidly over the last few years that these changes had to be acknowledged in the syllabus and title of the course, which from January 1968 would be known as the General Duties Aero-Systems Course, or ASC (the GD prefix was felt to be necessary since the RAF's Technical Branch had instituted its own Aero-Systems Course at the RAF Technical College Henlow). In any event the Spec N Course had been evolving in this direction for the last few years under my predecessor, Pinky Grocott, and the syllabus for the newly titled course needed little more than 'tweaking' to fit the requirements laid down by the Ministry of Defence, with whom we had had many discussions. Some concern was felt by the Specialist Navigation Association with its membership of Spec Ns going back for some forty years and with an annual get-together at the College of Air Warfare, but the problem was solved by re-christening it the Aries Association (the name Aries having an astronomical rather than an astrological significance), and it is still flourishing today.

In 1966, although the directing staff were concerned to some extent with planning for the new course, No. 24 Spec N Course continued with its usual busy summer programme: visits were made to the major aircraft and systems manufacturers (including a look at the Concorde mock-up at BAC Bristol), R&D establishments and RAF operational stations, while preparations for the North American tour were going on. In October we made a short visit to Paris, first to the French Centre d'Essais En Vol at Brétigny, the approximate equivalent of RAE Farnborough, to hear talks on their aircraft systems programme. This was the era of de Gaulle, when the French had declined to join NATO, and it had been decreed that the scientists talking to us should speak in their native language throughout, which for most of us was not helpful; I followed some of it with my rusty schoolboy French, and luckily we had a course student, Hugh Coriat, who was a fluent French speaker and took notes. However, we were taken out to lunch and our friendly hosts were mostly excellent English speakers; I recall that, on the way there, I scribbled a short speech of thanks in French which Hugh Coriat kindly vetted for me. Our hearts sank a little when we arrived at the chosen rather scruffy restaurant, but it turned out to be a notable meal, and as it proceeded through course after course with a different wine for each, my apprehension subsided somewhat and I was able to make a passable speech over the cognac which was well received. Our other visit near Paris was to Breguet, the aircraft manufacturer at Vélizy-Villacoublay, where we were given information – thankfully in

English – on its current aircraft and systems projects, supplementing and enlarging on the details we had been given at CEV Brétigny.

It was soon time for our annual North American tour, and this year, although the outward and return flights would be via Air Canada and BOAC respectively, we were to have a Transport Command Argosy at our disposal for all the internal travel, a great improvement on the previous year's use of a variety of US and Canadian domestic airlines. The party was led by Air Commodore Brown, and the programme was similar to that of 1965, including the traditional visits to the RCAF Central Navigation School at Winnipeg and the USAF's Mather Air Force Base, with their equally traditional and lavish hospitality. In Washington we visited the Bureau of Naval Weapons to discuss close air support from carrier-borne aircraft, developments in anti-submarine warfare, and the Omega project for long-range low-frequency navigation. In Atlanta we also took in the Lockheed-Georgia Company to look at the C-5A project for a very large military transport aircraft for the USAF – an impressive aircraft that dwarfed any other transport of that time. The Hughes Aircraft Company near Los Angeles (formed by the eccentric and reclusive Howard Hughes to build aircraft, but now also concerned with systems development) gave us presentations on current weapons systems, with emphasis on those for the F-111, on work going on in a satellite programme, and – of particular interest – on developments in laser techniques such as target ranging. In all the US bases and companies that we visited it was evident that the pressure was on to improve existing systems and produce new ones with the US involvement in the ill-fated Vietnam war now under way.

Back at Manby in time for Christmas, the current Spec N Course graduations and farewells took place amid preparations for the last course so named, No. 25, in 1967. Once the new course students were settled and grappling with the first intensive study phase, I took the opportunity to do some Dominie flying, including Staff n Course low-level exercises, always enjoyable, and an exercise to Gibraltar, conveniently over a weekend. In April I was able to attend a conference in Paris organized jointly by the Institute of Navigation and its French, German and Italian equivalents with co-operation from the Institutes in Australia and the USA: its purpose was to discuss, according to the official title, 'Automation as Applied to the Conduct of Craft by Sea and in the Air', and many papers were given by eminent authorities in the field (including my old friend and colleague Freddy Stringer, who spoke on 'The En-Route to Terminal Area Interface' – typical boffin-speak). As far as air navigation was concerned, the emphasis was on the use of multiple aids, including digital computers, and most of the papers were related to the operation of civil aircraft and ways of improving safety, reducing route time (and therefore cost), and obviating the need to employ a separate navigator (also cost reducing).

One interesting French contribution (by M. Le Bouar of Sud Aviation) concerned the navigational equipment which would be available in the supersonic Concorde when it became operational in 1970 at a cruising speed of Mach 2.2 (1,300 knots). The aircraft would be fitted with conventional ground-based systems such as VOR, DME, ADF and ILS, but for effective operation Concorde's navigational system must provide the 'information that allows the aircraft to be directed to any point on the globe, while its own position is known at any moment'. The problems of determining the true local vertical with the lengthy periods of longitudinal acceleration involved in supersonic flight were to be solved by the use of a Schuler-tuned inertial platform, and it was thought that the best automatic navigation system would be a digital computer combined with such an inertial platform, the intention being to provide two or even three identical inertial systems. There would be a moving map display allowing comparisons of information from the different IN systems, and if necessary resetting, by the pilot. Evidently the thinking on Concorde navigation systems (by both Sud and BAC) was as far ahead as was the design and performance of the aircraft.

Other presentations also dealt with future airborne computers, with the automation of long-range air navigation aids, with the integration of multiple-sensor systems, and with civil aircraft requirements for automation. Most were looking fairly well ahead, but it was evident from our North American tours that progress in the field was going to be comparatively rapid and that – certainly as far as civil aircraft were concerned – multi-redundancy (the doubling or tripling of systems to increase safety and efficiency) would be of some importance. Papers at the conference were almost equally divided between maritime and air operations, and there was little if any direct reference to military requirements; this meant that there was no need to attend a proportion of sessions.

So it happened that for once I was able to mix business with pleasure: Frank Lonie, formerly the RAAF student on No. 23 Spec N Course, and now in charge of the Guidance Section on my staff, accompanied me to Paris, and we took our wives with us (at our expense, of course). Joan got on well with Pat Lonie, and the two of them were able to do a little shopping and also take a guided tour out to Versailles when Frank and I were gainfully occupied. We had arrived at Le Bourget via BEA late in the evening, and we were hungry and tired by the time we reached our hotel (the Hôtel Electrique in the Seventeenth Arondissement, no doubt very up to date when it was named, probably early in the century, but with only bed and breakfast facilities). We walked around the local streets to find a restaurant, but the only one we could find open was almost empty, with only two or three people at one table: these turned out to be the proprietors and friends chatting over coffee and cognac. They could not provide a hot meal as the kitchen had closed, but produced a magnificent cold buffet with meats of various sorts, pâtés, salad and fruit, with a bottle of Valpolicella – a splendid repast and a memorable occasion.

Paris in the spring was a pleasure: on one day, between sessions, Frank and I met Joan and Pat in the Tuileries gardens and had a delightful luncheon picnic bought by our thoughtful wives in the local shops. One odd incident occurred when Frank and I were waiting for a train at a Metro station: a man started to cross the line between platforms but collapsed half way. The platforms were crowded but nobody moved to help. Frank and I got down on the line, and carefully avoiding what we assumed to be the live rail, managed to lift the man out on to the platform; by this time somebody had called for medical help, and a doctor or paramedic attended to him – whether he was ill, drunk, or drugged we never discovered, as our train arrived and we departed. But our visit was otherwise very enjoyable; we made the statutory ascent of the Eiffel Tower, and on the final evening attended the cocktail party held for those attending the conference and hosted at the Palais de Chaillot by the Mayor of Paris – an enjoyable function with a few familiar faces from the navigation world.

* * *

My engagement diary shows that the summer of 1967 was as busy as ever. We had the usual visits from the Canadian Central Navigation School and the Aerospace Systems Course. The Assistant Commandant, Group Captain Jackie Holmes, was replaced by Group Captain Bob Weighill, a former RAF rugby player and genial character. No. 113 Staff n Course arrived. The coming Aero-Systems Course syllabus and administrative arrangements were finalized, and I attended the selection board for the new course in the Air Secretary's Department at MOD. The Spec N Course enjoyed their usual visits to R&D organizations, operational stations, and the air industry, and undertook two polar flights (one of which I accompanied) to study high-latitude navigation and gyro performance. As light relief I went on a Staff n training flight in a Dominie to Malta as well as a one-day trip to Bodø in Norway. Flying was complicated by the five-week closure of Strubby airfield, from which our navigation flying took place, for runway resurfacing, but we operated from RAF Binbrook without too much disruption. The busy social life continued with drinks parties, farewell parties, dinner parties, and lunch in the mess for visiting lecturers, culminating in the annual summer ball. Looking back now from quiet retirement, we find it difficult to understand how we found the energy to cope.

In addition to my normal duties I somehow found myself committed to marking RAF Promotion Examination B papers, those from flying officer to flight lieutenant. The MOD made a practice of asking the various senior colleges to provide markers for the range of promotion and Staff College entrance examinations, and the Air Warfare College was an obvious choice. I found the work of great interest, though mostly having to be done in off-duty hours and usually late into the evenings. I was a little surprised at what I felt to be the low standard of English from these young officers, particularly in punctuation and spelling, but I remembered from my time at Farnborough that quite well-qualified scientists with university degrees did not always find it easy to express themselves in clear and correct English when writing their scientific papers, and often leant heavily on technical jargon only comprehensible to those involved in the same sort of work. Reading the latest edition of the RAF Handbook (2006) published by the MOD, I see that the use of techno-speak is increasing (although I must concede that, as one would expect, I cannot find much fault with spelling or punctuation).

The College was asked to send a briefing team to Near East Air Force to spread the message of the training available at Manby, a request probably not unconnected with the appointment of my predecessor, Pinky Grocott, as Group Captain Operations, HQ NEAF, based at Akrotiri in Cyprus.

Our Commandant, as always keen to fly, decided to take a Varsity aircraft from Strubby (more easily spared from the flying programme), and asked me to be his navigator and part of the briefing team. After a couple of shakedown flights in the UK, we left Strubby early in October 1967 and flew to Naples for a night-stop via Lyon. At Capodichino airport we were met by a party including the British NATO representative and a senior Italian Air Force officer, whom we could see lined up awaiting us as we taxied in. Cyclops changed rapidly out of his flying overalls and into his uniform, and walked down the steps to meet our hosts. After the usual exchange of courtesies, he was about to be driven off in an official car when an airport worker asked if the aircraft could be moved to another dispersal. So as the only pilot aboard formally cleared to operate the aircraft, Cyclops had climb in again and move the Varsity to another part of the airfield while the greeting party hung around a little longer. Eventually we arrived at our hotel and had a pleasant dinner, but had no opportunity to see Naples (although the clamour of the horrendous traffic did register with us).

We were off early the following morning for Akrotiri, with a refuelling stop in Athens, where we had a brief glimpse of the Acropolis as we came in to land. Although I was familiar with the Varsity, it was something of a retrograde step as far as navigation was concerned, certainly in comparison with the Dominie. Once we were out of Gee and Decca coverage, it was back to drifts, the occasional visual bearing, and radio compass. But in any event we were using the airways system now almost universal in Europe and the Mediterranean, navigating between radio beacons on the standard green airways charts, just as aircraft in the USA had done for so long.

Arriving in Akrotiri late on Sunday, we gave our presentation to staff of HQ NEAF the following day: the Commandant talked about the role of the College, a member of the directing staff covered our operational studies, I dealt with navigation and aero-systems training, and our weapons specialist described the weapons courses. Finally the College astronautics team put on its always spectacular show on the use of space for military purposes and the American Apollo programme to land men on the moon by 1970. Our efforts were well received, and in turn we were later given a briefing on NEAF's operational roles, covering a wide area of the Middle East, providing staging facilities, and maintaining the integrity of the sovereign base area against a background of the uneasy truce between the Greek and Turkish Cypriots, now policed to some extent by the UN Peace-Keeping Force set up in 1964. We repeated our presentation to RAF Akrotiri the following day, and again at Air HQ Malta in Luqa after flying via Iraklion in Crete. After a welcome free day in Malta we flew back to the UK, refuelling at Naples and Lyon as before.

After just under a week to catch up with work in the College, I accompanied 25 Spec N Course on their European tour, also led by the Commandant. We visited the Dutch air force base at Twenthe, the huge British military base at Rheindahlen, RAF Wildenrath, and the USAF base at Bitburg, getting some grasp of the NATO Cold War policy, tasks and weapons systems. We finished up in Paris where we had another informative visit to Breguet, being given *inter alia* details of the anti-submarine avionics system in their Atlantic maritime patrol aircraft, then in service with the French and German navies and later with the Netherlands and Italy. We were also briefed on the Anglo-French fighter-bomber project, the Jaguar, still to make its first flight and eventually to give long and sterling service to the RAF.

Arriving back on the Manby merry-go-round, we had just eight days before setting off on the North American tour, again flying out and back courtesy of BOAC but with our own Argosy for the internal flights. Since we had visited them last, the Royal Canadian Air Force had lost its identity and become part of the joint Canadian Armed Forces, a move of which most of the former RCAF officers we met did not approve, army ranks and green uniforms included. The only addition to the previous year's itinerary was a visit to the Boeing Aircraft Company at Seattle, mainly to study their supersonic aircraft project which seemed to be a response to the Anglo-French Concorde: I have retained no notes of this, but I seem to recall that the intended design looked ungainly, with two sponsons (small wings) projecting either side of the nose. In the event the project was abandoned and there is still no American supersonic passenger aircraft.

The end of 1967 saw the end of the Specialist Navigation Course after nearly forty years, and No. 25 Course was suitably dined out. As I have said, the long-standing Specialist Navigation Association, with a membership of almost 300 graduates of the course, continued as the Aries Association and flourishes to this day with its annual dinner (now usually at Cranwell), its newsletter and often a cocktail party once a year in London.

No. 1 Aero-Systems Course (in later years the hyphen was dropped) began in January 1968, with six pilots, four Air Electronics Officers (the recently-adopted title for commissioned air signallers), ten navigators, two RAAF navigators and one USAF navigator. As I have already written, the syllabus did not change dramatically – there was a more detailed study of aerodynamics and some reduction in the navigation flying exercise programme. The visit programmes and the polar flights were of course retained. I had been involved in the selection of the students and as I interviewed them after arrival I felt that they were well suited to the new course and were prepared for some hard work, especially in the first few months with the emphasis on maths, science and theory generally. They settled down well.

The senior course at Manby, the Air Warfare Course, also included overseas visits in their programme. The current course, No. 15, was due to go to the Far East in May, and the Commandant thought that it would be useful to repeat the sort of College presentations we had done in the Middle East the previous year (although none of our own aircraft would have been suitable for the long hauls involved and we would have to rely on Transport Command). I was therefore co-opted into the team, and we set off, with the AWC students, at the beginning of May, flying to Changi, Singapore, in a VC10 via Bahrain and Gan. The ground time at Gan was short – for refuelling only – but I was able to see a little of the station: my main impression was of the greenness of the island compared with its state in my time, when we were still building up and there were great areas which had been cleared of vegetation. Now most building was finished and the place looked much less bare, with tidy garden areas and well-kept roads. I paid a hasty visit to the mess and had the satisfaction of seeing my name among the list of Station Commanders on the wall at the mess entrance.

We stayed in the Hotel Ambassador in Singapore and our first visit was to the joint Far East Command and Far East Land Forces HQ, followed by HQ Far East Air Force and RAF Changi the following day, when we gave our College team lecture (or 'presentation', as it was inevitably called). It was strange to be back in the humid and bustling atmosphere of Singapore after seven years or so, and fascinating as it was, I was glad that I had never had to undergo a full tour of duty there. The Air Warfare students also spent some time at the other RAF stations on the island – Seletar and

Tengah – but if I accompanied them I don't recall what they learned about their organization and role. We went on to Butterworth, close to Penang in the former Malaya, which had recently become the Federation of Malaysia (from which Singapore had seceded in 1965 and was now fully independent). Butterworth was an airfield run by the Royal Australian Air Force, Australia being understandably concerned for peace and stability in this new country (and indeed still maintains some air and army capability there). We also visited Kuala Lumpur, the capital, and I have an abiding memory of the beauty and tranquillity of a newly built mosque there.

We flew back from Singapore, via flag-stops at Gan and Bahrain, and arrived back at Lyneham early one mid-week morning to be picked up by one of our own aircraft and taken back to Manby. The Canadian Armed Forces Aerospace Systems Course had just arrived for their annual exchange visit, and so, jet-lag notwithstanding, I was immediately in the thick of it, with a welcoming buffet supper that evening at which I could hardly keep awake. They had a full programme the following day, and departed after luncheon the day after that. The weekend was very welcome before it was back to work again.

*   *   *

I was now well into my third year at the College. It had been sensible to extend my tour of duty sufficiently to see the new Aero-Systems Course satisfactorily into its stride, but now I was thinking about my next move. I had held the rank of wing commander for nearly ten years, eight of them in the substantive rank, and I was naturally hoping for promotion, although I realized that with my age and seniority I was one of a large group at the same stage. A flying job was too much to hope for after two (virtually three) in a row, but I had hoped that the unrivalled knowledge and contacts I had built up in the systems and navigation field would lead to a job in research and development or in framing operational policy and requirements. I should have known better: I was posted to the Air Secretary's Department in the MOD dealing with policy for officers' careers and appointments, in a wing commander's post, indicating that promotion was not likely this year.

Joan was equally unhappy with the thought of moving from our pleasant house to the London area, but we had known that some sort of move was inevitable and that we would have to put up with it. I was due to report to MOD on 17 June, and my replacement, John Bore, would arrive three weeks earlier, giving time for a handover and a few days' leave; he had come (if I remember correctly) from the MOD Operations (Navigation) branch and had accompanied us on one North American tour, so we knew him and he was familiar with our work at Manby.

I was sorry to leave this unique and rewarding job (one of our USAF hosts at Mather AFB had rather exaggeratedly referred to it as 'the RAF's lead navigator'), and I would have been even more depressed if I had known that this was to be my last posting in the navigation world. I had made many friends at Manby, as had Joan, and we are still in touch with some of them after some forty years. The Aerosystems (*sic*) Course, surprisingly enough, is still in existence, though the College of Air Warfare became an Air Warfare Centre at the RAF College Cranwell with an Aerosystems Department. The latest information I have on the course (2006) is that it 'is a 45-week, international, multi-service, graduate-level course ....' Its aim is:

> to provide specialist education for selected Officers, Senior Non-Commissioned Officers and Civilians in advanced avionics and aerospace concepts to prepare them for appointments in procurement, research, development and testing. The course comprises 3 major phases: Academic, Applied Technology, Acquisition. The 3 phases and their associated modules flow sequentially to make up the ASC. They are interspersed with 2 major syndicate exercises, 4 UK and 2 international tours with industry. Course members must write a 14,000 word technical thesis on an Aerosystems related topic. ... Graduates of the ASC earn a Master of Science degree from Kingston University.

So the course has not changed radically from No. 1 ASC, but has the added bonus – well deserved by the detailed syllabus I have seen – of an MSc at the end, no doubt an attraction for prospective students. What has changed in the service is that the aircrew designation of Navigator seems to have disappeared: flying training is done at Cranwell, and the graduation lists given in the *Daily Telegraph* show Pilots and Weapons Systems Officers, but no Navigators, though no doubt many serving officers still wear the 'N' flying badge. I should not have been surprised, since in my three years at the College of Air Warfare the transition from navigation to systems had already started; perhaps the only surprise is that it took so long to complete. I wonder if any basic navigation is still taught.

CHAPTER EIGHTEEN

End of Story

Since this book is sub-titled 'A Navigator's Tale' there seems little point in going into great detail about my last three postings in the RAF, all behind a desk and with virtually no connection with navigation. But for the sake of completeness it may be worth writing about what happened in these final few years and how our family life was affected.

When I was posted to the Air Secretary's Department in June 1968 no married quarter was immediately available, although we were on the waiting list for one at RAF Northwood, in a suburban area north-west of London, which provided housing for officers at the MOD. Meanwhile I lived in the Mess at RAF Bentley Priory, the former HQ of RAF Fighter Command in the Battle of Britain, and commuted daily to London by tube. The department was located in Adastral House on Theobalds Road, an unlovely office block in an anonymous area that I found depressing – characterless compared with Richmond Terrace in Whitehall where I had worked in the early 1950s. The job was interesting enough, dealing with the policy aspects of officers' careers, their appointments, promotions and terms of service; the Directorate was a small one headed by a Secretarial Branch group captain, and I was the only General Duties officer in it. My boss, Group Captain Kemp, was an able, decisive and friendly Director with whom I got on well, and my small staff were a competent and equally friendly lot, luckily for me. The other two directorates in the department, headed by air commodores, were Postings (Air) and Postings (Ground), which is self-explanatory: besides the postings of officers they dealt with promotions, terms of service, and any other personnel problems that might affect individuals.

When I had been in the department for a little while I began to realize what a difficult and complicated job the posters had, and how inevitably there were some dissatisfied customers (like myself!). Eventually I sat in on appointments boards and promotion boards and saw at first hand the complicated jigsaw that was the posting process and the (usually unbiased and balanced) making of the promotion lists. I saw, too, the weight placed on the officers' annual confidential reports (Form 1369) – which at that time could not be seen by the subjects – and the way in which the idiosyncrasies of some reporting officers were known and allowed for. On the whole it was as fair a system as could be expected in the constantly changing background of service requirements.

* * *

Our Northwood married quarter came up in a few weeks, and we left our Manby house with many regrets, driving south in convoy, with Joan and Jenny in the little Morris 1000, and the Rover towing the caravan and driven by me. We were not particularly impressed with the Northwood quarter (which had just been vacated by Paddy Forsyth, my old friend and colleague from 'X' Flight, now a group captain): it was a post-war house surrounded by an 'estate' of similar houses which had a definite suburban air. There was a small, steep garden in the rear with a tree which was home to cheeky grey squirrels – as we were unpacking crockery and glassware in the dining-room one sat on the window sill and chattered at us.

Susan, at this time living in north London, now dropped a small bombshell: Keith, her fiancé, was posted (at the usual short notice) to the Andover squadron at Sharjah in the Gulf, and they wanted to get married before he left. This left us about eight weeks to make all the necessary arrangements – church, vicar, reception, dress and so on – in a completely strange area and a house into which we were just settling. As always, the majority of the task devolved on Joan – with a little help from Susan – and she performed wonders to plan the wedding at the local church, hire the necessary caterers so that we could have the reception at home, send out the invitations, help Susan with her wedding dress, and do all the other tasks involved. Susan and Keith were married in Northwood, and after a pleasant reception departed for their honeymoon in Devon and Cornwall. Joan's parents stayed with us for the occasion, and after a couple of days' much needed break Joan and I took off with the caravan for a holiday in the Dales, staying at a quiet site near West Witton in Wensleydale. Never was a holiday more welcome.

By this time Jenny had found herself a job in a small publishing firm in nearby Watford which produced trade magazines, one of which, I remember, was called *Toy World*. (This was the start of a successful career in public relations and marketing, and she now runs her own flourishing business.) I commuted daily from Northwood station, to which Joan would take me in the morning and from which she would pick me up in the evening – a dreary business, but with the benefit of a good walk to the office at the other end, with which and a snack lunch I managed to lose some of the weight I had put on in the social life at Manby.

As it happened I returned to Manby twice before the end of 1968 – first for the reunion dinner of the Spec N Association (soon to become the Aries Association), and then to talk to the Aero-Systems Course about career and postings policy. There were the usual difficult questions to discuss – the students had just been notified of their postings – but as they had recently returned from their North American tour and Christmas was approaching they were well disposed, and I got away lightly.

One of my jobs as P Pol 1(RAF) was to draft talks ('presentations') on personnel policy for officers to be given by the Air Secretary to various service institutions, such as the Staff College, the College of Air Warfare, the Joint Services Staff College and so on. Air Chief Marshal Sir Brian Burnett was the Air Secretary at this time, and I found him very easy to work for and appreciative of my efforts. Towards the end of 1969 he undertook a tour of almost all RAF overseas stations to talk to the officers, and I was fortunate to be included in the small team giving presentations on the work of the department. We had our own Comet IV, and our first stop was in Luqa, Malta, followed by Nairobi in Kenya, which had become a republic in 1964 but where there was still an RAF presence. We stayed a couple of days here and I was kindly put up by Wing Commander Ian Panton in his pleasant home; he had been a College Flight Commander at Cranwell in my time, and so was a friend. We were lucky enough to be taken to the game reserve just north of Nairobi by another officer who knew it well, and I still have a collection of slides taken that day – a great variety of wildlife from ostrich (with young), to antelope, bush buck, warthog, wildebeest, zebra, Grant's gazelle, giraffe, hippo and even rhino, not always easy to see. The finale was a family of lions sleeping off a meal in the shade, and as we drove home in the short twilight our path was crossed by a troop of baboons. As a boy I had been a keen reader of books on African big game, and it was an unexpected delight to have had the chance to see so much in one day.

From Nairobi we went on to Gan, where in the usual short flag-stop the Air Secretary was able to speak to most of the officers who wanted to see him. I was again pleased to see the island looking green and tidy, a great improvement in nine years. Our next stop was Singapore, where we visited all the RAF stations – HQ FEAF, Changi, Seletar and Tengah – in four days and then flew on to Hong Kong. This was my first visit, and I was duly impressed as we came in over the sea to land on the Kai Tak runway; at that time the big high-rise developments were just starting, and it was surprising to see these towering buildings going up apparently alongside the airfield. While we were there I had the opportunity to fly as navigator in a Whirlwind 10 helicopter on a comprehensive tour of Hong Kong and the New Territories: it was interesting to see the ubiquitous building in Hong Kong itself, and the amount of land that had been reclaimed (and was still being reclaimed) from the sea.

After a weekend in Kuala Lumpur we returned to Singapore and then went on to the Gulf via Gan, visiting Masirah Island, Sharjah (from which my son-in-law Keith had recently returned to the UK), and Muharraq. I was to become more familiar with these places at a later date, but thankfully was not aware of this then. The British had a considerable presence in the Gulf at this time, and the United Arab Emirates had still to be formed, with the astonishing progress physically and financially which some of them have made in the twenty-first century.

We pressed on to Cyprus, visiting HQ Near East Air Force and RAF Akrotiri; at all the service establishments at which we had stopped along our route, we gave our talks on postings and promotions, and some officers had the opportunity of speaking to the Air Secretary personally. We had intended to include Gibraltar as our final stop, but had to cancel because of some temporary runway problem there. Arriving back at Lyneham, we were all fairly tired but felt that the tour had been a worthwhile exercise and that we had been well received; the Air Secretary certainly appreciated his contacts with a wide range of the department's 'customers'. My diary says that there was a day off after we arrived back in the UK, and then it was back to work.

* * *

During the summer of 1969, we (Joan, Jenny and I) took the caravan across to France on the Channel ferry, staying a night in Normandy (with the regulation tourist visit to Mont St Michel) before driving to Concarneau on the south Brittany coast. The site we had booked was busy but acceptable, and we enjoyed the sunshine and the opportunity to buy good French food – we would pay morning visits to the boulangerie for bread and the local fisherman for fish caught that morning. Concarneau market was bustling, with stalls full of local food and other products (I still have a straw hat bought there), and the old town area and harbour of Concarneau was attractive, if a little touristy. We explored the local area, and particularly liked Quimper, where we spent a day looking round the cathedral and shops.

After a pleasant week or ten days in Brittany we left for Paris, routeing ourselves via Le Mans but not realizing that the motor-racing Grand Prix was being held, with substantial traffic problems that held us up for a while. But after a short stop at Chartres to see the magnificent cathedral we reached our caravan site in the Bois de Boulogne – a very crowded one but highly organized. Taking the Metro into the city, we found a suitable place for a drink on the Champs d'Elysées, and suddenly were in the midst of a tremendous hubbub, with cars driving up and down the street hooting and people shouting, 'Ou, ou, Pompidou!' Georges Pompidou had just been elected President, bringing to an end the de Gaulle era, and Paris was celebrating: our arrival had been well timed.

We spent two or three days in Paris, visiting the usual tourist venues, and Joan and I particularly enjoyed the formal park across the road from our site in the Bois de Boulogne, with its rose gardens, miniature château, and lily pond – a peaceful place away from the noise and traffic. We returned home via the Calais–Dover ferry (being flagged down on the way by two motor-cycle gendarmes who asked to see our papers and then waved us on), and were glad to be back again after a long day and an enjoyable holiday.

During that summer our faithful but very elderly spaniel, Candy, had died, and after our holiday we acquired a new puppy, a lively black and white cocker christened Biddy by Jenny; she was something of a handful, but soon settled down with us, and became part of the family for the next ten or more years – a very different dog from our shy Candy.

Keith had now been posted to Abingdon to fly Andovers, and he and Sue were allotted a married quarter, where we were able to go and see them from time to time. It was strange to revisit the station where we had spent so much time and energy, but no longer be part of the life there.

Joan would come up to London occasionally, sometimes with Jenny, and they would go shopping (usually in Harrods) and often meet me for lunch at the RAF Club or elsewhere. Though there was of course no social life to compare with that at Abingdon and Manby, old friends would surface in London from time to time, and we would have lunch or dinner somewhere – I recall Cyclops Brown, Mike Banfield also from Manby, Occ Tarry (last seen in Alaska), Bryan Lamb from Abingdon, and one special occasion which was a sort of miniature Gan reunion, with Bob Lewis, Vic Kendrick, Peter Surman and Bill Hart (the latter now a squadron leader and living across the road from us at Northwood). So MOD life was not all grim and earnest.

*   *   *

Group Captain Kemp was replaced by Group Captain Russell as Director of Personnel Policy – another pleasant and capable boss to work for. My own small staff underwent some changes, and by 1970 I was beginning to wonder if I would be required to complete a full three-year MOD tour or if I would again get away with two years, as I had done at the old Air Ministry. In the event my long-awaited promotion to group captain took place on the 1 July 1970 list: Joan and I were of course delighted, but like many good things this came with a downside – I was posted to HQ Air Forces Gulf in Bahrain as Senior Officer i/c Administration (SOA), to take up the job at the beginning of September. We felt no regret to be leaving Northwood and the MOD, but did not particularly look forward to a job in the Gulf, especially as it would be largely divorced from any flying activities. On the other hand, there was an ex-officio married quarter almost immediately available, and the likelihood was that we would spend no more than a year or so in Bahrain: in 1968 the Labour government had decided to withdraw all our military forces from the Far East and the Persian Gulf by the end of 1971, and it was too late for the new Conservative regime in 1970 to reverse this policy, drastic as it was.

The family had a lot to do before the posting took effect. Jenny did not wish to come with us, and was making arrangements to move north, find somewhere to live in Yorkshire (probably Ilkley, where most of her old school friends were), not far from her grandparents in Leeds, and look for another job there. We corresponded with my predecessor in HQ AFG (Group Captain Peter Stembridge), who gave us some idea of what we would need to take out with us in the way of household equipment; he was also willing to pass on his small private car to us, as an official car and driver came with the job. We therefore had some idea of what to pack up for transit and what to put in store. Our own car, now an Austin estate car, we arranged to put into storage close to RAF Lyneham, from where we would be departing for, and arriving back from, the Gulf. We took our caravan up to a pleasant site near Arncliffe in Coverdale, where Jenny would be able to keep an eye on it, and I hired a small van to move her effects up to Yorkshire, while she took over Joan's little car.

Finally I took our heavy baggage to Lyneham and we 'marched out' of our house at Northwood. There had been the usual farewell drinks parties at MOD, as well as the odd celebration of promotion, but it was a relief to leave it all behind and fly out of Lyneham on the way to our new posting.

*   *   *

The British had been involved in the Arabian (or Persian) Gulf for well over a century. The Royal Navy played a leading part in the suppression of the slave trade and of the piracy that was rife along the Gulf coasts. Several small tribal kingdoms were brought into treaty relationship with the UK, and became known as the Trucial States. Of these, Bahrain had been a British protected state since 1861, although treaty relationship went back to 1820; the rulers came from the al Khalifa family, with the advice of a British Political Agent (and the Political Resident in the Arabian Gulf was also based in Bahrain). The British influence was strong, and in many respects Bahrain was the most advanced of the Gulf states at that time (1970): it was a natural trade centre, and at one time the pearl-fishing industry had been very lucrative. This was now declining, and oil was the important product, the Bahrain Oil Company (BAPCO) starting operations in 1930, and in 1968 producing 75,000 (US) barrels a day, with the refinery producing 230,998 barrels daily using oil imported from Saudi Arabia and elsewhere. In addition, a new port, Mina Sulman, had been built near Manama, the capital, with up-to-date facilities, and there were plans for an aluminium smelter, a graving dock and a flour mill. A prawn-fishing industry had also been established.

The state of Bahrain comprises several islands, of which Bahrain Island is the largest (some thirty miles long and eight to ten miles wide), about fifteen miles from the Arab coast and a little more from the Qatar peninsula. Manama, the capital, is on the north-east tip and is joined by a causeway to the town of Muharraq with its international airport, then shared with RAF Muharraq. It was here that we arrived on the first of September 1970.

Although the really hot season was coming to an end, we felt the heat and humidity as we stepped off the aircraft, to be met by Peter Stembridge. We spent the next two or three nights in temporary accommodation reserved for service personnel in transit, but soon took over the Stembridges' house, known as 3 Knightsbridge, in a small enclave (leased to the RAF for senior officers by a member of the Ruler's family) on the outskirts of Manama; it was not unpleasantly situated, with a small garden around it with date palms and other tropical plants. There were four bedrooms and four bathrooms, air conditioning (except in the kitchen where it was most needed), and terrazzo floors, and it was adequately furnished and equipped, although the household china, which we had been told was acceptable, turned out to be standard thick, white, service issue, which we had to replace by more presentable Noritake. Our heavy baggage arrived in a day or so and we began to feel more at home. There was an Arab 'houseboy', Ahmed, who reminded me somewhat of Idle Ali at Gan – he was not particularly industrious, spending a lot of time washing the floors with a none-too-clean mop; Joan was understandably not very appreciative of his efforts, though tickled to be addressed as 'Memsahib'.

Our neighbours were the Senior Engineering Officer (Jock Hunter, a jovial Scot) and his wife Marjorie; the Senior Meteorological Officer, Don Forsdyke and Sheila; and Colonel and Mrs Alan Woolford (he was on the Army staff). We formed a friendly and supportive group, and exchanged social visits fairly frequently, and their help and advice was much appreciated in our first weeks in Bahrain.

The Stembridges departed after a very short handover, and I took up my new job at HQ Air Forces Gulf based at Jufair, just outside Manama. As SOA I reported directly to the Air Commodore, who was Commander AFG, and my responsibilities covered the usual administrative services – supply, personnel, organization, catering, the RAF Regiment, the fire service and all the other areas not covered by the other two group captains in HQAFG (Jock Hunter, already mentioned, and the Senior Air Staff

Officer, David Rhodes, an ex-fighter pilot, who was a bachelor). I was lucky enough to inherit an experienced deputy, Wing Commander Ken Allport, and an efficient sergeant PA.

The Royal Navy and the British Army had corresponding staffs at Jufair, and we all came under a major-general who was Commander British Forces Gulf. The RAF units under Air Forces Gulf's command were Muharraq on Bahrain Island, Sharjah in the sheikhdom of that name, and Masirah on Masirah Island off the east coast of Oman; all these were active airfields operating a variety of aircraft or acting as staging-posts. We also had some responsibility for those RAF personnel who were seconded to the Sultan of Oman's Armed Forces, including pilots at Bait-al-Falaj (Muscat) and Salalah on the south Oman coast, where the Omanis were fighting a guerrilla war with dissident tribes.

I visited all these locations, some several times, during my tour of duty, and it was a relief and a pleasure to get away from the office, although there was usually some intractable problem to wrestle with.

We all knew that the British would be pulling out of the Gulf in the latter part of 1971 (although many Bahrainis professed not to believe it), and all our work was under the shadow of the 'rundown'; I remember that my senior personnel officer presented me with a supposed medal bearing the inscription 'Think Rundown!' – an unnecessary injunction in the circumstances. I was a member of a tri-service committee planning all the administrative aspects of the withdrawal, and many difficult decisions had to be made. One minor problem which exercised us was how to dispose of all the furniture and effects in the many service married quarters: the cost of packing and transit to the UK would have been formidable, but we solved it by selling everything to the occupants at a nominal sum, leaving them to pack up and bear the cost of transferring them to the UK. Nearly forty years on we still have and use some of those items, and have only recently disposed of a pair of curtains as well beyond their 'use-by' date.

*   *   *

So there was plenty of work to keep me busy at HQAFG, and I would leave home every morning in the Army car and driver provided, sometimes lunching at home and sometimes not. But the social life seemed to be never ending, with frequent lunches, dinners, and parties of every sort. We entertained a great deal at home, and frequently had house guests who were visiting or passing through, sometimes old friends and sometimes not. Esther and Harry Phair (they had been great friends at Abingdon, and he was now the Padre at Lyneham) came out for a week, and with several chaplains passing through I remember a very ecclesiastical lunch party at home. As usual Joan bore most of the burden of these occasions, still having to do the cooking and preparation despite the so-called help in the house.

She was also called upon, as was Marjorie Hunter, for advice and assistance by our Commander's wife, who was recently married and had no experience of service life, but had to entertain high-ranking guests such as the Under-Secretary of State for Defence (Air), Lord Lambton, for whom she gave a dinner party at which we were present; he seemed a pleasant enough chap, if not particularly forceful (notoriety came later).

Joan enjoyed going down to the souk in Manama, driving herself in our shabby little Austin or taking one of the plentiful and cheap taxis. Thanks to the long connection of the British with Bahrain, she never felt threatened in the crowded streets full of Arabs from all over the Gulf, as well as Bahrainis, Indians, and Europeans; local ladies usually wore the abba but often had very smart Western-style clothing beneath, and European ladies normally followed a modest dress code. The souk sold everything from fruit, vegetables and spices (always colourfully displayed), to clothes, dress materials, and haberdashery, with a separate gold souk with shops displaying bracelets and necklaces of heavy gold in the windows. Shopkeepers and stallkeepers were always keen to sell without being overbearing, and would offer customers chairs and cold drinks. I had two excellent tropical suits made up for me in a few days, and Joan would often buy dress material in the morning and make it up into a smart dress at home during the afternoon.

When we had a free evening we would often sit on our flat roof as the sun went down, enjoying the cooler atmosphere and watching the happenings in the 'Ladies' Park', reserved for women and children, just across the road; we also enjoyed the nightly fly-round by a group of rose-ringed parrakeets, apparently a popular cagebird brought from India to Bahrain, where many had escaped and were now breeding (just as green-winged parrakeets have done in the London area in the last few years). Ordinary sparrows mixed with bulbuls in the garden, and there was the occasional hoopoe, which Joan managed to photograph on one occasion. With water plentiful on the island, we would keep a garden hose trickling in the hot weather to keep what passed as grass alive; the odd passing Arab would ask if he could drink from it, and would do so, illustrating one of the basic Arab hospitalities of never refusing water if you have it.

Although the island was small, it had a varied terrain with even a miniature desert – the Jebel Dukhan – almost in the centre. We drove down there once or twice and had a quiet walk, passing bee-eaters on the way and disturbing small unidentified birds in the empty desert area. On one of these occasions we were lucky enough to see a small herd (if that is the right collective noun) of gazelles, which, though no longer hunted in Bahrain, were rare and possibly heading for extinction.

At Budaiya, on the north-west coast, the Bahrain government had established an Agricultural Experimental Centre and Model Farm to study local problems of agriculture in this poor soil and hot climate, and give advice to those involved with both livestock and crops. It was pleasant to walk there in the shade of the date-palms and of many other types of tropical tree, some with spectacular flowers. Another place of great interest to us was the Qalat Al-Bahrain, the remains of the fort built by the Portuguese in the sixteenth century when they occupied the island (part of a long history of occupation by the Persians, Arabs and Omanis at various times). The five-sided walls, with square towers at four corners and a turret at the fifth, were all in poor repair, as might be expected, but had obviously been skilfully built and still looked massive. Geoffrey Bibby, the archaeologist, describes in his book *Looking for Dilmun* how his team excavated parts of the fort in 1956 and 1969, and found not only earlier Arab constructions below the Portuguese work, but pottery going back to 2000 BC – a long history and prehistory indeed. Joan and I had been visiting the fort one afternoon when our elderly car broke down; luckily there was a small garage a few hundred yards down the road, and the friendly Bahraini mechanics fixed it temporarily so that we could drive home, but would take no payment – a pleasing experience.

Just before Christmas we were able to take a week's leave, and visited Diana and Peter Hammond in Cyprus: Peter had been on the Spec N Course at Manby, then on my staff, and now was a squadron leader flying with a squadron from Akrotiri. He had stayed with us in Bahrain and said that we would be welcome in Cyprus, so we were taking up his offer. Although it was the so-called cold season in Bahrain, we found Cyprus even colder, but we hired a car and explored the island: we particularly remember visiting the ruins of Salamis, the city established by the Greeks in the fourth or fifth century BC, but changing hands several times, as many of these Mediterranean cities did, being later under Roman rule and suffering from an earthquake in the fourth century AD. The ruins were impressive: we had the place to ourselves and wandered round in the silence, admiring the remaining columns of the gymnasium, the theatre and the basilica. Walking through the site of the agora, the market-place, we met a goatherd playing his pipe and followed by his shaggy goats, just as he might have done a thousand years earlier. The ruins are close to the sea, and we found a small kafeneion near the beach where we had a pleasant lunch: a day to remember.

We also visited Kyrenia, with its ancient harbour, pharos and museum, and the Hammonds took us to Paphos, then just a fishing village without the hotels and other tourist attractions of today; we lunched outside in the sun, and were amused by the sight of a pelican perched on the saddle of someone's parked motor-cycle. We looked at the Roman mosaics nearby, and stopped on the coast at the spot where Venus is said to have emerged from the waves. It was an enjoyable holiday, and we returned to Bahrain relaxed (and with a basket of Cypriot fruit).

* * *

In March the Air Secretary, now Air Marshal Sir Denis ('Splinters') Smallwood, came to Bahrain to visit Air Forces Gulf as part of his annual overseas itinerary. By this time I had received advance notice of my next posting as Senior Personnel Staff Officer at HQ Maintenance Command, and was very disappointed at yet again getting an administrative post and one not in an operational command. A new redundancy scheme for officers, allowing them to retire early at the age of 50, while still retaining some benefits, had just been announced, and after discussing it with Joan we felt that this was something we should seriously consider. I was fortunate enough to have an interview with the Air Secretary, and discussed with him frankly how I felt: he told me that I had been specially selected for the Maintenance Command job since some improvement was needed there in the personnel field, and urged me not to consider redundancy at this point, hinting that a more acceptable post would be found for me later. He was frank and friendly, but knowing how his department worked from the inside I did not place too much reliance on his forecast. Interestingly enough, he found the opportunity to talk to Joan at one of the social events we were involved in during his visit, and asked her to encourage me to stay in the service: she said, of course, that I would have to make my own decision.

Our air commodore and his lady had arranged a picnic for Sir Denis and Lady Smallwood in the desert area at the southern tip of the island, an ambitious venture somewhat marred by the very windy conditions, which among other things made it hazardous for the ladies to use the canvas-screened conveniences that had been erected – amusing in retrospect but not very funny for them at the time. As we walked down to the very tip of Bahrain Island, Sir Denis, a bird watcher, was interested in the migrating swallows coming up from the south across the sea, battling the strong wind and often landing exhausted at our feet. Later we were driven back to a marquee erected further north, in which a military band played as we had drinks, something of an anti-climax, as the sand was still being whipped up and conditions were not pleasant; on the whole the day was not a success.

Meanwhile, work had to carry on, although there were some compensations. No. 47 Squadron, now equipped with the Hercules (C-130 to the USAF), had a detachment at Sharjah, and I was able, on the strength of being an ex-CO, to fly as second navigator on a local low-level cross-country and supply drop; the contrast with the Beverley was remarkable, both in performance and in improved navigation equipment. On a visit to Oman I was again able to act as navigator (on this occasion mainly map reading) in a Whirlwind helicopter of the Sultan of Oman's Armed Forces from Bait-al-Falaj, the airfield near Muscat. We flew over the local jebel terrain, arid and hilly, with small villages and their camels and goats. As it happened, these two flights were the last I was to make as a practising navigator – for me the end of an era, though luckily I did not know this at the time.

At Bait-al-Falaj I had the pleasure of a brief meeting with one of my old co-pilots from 53 Squadron, Hamish Raynham, who had been seconded to SOAF to fly transport aircraft. SOAF was being brought up to date by the new young Sultan Qaboos, Sandhurst trained, who had supplanted his father in a coup in July 1970; the old Sultan Said had ruled for thirty-eight years, and had kept Oman as a medieval kingdom (it was rumoured that he kept weapons and gold under his bed). Qaboos now had the task of dragging Oman out of the Middle Ages and into the twentieth century, and it seemed that he was so far making a good job of it, gradually introducing more education and health services, modernizing the capital, Muscat, and coping with the left-wing rebels in the south-west of the country. I visited Salalah, which had an airfield in this area operating Provost V aircraft (also flown by seconded RAF pilots) against the dissidents, who the day before my visit had mounted a mortar attack against the camp, fortunately with no casualties. The pilots I talked to were full of enthusiasm for their work and approval of Qaboos, who they said had recently dropped in to see them and had made a good impression.

Back in Bahrain, the rundown of the British forces continued, with my own departure from the depleted headquarters due at the end of July 1971. At home we were busy packing and making preparations to leave when, two weeks before our departure date, we had the sad news that Joan's father had died unexpectedly. We managed to get a flight back to the UK almost immediately, and drove up from Brize Norton to Leeds in a hire-car to give Joan's mother what help we could and to attend the funeral – a traumatic time for the family. We arrived back in Bahrain just one week before our planned leaving date, with many official and personal things to be done, including farewell drinks and dinners which neither of us felt much like attending. We finally left the island on 29 July, arriving at Brize Norton very early the following morning and driving almost immediately to RAF Andover in Hampshire (the location of HQ Maintenance Command), to 'march in' to a married quarter which was fortunately awaiting us. We had several weeks' leave to come, and after spending a night with Sue and Keith at Abingdon, we drove up to Leeds to stay with Joan's mother.

Reluctant as we had been to go to Bahrain, we have some pleasant memories of the place, and met many people who became good friends for the comparatively short time we spent there. As usual in these memoirs, there are faces and places which I have not mentioned: we were honorary members of the BAPCO Club at Awali, and would often visit their cinema or have an evening meal there (or both), and the airport restaurant at Muharraq was another favourite spot for dinner. Joan recalls patronizing what might be called a junk shop (known to the Brits as 'Steptoes' after the TV series) which sold brass and copperware now being discarded by the Bahrainis and Arabs generally in favour of modern plastic, and often used as ballast in dhows: we have various brass bowls, a traditional brass coffee-pot with a round base to sit in a fire, and two rosewater dispensers which were for sprinkling hands after meals – all these things bring back our Gulf memories.

After our leave in Yorkshire we drove down to Andover, took over our new married quarter, and were reunited with our heavy baggage. We had also been reunited with our spaniel Biddy, who had lived with Joan's parents while we were in the Gulf, and now settled in with us again quite happily. The house was a post-war one among others of its kind, similar to our Northwood house but in a more attractive setting, looking across a wide field to the main headquarters building and the hills beyond. Andover was an early RAF station, a couple of miles from the pleasant market town, and had been the home of the original RAF Staff College from 1922 to 1942, and again later until 1970, when it was merged with the Staff College at Bracknell; there was still a small grass airfield, little used except by the Ansons (still going strong) employed for staff visits around the far-flung command.

Maintenance Command did mainly what its name implied, supplying aircraft and equipment to the RAF and undertaking major servicing at maintenance units up and down the UK. But it also had under its umbrella a variety of units, mostly small, for which it was responsible: the RAF elements of RAE Farnborough and A&AEE Boscombe Down, for example; the RAF Personnel Management Centre at Gloucester; the RAF Hospital at Wroughton (soon to be handed over to the Royal Navy); the RAF Chaplains' School at Amport House near Andover; RAF Uxbridge, a station with many roles in north London; and several more.

During my tour at Andover its name was changed to Support Command. Air Support Command (formerly Transport Command) was subsumed by Strike Command (formerly Bomber Command), and Training Command had taken over the roles of both flying and technical training which had originally been separate commands. This was said to be in the interests of a leaner and more efficient Air Force, but I imagine that the main thrust was to save money and reduce manpower.

Our Air Officer-Commanding-in-Chief was Air Marshal Sir John Rowlands, the second most senior officer in the RAF's Engineer Branch and a holder of the George Cross, not a decoration lightly given. I had direct access to him on disciplinary and other matters, and found him astute and sympathetic. My immediate boss was Air Vice-Marshal Frith, Air Officer i/c Administration, of the Secretarial Branch. In fact, almost all the staff officers at the headquarters were, as might be expected, members of the Engineer, Supply or Secretarial Branches (except for specialist areas such as medicine and dentistry), and I believe I was one of the only two General Duties officers there, although the unit commander, Wing Commander Ted Dunne, was a GD navigator. Certainly there were few, if any, people we had known previously, and I was a little like a fish out of water, though as we settled in we made many good friends.

My job was the oversight of the several thousand service personnel of all ranks in the command (thankfully the many civilian employees were looked after by a separate civilian personnel officer). I had a small staff, mainly Secretarial Branch officers, with an excellent deputy in Wing Commander Ian Miller, a very experienced flight lieutenant and a warrant officer who dealt with airmen's disciplinary problems, and a most efficient and pleasant secretary, Mrs Margaret Thompson. An ex-officio job was as the command representative on the RAF Club's General Committee, which involved occasional days in London (with the compensation of a good lunch). After a few months I also got the job of President of the Mess Committee in the Officers' Mess: not an onerous job in itself, as there were other committee members and a Mess Manager, but requiring my presence at Mess functions and when the C-in-C or senior visitors were lunching or dining, which was not infrequently. However, after a stint of nine months or so I was able to hand over to one of the other six or seven group captains in the headquarters.

Joan and I had been discussing the future, and we had come to the conclusion that I should apply for retirement at the age of 50 under the redundancy scheme recently announced. Though there was a slight possibility of further promotion, by the time I reached 50 I should have been away from the sharp end of the RAF for nearly six years, away from my own specialization, and unlikely to return to it. The thought of further postings to MOD or a personnel job was not encouraging: not only that, but we were both beginning to hanker after a settled home of our own, and house prices were beginning to rise (and would continue to do so alarmingly over the next few years). The redundancy scheme offered a reasonable proportion of retired pay, a somewhat reduced terminal grant, and a special capital payment, all of which would give us more capital than we had had previously (not a difficult task). Shortly after our arrival at Andover, I applied to retire under the scheme, and MOD approval was notified at the beginning of 1972, with a retirement date set for March 1974.

In May of 1972, Joan went into Wroughton Hospital for a comparatively minor operation, as a result of which it was discovered that a major operation was necessary. She remained in hospital for a fortnight, and I visited as often as possible; she had a room to herself and was given excellent treatment, but was very weak when she came home. As she gradually recovered strength I remember that we would go for short walks on the field behind our house and identify the many wild flowers that grew there; I still have a notebook in which we recorded over thirty species. Eventually we were able to take some leave, and we went to stay at Grassington in Wharfedale (where we had had our honeymoon in 1945). The Dales air and the familiar countryside did wonders, but it was some time before Joan was her normal lively self again.

This holiday boosted our determination to go back to Yorkshire when we left the service. Jennifer was now settled in her flat in Ilkley, and early in 1973 told us that she had spotted a small housing development not far from where she lived, comprising a couple of three-storey 'town houses' inserted between existing dwellings and being built by a reputable local builder. Having looked at it, we decided that it would do as a *pied-à-terre* until we could find a more suitable and permanent house. We organized a mortgage and furnished it very basically, and Jenny moved in to keep the place occupied until we came up from Andover.

By now Sue and Keith had moved to Manby: Keith had qualified as a flying instructor at the Central Flying School, and was now working on the refresher courses at the College. We visited them at their small rented house in the local village, and before long they were able to move into married quarters on the station. While they were still at Abingdon we had seen something of them, and I remember that we had had an enjoyable day together at the Farnborough Air Show (driving past the old site of our house, Mytchett Heath, and finding it demolished and crammed with small modern houses). We had sensed then that all was not well with their marriage, and indeed they parted not long before we moved to Ilkley when I retired – Sue finding a flat and a job in Ilkley, of all places; family ties were evidently still strong. For me my last few months passed quickly. There was plenty of work to occupy me – visits to stations to be made, and the handling of some difficult disciplinary cases, as well as a detailed review of manpower in the headquarters (with a view to a reduction, naturally). Joan and I had the good fortune and pleasure of attending a Royal Garden Party at Buckingham Palace, a special experience which we thought could never be repeated, but which in fact did happen again some years later, for different reasons. Early in 1974 I attended a four-week resettlement course run by the Army in Aldershot for retiring officers. Several areas of study had been available, and I chose house maintenance as being the most practically useful in the immediate future (as it indeed proved to be). I had dabbled with 'do-it-yourself' work for the last few years, but in a very amateurish fashion; now we were taught very professionally by experts in the field – plastering, bricklaying, painting and decorating, carpentry, damp-proofing – all taught in a 'hands-on' way that was very satisfying, by experienced and skilful instructors. This was a refreshing change from my daily work, and it was to stand me in good stead in the years to come. For the day eventually arrived when I had handed over to my successor, been dined out, and attended various farewell parties. We 'marched out' of quarters for the last time and set course for Yorkshire. When we arrived at our house in Ilkley, Jenny gave us details of two properties just come on the market which she thought might interest us, and the following day we went to look at them. The first turned out to be unsuitable, but the second – a cottage in a Domesday Book village between Wensleydale and Nidderdale – attracted us immediately. We are still there thirty-six years later.

* * *

This, then, was the end of 'a navigator's tale', after thirty-two years in the Royal Air Force. If my time in the service did not end in the way I would have liked, I had done some worthwhile work and had seen the growth of air navigation from the days of maps and compasses to orbiting satellites. Flying in nearly fifty types of aircraft during my service, I had been lucky to survive against the odds in 1944, and lucky to have commanded a flying squadron and to have seen a great deal of the world. I had been blessed (and am still blessed) with a wife who took many different dwellings in her stride and made a home in all of them, in whatever part of the world they were. We have made many good friends, some of whom are still with us, and have a store of remarkable memories. As for the last thirty-six years, that is another story.

Bibliography

Armitage, Air Chief Marshal Sir Michael, *The Royal Air Force*, Cassell & Co., 2nd Edn, 1999.

Belgrave, James H.D., *Welcome to Bahrain*, Augustan Press, 1970.

Bennett, D.C.T., *The Complete Air Navigator*, Pitman, 1942.

Bibby, Geoffrey, *Looking for Dilmun*, Collins, 1970.

Cooper, Peter J., *Forever Farnborough: Flying the Limits 1904–1996*, Hikoki Publications, 1996.

Critchley, Julian, *A Bag of Boiled Sweets*, Faber & Faber, 1994.

Doling, Peter, *From Port T to RAF Gan*, Woodfield Publishing, 2003.

Harris, Sir Arthur, *Bomber Offensive*, Collins, 1947.

Hastings, Max, *Bomber Command*, Michael Joseph 1979/Pan Books 1981.

Hearley, M.J., *Examples and Exercises in Elementary Air Navigation for Use of the Air Crews of the RAF, Army Co-operation, Fleet Air Arm, and Cadets of the ATC*, Longman, 1940?

Jacobin, Lou, *Lou Jacobin's Guide to Alaska and the Yukon*, 10th Anniversary Edition, Guide to Alaska Co., Juneau, Alaska, 1957.

Johnstone, Group Captain E.A., *In My Element*, Geo Mann of Maidstone, 1999.

Manson, Jack, *United in Effort: The Story of No. 53 Squadron RAF, 1916–76*, Air Britain (Historians) Ltd, 1997.

Mason, Wing Commander R.A., *The RAF Staff College 1922–1972*, unpublished document, Bracknell, 1972.

Mills, James, *Airborne to the Mountains*, Herbert Jenkins, 1961.

Morris, Richard, *Guy Gibson*, Penguin (paperback edition), 1995.

Overton, Bill, *Blackburn Beverley*, Midland Counties Publications, 1990.

Richardson, Group Captain 'Dickie', *Man Is Not Lost: The Log of a Pioneer RAF Pilot/Navigator 1933–1946*, Airlife, 1997.

Simms, Eric, *Birds of the Air*, Hutchinson, 1976.

Terraine, John, *The Right of the Line. The Royal Air Force in the European War 1939–1945*, Hodder & Stoughton, 1985/Sceptre, 1988.

Turnill, Reginald and Reed, Arthur, *Farnborough – The Story of RAE*, Robert Hale, 1980.

Yates, Jack, and Thorold, Henry, *A Shell Guide to Lincolnshire*, Faber & Faber, 1965.

—— *Royal Air Force Handbook, The – The Definitive MOD Guide* (produced by the Directorate of Public Relations (RAF) with the Defence Procurement Agency), Conway, an imprint of Anova Books, 2006.

—— 'Royal Air Force Manual of Air Navigation', Air Publication 1234, HM Stationery Office, 1944.

Index